An Annotated Bibliography
of Jane Austen Studies
1973–83

An Annotated Bibliography
of Jane Austen Studies
1973–83

Barry Roth

Published for the Bibliographical Society of
the University of Virginia

The University Press of Virginia
Charlottesville

THE UNIVERSITY PRESS OF VIRGINIA
Copyright © 1985 by the Rector and Visitors
of the University of Virginia

First Published 1985

Library of Congress Cataloging in Publication Data

Roth, Barry, 1942–
  An annotated bibliography of Jane Austen studies,
1973–83.

  Includes indexes.
  1. Austen, Jane, 1775–1817—Bibliography. I. Title.
Z8048.R68   1984   [PR4037]   016.823'7   84-20814
ISBN 0-8139-1054-4

Printed in the United States of America

For the other women in my life:

my mother, Sarah

my sister, Janna

my daughters, Alexis and Miranda

and my wife, Nancy

Contents

To hand people along a ways in their dark journey
and be handed along, and for good and selfish reasons

Preface

My first bibliography of Jane Austen studies (1973),
written with Joel Weinsheimer, covered the years 1952-72
and included 794 items. In comparison the present
bibliography spans only eleven years, 1973-83, yet has
about a third more entries, over 1,060. These figures
attest to the tremendous development in the recent
literary criticism of Austen. While work on her during
the fifties and sixties proved the most concentrated and
illuminating that had yet appeared, the attention paid her
in the seventies and early eighties has intensified, and
our understanding of her significance has grown even
richer. The bicentennial of her birth, in 1975, may have
stimulated many to contribute new viewpoints about her
fiction, but, with that anniversary well in the past now,
fresh interpretations continue to be published at a rate
never before experienced. The course of Austen studies
thus appears well set for the foreseeable future.

Given what has been accomplished, we need now, even
more than at the time of the earlier bibliography, a
scholarly tool locating and summarizing research, so as to
determine the present state of our knowledge and help
future work proceed fully informed of past efforts.
Consequently, to fulfill these functions the present
bibliography includes all Austen studies first published
in the period 1973-83 (and those from 1984 as they became
available). Specifically, I list and annotate every book,
essay, article, and doctoral dissertation on her, the
critical matter appended to every edition of her works in
English and to selected translations, and significant
mentions. By presenting this range of material, I offer
the reader a comprehensive and up-to-date guide to Austen
studies.

The needs the bibliography will supply determine the
work's format. For clarity and ease of reference the
bibliography has three main sections. The first covers
books, essays, and articles devoted entirely or in good
part to Austen, including reviews of all the book-length
studies. The second presents doctoral dissertations
wholly or partly about her. The third offers significant

mentions, included regardless of length when they offer an unusual, perceptive, or otherwise striking idea. Within the divisions entries appear chronologically and, within each year, alphabetically by critic's name. I arrange book reviews alphabetically by journal for each year, append three indexes--authors, titles of Austen's works, and subjects--and provide a list of journal and other abbreviations before section one.

All entries have annotations, which provide a concise statement of the critic's thesis. These annotations let the author speak for himself and aim at objectivity and avoid evaluation. In general the maximum length of annotation for an average essay-length study or dissertation is about seventy-five words. Though I enter all discrete Austen items, I do not duplicate annotations. Thus, an article later incorporated in a book has its own annotation only if its thesis would otherwise be omitted. I locate, in the original entry, all reprinted forms of an essay and indicate if a work contains a bibliography when the bibliography proves extensive or otherwise noteworthy. I cross-reference continuing critical disputes and bring together under one entry all extended correspondence within a journal.

For books published simultaneously in the United States and abroad, I supply only the American publisher; otherwise, of course, I give the earliest publisher. I treat only original editions, and all book reviews, even if they pertain to a reprint, paperback or otherwise, appear with the reviews of the original edition. While I have tried to be as full as possible in my listings, to include all printed material, whether in books and scholarly journals, in newspapers and magazines, or in other forms, some exclusion has proved necessary. The bibliography thus does not treat editions and translations without critical matter, abridgments, master's theses, materials in other than printed media, items such as T-shirts and bumper stickers, and study-note series for high school and college students.

I would like to acknowledge the many people who have helped me compose this bibliography. I owe a great debt to employees of the Ohio University Library, who have ably assisted me throughout the more than three years of my project. The Reference Department and particularly the Interlibrary Loan Department, headed by Donna Chen and staffed by Cathy Sitko and LaDawna Harrington, have proved invaluable. Likewise, James E. Davis, R. Vance Ramsey, and Duane B. Schneider of Ohio University's English Department, as well as other of my colleagues, have given generously of their time and intelligence. I could not have completed the work without the liberal financial support of the Penrose Fund of the American Philosophical Society, the Dean of Ohio University's College of Arts and

Sciences, the Ohio University Research Committee, and the Ohio University Baker Awards Committee. In addition, the Ohio University Office of Research and Sponsored Programs, managed by Adam Marsh, has encouraged me throughout.

Many others have contributed much to my efforts, chief among them David Gilson, whose industry and cooperation have improved my work greatly, and I. B. Cauthen, Jr., Alistair M. Duckworth, and A. Walton Litz, who have written often in my behalf during the project. I have asked Bartolomeo Martello, Ewa Stawecka, and others at Ohio University for occasional assistance in translation, which they have always willingly undertaken. Martha P. Pinter also aided in this area. Let me note as well my gratitude to all those who have helped me obtain various items, many difficult to find, including Joan Austen-Leigh, Diana Beacom, J. C. Beard, Claire Booss, Christian Bourgois, Katie Burgess, J. F. Burrows, Robert S. Coggins, Diana K. Coldicott, Peter Conrad, Victor Crittenden, Lynette P. Edwards, Don Erickson, Mary L. Fahnestock, Joseph I. Fradin, Karl-Peter S. Frenger, Eileen Fuller, K. H. Göller, Pierre Goubert, Christian Grawe, J. David Grey, Jocelyn Harris, Yasuo Hashiguchi, Donald M. Hassler, Lia Hunt, Indulis Kepars, Michael Khan, S. Korninger, Patricia A. Kosobud, B. S. Lee, Robert Lowrey, Karen Mateyak, Dona Morey, Vincent Newey, Seikei Okamoto, P. A. Packer, Lisa A. Parente, Atma Ram, Joan Reckitt, Heinrich Reclam, Noboru Shimomura, Sir Hugh Smiley, Michael Smith, Dennis Stevens, Geoffrey Turner, Charlotte Unwin, Katsuo Wakiyama, David Welsj, and Patricia M. Woodall. Though I may not have mentioned all who sought to insure the bibliography's thoroughness, I remain grateful to them nonetheless.

Finally, I owe much to my family's unfailing support, to their interest, understanding, and patience: to Alexis and Miranda, who faithfully and happily accompanied their daddy to libraries on both coasts and in between, and to Nancy, who also lovingly went with me and who was always right.

Short Titles and Abbreviations

ABC	American Book Collector
ABMR	Antiquarian Book Monthly Review
Acme	Acme: Annali della Facoltà di Lettere e Filosofia dell'Università degli Studi di Milano
AI	American Imago: A Psychoanalytic Journal for Culture, Science, and the Arts
AJES	The Aligarh Journal of English Studies
AN&Q	American Notes & Queries
Anglia	Anglia: Zeitschrift für Englische Philologie
AnUILit	Analele ştiinţifice ale Universităţii "Al. I. Cuza" din Iaşi. (Serie nouă.) Secţiunea III. f. Literatură
ARBA	American Reference Books Annual
Archiv	Archiv für das Studium der neueren Sprachen und Literaturen
ArielE	Ariel: A Review of International English Literature
Arnoldian	The Arnoldian: A Review of Mid-Victorian Culture
ArQ	Arizona Quarterly
ASch	The American Scholar: A Quarterly for the Independent Thinker
Atlantis	Atlantis: A Women's Studies Journal/Revue des Études sur la Femme
AUMLA	AUMLA--Journal of the Australasian Universities Language and Literature Association: A Journal of Literary Criticism, Philology, & Linguistics
Austenilia	Austenilia: A Compendium of News, Reviews, and Entertainment
AWR	The Anglo-Welsh Review
B&B	Books and Bookmen
BBNews	British Book News: A Monthly Review of New Books
BC	The Book Collector
BestS	Best Sellers: The Monthly Book Review
BJECS	British Journal for Eighteenth-Century Studies
BKBS	Bibliographische Kalenderblätter der Berliner Stadtbibliothek

BkIC	Books in Canada: A National Review of Books
BkW	Book World (The Washington Post)
BLJ	The British Library Journal
BMMLA	The Bulletin of the Midwest Modern Language Association
BP	The Banasthali Patrika
BRH	Bulletin of Research in the Humanities
BRMMLA	Rocky Mountain Review of Language and Literature
BSEAA	Bulletin de la Société d'Études Anglo-Américaines des XVIIe et XVIIIe Siècles
BuR	Bucknell Review: A Scholarly Journal of Letters, Arts, and Sciences
BW	Book World (Chicago Tribune)
BWA	Book World Advertiser
Bygone Kent	Bygone Kent: A Monthly Journal on All Aspects of Local History
C&L	Christianity & Literature
CB	The Crane Bag
CdS	Corriere della sera
CE	College English: An Official Journal of the National Council of Teachers of English
ChLB	The Charles Lamb Bulletin: The Journal of the Charles Lamb Society
ChrT	Christianity Today: A Fortnightly Magazine of Evangelical Conviction
CL	Comparative Literature
CLAJ	CLA Journal: Official Quarterly Publication of the College Language Association
ClioI	Clio: A Journal of Literature, History, and the Philosophy of History
CLM	The Central Literary Magazine
CLS	Comparative Literature Studies
College	The College (St. John's College, Annapolis, Md.)
Colóquio	Colóquio: Revista de Artes e Letras
Comunità	Comunità: Rivista quadrimestrale di informazione culturale
Confrontation	Confrontation: A Literary Journal of Long Island University
ContempR	Contemporary Review
Cornhill	The Cornhill Magazine
CQ	The Cambridge Quarterly
CR	The Critical Review (Australian National Univ.)
CRCL	Canadian Review of Comparative Literature
CritI	Critical Inquiry
Criticism	Criticism: A Quarterly for Literature and the Arts
CritQ	Critical Quarterly
Crux	Crux: A Journal on the Teaching of English

CSM	The Christian Science Monitor: An International Daily Newspaper
Cultura	La cultura: Rivista di filosofia, letteratura, e storia
Daedalus	Daedalus: Journal of the American Academy of Arts and Sciences
DAI	Dissertation Abstracts International
Descant	Descant: The Texas Christian University Literary Journal
DHS	Dix-Huitième Siècle: Revue Annuelle
Dial	The Dial (New York)
Dolphin	The Dolphin: Publications of the English Department, University of Aarhus
Dorset	Dorset County Magazine (England)
DownR	The Downside Review
DQ	Denver Quarterly
DQR	DQR: Dutch Quarterly Review of Anglo-American Letters
DR	Dalhousie Review
Drama	Drama: The Quarterly Theatre Review
DTelegraph	The Daily Telegraph (London)
DTMag	The Daily Telegraph Magazine (London)
DUJ	Durham University Journal
E	Emma
EA	Études Anglaises: Grande-Bretagne, États-Unis
EAA	Estudos Anglo-Americanos
EASG	English and American Studies in German--Summaries of Theses and Monographs: A Supplement to Anglia
ECLife	Eighteenth-Century Life
Economist	The Economist (London)
ECS	Eighteenth-Century Studies
Edda	Edda: Nordisk tidsskrift for litteraturforskning
EDH	Essays by Divers Hands
EHR	The English Historical Review
EIC	Essays in Criticism: A Quarterly Journal of Literary Criticism
EigoS	Eigo Seinen (The Rising Generation)
ELH	[Formerly Journal of English Literary History]
ELN	English Language Notes
ELT	English Literature in Transition, 1880-1920
ELWIU	Essays in Literature (Western Ill. Univ.)
EM	English Miscellany
EnglSt	English Studies (Seoul National Univ., Dept. of English Literature)
ES	English Studies: A Journal of English Language and Literature
ESA	English Studies in Africa: A Journal of the Humanities
ESC	English Studies in Canada
ESQ	ESQ: A Journal of the American

	Renaissance
ESRS	The Emporia State Research Studies: The Graduate Publication of the Emporia State University
FDMS	Farnham & District Museum Society Newsletter
FemSt	Feminist Studies
FJS	Fu Jen Studies: Literature & Linguistics
FLang	Foundations of Language: International Journal of Language and Philosophy
FMod	Filología Moderna
Focus	Focus: Teaching English Language Arts
Folio	Folio: The Quarterly Magazine of the Folio Society
GaR	Georgia Review
GardH	Garden History: The Journal of the Garden History Society
Genre	Genre: A Quarterly Devoted to Generic Criticism
Gourmet	Gourmet: The Magazine of Good Living
GRM	Germanisch-Romanische Monatsschrift
GSUFZF	Godišnik na Sofiiskiia Universitet, Fakultet po zapadni filologii/Annuaire de l'Université de Sofia, Faculté des Lettres
Guardian	The Guardian (Manchester)
HAB	The Humanities Association Review/La Revue de l'Association des Humanités
Hampshire	Hampshire: The County Magazine (England)
HartC	The Hartford Courant
History	History: The Journal of the Historical Association
HistS	Historical Studies
HistT	History Today
HSL	University of Hartford Studies in Literature: A Journal of Interdisciplinary Criticism
HudR	The Hudson Review
HUSL	The Hebrew University Studies in Literature
I&C	Ideology & Consciousness
IEY	Iowa English Bulletin: Yearbook
IFR	The International Fiction Review
IJES	Indian Journal of English Studies
IJWS	International Journal of Women's Studies
ILN	The Illustrated London News
IndSch	Indian Scholar
Insight	Insight (Mount Saint Vincent Univ., Halifax, Nova Scotia)
IntD	Intellectual Digest
JA	Jane Austen
JAAC	The Journal of Aesthetics and Art Criticism
JDEUC	Journal of the Department of English, University of Calcutta

JEGP	Journal of English and Germanic Philology
JEn	The Journal of the Department of English (Faculty of Arts) (Sana'a Univ., Yemen Arab Republic)
JKUH	Journal of the Karnatak University: Humanities
JLS	Journal of Literary Semantics: An International Review
JMJ	James Madison Journal
JNL	Johnsonian News Letter
JPC	Journal of Popular Culture
JRUL	The Journal of the Rutgers University Libraries
JuniorB	The Junior Bookshelf: A Review of Children's Books
KeyR	The Key Reporter
KFR	Kentucky Folklore Record
Kirkus	Kirkus Reviews
Lady	The Lady (London)
L&H	Literature & History: A New Journal for the Humanities
Lang&L	Language & Literature
Lang&S	Language and Style: An International Journal
LAT	Los Angeles Times
LCrit	The Literary Criterion
LibJ	Library Journal
Library	The Library: Transactions of the Bibliographical Society
Listener	The Listener (London)
MGW	Manchester Guardian Weekly
MLPS	Manchester Literary and Philosophical Society: Memoirs and Proceedings
MLQ	Modern Language Quarterly
MLR	The Modern Language Review
MLS	Modern Language Studies: A Publication of the Northeast Modern Language Association
ModA	Modern Age: A Quarterly Review
ModPhil	Modern Philology: A Journal Devoted to Research in Medieval and Modern Literature
Mosaic	Mosaic: A Journal for the Comparative Study of Literature and Ideas
MP	Mansfield Park
MQ	The Midwest Quarterly: A Journal of Contemporary Thought
MR	The Massachusetts Review: A Quarterly of Literature, the Arts, and Public Affairs
NA	Northanger Abbey
Nagyvilág	Nagyvilág: Világirodalmi folyóirat
N&Q	Notes and Queries: For Readers and Writers, Collectors and Librarians
NArg	Nuovi argomenti

Nation	The Nation (New York)
NatRev	National Review
NCF	Nineteenth-Century Fiction
NDFN	Nauchnye doklady rysshei shkoly. Filologicheskie nauki
NE	Nueva Estafeta
Neophil	Neophilologus: An International Journal of Modern and Mediaeval Language and Literature
NewB	New Blackfriars: A Monthly Review
NewLJ	New Law Journal
NewR	The New Republic: A Journal of Politics and the Arts
NewRev	The New Review
NL	Les Nouvelles Littéraires
NLH	New Literary History: A Journal of Theory and Interpretation
Novel	Novel: A Forum on Fiction
NRBR	News from the Rare Book Room (Univ. of Alberta Library)
NS	Die Neueren Sprachen: Zeitschrift für Forschung, Unterricht, und Kontaktstudium auf dem Fachgebiet der modernen Fremdsprachen
NUQ	New Universities Quarterly
NY	The New Yorker
NYRB	The New York Review of Books
NYT	The New York Times
Observer	The Observer (London)
Observer Mag	Observer Magazine (London)
OhR	The Ohio Review
P	Persuasion
P and P	Pride and Prejudice
PAPA	Publications of the Arkansas Philological Association
Paragone	Paragone: Letteratura
PBSA	The Papers of the Bibliographical Society of America
PHSL	Proceedings of the Huguenot Society of London
PLL	Papers on Language & Literature: A Journal for Scholars and Critics of Language and Literature
PMLA	PMLA: Publications of the Modern Language Association of America
Poetica	Poetica: Zeitschrift für Sprach- und Literaturwissenschaft
PoT	Poetics Today: Theory & Analysis of Literature & Communication
PQ	Philological Quarterly
PrS	Prairie Schooner
PsychoculR	Psychocultural Review: Interpretations in the Psychology of Art, Literature, and Society
PTL	PTL: A Journal for Descriptive Poetics

	and Theory of Literature
PURBA	Panjab University Research Bulletin (Arts)
PW	Publishers Weekly
QL	La Quinzaine Littéraire
QLL	Quaderni di lingue e letterature
QQ	Queen's Quarterly: A Canadian Review
RDigest	Reader's Digest (British ed.)
Redbook	Redbook: The Magazine for Young Women
Renascence	Renascence: Essays on Values in Literature
RES	The Review of English Studies: A Quarterly Journal of English Literature and the English Language
RLet	Revista Letras: Publicação do Curso de Letras do Setor de Ciências Humanas, Letras, e Artes, da Universidade Federal do Paraná
RomMov	The Romantic Movement: A Selective and Critical Bibliography
Room	Room of One's Own: A Feminist Journal of Literature and Criticism
RSRev	RSR: Reference Services Review
RUSE	Rajasthan University Studies in English
SAB	South Atlantic Review: The Publication of the South Atlantic Modern Language Association [formerly South Atlantic Bulletin]
Samlaren	Samlaren: Tidskrift för svensk litteraturvetenskaplig forskning
S and S	Sense and Sensibility
SAQ	The South Atlantic Quarterly
SBHT	Studies in Burke and His Time: A Journal Devoted to British, American, and Continental Culture, 1750-1800
SCB	The South Central Bulletin
ScLJ	Scottish Literary Journal: A Review of Studies in Scottish Language and Literature
SEL	Studies in English Literature, 1500-1900
Selecta	Selecta: Journal of the Pacific Northwest Council on Foreign Languages
SELit	Studies in English Literature (English Literary Society of Japan)
SHR	Southern Humanities Review
Signs	Signs: Journal of Women in Culture and Society
SIR	Studies in Romanticism
SJS	San Jose Studies
SLPD	St. Louis Post-Dispatch
SN	Studia Neophilologica: A Journal of Germanic and Romance Languages and Literature
SNNTS	Studies in the Novel (North Tex. State Univ.)

SocEd	Social Education: Official Journal of the National Council for the Social Studies
SoR	The Southern Review (La. State Univ.)
SoRA	Southern Review: Literary and Inter-disciplinary Essays (Univ. of Adelaide)
Soundings	Soundings: An Interdisciplinary Journal
SP	Studies in Philology
Spectator	The Spectator (London)
Sprachkunst	Sprachkunst: Beiträge zur Literaturwissenschaft
SR	The Sewanee Review
SSEng	Sydney Studies in English
StAR	St. Andrews Review: A Twice-Yearly Magazine of the Arts and Humanities
STelegraph	Sunday Telegraph (London)
STimes	The Sunday Times (London)
STimes Mag	The Sunday Times Magazine (London)
SVEC	Studies on Voltaire and the Eighteenth Century
TES	The Times Educational Supplement (London)
THES	The Times Higher Education Supplement (London)
This England	This England: A Quarterly Reflection of English Life
Time	Time: The Weekly Newsmagazine
Times	The Times (London)
TLS	The Times Literary Supplement (London)
TofE	The Teaching of English: Journal of the English Teachers' Association of New South Wales
TQ	The Texas Quarterly
Triveni	Triveni: Journal of Indian Renaissance
TSLL	Texas Studies in Literature and Language: A Journal of the Humanities
TV Guide	TV Guide: America's Television Magazine (N.Y. Metropolitan ed.)
UCTSE	UCT Studies in English
UE	The Use of English
UES	Unisa English Studies: Journal of the Department of English
UTQ	University of Toronto Quarterly: A Canadian Journal of the Humanities
UWR	The University of Windsor Review
VMU	Viestnik Moskovskovo Univiersiteta: Nauchnii zhurnal. Seria X, Filologia
VQR	The Virginia Quarterly Review: A National Journal of Literature & Discussion
VSun	The Vancouver Sun
VWQ	Virginia Woolf Quarterly
WallStJ	The Wall Street Journal
W&L	Women & Literature
WC	The Wordsworth Circle
WCR	West Coast Review
WLB	Wilson Library Bulletin

WLH	Wye Local History
WLWE	World Literature Written in English
Women	Women: A Journal of Liberation
WPost	The Washington Post
YES	Yearbook of English Studies
YR	The Yale Review: A National Quarterly
YWES	The Year's Work in English Studies

I. Books, Essays, and Articles

1973

1 Aers, Lesley. "Jane Austen and the Social Revolution."
      UE, 24 (1973), 313-17.

      Students tend to be suspicious of E partly because
   it is not revolutionary and partly because they do not
   appreciate subtlety.

2 Anderson, Walter E. "The Plot of Mansfield Park."
      ModPhil, 71 (1973), 16-27.

      MP achieves unity and coherence through its plot
   rather than its themes. The main interest lies not in
   a love story but "the question of Fanny Price's finding
   a home at Mansfield Park." The relationship between
   her and Sir Thomas, the Park's guardian, is thus
   central, and the plot, which begins with his bringing
   Fanny to Mansfield, culminates only when he recognizes
   her moral position within his home and selects her "as
   his preferred daughter."

3 Bellman Nerozzi, Patrizia. Jane Austen. (Biblioteca
      di studi inglesi, 25.) Bari: Adriatica, 1973.

      (This book includes chapters on JA's life, novels,
   and minor works. It discusses her fiction in terms of
   irony, structure, and style and treats such subjects as
   morality and human relationships. Among other things
   it argues that JA focuses on the conflicts between the
   individual and society, appearance and reality, and
   emotion and intellect.)

4 Bennett, James R. "'Doating on You, Faults and All':
      Mr. George Knightley." SNNTS, 5 (1973), 248-50.

      Mr. Knightley is more often unconscious of his
   motives and irrational in his behavior than critics
   have realized. And JA's "deflations of her otherwise
   inhuman hero" provide additional evidence of her genius
   for irony.

5 Bogh, Kirsten. "Aspects of Three Novels by Jane
      Austen. Part Three. <u>Persuasion</u>: Love and
      Marriage, or 'Bad Morality to Conclude With'?"
      <u>Lang&L</u>, 2 (Nov. 1973), 72-94.

      Though in <u>P</u>, as in her other novels, JA criticizes
   "matrimonial bargains" and women's dependent position,
   the marriage of Anne and Wentworth remains "an exchange
   of economic security with sexuality." And, convinced
   of the naturalness of social class, JA here shows "that
   the best people belong to the upper classes--with a few
   deplorable exceptions--and that those who are by nature
   in possession of valuable qualities" can rise socially.

6 Bogh, Kirsten, et al., eds. "Jane Austen: Criticism
      and Ideological Debate." <u>Lang&L</u>, 1 (Spring 1973),
      17-31.

      (This essay, which criticizes a teacher in the
   English Department at the University of Copenhagen for
   having judged unfairly a student's paper on JA, argues
   that the student's sociological approach to JA is sound
   and that all literary study implies value judgment, as
   well as urges "that the people who correct papers make
   their evaluation explicit to avoid our falling victims
   to unconscious political censorship." The essay
   includes as appendixes the student's paper and the
   teacher's commentary.)

7 Bradbrooková, B. R. "Rozumíme Jane Austenové?"
      <u>Proměny</u>, 10 (Oct. 1973), 44-59.

      (This essay discusses JA's life, the importance of
   love and marriage in her books, and the limits she
   imposed on her art despite her knowledge of the world
   outside Chawton.)

8 Bradbury, Malcolm. "Persuasions: Moral Comedy in <u>Emma</u>
      and <u>Persuasion</u>," in <u>Possibilities</u>: <u>Essays</u> <u>on</u> <u>the</u>
      <u>State</u> <u>of</u> <u>the</u> <u>Novel</u>. New York: Oxford Univ. Press,
      1973, pp. 55-78. Parts of Bradbury's essay ap-
      peared originally, with the title "Jane Austen's
      <u>Emma</u>," in <u>CritQ</u>, 4 (1962), 335-46, and, with the
      title "<u>Persuasion</u> Again," in <u>EIC</u>, 18 (1968), 383-
      96.

      The very visible differences between <u>E</u> and <u>P</u>
   demonstrate that no single society in the canon is
   identical to any other. In JA's fiction "nothing is
   given"; rather, she consciously makes "her society, her
   moral world, her compositional form," and she makes
   them, as do all good novelists, "for the purpose of

persuading us into a total, coherent impression in
which arrangement and authorial management are of the
essence."

9   Brogan, Hugh. "Jane Austen's Cities." Letter in
       Times, 16 Feb. 1973, p. 19.

       Bath and Winchester, both closely associated with
    JA, need money to save them from "near-total devasta-
    tion."

10 Brown, Lloyd W. _Bits of Ivory: Narrative Techniques
       in Jane Austen's Fiction_. Baton Rouge, La.:
       Louisiana State Univ. Press, 1973. Parts of
       Brown's book appeared originally, with the title
       "Jane Austen and the Sublime: A Note on _Mansfield
       Park_," in _SBHT_, 10 (1968), 1041-43, and, with the
       title "The Comic Conclusion in Jane Austen's
       Novels," in _PMLA_, 84 (1969), 1582-87.

       Rev. in _Choice_, 10 (1973), 1188 and 1190; by G. M.
    Harvey in _DR_, 53 (1973-74), 788-90; by H. G. Hahn in
    LibJ, 98 (1973), 2105; by Stuart M. Tave in _NCF_, 28
    (1973), 364-66; in _VQR_, 49 (1973), cxlv; by J. A. V.
    Chapple in _YWES_, 54 (1973), 342; by C. C. Barfoot in
    _ES_, 55 (1974), 372; by Mary A. Burgan in _JEGP_, 73
    (1974), 127-29; by Juliet McMaster in _QQ_, 81 (1974),
    306-8; by F. B. Pinion in _RES_, NS 25 (1974), 354-56;
    by Susan Gubar in _Novel_, 8 (1975), 246-59; by J.
    Donald Crowley in _SNNTS_, 7 (1975), 137-60; by Alistair
    M. Duckworth in _SR_, 83 (1975), 493-502; by Norman Page
    in _YES_, 5 (1975), 304-5; by Joel J. Gold in _ModPhil_,
    73 (1976), 316-18; by Joel Weinsheimer in _PLL_, 12
    (1976), 209-23.

       Diction: Following a tradition of eighteenth-
    century philosophy, JA exploits ambiguous connotations
    of words like "sensibility," "pride," and "persuasion"
    for satiric ends, as part of her moral and in-
    tellectual discrimination between the ideal and the
    real. She thus uses the multiple definitions of such
    key terms to help in characterization and the develop-
    ment of her ideas and form, as well as, more
    specifically, to study social and psychological
    contradictions and problems of communication and
    judgment.

       Imagery: Close to rhetoricians like Blair, JA
    distrusts hackneyed, inappropriate, or excessive
    imagery, not imagery itself, which she handles in
    diversified ways, "ranging from the burlesque of
    florid styles to the analytic and the emotive." She
    makes the individual's metaphoric language "relevant

not only to the ironies of the human personality but
also to the unfolding of theme and structure." She
proves as versatile, too, in adapting figurative
patterns to her narrative commentary.

Symbolism: Especially in the last three novels JA
relies on fully developed, complex symbols to suggest
meaning, stressing in MP the emblematic importance of
acting and the priesthood, in E of the riddle and the
weather, and in P of the seasons and time. In addition, because symbols serve as moral experiences for
the characters, who interpret the significance of
their surroundings, she internalizes the process of
making symbols, integrates consciousness and situation.

Conversation: JA believes, like Addison, Cowper,
and others, that one's conversation or mode of
communication defines one's morality and taste, but
she also has individual style impinge on a novel's
total content and shape. In NA, for example, the
hero's fondness for parody accords with the general
attention paid Gothic fantasy and social awareness,
and in P and P, as Elizabeth matures, her comic sense
grows more self-questioning, less likely to accept the
trite and superficial.

Letters: In JA, as in Richardson before her,
letters allow characters to disclose their own nature,
through confession and self-betrayal, and describe
others. She explores the structural, moral, and
psychological dimensions of the epistolary mode
throughout the canon, focusing in the later novels on
the emotional value of included correspondence, the
handling of narrative point of view, and themes like
prejudice and imagination.

Dialogue: Generally signifying "an exercise in
noncommunication," dialogue dramatizes "barriers to
meaningful human relationships." Evidence of her
art's complexity and her abiding concern for irony and
ambiguity, nonreciprocal exchanges reveal JA's parodic
interest, further plot, allow for dramatic conflict
and ethical debate, portray character, and provide a
kind of catalyst for reevaluation and growing self-
awareness.

Parody: From the very start of her career a
penchant for burlesque leads JA to study the
"rhetorical relationship between narrator and reader,"
and, as she develops her art, in S and S and especially E, for instance, she subordinates parody's
literary motifs "to the primary goals of characterization and social analysis." Parody helps determine,
too, the shape and ideas of her comic conclusions,

which, ironically self-conscious, paradoxically confirm her own uncompromising realism and the novel form's artificiality.

11 Brown, Lloyd W. "Jane Austen and the Feminist Tradi-
        tion." NCF, 28 (1973), 321-38.

        JA writes within "the eighteenth-century feminist
    tradition," sharing many "liberationist" ideas with
    Mary Wollstonecraft. She questions male attitudes to
    woman's identity, especially "conventional, restrict-
    ing notions of 'female feelings,' education, and
    sexual passion," and uses marriage in her novels not
    "as a socially sanctified and self-justifying goal"
    but as a symbol of "the successful maturation of
    human relationships."

12 Chechetko, M. V. "Dzhein Osten v anglo-amerikanskoi
        kritike" [Jane Austen in Anglo-American
        criticism]. VMU, no. 6 (1973), pp. 39-47.

        Many of JA's twentieth-century critics have
    neglected to examine her social concerns. "The point
    is to understand her heritage as realistic and true
    in its social opinions, although not devoid of well-
    known limitations." In the Soviet Union, study of her
    is only beginning and concentrates on S and S and P
    and P.

13 Chechetko, M. V. "Rannie parodii Dzhein Osten" [Jane
        Austen's early parodies]. NDFN, no. 6 (1973),
        pp. 34-45.

        Through irony JA's early parodies attack the
    values and plot devices typical of the novel of
    sensibility. Works like "Love and Friendship" show
    that the refinement and idealization the novel of
    sensibility claimed for itself are actually based on
    "the most negative actions and features."

14 "Crime Report." Times, 26 Sept. 1973, p. 16. See
        also no. 40.

        (On the theft of JA's water pump, "the only
    remaining relic of the rectory in Steventon.")

15 Friebe, Freimut. "Von Marianne Dashwood zu
        Anne Elliot: Empfindsame Motive bei
        Jane Austen." Anglia, 91 (1973), 314-
        41.

JA depicts intense emotion throughout her career, particularly in S and S, MP, and P, portraying both its value and danger to her heroines. Among other aspects of the subject, she develops the motif of first attachments and shows that the love Marianne Dashwood, Fanny Price, and Anne Elliot feel for nature and music causes them to be misunderstood and tends to isolate them within their own environment.

16 Gane, Gill, et al. "Austen, Jane (1775-1817)," in Women and Literature: An Annotated Bibliography of Women Writers. 2d ed. Cambridge, Mass.: Sense and Sensibility Collective, 1973, p. 48. A third edition of this bibliography, adding new references to JA, appeared in 1976, published by the Women and Literature Collective.

(Expands the bibliography of writings by JA found in the original, 1972 edition.)

17 Gilson, D. J. "Letters of Jane Austen." Letter in TLS, 9 Nov. 1973, pp. 1372-73.

Contrary to a remark made in TLS, 20 July 1973, p. 840, St. John's College, Oxford, owns not seven but five JA letters, including one, number 98 in the standard edition, with "a second postscript not printed by Dr Chapman"; the College also possesses one letter written by her father.

18 Goetsch, Paul. "Jane Austen: Persuasion," in Der englische Roman im 19. Jahrhundert: Interpretationen zu Ehren von Horst Oppel. Ed. Paul Goetsch, Heinz Kosok, and Kurt Otten. Berlin: Schmidt, 1973, pp. 36-55.

P differs significantly from JA's other works. Among other things it focuses more exclusively on the protagonist and has a freer style and a new element of personal emotion. For the first time, too, JA treats a reality dependent on historical and temporal processes and renounces it. She relies to such an extent on luck and accident to reach her conclusion that the happy ending appears providential.

19 Halperin, John. "Jane Austen (1775-1817)," in The Language of Meditation: Four Studies in Nineteenth-Century Fiction. Ilfracombe, Devon: Stockwell, 1973, pp. 19-50. Part of Halperin's essay appears also, with the title "The Victorian Novel and Jane Austen," in his Egoism and

<u>Self-Discovery</u> in the <u>Victorian</u> <u>Novel</u>: <u>Studies</u> in
the <u>Ordeal</u> of <u>Knowledge</u> in the <u>Nineteenth</u> <u>Century</u>
(New York: Franklin, 1974), pp. 1-30; see no. 68.

The heroines of <u>P</u> and <u>P</u> and <u>E</u> complete their moral
education when they meditate about the evils of
subjectivity. When they do so, they move from egoism
to self-knowledge, from blindness to clear vision.
During this crisis they remain logical and articulate,
and the language describing the experience tends to be
abstract, unfigurative, and balanced.

20 Hamilton, Jack. "A Conversation with Jane Austen."
    <u>IntD</u>, 3 (May 1973), 16-18. Hamilton's essay
    appears also, with the title "Conversation with
    Jane Austen," in <u>DTMag</u>, 14 Sept. 1973, pp. 63, 66,
    68, and 70.

    (An imaginary interview.)

21 Hamouchene, Ulla, Gerd Lemvig, and Else Thomsen.
    "Aspects of Three Novels by Jane Austen. Part
    Two. <u>Emma</u>: Love and Marriage, or How the Rigid
    Class Division Should Be Mollified a Little."
    <u>Lang&L</u>, 2 (Nov. 1973), 56-71.

    <u>E</u> describes "a process of self-realization." At
    the start the heroine is blind, dividing people into
    social ranks according to external qualities, and
    later develops rationality when she makes class
    distinctions on the basis of what is internal. She
    learns as well that "woman ought to submit to the
    greater judgment of man."

22 Hanson, C. "Austen, Jane," in <u>Webster's</u> <u>New</u> <u>World</u>
    <u>Companion</u> to <u>English</u> and <u>American</u> <u>Literature</u>. Ed.
    Arthur Pollard. New York: World, 1973, pp. 23-26.

    Fundamentally serious and complex, JA's novels
    value social hierarchy, proper conduct, "active
    principle," and strong feeling; they condemn snobbery,
    selfishness, and "unmannerly display."

23 Hardwick, Michael. <u>A</u> <u>Guide</u> to <u>Jane</u> <u>Austen</u>. New York:
    Scribner's, 1973. Hardwick's book appears also
    with the title <u>The</u> <u>Osprey</u> <u>Guide</u> to <u>Jane</u> <u>Austen</u>
    (Reading, Berkshire: Osprey, 1973).

    Rev. in <u>TLS</u>, 31 Aug. 1973, p. 1005; by Richard
    Heinzkill in <u>LibJ</u>, 99 (1974), 1115; by Chester S.
    Bunnell in <u>ARBA</u>, 6 (1975), 614; by Alistair M.

Duckworth in NewR, 25 Jan. 1975, pp. 24-25; by
Alistair M. Duckworth in SR, 83 (1975), 493-502; by
Joel Weinsheimer in PLL, 12 (1976), 209-23.

(Provides an outline of JA's life, catalogues the
characters, and summarizes the plots of the major
novels and some minor works.)

24 Hennedy, Hugh L. "Acts of Perception in Jane Austen's
      Novels." SNNTS, 5 (1973), 22-38.

Though JA uses metaphors of perception extensively
in all six novels, in NA and P "literal acts of
perception dominate or are as important as the
metaphoric ones." NA records the difficulty both the
characters and readers of the novel have seeing
clearly, and P concerns hearing, an appropriate
subject for a novel whose major theme is the trouble
people have communicating with each other.

25 Hummel, Madeline. "Emblematic Charades and the
      Observant Woman in Mansfield Park." TSLL, 15
      (1973), 251-65.

Extremely cynical, "harshly derisive," JA treats
events in MP "as emblematic charades" affording Fanny
and herself the opportunity to observe and measure the
shortcomings of others and the whole society. By
means of Fanny's double role as victim and reflector
of a decaying society, JA offers her "most unequivocal
condemnation of her own environment's propensity to
relegate its women to a state of total subjection."

26 Jackel, David. "Jane Austen and 'Thorough Novel
      Slang.'" N&Q, NS 20 (1973), 46-47. See also no.
      224.

(Cites occurrences in various novels of the phrase
"vortex of dissipation," which JA in a letter
complained of as "thorough novel slang.")

27 The Jane Austen Society: Report for the Year, 1972.
      Alton, Hampshire: Jane Austen Society, [1973].

(In addition to the guest speaker's address to the
Society's annual general meeting, abstracted below,
this report includes, among other things, several
brief notes.)

Rosalind Wade, "The Anatomy of Jane Austen," pp.
12-21. Historically, the rather fierce disagreement

between JA's supporters and detractors concerns not
just the value of her books but her private personality as well. Yet we cannot infer from the novels
her personal "opinions and ultimate dispositions."
Perhaps it is her correspondence that best reveals
"the real woman" buried beneath accumulated "layers
either of sentimental regard or unfair blame."
[Wade's essay, part of which appeared originally, with
the title "The Anatomy of Jane Austen (1775-1817)," in
ContempR, 218 (1971), 132-36, appears also, with the
title "The Anatomy of Jane Austen," in Collected
Reports of the Jane Austen Society, 1966-1975
(Folkestone: Dawson, 1977), pp. 178-87.]

28 Lading, Åse. "Love and Marriage, or How Sexuality
       Becomes Integrated in the Family." Lang&L, 2
       (Nov. 1973), 94-103.

       In P, JA defines different sexual roles of the
early nineteenth century. While Anne represents the
"reality principle," or tradition and reason,
qualities associated with women, Wentworth embodies
the "pleasure principle," or emotion and sexuality,
traits connected with men. Her restraint and
dependence on her family contrast with his outgoing
nature and ability to make his own way in the world.
At the end their marriage unites the two opposing
sets of characteristics.

29 Lock, F. P. "A Jane Austen Quotation Identified."
       N&Q, NS 20 (1973), 289.

       (Identifies James Townley's High Life below Stairs
as the source of a remark in JA's early work "The
Visit.")

30 Mansell, Darrel. The Novels of Jane Austen: An
       Interpretation. New York: Barnes & Noble, 1973.

       Rev. in Booklist, 70 (1973), 269; in Choice, 10
(1973), 1551; by C. J. Rawson in English, 22 (1973),
118; by H. G. Hahn in LibJ, 98 (1973), 3561; in TLS,
17 Aug. 1973, p. 950; by J. A. V. Chapple in YWES, 54
(1973), 342; by John E. Jordan in ELN, 12 Supplement
(1974), 27; by C. C. Barfoot in ES, 55 (1974), 372-73;
by Walter E. Anderson in NCF, 29 (1974), 110-12; by
A. van der Loop in DQR, 5 (1975), 210-11; by Frank
McCombie in N&Q, NS 22 (1975), 86-87; by Susan Gubar
in Novel, 8 (1975), 246-59; by W. A. Craik in RES, NS
26 (1975), 95-97; by Erik Frykman in Samlaren, 96
(1975), 299-300; by Alistair M. Duckworth in SR, 83
(1975), 493-502; by John Halperin in ClioI, 5 (1976),

262-65; by Joel Weinsheimer in <u>PLL</u>, 12 (1976), 209-23.

<u>NA</u>: As in all the novels, in <u>NA</u> the heroine learns to distinguish between appearance, here founded on the exaggerations common to sensibility and Gothicism, and real life. As in all the novels, too, JA herself follows a stylized plan, one far from realistic in an ordinary sense, because the few concrete particulars she provides serve symbolic ends: they exist not for their own sake but to help her attain her general goal, which in this case is to alter Catherine's psychology.

<u>S</u> and <u>S</u>: To allow her protagonists to define themselves by projecting their illusions onto relatively neutral surroundings, JA offers as little certainty about the other characters as about objective facts. In <u>S</u> and <u>S</u> both Elinor and Marianne (as well as the heroes), after similar errors of imagination, come to qualify the ways they interpret people, balancing sense and sensibility and approaching a unity represented by their family relationship.

<u>P</u> and <u>P</u>: In the course of <u>P</u> and <u>P</u> Elizabeth and Darcy exchange habitual modes of perception, which have created "a pleasing little aesthetic world to live in," for the mortifying recognition that they have ignored truth and denied their kinship with others. To signify stages in their inner development and have these individuals overcome their pride and detachment, JA invents patently improbable episodes, showing her increasing tendency to subordinate verisimilitude to thematic necessity.

<u>MP</u>: Suffering from a "leaden and witless" narrative and reading more like an essay or sermon than a novel, <u>MP</u> reveals the guilt, evident from the start of her career, that JA associates with irony and playfulness. She here scourges the spirit of youthful independence found in some of the characters and in herself and judges all by a simplistic, conventional morality, which approves of Fanny and Edmund for shedding artistic masks and seeking harmony in retirement.

<u>E</u>: Though, in <u>E</u>, JA largely abandons her "workaday plot business as a makeshift for psychological action," she still tells her usual story of a young woman's entering the world filled with misconceptions that eventually give way to facts. Conceived quite broadly, the heroine's misconceptions in this novel seem "simply the causeless state of the mind itself" as the individual leaves the parent's home, an encapsulated little universe, for "another house, another heart, and another name."

_P_: _P_ goes over much of the same ground as the earlier novels, contrasting false and true heroes, for example, and using letters as crucial sources of objective reality. But it also strikes out in new directions, notably in its Romantic treatment of nature, which, in the form of the sea, draws Anne from her traditional, inland origins toward an acceptance of fluidity and danger, of "the sheer redemptive power of experience itself."

31 Mirak, Muriel. "La visione della conoscenza umana in _Emma_ di Jane Austen." _Acme_, 26 (1973), 167-74.

JA's handling of language in _E_ functions structurally and morally, allowing her to show the formation of social consciousness. In order for this process to be completed Emma must free herself from her early and partial opinions of the world and enter into direct dialogue with Mr. Knightley.

32 Mortensen, Margit, Annemette Goldberg, and Marianne Sørensen. "Aspects of Three Novels by Jane Austen. Part One. _Mansfield Park_: Love and Marriage, or How to Catch a Husband without Really Trying." _Lang&L_, 2 (Nov. 1973), 39-56.

_MP_ concerns the conflict between what is external, defined here in terms of economic and social value, and what is internal, namely, moral principle. "Generally speaking, it may be said that . . . the more importance a person attaches to internal qualities, the higher a rank in society will the person obtain." Conversely, those lacking a true inner dimension either reform or suffer a social and economic fall.

33 Munday, M. "Jane Austen, Women Writers, and _Blackwood's Magazine_." _N&Q_, NS 20 (1973), 290.

Contemporary references in _Blackwood's Magazine_ to JA and to women writers as a group show that, even if she "was not generally recognized, she was at least better known than has often been thought."

34 Nardin, Jane. _Those Elegant Decorums_: _The Concept of Propriety in Jane Austen's Novels_. Albany: State Univ. of New York Press, 1973.

Rev. by H. G. Hahn in _LibJ_, 98 (1973), 2862; by J. A. V. Chapple in _YWES_, 54 (1973), 341; in _Choice_, 10 (1974), 1720; by Rosalind Wade in _ContempR_, 224

(1974), 161-62; by Walter E. Anderson in NCF, 29
(1974), 112-14; by Juliet McMaster in QQ, 81 (1974),
306-8; by Stuart Curran in SEL, 14 (1974), 654-55; by
Gertrude M. White in ABC, 25 (Mar.-Apr. 1975), 6; by
Susan Gubar in Novel, 8 (1975), 246-59; by J. Donald
Crowley in SNNTS, 7 (1975), 137-60; by Alistair M.
Duckworth in SR, 83 (1975), 493-502; by John Halperin
in ClioI, 5 (1976), 262-65; by Joel Weinsheimer in
PLL, 12 (1976), 209-23.

Introductory: Though her ideas about propriety
vary from novel to novel, JA consistently defines an
individual's social behavior as "the external manifestation of his internal moral and psychological
condition." She handles irony and narrative point
of view in complex ways, to give critical and unsentimental affirmation to her culture's values and
help her "redefine them in a more acceptable and
durable form."

S and S: Largely, though not completely, S and S
justifies Elinor's system of dealing with the world
around her, a system entailing duty, conventionality,
and reasoned observation, rather than Marianne's,
which emphasizes personal impulse and romantic
preconceptions. The book concludes that the rules of
propriety, while repressive, do indeed provide people
"with generally workable ways of structuring their
relationship to society" and protect them from "the
forces of selfishness, destructive feeling, and
uncertain judgment."

P and P: P and P enforces a healthy "respect for
the rules of decorum, combined with an intelligent
realization that merely to obey the rules in their
strictest sense does not constitute the whole of good
breeding." Because the novel simply and directly
equates manners and moral character, proper assessment of others becomes almost entirely a question of
evaluating social actions.

NA: In NA Catherine learns that, to understand
others, she must consciously and continually question
their pretensions to proper manners. Distinguishing
between the conventions of ordinary life and those of
fiction, she comes to recognize that the former,
"though basically moral in intention, in practice are
quite flexible enough to permit bad people to express
the evil in their hearts without getting themselves
into serious trouble."

MP: MP's principled figures, who combine low
status with the need to work, attempt to integrate
morals and manners, while the unprincipled ones, who
possess both high position and money, see only the

social value of propriety. <u>MP</u> thus opposes two standards of decorum, attacking corruption in the fashionable world, where restless energies find only dangerous outlets, and praising hardship, vocation, and the renunciation of desire as a moral guide.

<u>E</u>: In the beginning Emma overvalues polished manners, priding herself on her own decorous behavior, but later learns that true propriety consists rather in good feeling toward others and plain speaking. Her experiences with Robert Martin, Mr. Elton, Jane Fairfax, and Mr. Knightley, culminating in the failure of the Box Hill expedition, show her that elegance, really only a superficial part of social conventions, has little to do with character and virtue.

<u>P</u>: More ironically and in a less doctrinaire way than the earlier novels, <u>P</u> questions the role that manners play in one's life, "examining both the possibility that the fallible individual may sometimes be wiser than the major laws of decorum and the possibility that trusting even the best feelings to determine the minor aspects of social behavior may not be an acceptable solution to the problem of how to promote true propriety."

35   Odumu, Ocheibi. "Women Talk about Women: The Image of Women in the Novels of Jane Austen and Emily Brontë." <u>Horizon</u> (Ibadan), 9 (1973), 47-54.

(Not seen.)

36   Ørum, Tania. "Love and Marriage, or How Economy Becomes Internalized: A Study of Jane Austen's <u>Pride and Prejudice</u>." <u>Lang&L</u>, 2 (Nov. 1973), 3-37.

Though it begins by contrasting economic and spiritual or emotional values, <u>P and P</u> ends with "internalization of . . . economic distinctions," so that one's social and spiritual positions coincide. Really "an apology for the existing capitalist class-society," the novel ultimately prefers "the rule of economy over emotion" rather than "the revolt of emotions against economy" and bases social relationships "on property, not on 'aristocratic' or ideologically founded privileges."

37   Palmer, Helen H., and Anne Jane Dyson, comps. "Jane Austen," in <u>English Novel Explication: Criticisms to 1972</u>. Hamden, Conn.: Shoe String Press, 1973, pp. 3-10.

(Bibliography.)

38 Papančev, Georgi. "Interior Monologue (Internal
        Speech) in Jane Austen's Novels." GSUFZF, 67, no.
        1 (1973), 193-246. Papančev's essay includes a
        Bulgarian summary.

"One of the anticipators of the interior monologue
(internal speech) as a literary technique for presenting human psychology," JA uses inner speech to achieve
many effects, such as individualizing the characters,
establishing the point of view, dramatizing the story,
and expressing her ideas unobtrusively. Although she
experiments with all the different manifestations of
inner speech found in fiction of the time, perhaps as
"a reflection of her preferences for oblique presentation" she relies especially on the indirect forms.
In general she closely connects this stylistic element
to "the third person narrative perspective" and
novelistic structure, making it "part of an orderly
system of artistic devices."

39 Pinion, F. B. A Jane Austen Companion: A Critical
        Survey and Reference Book. New York: St. Martin's
        Press, 1973.

Rev. in Choice, 10 (1973), 1197; by Geoffrey
Grigson in Country Life, 18 Jan. 1973, pp. 178-79; by
C. J. Rawson in English, 22 (1973), 117; by Harold
Stolerman in LibJ, 98 (1973), 2300-2301; by Hilary
Carnell in RES, NS 24 (1973), 533; in STimes, 11 Feb.
1973, p. 30; in TLS, 26 Jan. 1973, p. 99; by J. A. V.
Chapple in YWES, 54 (1973), 341; in ARBA, 5 (1974),
515; by R. Gordon Cox in CritQ, 16 (1974), 95-96; by
J. Donald Crowley in SNNTS, 7 (1975), 137-60; by
Alistair M. Duckworth in SR, 83 (1975), 493-502; by
Joel Weinsheimer in PLL, 12 (1976), 209-23.

(In addition to the commentary on the novels,
abstracted below, this illustrated review of JA's life
and writings includes, among other things, a background of her times, sections on the minor works and
letters, a discussion of her literary reputation, a
list of people and places she mentions, a glossary of
her diction, a bibliography of writings by and about
her, and appendixes on the chronology of composition,
the "Plan of a Novel," The Mirror, and the Austen
family.)

Subtle and scrupulous, dramatic and psychologically realistic, JA's art analyzes human character
and social conduct and takes its shape from her
uncompromising moral standards, which stress

"individual responsibility and choice." Her novels,
more unified, coherent, and disciplined than earlier
English fiction, develop such themes as "the hypocrisy
and heartlessness of mercenary people," the connection
between love and "natural attraction" rather than
wealth or social rank, education "as a preparation for
life," and "the fallibility of human judgment." Often
unconventional and technically original, and varying
significantly in their gaiety or gravity as well as
their ironic emphasis, the novels show the influence
of Johnson, Gilpin, Richardson, Shakespeare, and a
number of contemporary poets and novelists.

40   "Pump Sensation." _Times_, 28 Sept. 1973, p. 18.

The water pump reported stolen on 26 Sept. 1973
(see no. 14) may not have been JA's.

41   Quennell, Peter. "[Jane Austen]," in _A History of_
     English Literature. Springfield, Mass.: Merriam,
     1973, pp. 327-31.

(Provides biographical information and comments on
her limitations and strengths.)

42   Roth, Barry, and Joel Weinsheimer. _An Annotated_
     Bibliography of Jane Austen Studies, 1952-1972.
     Charlottesville, Va.: Univ. Press of Virginia for
     the Bibliographical Society of the Univ. of
     Virginia, 1973.

Rev. by J. A. V. Chapple in _YWES_, 54 (1973), 341;
by John E. Jordan in _ELN_, 12 Supplement (1974), 27; by
Stuart Curran in _SEL_, 14 (1974), 655; in _TLS_, 5 Apr.
1974, p. 376; by Peter Miles in _Library_, 5th ser., 30
(1975), 59-61; by David Gilson in _NCF_, 29 (1975), 466-
69; by Renate Mann in _NS_, 74 (1975), 472-73; by J.
Donald Crowley in _SNNTS_, 7 (1975), 137-60; by Alistair
M. Duckworth in _SR_, 83 (1975), 493-502; by Lawrence S.
Thompson in _PBSA_, 70 (1976), 149-50; by Joel
Weinsheimer in _PLL_, 12 (1976), 209-23.

(This bibliography includes sections on books,
essays, and articles, doctoral dissertations, and
significant mentions of JA.)

43   Sabiston, Elizabeth. "The Prison of Womanhood." _CL_,
     25 (1973), 336-51.

"Emma Woodhouse is in many ways the prototype of
the creative provincial, self-deceived, and mentally

blind who, in trying to rise above her society, often
merely reinforces its values." Like Madame Bovary,
Dorothea Brooke, and Isabel Archer after her, Emma,
conceiving life according to romantic ideals, becomes
a victim of the tension between public and private
worlds and of her own personal limitations.

44   Shrubb, Peter. "Emma." TofE, no. 25 (Aug. 1973), pp.
      26-38.

      Though E, a "serious comedy," pictures "the
balance that tragedy shows overthrown," it yet
"acknowledges what it does not allow to enter in full
force." It describes both "the strengths civilisation
may call on, and the weaknesses it may encourage." In
an intelligent and subtly discriminating manner the
novel explores, among other subjects, love, judgment,
and conscience, as well as integrity, the state "in
which the individual, without submitting, nevertheless
comes to recognise the independence of other people."

45   Steig, Michael. "Psychological Realism and Fantasy in
      Jane Austen: Emma and Mansfield Park." HSL, 5
      (1973), 126-34.

      MP is unique among JA's novels. Especially as
distinct from E, which emphasizes psychological
realism, MP explores unconscious fantasy, notably
"infantile megalomania and brother-sister marriage."
The heroine, whose environment adapts to her rather
than the reverse, does not change, has no serious
flaws, and triumphs "through a kind of negative moral
force."

46   Strimpel, Mathilde. "The Marriage Theme in Jane
      Austen." Acme, 26 (1973), 257-304.

      JA treats the theme of marriage, which constitutes
"a metaphor for the individual's engagement with
society," in a doubly ironic manner. In each novel
she juxtaposes to the heroine's "ideal" union many
failed marriages, allowing the two contrasting views
"to confront and comment on each other" and thus cast
doubt on what the heroine achieves. She also points
to contradictions or flaws in the protagonist's
marriage by presenting it as a compromise between
extremes, as "a combination of divergent points of
view not entirely resolved."

47   Szladits, Lola L. "Jane Austen," in Other People's
      Mail: Letters of Men and Women of Letters,

Selected from the Henry W. and Albert A. Berg
Collection of English and American Literature.
New York: New York Public Library, 1973, pp.
21-27.

(Facsimile reproduction of a letter from JA to her
sister, 26 Nov. 1815.)

48   Tanaka, Ronald. "The Concept of Irony: Theory and
        Practice." JLS, 2 (1973), 43-56.

        As a study of Mark Schorer's interpretation of E
makes clear, "a particular literary concept," in this
case irony, "can be analyzed in terms of a more
general theory of meaning and . . . these can then be
applied to explain particular literary phenomena."
And, unless we accept literary theory's inter-
disciplinary nature, literary specialists cannot
"solve the kinds of individual problems required of
their work."

49   Tave, Stuart M. Some Words of Jane Austen. Chicago:
        Univ. of Chicago Press, 1973.

        Rev. by B. Gilbert Cross in LibJ, 98 (1973), 3563;
by J. A. V. Chapple in YWES, 54 (1973), 341-42; by
Gene Koppel in ArQ, 30 (1974), 181-83; by John Lauber
in ELN, 12 (1974), 151-52; by John E. Jordan in ELN,
12 Supplement (1974), 27-28; by C. C. Barfoot in ES,
55 (1974), 372; by Darrel Mansell in JEGP, 73 (1974),
556-58; by Walter E. Anderson in NCF, 28 (1974), 492-
97; by Kenneth L. Moler in PrS, 47 (1973-74), 367; by
Stuart Curran in SEL, 14 (1974), 654; by Joel
Weinsheimer in SNNTS, 6 (1974), 501-2; in VQR, 50
(1974), lxxiv; by A. van der Loop in DQR, 5 (1975),
210; by Juliet McMaster in HAB, 26 (1975), 146-48; by
Michael Taylor in IFR, 2 (1975), 88-89; by Howard S.
Babb in MLQ, 36 (1975), 89-91; by Frank McCombie in
N&Q, NS 22 (1975), 422-23; by Susan Gubar in Novel, 8
(1975), 246-59; by J. Donald Crowley in SNNTS, 7
(1975), 137-60; by Alistair M. Duckworth in SR, 83
(1975), 493-502; by Wayne C. Booth in WC, 6 (1975),
133-36; by Ann P. Messenger in WCR, 9 (Apr. 1975), 20-
21; by John Halperin in ClioI, 5 (1976), 262-65; by
Joel Weinsheimer in PLL, 12 (1976), 209-23; by Andrew
Wright in YES, 6 (1976), 294-96.

        Introductory: Neither problematic nor oppressive,
time, space, and language in JA represent given,
common conditions, necessary, fulfilling forms that
shape life, offer choices, and test the individual's
ability to use them well. "In a world of real meaning
and proper naming, of degree and of balance,

definition is limitation, but it is also liberation."

NA: About the heroine's expectations and our own, as readers, NA teaches us to avoid rigid responses to experience because they lessen our freedom and to make observations and calculate probabilities because only then may we know and act morally. Having explored romance's delusions and the deceptions of ordinary existence, the novel concludes "that though strange things can be accounted for, common life will always be presenting what is never expected."

S and S: S and S, the story of Elinor, not Marianne, distinguishes false sensibility, "conventional, selfish, and weak," from true, which makes the individual larger, more loving, and more capable, and mere activity from genuine exertion. For JA exertion, "the outward and social manifestation of the inward and religious conquest," proves "powerful in proportion to what is required, because it is that dynamic relation of exertion and emotions that makes Elinor's sensibility credible."

P and P: In P and P Elizabeth learns the difference between the agreeable, "an insipid fictive perfection that offers itself for immediate admiration," and the amiable, a reality demanding moral character "that frequently takes time to disclose itself." As the novel progresses, she painfully defines the basis of affection and earns her final happiness by bearing mortification, a renovative force generating humility and self-recognition.

MP: MP concerns liveliness, which, as in the case of the Crawfords, may amount to no more than animation lacking intelligence or endurance, and idleness, a word signifying a mind without direction. The book also contrasts versions of propriety--such as Maria's substitution of external forms for inner meaning and Fanny's sense of the term as a difficult "attainment of spirit"--and describes memory's importance as a foundation for the moral life.

E: Using imagination to reshape the world to her own desires, Emma, like most characters in the novel, actually limits what she sees and loses the power she craves. But with the guidance of Mr. Knightley, whose imagination derives from a clear vision and helps him to understand the feelings of others, she discovers that beauty and freedom reside only "in the simple truth."

P: P starts "when Anne's word has no weight," when she hears but is unheard, and ends, as the revised conclusion emphasizes, "when her word pierces a man's

soul." Wentworth then appreciates the strength and
self-control required by "the right kind of submission" and the "fineness of mind that enables her to
make distinctions" and act more usefully than anyone
else in the novel.

50 Tsuchiya, Shizuko. "Heroine no henbo--Jane Austen:
    Emma" [Evolution of the heroine--Jane Austen:
    Emma]. EigoS, 119 (1973), 402-3.

Using dramatic irony as its principal narrative
technique, E concerns a heroine who begins as a snob
but corrects her faults in the course of the novel.
She changes mostly through the influence of Mr.
Knightley's sense of value, gaining a better understanding of human dignity and the relation between the
individual and his social position.

51 Welcher, Jeanne K. "Jane Austen's Men: A Fair Share
    of Excellence." Confrontation, no. 7 (1973), pp.
    97-102.

Realistic in her portrayal of the sexes, JA
ignores stock images of the distinctions between men
and women in favor of the view that we are all "more
alike than different," especially as regards the
capacity for personal development. Her men, "sharply
defined figures, who hold their own alongside the
ladies," reveal "her confident assessment of the
masculine potential as tremendous and various."

1974

52 Ames, Carol. "Fanny and Mrs. Norris: Poor Relations
    in Mansfield Park." DR, 54 (1974), 491-98.

Though otherwise so dissimilar, Fanny and Mrs.
Norris are ironically alike in being poor relations to
Sir Thomas. Their different personalities derive
"from the age and way each becomes aware of being a
poor relation," and Fanny is rewarded for accepting
her dependent position, "while Mrs. Norris is punished
for denying her dependence."

53 Beasley, Jerry C. "Fanny Burney and Jane Austen's
    Pride and Prejudice." EM, 24 (1973-74), 153-66.

JA transforms the novelistic materials she derives
from Burney, achieving more concentrated effects and
creating more dynamic and complex characters in P and

P than Burney does in Evelina and Cecilia. JA also
enlarges on the significance of the action: P and P
"is a study not only in manners but in personality,
in the discovery of self."

54   Beer, Patricia. "[Jane Austen]," in Reader, I Married
        Him: A Study of the Women Characters of Jane
        Austen, Charlotte Brontë, Elizabeth Gaskell, and
        George Eliot. New York: Barnes & Noble, 1974, pp.
        45-83.

     There are hints of stress between the ideals JA
held for women and her essential acceptance of a
masculine-dominated world. All the women in the
novels seek marriage as their natural goal in life, a
goal they systematically strive for while having to
appear passive. They cultivate talents not to please
themselves but to allure men sexually. And the men,
with their well-concealed "traces of arrogance,
conceit and sadism," cause the women much suffering.

55   Blakesley, Mildred Lenoré. The Dashwoods: A Play in
        Three Acts. New York: Vantage Press, 1974.

     (Adaptation of S and S.)

56   Bradbrook, Frank W. "Jane Austen's Bicentenary."
        Letter in TLS, 18 Oct. 1974, p. 1164. See also
        letter in TLS, Denys Parsons, 8 Nov. 1974, p.
        1261.

     Celebrations of the two-hundredth anniversary of
JA's birth should coincide with the actual date of her
birth.

57   Brereton, Anne. "Jane Austen." CLM, 40 (1974), 209-
        12.

     Comic and ironic, subtle and deep, JA depicts
truthfully human nature and relationships, studying
the conflicts between reality and illusion and
prudence and love. While "she seems more concerned
with moral issues" in MP than elsewhere, "guilt and
misery play only a minor part and are successfully
overcome in Emma and Persuasion."

58   Brower, Reuben. "From the Iliad to the Novel, via the
        Rape of the Lock," in Mirror on Mirror: Transla-
        tion, Imitation, Parody. Cambridge, Mass.:
        Harvard Univ. Press, 1974, pp. 77-95. Brower's

essay appears also, with the title "From the _Iliad_ to Jane Austen, via _The Rape of the Lock_," in _Jane Austen: Bicentenary Essays_, ed. John Halperin (New York: Cambridge Univ. Press, 1975), pp. 43-60.

In her mastery of wit and sentence rhythm, her precision and intricacy, JA is naturally allied with the Augustans, especially Pope. Like him she brings "the multiple perspectives of irony _and_ tenderness to bear simultaneously on the social case." More particularly, _P and P_ thematically and structurally resembles _The Rape of the Lock_.

59 Cahoon, Herbert. "Jane Austen, 1775-1817," in
        Autograph Letters & Manuscripts, vol. 1 of _Major
        Acquisitions of the Pierpont Morgan Library, 1924-
        1974_. New York: Pierpont Morgan Library, 1974,
        pl. 22.

    (Describes the Library's manuscript of _Lady
Susan_.)

60 Carr, Stanley. "Jane Austen's Birthday." _NYT_, 22
        Dec. 1974, sec. 10, p. 3.

    (On the bicentennial.)

61 Chechetko, M. V. "Esteticheskie vzgliadi i hudozh-
        estviennie principi Dzhein Osten" [Aesthetic views
        and artistic principles of Jane Austen], in
        Problemi Angliiskoi literaturi XIX i XX vv
        [Problems of nineteenth- and twentieth-century
        English literature]. Ed. V. V. Ivasheva. Moscow:
        Izdatielstvo Moskovskovo Univiersiteta, 1974, pp.
        7-38.

    JA bases her aesthetics on the need for truth in art, a truth that involves creation, not reproduction, and that derives from reason, experience, and emotion. She studies man as a moral and economic creature, his intricate, often contradictory nature, and the significance of environment and education, especially self-education, on his development. While she owes much to the Enlightenment, including the idea of ridiculing the monstrous and affected, she has ties as well to nineteenth-century romanticism and realism.

62 Drabble, Margaret. "Introduction" to her ed. of _Lady
        Susan, The Watsons, Sanditon_. Baltimore: Penguin,
        1974, pp. 7-31. This edition includes a note on
        "Social Background," pp. 33-36, which describes

such topics as the difficulty of travel and the significance of one's dinner hour.

These minor works illuminate the major novels and are pleasing in their own right. Lady Susan's limitations, including the letter format and the heroine's character, appear only when set beside JA's own later achievements. The Watsons, written with "vitality and optimism," treats her typical themes of marriage, money, and love. When she wrote Sanditon, which concerns speculation and change, issues on which she had mixed feelings, "she was too ill to moralize in fiction, and cheered herself up by seeing the world as a joke."

63 Fleishman, Avrom. "The Socialization of Catherine Morland." ELH, 41 (1974), 649-67. Fleishman's essay appears also in his Fiction and the Ways of Knowing: Essays on British Novels (Austin, Tex.: Univ. of Texas Press, 1978), pp. 23-36.

NA explores how the heroine comes to understand better her cultural milieu, including literature, ethical dicta, aesthetic and linguistic norms, historiography, and rhetoric. She "moves from an unformulated openness to experience, through a naive notion of the direct applicability of symbols (like those of the Gothic novels), to a more sophisticated use of cultural forms--which she treats no longer literally but metaphorically."

64 Fowler, Marian E. "The Courtesy-Book Heroine of Mansfield Park." UTQ, 44 (1974), 31-46.

In Fanny Price, JA "has drawn the full-length portrait of a courtesy-book girl, a paragon of propriety. Fanny is reserved and modest, shrinking from notice, speaking seldom in company, never attempting wit. She blushes easily, shuns flirting and the company of rakes, is delicate both physically and mentally, and has been educated according to the Evangelical prescription to have fine moral principles and excellent judgment."

65 Gillie, Christopher. A Preface to Jane Austen. (Preface Books.) London: Longman, 1974.

Rev. in Choice, 12 (1975), 998; by Stephen R. Rounds in LibJ, 100 (1975), 1324; by John E. Jordan in SEL, 15 (1975), 688; by Robert Nye in MGW, 8 Feb. 1976, p. 22; by Barry Roth in SNNTS, 9 (1977), 233-35.

(In addition to the commentary on the novels, abstracted below, this book includes, together with more than twenty-five illustrations, sections devoted to JA's life and literary background, a bibliography of writings by and about her, information about people and localities important to her, discussion about her vocabulary, and maps of places in the novels.)

Characterization: JA's heroines, partly defined in contrast to her caricatures and minor characters and to the unrealistic protagonists of inferior literature, are dynamic, for they grow in self-awareness and "by the slow fruition of innate virtues." Her heroes, because of social conventions, prove mysterious figures to the heroines, in general provoking, offsetting, and magnetizing them.

Structure: Each of JA's novels has two parts: the first pictures the heroine in "a psychologically confining space," and the second, by confronting her with external and internal obstacles to happiness, shows her gaining new, often painful insight into her situation, a precondition for her final release. In her attempts, like Sterne's starling, to "get out," she must balance feeling and judgment, personal and social demands.

E: The comparison between Emma and Miss Bates, Jane Fairfax, and Mrs. Elton dramatizes the heroine's nature, and that between Frank Churchill and Mr. Knightley illuminates the novel's central theme: "when a game transgresses human feelings, it ceases to be a game and becomes a crime."

JA's Place in the English Novel Tradition: JA connects the eighteenth- and nineteenth-century English novel. Like writers before her she assumes society's permanence and value but looks ahead to a time when social class would express less and less of a character's personality. She emphasizes the existing order, and "the possibilities of change and decay are within or imminent, rather than actual."

66 Gilson, D. J. "Jane Austen's Books." BC, 23 (1974), 27-39.

(Offers a "provisional list" of eighteen titles "with a fair claim to having been Jane Austen's.")

67 Gilson, D. J. "Serial Publication of Jane Austen in French." BC, 23 (1974), 547-50.

Before being issued in book form in French, P and

P and MP appeared in "a series of connected extracts" in French translation. NA and E also were published serially in French.

68 Halperin, John. "The Victorian Novel and Jane
        Austen," in Egoism and Self-Discovery in the
        Victorian Novel: Studies in the Ordeal of
        Knowledge in the Nineteenth Century. New York:
        Franklin, 1974, pp. 1-30. Part of Halperin's
        essay appeared originally, with the title "Jane
        Austen (1775-1817)," in his The Language of
        Meditation: Four Studies in Nineteenth-Century
        Fiction (Ilfracombe, Devon: Stockwell, 1973), pp.
        19-50; see no. 19.

    JA has many ties to the Victorian novelists,
including the use of the Cinderella motif, the preoccupation with money, and the development of point
of view. Most important, perhaps, is "the ordeal
leading from egoism to self-discovery," a formula
governing their work and one that actually starts with
her novels, specifically P and P and E.

69 Hayter, William. "Brothers and Sisters." Letter in
        TLS, 23 Aug. 1974, p. 906. See also letters in
        TLS, Alethea Hayter, 9 Aug. 1974, p. 859; Donald
        H. Reiman, 13 Sept., pp. 979-80; Roger Fulford,
        4 Oct., pp. 1078-79; Mary Moorman, 4 Oct., p.
        1079; Donald H. Reiman, 1 Nov., p. 1231; Molly
        Lefebure, 8 Nov., p. 1261; Mary Moorman, 15 Nov.,
        p. 1288; John Wardroper, 15 Nov., p. 1288; Roger
        Fulford, 15 Nov., p. 1288; Alethea Hayter, 22
        Nov., p. 1317.

    The relationship between Fanny and William Price
exemplifies the closeness many brothers and sisters
in the nineteenth century felt for each other, a
closeness with no hint of incest. "It would be as
absurd to impose any incestuous interpretation on
this relationship, and on the other very intense
fraternal and sororal relationships described in her
novels, as to make any such supposition about Jane
Austen's own very close relationships" with her
siblings.

70 Higuchi, Kinzo. "Persuasion: Keiken no oshieta
        mono" [Persuasion: What experience teaches], in
        Eikoku shosetsu kenkyu [Studies in English
        novels]. (No. 11.) Tokyo: Shinozaki Shorin,
        1974, pp. 45-66.

    P shows how, in spite of her cold, unaffectionate

family, lové develops Anne Elliot's character. This
love, partly physical in nature and based also on
mutual respect and understanding, represents JA's hope
for a pure personal relationship in an egotistical,
irrational world hedged with death.

71   Ishizuka, Torao. Jein Ōsuten shosetsuron [Various
        views of Jane Austen]. Tokyo: Shinozaki Shorin,
        1974.

(This book, which includes chapters on the
juvenilia, Lady Susan, The Watsons, Sanditon,
NA, and MP, studies JA's irony, characterization,
and romanticism and compares her to Shakespeare as
well as to English novelists from the eighteenth
century to modern times. It also offers a
bibliography of writings by and about her.)

72   Ivasheva, V. "Niesravniennaia Dzhein: Dzhein Osten,
        1774-1817 [sic]" [Incomparable Jane], in
        Angliiskii realisticheskii roman XIX vieka v ievo
        sovremiennom zvuchanii [The English realistic
        novel of the nineteenth century in its modern
        resonance]. Moscow: Hudozhestviennaia
        Litieratura, 1974, pp. 41-88.

JA, "without whom there is no English realism in
the nineteenth century," derives strength from her
artistic methods rather than her range. While
interested mainly in deep psychological analyses of
her characters, she studies as well significant
contemporary events and ideas. She also treats the
power of money and creates a complex world, one many
critics mistakenly label conservative.

73   The Jane Austen Society: Report for the Year, 1973.
        Alton, Hampshire: Jane Austen Society, [1974].

(In addition to the guest speaker's address to the
Society's annual general meeting, abstracted below,
this report includes, among other things, several
brief notes.)

Joan Hassall, "On Illustrating Jane Austen's
Works," pp. 15-22. Before illustrating a work, one
must study not only "costume, furniture, architecture
and so on, but the inner moods and probabilities of
the book in question." And, as various illustrated
editions of JA in the British Museum Library testify,
though the artist strives for historical accuracy, he
cannot fully detach himself from his own time period.
[Hassall's essay appears also, with the title

"Illustrating Jane Austen," in Folio (Summer 1975),
pp. 3-9, and, with the title "On Illustrating Jane
Austen's Works," in Collected Reports of the Jane
Austen Society, 1966-1975 (Folkestone: Dawson, 1977),
pp. 201-8.]

74   "Jane Austen Stamps." Times, 10 Dec. 1974, p. 2.

In honor of the bicentennial of her birth JA will
be "the first woman author to be commemorated by a
special issue of British stamps."

75   Jason, Philip K. "Off-Stage Characters in Jane
Austen's Novels." SHR, 8 (1974), 55-66.

"Off-stage characters" in the novels economically
provide, among other things, "a background or milieu
in which the major characters move, and they give that
world a sense of roundness and verisimilitude; they
provide a measure or touchstone for the values under
discussion in the novels and help to delineate the on-
stage characters in terms of those values; they aid in
the development of plot."

76   Joukovsky, Nicholas A. "Another Unnoted Contemporary
Review of Jane Austen." NCF, 29 (1974), 336-38.

(Reprints a previously unnoted review of P and P
from 1813.)

77   Kaplan, Fred. "Austen, Jane. 1775-1817," in The Best
in American and British Fiction, Poetry, Essays,
Literary Biography, Bibliography, and Reference,
vol. 1 of The Reader's Adviser: A Layman's Guide
to Literature. Ed. Sarah L. Prakken. 12th ed.
New York: Bowker, 1974, pp. 374-77. Kaplan's
comments on JA include a bibliography of writings
by and about her.

"Underlying her fiction is a vision of the partial
perfectability of the moral sensibility which can,
despite pervasive obstacles, create a balance of
interests and an almost pastoral resolution of tensions."

78   Kestner, Joseph A., III. Jane Austen: Spatial
Structure of Thematic Variations. (Romantic
Reassessment, 39.) Salzburg: Institut für
Englische Sprache und Literatur, Universität
Salzburg, 1974. Parts of Kestner's book, which

includes a bibliography of writings by and about
JA, appeared originally, with the title "Intimacy
in the Novels of Jane Austen," in IEY, 21 (Fall
1971), 52-59, with the title "Silence and Shyness
in the Novels of Jane Austen: 'The Quietness of It
Does Me Good,'" in Descant, 16 (Fall 1971), 40-47,
and, with the title "The 'I' Persona in the Novels
of Jane Austen," in SNNTS, 4 (1972), 6-15.

Rev. by J. A. V. Chapple in YWES, 55 (1974), 422;
by John E. Jordan in ELN, 13 Supplement (1975), 28; by
John E. Jordan in SEL, 15 (1975), 688; by Jeffrey R.
Smitten in WC, 6 (1975), 137-38; by Joel Weinsheimer
in PLL, 12 (1976), 209-23; by Margaret A. Doody in
YES, 6 (1976), 296-97.

Six key word clusters, serving both ethical and
aesthetic functions in the novels, relate to improvement, intimacy, concealment, imagination, silence, and
shyness. To distinguish between genuine improvement,
which is moral in nature, and mere change, which is
artificial, JA studies, among other things, architecture, the emancipation of women, and alterations
brought about by marriage, adoption, inheritance, and
social mobility. She carefully demarcates the grada-
tions in personal relationships "as acquaintance,
attachment, friendship, intimacy, familiarity, and
sexual love" and explores the tension between the
selfish and disinterested in these relationships.
Just as contact between people may lead to intimacy,
so may it provide possibilities for concealment,
deception, and insincerity, with harm resulting to
those manipulated and to the schemers. The characters
who do not follow reason or rationally control the
power of imagination cause mischief as well because,
treating life as a play, they "act," "pretend,"
"assume roles," and "perform." Finally, the novels
also treat the value of silence and shyness, terms
relevant to JA's technique of understatement and the
themes of pride, love, and restraint. Partly through
her handling of these six word groupings and partly
through her use of three distinct identities for the
"I" of the novels, JA achieves "harmony," "the union
of life and art."

79 Kramer, Richard. "Reading: Emma." Mademoiselle, 79
    (Aug. 1974), 95 and 183.

"Austen's Regency daydream," E "resounds with the
hum of real things." It is "sublime chamber music for
out-of-tune instruments. By the end of the novel,
these instruments have all hit their proper tone, but
until they do, Emma is a particularly sour comedy that
always teeters on the edge of becoming a tragedy of

manners" owing to the heroine's blindness about love.

80 Lancaster, Osbert. "Literary Properties: Mansfield
        Park." TLS, 11 Oct. 1974, pp. 1124-25.
        Lancaster's piece appears also, with the title
        "Mansfield Park," in his Scene Changes (London:
        Murray, 1978), pp. 11-13.

        (Cartoon and accompanying text that continue the
    story of Sir Thomas's estate, describing the "Mans-
    field Park School for Girls . . . first established
    in the old home of the Bertrams shortly before the
    1914 war.")

81 Lauber, John. "Jane Austen's Fools." SEL, 14 (1974),
        511-24.

        JA's fools, evidence of her comic playfulness and
    fertile invention, serve a double function, providing
    us with pleasure and helping to develop plot and
    theme. Though they vary morally and in manner of
    presentation, they are all "self-made" and necessarily
    "rigid, unchanging, predictable." Through their
    mechanical attitudes JA clearly and sharply juxtaposes
    "the personal life and the external life, the life of
    feeling and the life of ceremony."

82 Leeming, Glenda. Who's Who in Jane Austen and the
        Brontës. New York: Taplinger, 1974.

        Rev. by B. Gilbert Cross in LibJ, 99 (1974), 47;
    in RSRev, 2 (July-Sept. 1974), 30; by Stuart Curran in
    SEL, 14 (1974), 658.

        (Lists and describes the characters in JA's
    novels.)

83 McMaster, Juliet. "Surface and Subsurface in Jane
        Austen's Novels." ArielE, 5 (Apr. 1974), 5-24.

        (See no. 351.)

84 Masuda, Izuru. "On Speech in Emma," in Gengo to
        buntai: Higashida Chiaki kyoju kanreki kinen
        ronbunshu [Language and style: Collected essays
        commemorating the sixtieth birthday of Professor
        Chiaki Higashida]. Osaka: Osaka Kyoiku Tosho,
        1974, pp. 113-21.

        JA greatly varies forms of speech in E, including

the narrative, represented, and direct kinds. She
subtly adjusts the distance between speaker and
audience to help in characterization and to enhance
her dramatic effects.

85 Maxwell, J. C. "Jane Austen and _Belinda_." _N&Q_, NS 21
       (1974), 175-76. See also no. 217.

    (Connects JA's defense of novels in _NA_ to a
    passage in Edgeworth's _Belinda_ where Lady Delacour
    expresses an attitude hostile to "indiscriminate,
    stock condemnation of novels.")

86 Mertens, Susan. "Austen Tradition Alive and Well in
       Victoria." _VSun_, 25 Oct. 1974, pp. 4A-5A.

    (This article describes the University of Vic-
    toria's bicentennial commemoration and a Canadian
    descendent of JA and prints a facsimile of an 1806 JA
    poem.)

87 Munro, Hector. "_Pride and Prejudice_ and Its Entail."
       NewLJ, 18 Apr. 1974, pp. 375-76. See also letter
       in _NewLJ_, A. M. Prichard, 9 May 1974, p. 446.

    JA's view of the Longbourn entail appears in-
    correct. "There seems to have been nothing to stop
    Mr. Bennet from levying a fine, or suffering a re-
    covery, and thus providing for his daughters, and
    disposing of Mr. Collins' pretensions. Blackstone
    [12th ed., 1794] even has an appendix of precedents
    of the forms in common use in his time."

88 Rothstein, Eric. "The Lessons of _Northanger Abbey_."
       UTQ, 44 (1974), 14-30.

    In _NA_ "the protagonist and the reader undergo
    parallel, but in almost no way identical, educations."
    While Catherine comes to realize the need for
    "complementary perspectives" in "'reading' real life,"
    the reader learns of the narrative's "necessary
    ambiguity . . . in terms of its freedom from and
    dependence upon the hackneyed devices of fiction, and
    in terms of its priority to and dependence upon the
    characters whose lives it describes."

89 Sabbadini, Silvano. "L'avorio ideologico di J.
       Austen." _Paragone_, 25, no. 294 (1974), 90-112.

    JA lets her characters choose between a

consciousness or ignorance of living within a certain
ideological context, a context based on social, not
individual, psychology. Setting her heroines on the
road from the father's house to that of the future
husband, a journey allowing the greatest freedom in
terms of the choices available, she structures her
novels like Bildungsromane and contrasts various
responses to the initiation rites of the bourgeoisie.

90 Southam, B. C. "Austen, Jane," in The New
      Encyclopaedia Britannica. 15th ed. Chicago:
      Encyclopaedia Britannica, 1974. Macropaedia, II,
      377-80. Southam's essay includes a bibliography
      of writings by and about JA.

      "It is with Jane Austen that the novel takes on
its distinctively modern character," particularly as
regards the concentration on personality and the
relationship between the individual and his society.
"It is this modernity, together with the wit, realism,
and timelessness of her prose style; her shrewd,
amused sympathy; and the satisfaction to be found in
stories so skillfully told . . . that helps to explain
her continuing appeal for readers of all kinds."

91 Southam, B. C. "Jane Austen," in The English Novel:
      Select Bibliographical Guides. Ed. A. E. Dyson.
      London: Oxford Univ. Press, 1974, pp. 145-63.

      (Narrative survey and bibliographical listing of
works by and about JA.)

92 Tanaka, Ronald. "A New Model in the Analysis of
      Literary Texts." JLS, 3 (1974), 23-55.

      The problems critics experience in interpreting
E derives from inconsistencies of "at least the text
and very likely Austen's own assumptions." JA morally
praises her heroine while exonerating her because of
the character's self-deception. But "given Austen's
concepts of rationality and causality, and given
general conditions on agency and moral judgment which
Austen tacitly accepts . . . Emma cannot be both a
fully rational agent and excused on the grounds that
she is self-deceived."

93 Weinsheimer, Joel C. "Mansfield Park: Three
      Problems." NCF, 29 (1974), 185-205.

      The antithesis of Fanny and Mary, which allows no
possibility of mediation, the three discrete and

sometimes irreconcilable standards of evil--the
personal, the social, and the religious--and the
presentation of Mansfield as an ideal, a presentation
based less on empirical observation than wish-
fulfillment, constitute "interrelated sources of
ambiguity" rendering MP simplistic, reductive,
unclear, and confusing.

94   Whitten, Benjamin. Jane Austen's Comedy of Feeling:
     A Critical Analysis of Persuasion. (Hacettepe
     University Publications, B12.) [Ankara]:
     Hacettepe Univ. Press, 1974.

     Rev. by Alan Roper in NCF, 29 (1975), 491 and 493-
     95; by Andrew Lincoln in YWES, 57 (1976), 254.

     In P, JA "successfully integrates both the
     subjective views of personal feeling and the objective
     view of irony to make a distinctive form, a 'comedy of
     feeling.'" Controlling and varying her tone through
     careful manipulation of style, point of view, and
     narrative distance, she tells two stories--one
     concerning the misunderstandings between Anne and
     Wentworth, the other their emotional changes.

     P's first five chapters establish the narrator's
     reliability, indicate that the book's form is comedy,
     and increasingly focus on the heroine, for whom we
     feel deep sympathy. The opening emphasizes Kellynch's
     sterility, but the movement to Uppercross provides
     relief and hope for Anne's future. In the remainder
     of the first volume Anne's renewed activity coincides
     with her improved spirits and growing sense of her own
     physical attractiveness, qualities necessary to insure
     her eventual happiness. Though we experience the
     intensity of her love and understand the strength of
     her judgment, our view remains broader than hers
     because we are also let into the consciousness of
     others. And understanding Wentworth's motives for now
     rejecting Anne, including his continuing sense of
     injury from the past, helps us anticipate the pro-
     tagonists' reunion. Toward the close of volume one
     the striking romantic quality of the description of
     Lyme heralds approaching changes.

     In the second volume Anne, able to see her family
     and herself with fresh objectivity, even irony, can
     turn with developed confidence and independence to the
     new Bath setting. Though cold and impersonal, it will
     at least offer her opportunities for exertion.
     William Walter Elliot's interest in her confirms our
     sense of her restored vitality, but the reader is led
     to believe, partly because of the book's comic form
     and the expectations earlier built up about Wentworth,

that this new suitor will prove unsatisfactory. The
presentation of Mrs. Smith, needed for the book's ending, helps show by contrast the heroine's superior
character. The last half of volume two "allows us
simultaneously to feel compassionately with our
heroine and hero and laugh sympathetically at them
through their anxieties and frustrations to the
inevitable happy conclusion."

95 Wiesenfarth, Joseph. "History and Myth in Jane
        Austen's _Persuasion_." _LCrit_, 11 (Winter 1974),
        76-85.

    (Wiesenfarth's essay appeared originally, with the
title "_Persuasion_: History and Myth," in _WC_, 2 [1971],
160-68.)

96 Williams, Ioan. "The Novels of Jane Austen: Con-
        servatism and Innovation," in _The Realist Novel
        in England: A Study in Development_. London:
        Macmillan Press, 1974, pp. 12-24.

    Though the material and techniques of _E_ are new,
we should not exaggerate JA's originality. She "took
no step towards accepting that value itself can be
established through internal individual experience,
but instead brought the emotional sensitivity of the
individual to serve as a qualifying factor in a system
of judgement which was basically external and arbitrary."

97 Yamamoto, Tadao. "Jane Austen no kamen" [Jane
        Austen's mask], in _Gengo to buntai: Higashida
        Chiaki kyoju kanreki kinen ronbunshu_ [Language and
        style: Collected essays commemorating the sixtieth
        birthday of Professor Chiaki Higashida]. Osaka:
        Osaka Kyoiku Tosho, 1974, pp. 103-12.

    _E_'s realism depends on the economical and proper
use of words and its structure on the comparison of
characters. More specifically, Mr. Knightley tends to
speak sensibly and Emma inconsistently.

                            1975

98 Amis, Martin. "Enigma and Variations." _Radio Times_,
        13-19 Dec. 1975, pp. 7 and 10.

    "A conscious artist," who "like all geniuses . . .
renews herself for every age," she will never seem

less complex than now. "Everything that is written about Jane Austen may not add to an understanding of her work, but it salutes the depth of her enigma."

99 Austen, Jane, and Another Lady. Sanditon. Boston: Houghton Mifflin, 1975. This book appears also, in condensed form, in Redbook, 144 (Feb. 1975), 135-58, and in Woman's Journal (London), May 1975, pp. 98-102, 105, 107-10, 112, and 115-18; June 1975, pp. 78-79, 81, 83-84, 86-87, 89-90, and 92-93; July 1975, pp. 78-81, 83-84, 86, 89-90, 92-93, and 95; Aug. 1975, pp. 72-75, 77-78, 80-81, 83-86, and 88-89.

Rev. in Kirkus, 15 Dec. 1974, p. 1326; by Anthony Siaulys in BestS, 35 (1975), 29; by Richard Freedman in BkW, 16 Mar. 1975, p. 3; in Booklist, 71 (1975), 483 and 500; by Gail Godwin in BW, 23 Feb. 1975, p. 1; in Choice, 12 (1975), 528; by Robert Nye in CSM, 12 Mar. 1975, p. 9; by John Agar in LibJ, 100 (1975), 144; by Gabriele Annan in Listener, 24 July 1975, p. 125; by Annette Flower in Ms., 4 (Aug. 1975), 38-39; by Craig Raine in New Statesman, 25 July 1975, pp. 117-18; in NY, 14 Apr. 1975, p. 127; by V. S. Pritchett in NYRB, 17 July 1975, p. 26; by Martin Amis in Observer, 20 July 1975, p. 23; by Barbara A. Bannon in PW, 13 Jan. 1975, p. 58; by Olivia Manning in Spectator, 9 Aug. 1975, pp. 188-89; in STimes, 14 Sept. 1975, p. 41; by Christopher Porterfield in Time, 10 Mar. 1975, pp. 80 and 82; by Philippa Toomey in Times, 21 July 1975, p. 9; by Patricia Beer in TLS, 25 July 1975, p. 821; by Edmund Fuller in WallStJ, 23 July 1975, p. 14; by J. A. V. Chapple in YWES, 56 (1975), 327-28; by Genevieve Stuttaford in PW, 23 Feb. 1976, p. 122; by Thomas McFarland in SEL, 16 (1976), 714-15; by Luke Flaherty in W&L, 4 Supplement (Fall 1976), 33; by Bernard Jones in B&B, 23 (Jan. 1978), 28-30.

(Finishes the fragment.)

100 Barr, John, and Hilton Kelliher, comps. Jane Austen, 1775-1817: Catalogue of an Exhibition Held in the King's Library, British Library Reference Division, 9 December 1975 to 29 February 1976. London: British Museum Publications for the British Library, 1975.

(The listing for the exhibition coinciding with the bicentennial of JA's birth includes, among other things, items about her family, residences, portraits, and writings.)

101   Beer, Patricia. "Jane Austen and Charlotte
          Brontë--An Imaginary Conversation." Listener,
          31 July 1975, pp. 144-47.

       (Humorous sketch in which the two authors discuss
    what "is now inelegantly designated 'The Woman
    Question.'")

101a   Beinlich, Ursula. "16 Dezember: 200. Geburtstag
          der englischen Schriftstellerin Jane Austen."
          BKBS, 17, no. 12 (1975), 30-32.

       (Chronology of the main events of JA's life and
    list of modern East German editions, translations,
    and studies.)

102   Berger, Carole. "The Rake and the Reader in Jane
          Austen's Novels." SEL, 15 (1975), 531-44.

       JA's "deceptive portrayals of her rake figures
    . . . implicate us, as we read, in the moral and
    thematic concerns of each novel." This rhetorical
    strategy emphasizes the difficulty of uncovering
    villainy "in its subtle real-life forms," obliging
    us, like the heroine, to try to distinguish between
    "the true hero and his rakish rival." The process
    makes us aware of our own tendency to make "judgments
    formed under emotional or conventional pressures."

103   "[The Bicentennial.]" Times, 15 Dec. 1975, p. 13.

       (Photograph taken in JA's Chawton home, in honor
    of the bicentennial of her birth.)

104   Blake, J. E. "Chawton: Hampshire's Literary Shrine."
          This England, 8 (Autumn 1975), 23.

       (On Chawton, JA's connection to it, and the
    bicentennial.)

105   Bompiani, Ginevra. "Il romanzo e il labirinto:
          Studio su Jane Austen." NArg, nos. 43-44 (1975),
          pp. 159-88. Bompiani's essay appears also, with
          the title "Jane Austen: Il romanzo e il
          labirinto," in her Lo spazio narrante: Jane
          Austen, Emily Brontë, Sylvia Plath (Milan: La
          Tartaruga, 1978), pp. 11-57.

       JA treats the reality underlying society's net-
    work of rules and principles. In the juvenilia she

reveals the emptiness of most novels and in NA the terror hidden behind the social mask. For her both language and money help transform nature into culture, and marriage represents the happiness of those who accept the world's artificial constructions.

105a   Brann, Eva. "The Perfections of Jane Austen." College, 27 (Apr. 1975), 1-14.

JA's perfections include, among other things, her singleness of story, exclusion of the alien and election of the known, union of sense and sensibility, presentation of a dignified, shapely world, clear sense of moral value combined with an unflinching awareness of life's realities, light, unstrained, and profound humor, ability to perceive distinctions, formal symmetry, felicitous language, and knowledge of the heart.

106   Burgan, Mary A. "Mr. Bennet and the Failures of Fatherhood in Jane Austen's Novels." JEGP, 74 (1975), 536-52.

JA persistently criticizes the patriarchal organization of society, especially its moral and emotional failures, and searches "for a more responsible and humane source of order to re-create the social possibilities betrayed by the elders." She comes to favor "a kind of democratic individualism in which a man gets authority and approval through what he does as well as through the position into which he has been born."

107   Burrows, J. F. "Habits of the Mind: The Vocabulary of Mansfield Park," in Proceedings and Papers of the Sixteenth Congress of the Australasian Universities Language and Literature Association, Held 21-27 August 1974 at the University of Adelaide, South Australia. [Adelaide: Australasian Universities Language and Literature Association, 1975], pp. 148-49.

(Synopsis of an essay on the "astonishing exactitude" with which JA uses vocabulary in MP to define character and study the mind's processes.)

108   Bush, Douglas. Jane Austen. (Masters of World Literature Series.) New York: Macmillan, 1975.

Rev. in Kirkus, 15 Nov. 1974, p. 1248; by

Harriett Straus in <u>LibJ</u>, 99 (1974), 2478; by Albert
H. Johnston in <u>PW</u>, 30 Dec. 1974, p. 97; by William
Haley in <u>ASch</u>, 44 (1975), 684-86; by Albert Solomon
in <u>BestS</u>, 34 (1975), 488; by Richard Freedman in <u>BkW</u>,
16 Mar. 1975, p. 3; by Gail Godwin in <u>BW</u>, 23 Feb.
1975, p. 1; in <u>Choice</u>, 12 (1975), 838; by Alistair M.
Duckworth in <u>NewR</u>, 25 Jan. 1975, pp. 24-25; by V. S.
Pritchett in <u>NYRB</u>, 17 July 1975, p. 26; by Susan
Greenstein in <u>OhR</u>, 17 (Fall 1975), 120-21; by Kenneth
L. Moler in <u>PrS</u>, 49 (1975), 169-70; by John E. Jordan
in <u>SEL</u>, 15 (1975), 687-88; by Alistair M. Duckworth
in <u>SR</u>, 83 (1975), 493-502; in <u>VQR</u>, 51 (1975), xcvii;
by J. A. V. Chapple in <u>YWES</u>, 56 (1975), 327; by
Kenneth Graham in <u>English</u>, 25 (1976), 52-60; by C. C.
Barfoot in <u>ES</u>, 57 (1976), 440; by G. B. Tennyson in
<u>NCF</u>, 31 (1976), 77-83; by Joel Weinsheimer in <u>PLL</u>, 12
(1976), 209-23; by Barry Roth in <u>SNNTS</u>, 8 (1976),
474-81; by Nirad C. Chaudhuri in <u>TLS</u>, 16 Jan. 1976,
p. 55; by Ian Gregor in <u>L&H</u>, no. 5 (1977), pp. 96-
104; by Stuart M. Tave in <u>MLR</u>, 72 (1977), 409-10; by
Marilyn Butler in <u>N&Q</u>, NS 24 (1977), 374-76; by
Juliet McMaster in <u>QQ</u>, 84 (1977), 141-42; by Atma Ram
in <u>RUSE</u>, 10 (1977), 71-75; by Nol van der Loop in
<u>DQR</u>, 8 (1978), 144-45.

(In addition to the commentary on the novels,
abstracted below, this book includes sections on JA's
life and minor works, a background of her times, and
a bibliography of writings about her.)

<u>NA</u>: Except in the unreal and unconvincing episode
at the Abbey, which "threatens to warp moral judgment," <u>NA</u> marks an immeasurable advance over the
juvenilia, especially as regards characterization and
dialogue. It treats, in a youthful and relatively
simple way, JA's abiding concern for love and her
heroine's progress from delusion to a recognition of
truth.

<u>S</u> <u>and</u> <u>S</u>: Central in her work, too, is the moral
opposition of sense and sensibility, of reason and
emotion, though here the plot and arrangement of
characters appear artificial and the speech sometimes
stilted. Nevertheless, as in the mature JA,
style--whether the formality of civilized utterance
or vulgarities--helps to define the individual's
worth.

<u>P</u> <u>and</u> <u>P</u>: Richer and more complex than its
predecessor, <u>P</u> <u>and</u> <u>P</u> "combines mature or semi-mature
art with the ebullient spirit of youth and comedy."
With great ease and spontaneity it reveals the operation of the title's abstract qualities, creates
fully developed individuals, and blends wit and
feeling.

MP: MP, her profoundest and most urgent novel, explores education, considered both religiously and culturally, as well as self-knowledge and selfishness. In a manner "far from being crudely simplistic" it confronts the problem of upholding personal and social moral values "against the pressure of the looser values of the world at large."

E: Exquisitely crafted and subtle, E tells of the heroine's mistakes in judgment and the harm she accomplishes trying to arrange people's fates. The novel traces her education and increasing involvement in life, her movement from a privately imagined world to membership in the community, from romantic illusion to actuality.

P: Like the rest of the canon P contrasts attitudes to love and marriage and "has a vein of sharp satire," but it pays more attention than the earlier novels to the themes of time, change, and continuity. P's uniqueness lies in the isolated Anne's "sad, rich experience and character," which enable her decisively to break free of an outworn society and find happiness in a new setting.

109 Bussby, Frederick. _Jane_ _Austen_ _in_ _Winchester_. 2d ed. The Close, Winchester: Friends of Winchester Cathedral, 1975. A third edition of Bussby's work--a slightly altered version of the second--appeared in 1979.

(Bicentennial edition of a booklet on JA's association with Winchester, including events from 1975.)

110 Butler, Marilyn. _Jane_ _Austen_ _and_ _the_ _War_ _of_ _Ideas_. Oxford: Clarendon Press, 1975. Part of Butler's book appears also, with the title "The Anti-Jacobin Position," in _Jane_ _Austen_, Northanger Abbey _and_ Persuasion: _A_ _Casebook_, ed. B. C. Southam (London: Macmillan Press, 1976), pp. 106-21.

Rev. in _Economist_, 20 Sept. 1975, p. 126; by Alasdair MacIntyre in _New_ _Statesman_, 24 Oct. 1975, pp. 508-9; by Angus Wilson in _Observer_, 14 Dec. 1975, p. 24; in _Choice_, 13 (1976), 66 and 68; by John E. Jordan in _ELN_, 14 Supplement (1976), 26; by Laurence Lerner in _Encounter_ (London), 47 (July 1976), 66-71; by Kenneth Graham in _English_, 25 (1976), 52-60; by C. C. Barfoot in _ES_, 57 (1976), 439-40; by Gabriele Annan in _Listener_, 22 Jan. 1976, pp. 93-94; by Robert Nye in _MGW_, 8 Feb. 1976, p. 22; by Avrom Fleishman in

MLQ, 37 (1976), 281-89; by Frank W. Bradbrook in N&Q,
NS 23 (1976), 466-69; by G. B. Tennyson in NCF, 31
(1976), 77-83; by F. B. Pinion in RES, NS 27 (1976),
223-26; by Barry Roth in SNNTS, 8 (1976), 474-81; by
Stuart Hampshire in TLS, 16 Jan. 1976, p. 54; by
Pierre Goubert in EA, 30 (1977), 365; by John Casey
in EIC, 27 (1977), 348-54; by Alexander Welsh in
JEGP, 76 (1977), 255-57; by Ian Gregor in L&H, no.
5 (1977), pp. 96-104; by Atma Ram in RUSE, 10 (1977),
71-75; by Keiko Izubuchi in SELit, English no.
(1977), pp. 183-91; by Mey Hurter in UES, 15 (Apr.
1977), 66-68; by Nol van der Loop in DQR, 8 (1978),
144-45; by David McCracken in SBHT, 19 (1978), 179-
82; by Gina Luria in Signs, 4 (1978), 377 and 379-80;
by Andrew Wright in YES, 8 (1978), 345-46.

Background: Novels of the revolutionary period
are not only didactic but partisan, arguing like the
sentimentalist Mackenzie for spontaneous feeling and
man's benevolence, or like the Jacobin or progressive
Godwin and Bage for the individual's conscious understanding as his guarantee of dignity and protection
against social tyranny, or like the anti-Jacobin or
conservative Jane West for Christianity, the existing
order of things, reason as opposed to emotion, and a
skeptical attitude to man's claims for himself. In
this "war of ideas" JA belongs undeniably to the
conservative camp because, among other things, she
endorses rationality and a "preconceived and
inflexible" morality and disapproves of the
unorthodox, the sensuous, and the intuitive. Not a
realistic writer, she offers "an ideal programme,"
one suggested by her "confident and generalizing"
style "and her openly apparent arrangement of
character and plot." In the manner of the era's
reactionary novelists she creates heroines who err
and later learn not to be presumptuous or who know at
the start the true value of principle and duty. Thus
deeply involved in contemporary issues (in contrast
to a common critical assumption about her), she gives
"life to a viewpoint that, in all other hands, proves
deficient in art as well as in humanity."

The Juvenilia and NA: Like the juvenilia, NA
criticizes "the conventional matter of the merely
subjective novel," including the revolutionary
individual's inherent selfishness and cynicism toward
marriage. Though clearly anti-Jacobin in ideology,
NA handles the conservative novel's clichés with
virtuosity and rethinks its material in "naturalistic
and intellectually consistent" terms.

S and S: S and S, resembling contemporary
conservative novels that contrast two protagonists,
proves "unremittingly didactic." It defends civility

against individualism, nurture against nature, and
objective against subjective forms of perception and
concludes by opposing sense--a moral ideal derived
from Christian tradition--to sensibility--defined as
"selfishness with merely a fashionable cover of
idealism."

P and P: While the theme of Elizabeth's moral
education "does not sanction but rebukes the
contemporary doctrine of faith in the individual,"
P and P bafflingly makes the heroine's wit and lively
vision so seductive that the book lacks a clear
message. "Partly because Elizabeth's thoughts are
insufficiently characterized, and partly because no
character within the novel effectively criticizes
her," P and P confuses virtue and vice and thus errs
"from orthodoxy, not wilfully, but through a fault in
the execution."

MP: MP's failure stems less from its ideas,
including the comparison of worldliness and sub-
jectivism with spirituality and skepticism of the
self, than its "attempt to use the inward life of a
heroine as a vehicle for them." And the work is
split into two parts, the first a skillful social
comedy--dramatic, open-ended, complex--the second,
which switches from Maria's testing to Fanny's, a
presentation of consciousness--static, exemplary,
thin.

E: E enacts the inner life only to deny it
validity. As in much conservative fiction, but here
in masterly fashion, the novel follows the heroine
from fallible beginnings through struggles toward
fixed truths external to herself, until, humbled, she
submits "her imaginings to common sense." Simultaneously, largely through language, which functions in
harmony with the form more thoroughly than elsewhere
in JA, the novel makes the reader distrust unaided
thought processes.

P and Sanditon: P is at worst a "muddle" and at
best an "uneasy compromise" between JA's usual "novel
of moral choices in which each choice is given
external bodily reality" and a new subjective
emphasis, which implies "that the senses have a
decisive advantage over reason and fact." Yet P
represents no radical departure for JA; its continuing "conservative social comment," coupled with
Sanditon's hostility to modern tendencies, underlines
"the striking intellectual consistency of her whole
career."

111 Cahoon, Herbert. Jane Austen: Letters & Manuscripts

in the Pierpont Morgan Library. New York:
Pierpont Morgan Library, 1975.

Rev. by Jenny Stratford in TLS, 5 Mar. 1976, p.
271 [and see letter, Jenny Stratford, 19 Mar. 1976,
p. 321].

(Checklist of the Library's manuscripts by and
about JA.)

112 Carr, Gladys E. "England's Jane: 1775-1975--
Bicentenary of the Birth of Our First Lady of
Literature." This England, 8 (Autumn 1975),
18-22.

(Biography.)

113 Chabot, C. Barry. "Jane Austen's Novels: The
Vicissitudes of Desire." AI, 32 (1975), 288-308.

The novels invariably argue that "less is more"
and "young is older." JA and her heroines "have it
both ways. They reconcile themselves to the demands
of their milieu by internalizing the imposed communal
ethic, by making their desires one with its ideals.
At the same time, their initial, overt resentment
toward the imposers of these restrictions vindicates
itself through the discovery of parental deviance
from the ideals."

114 Chessell, Henry. Jane Austen in Lyme. Lyme Regis,
Dorset: Lyme Regis Printing, [1975].

(Describes JA's visit to Lyme Regis, both
factually and through a short play using "as far as
possible her own words, as contained in letters to
her sister.")

115 "[Commemorative Stamps.]" Times, 10 Sept. 1975, p.
17.

(Photographs of the four stamps, portraying
characters from the novels, issued to commemorate the
bicentennial of JA's birth.)

116 "Compass Referred to by Jane Austen Found." Times, 7
Nov. 1975, p. 16.

"A compass-sundial mentioned in a letter written
by Jane Austen in 1805 has come to light."

117   "[The Crawfords of <u>Mansfield</u> <u>Park</u>.]"   <u>TLS</u>, 24 Oct.
       1975, p. 1254.

       (Photograph of "one of the stamps issued . . . to
commemorate the bicentenary of Jane Austen's birth.")

118   Devlin, D. D.   <u>Jane</u> <u>Austen</u> <u>and</u> <u>Education</u>.   New York:
       Barnes & Noble, 1975.

       Rev. in <u>Choice</u>, 12 (1976), 1570; by Laurence
Lerner in <u>Encounter</u> (London), 47 (July 1976), 66-71;
by Kenneth Graham in <u>English</u>, 25 (1976), 52-60; by
Gabriele Annan in <u>Listener</u>, 22 Jan. 1976, pp. 93-94;
by Frank W. Bradbrook in <u>N&Q</u>, NS 23 (1976), 466-69;
by Stewart Trotter in <u>NewRev</u>, 2 (Feb. 1976), 66-67;
by F. B. Pinion in <u>RES</u>, NS 27 (1976), 223-26; by
Barry Roth in <u>SNNTS</u>, 8 (1976), 474-81; by Stuart
Hampshire in <u>TLS</u>, 16 Jan. 1976, p. 54; by Andrew
Lincoln in <u>YWES</u>, 57 (1976), 254; by Stuart M. Tave in
<u>NCF</u>, 32 (1977), 334-39; by S. E. Capitini in <u>UES</u>, 16
(May 1978), 55-56; by J. F. Burrows in <u>MLR</u>, 76
(1981), 936-38.

       JA and John Locke: JA "continues and greatly
extends" Locke's ideas concerning education and
freedom. Like him she believes in moral growth as
the main goal of the learning process, in the
significance of the tutor-pupil relationship, and in
the power of environment, especially during childhood. But she goes beyond his notion that liberty
entails self-control by adding that love alone truly
frees the individual and completes one's education.

       Early Fiction: Several of the minor works and <u>NA</u>
begin to explore the connection among love, freedom,
and education that the major novels dramatize fully.
"Catharine, or the Bower" and <u>The</u> <u>Watsons</u> remain
incomplete because only limited development is
possible when the protagonists are "in love with
nobody." <u>Lady</u> <u>Susan</u> traces uncertainly a young
woman's movement to maturity and independence, and
<u>NA</u> successfully portrays love's ability to overcome
the heroine's faulty education.

       JA, the Earl of Shaftesbury, and Samuel Johnson:
JA owes more to Johnson than to Shaftesbury: she
separates art and virtue, rejects a sentimental or
non-rational ethic and the concept of man's in-
stinctive benevolence, and insists on the necessity
of education and free choice as well as the complex
nature of all moral action.

       <u>MP</u>: (Devlin's essay on <u>MP</u> appeared originally, in
shortened form, with the title "<u>Mansfield</u> <u>Park</u>," in

ArielE, 2 [Oct. 1971], 30-44.)

119 Duckworth, Alistair M. "Jane Austen Criticism on the
       Eve of the Bicentenary." SR, 83 (1975), 493-502.

       (Review-essay on nos. 10, 23, 30, 34, 39, 42, 49,
     and 108.)

120 Ek, Grete. "Mistaken Conduct and Proper 'Feeling': A
       Study of Jane Austen's Pride and Prejudice," in
       Fair Forms: Essays in English Literature from
       Spenser to Jane Austen. Ed. Maren-Sofie Røstvig.
       Totowa, N.J.: Rowman and Littlefield, 1975, pp.
       178-202.

       Contrary to the common view that P and P is a
     novel of antitheses, in which hero and heroine
     represent opposing qualities, the initial conflict
     between Darcy and Elizabeth is actually "in itself
     ironic: the very situations and the very response
     which create antagonism also reveal" their funda-
     mental affinity. Sharing the same values and
     "capacity for emotional commitment," they must
     clarify to themselves who they are rather than
     undergo significant change.

121 Ellis, H. F. "Sense and Centenaries." NY, 29 Dec.
       1975, pp. 26 and 31-32.

       (Humorous sketch.)

122 Franks, Lucinda. "Jane Austen's Fans Hail a Bi-
       centennial." NYT, 26 May 1975, pp. 17 and 30.

       (On the bicentennial.)

123 "Friendly Persuasion." TLS, 19 Dec. 1975, p. 1514.

       (An account of the British Library's JA bi-
     centennial exhibition; see no. 100.)

124 Garside, Peter, and Elizabeth McDonald. "Evan-
       gelicalism and Mansfield Park." Trivium,
       10 (1975), 34-50.

       MP "echoes Evangelicalism" in its social
     criticism, its themes, and its language. Like the
     religious movement, the novel attacks the fashionable
     world's immorality and the notion of feminine
     accomplishments; it advocates stillness, a meticulous

attention to time, and the belief that religion improves manners; and it stresses the importance of words and uses three kinds of language, which mirror "styles identified by the Evangelicals: the religious, the social, and the hedonistic."

125   Gilson, D. J.   "Eliza Giffard."   BC, 24 (1975), 608, query 296.

(Seeks information about Eliza Giffard, who may have "owned all Jane Austen in original boards.")

126   Goubert, Pierre.   Jane Austen: Étude psychologique de la romancière.   (Publications de l'Université de Rouen, Série Littéraire, 32.)   Paris: Presses Universitaires de France, 1975.   Goubert's book includes a bibliography of writings by and about JA.

Rev. by Michèle Bellot-Antony in DHS, 9 (1977), 464-65; by Irène Simon in EA, 30 (1977), 495-97.

(This book studies the novelist's thought about her chosen form, her characters, human psychology, and morality. It describes her attachment to the concept of probability and to lucidity and simplicity of style. It presents her complex reactions to the heroine of the novel of sensibility, reactions that help us understand JA's attitude to subjects like emotion, friendship, and love as well as education, money, and society. It defines the novelist's view of psychology as dominated by a concern not to lose contact with reality and by the consequent need for clear observation to avoid the chimeras of imagination, prejudice, and passion. Finally, it terms her morality rigorous, speaking of her belief in man's fundamental selfishness, the value she places on generosity, and the combined optimism and pessimism she expresses about human nature.)

127   Graham, Janet.   "Immortal Jane Austen."   RDigest, 107 (Dec. 1975), 95-99.

(Biography.)

128   Grigsby, Joan.   "When Jane Danced at Great Hampshire Houses: A Tribute to Jane Austen on Her 200th Birthday."   Hampshire, 16 (Dec. 1975), 53 and 60.

(Biography.)

129   Gubar, Susan. "Sane Jane and the Critics: 'Profes-
        sions and Falsehoods.'" Novel, 8 (1975), 246-59.

        (Review-essay on nos. 10, 30, 34, and 49.)

130   Hagan, John. "The Closure of Emma." SEL, 15 (1975),
        545-61.

        "Securely rooted in a convention of fictional
      realism which precludes . . . moral and psychological
      simplifications," E presents its two major characters
      as "complex, mixed, ambivalent" figures. Thus,
      Emma's reformation, while significant, is not total
      or unqualified, and Mr. Knightley, far from being a
      paragon of reason or a moral norm, proves "romantic"
      and engagingly fallible.

131   Hall, Judith. "Sanditon's 'Other Lady.'" Woman's
        Journal (London), Aug. 1975, p. 71.

        (Marie Dobbs discusses her completion of
      Sanditon.)

132   Halperin, John, ed. Jane Austen: Bicentenary Essays.
        New York: Cambridge Univ. Press, 1975.
        Halperin's book includes a bibliography of
        writings by and about JA.

        Rev. by Lorna Sage in New Statesman, 5 Dec. 1975,
      pp. 719-21; by V. S. Pritchett in NYRB, 17 July 1975,
      p. 26; by J. A. V. Chapple in YWES, 56 (1975), 327;
      in Choice, 13 (1976), 69-70; in ELN, 14 Supplement
      (1976), 27; by Laurence Lerner in Encounter (London),
      47 (July 1976), 66-71; by Gabriele Annan in Listener,
      22 Jan. 1976, pp. 93-94; by Robert Nye in MGW, 8 Feb.
      1976, p. 22; by Avrom Fleishman in MLQ, 37 (1976),
      281-89; by G. B. Tennyson in NCF, 31 (1976), 77-83;
      by Joel Weinsheimer in PLL, 12 (1976), 209-23; by
      F. B. Pinion in RES, NS 27 (1976), 223-26 [and see
      letter, F. B. Pinion, NS 27 (1976), 445]; by Thomas
      McFarland in SEL, 16 (1976), 715; by Barry Roth in
      SNNTS, 8 (1976), 474-81; by Hilary Spurling in
      Spectator, 10 Jan. 1976, p. 14; by Stuart Hampshire
      in TLS, 16 Jan. 1976, p. 54; in VQR, 52 (1976),
      xciii; by Ian Gregor in L&H, no. 5 (1977), pp. 96-
      104; by Mey Hurter in UES, 15 (Apr. 1977), 66-68; by
      Frank McCombie in N&Q, NS 25 (1978), 187-88; by J. F.
      Burrows in MLR, 76 (1981), 936-38.

        John Halperin, "Introduction--Jane Austen's
      Nineteenth-Century Critics: Walter Scott to Henry
      James," pp. 3-42. Between Scott's unsigned review

of E in 1816 and James's comments on her in "The
Lesson of Balzac" (1905), JA "passed through stages
of neglect, belated lionization, and revisionist
questioning." This period contributed very little to
her subsequent critical reputation. Yet, as in
George Henry Lewes's remarks about psychological
verisimilitude and Richard Simpson's analysis of
her treatment of love, education, and society, what
the nineteenth century did offer frequently an-
ticipated and gave shape to Austen criticism in
the twentieth century.

Reuben A. Brower, "From the Iliad to Jane Austen,
via The Rape of the Lock," pp. 43-60. (See no. 58.)

Stuart M. Tave, "Jane Austen and One of Her
Contemporaries," pp. 61-74. Though JA, unlike
Wordsworth, does not explore what is unlimited or
visionary, she does significantly resemble him.
Both treat the small, often unregarded incidents
of common life, in plain, unhackneyed language.
Both also write of duty and of the different effects
of city and country on individual integrity and the
life of the community.

Jane Aiken Hodge, "Jane Austen and Her Publishers," pp. 75-85. "Jane Austen was not lucky
with her publishers," earning less than ±700 in her
lifetime, a figure that compares very unfavorably
with the amounts others like Byron and Scott were
making. Although the climate for writers, and
particularly women writers, was not propitious, her
lack of success "was partly her fault. She did not
want to be a lion." [Part of Hodge's essay appeared
originally, with the title "Jane Austen and the
Publishers," in Cornhill, no. 1071 (Spring 1972), pp.
188-94.]

Katrin Ristkok Burlin, "'The Pen of the Con-
triver': The Four Fictions of Northanger Abbey,"
pp. 89-111. In NA four fictions, each with its own
kind of language, "battle for the heroine's understanding as well as her person." These fictions are
the extravagance of the Gothic novel, "the satiric,
educative fictions of Henry Tilney," "the manipulative, egotistical fictions of the Thorpes," and the
realism of NA itself. Structurally, the novel's
first volume creates all these fictions, and volume
two brings them "to their realization." [See also
no. 748.]

Everett Zimmerman, "Admiring Pope No More Than Is
Proper: Sense and Sensibility," pp. 112-22. JA
considers both sense and sensibility essential to
understand the deceptions of personal feeling and

society. In S and S she presents the horrors of "an
egocentrically distorted view of the world," in
Marianne, as well as of "the imprisonment of the self
within the hardened forms of a sometimes irrelevant
social structure," in Elinor. JA shows that, while
one needs to interact with society, one must also be
protected from it.

Robert B. Heilman, "E pluribus unum: Parts and
Whole in Pride and Prejudice," pp. 123-43. While JA
does not much develop the motif of prejudice in P and
P, she does significantly explore the themes of
humility, marriage, and, especially, pride. She
begins as if her central subjects were unproblematic
but then proceeds to her "drama of definition."
Although "'pride' can become a cliché of multiple
uses but limited usefulness, behind the cliché
currency there lies a profound human motive that
manifests itself in different ways."

Karl Kroeber, "Pride and Prejudice: Fiction's
Lasting Novelty," pp. 144-55. Like JA's other novels
P and P endures because it "enables us to discrimi-
nate underlying principles of personal relations."
By uncovering "ideal possibilities of relationship
beneath specialized manifestations constituting a
particular etiquette, her fiction persists as means
for judging all kinds of manners, including those
(inconceivable to her) of our time."

R. F. Brissenden, "Mansfield Park: Freedom and
the Family," pp. 156-71. MP owes much to the
eighteenth-century novelistic tradition. Like a
comic or non-tragic rendering of Clarissa, JA's novel
allows its virtuous and harassed protagonist to
reconcile successfully the desire to have free choice
and remain a member of the family. And like Pamela,
Joseph Andrews, and Tom Jones, MP explores, in the
relationship between Fanny and Edmund, the theme of
incest. [A synopsis of Brissenden's essay appears in
Proceedings and Papers of the Sixteenth Congress of
the Australasian Universities Language and Literature
Association, Held 21-27 August 1974 at the University
of Adelaide, South Australia (Adelaide: Australasian
Universities Language and Literature Association,
1975), p. 146.]

Kenneth L. Moler, "The Two Voices of Fanny
Price," pp. 172-79. We learn part of Fanny's moral
shortcomings through her two distinctive ways of
talking. She has a "'bookish' voice . . . that
sounds artificial and out of place in the real-life
conversations in which her speeches occur" as well as
a "schoolgirlish inarticulateness." These two styles
of speaking, both related to the schoolroom, point to

her failure to face the actual social world beyond
the East room.

Barbara Hardy, "The Objects in Mansfield Park,"
pp. 180-96. The objects in MP are not conspicuously
sensuous and acquire symbolic significance slowly and
unobtrusively. These objects, from the cast-off
items in the East room to the well-furnished chapel
at Sotherton, help us, among other things, understand
the characters. Fanny, for example, connects objects
to abstract qualities like gratitude and charity and
witnesses how others abuse things, while "objects are
too much for Mrs Price, no trouble at all to Lady
Bertram, and spoils for Mrs Norris." [Part of
Hardy's essay appears also, with the title
"Properties and Possessions," in her A Reading of
Jane Austen (London: Owen, 1975), pp. 136-65; see no.
133.]

John Halperin, "The Worlds of Emma: Jane Austen
and Cowper," pp. 197-206. Always a favorite of hers,
Cowper in The Task treats some of the same themes JA
does in E, including egoism, the mind's capacity for
self-deception, and the need for meaningful social
experience, and he does so from a similar moral
viewpoint.

Joseph Wiesenfarth, "Emma: Point Counter Point,"
pp. 207-20. JA's final and liveliest rendering of
the myth of Pygmalion and Galatea, E "affirms all
that is reasonable and natural in a society that
withstands fanciful delusions and snobbish willful-
ness." The book also concerns matchmaking, clever-
ness, and elegance. [Part of Wiesenfarth's essay
appears also, with the title "Austen and Apollo," in
Jane Austen Today, ed. Joel Weinsheimer (Athens, Ga.:
Univ. of Georgia Press, 1975), pp. 46-63; see no.
184.]

A. Walton Litz, "Persuasion: Forms of Estrangement," pp. 221-32. Evidence of JA's "new-found
Romanticism," P's first volume relies for its effects
on the physical, the internal, the passionate. But
to portray Anne's acute dislocation in volume two JA
reverts to the more objective techniques of her
earlier fiction, in which she largely ignores the
external world and derives her vocabulary from the
value terms of the eighteenth century rather than
from nature. [Litz's essay appears also in Jane
Austen, Northanger Abbey and Persuasion: A Casebook,
ed. B. C. Southam (London: Macmillan Press, 1976),
pp. 228-41.]

Mary Lascelles, "Jane Austen and the Novel," pp.
235-46. Excepting S and S, JA's novels conform to a

pattern: "in its very centre she develops the discovery of love by a young woman, and a man not much older; and this proves a kind of self-discovery, a growing up into self-knowledge." In addition, she creates an "extraordinary illusion of actuality" and unobtrusively sustains "a pervasive sense" of her own presence.

Marvin Mudrick, "Jane Austen's Drawing-Room," pp. 247-61. "The case against Jane Austen always comes down" to the issue of sexuality, particularly female sexuality. What bothered Charlotte Brontë was the articulateness of Austen and her heroines; they are "as strong and brave" in their talk as in their feeling. And that feeling is real because it was JA who discovered that what was going on in the drawing room was passion. Each of her novels tells "more about love and marriage than we could learn from a secret diary or any number of Brontë manuals." [Mudrick's essay appears also, with the title "Jane Austen," in his The Man in the Machine (New York: Horizon Press, 1977), pp. 61-78.]

Donald Greene, "Jane Austen's Monsters," pp. 262-78. A dedicated, unsentimental moralist and "no mean psychopathologist," JA recognizes that man "retains a hard core of original sin." She accordingly shows "the many grotesque forms which the perversion of native human potential can take, and the dangers inherent in that perversion." She creates a full range of monsters and freaks, all of whom lack a capacity for genuine feeling and who fit "the old medieval classification of the seven cardinal sins."

Alistair M. Duckworth, "'Spillikins, Paper Ships, Riddles, Conundrums, and Cards': Games in Jane Austen's Life and Fiction," pp. 279-97. JA uses trivial metaphors, like those pertaining to card and word games, to reveal character and theme, evaluate social performance, and analyze culture. To express her idea of play in a public setting she tries constantly to mediate between the word common as meaning "the trite" and as meaning "community," searching "for individual performance which both invigorates and respects inherited systems of value, for a 'playfulness' that vitalizes without distorting or destroying conventions."

Andrew Wright, "Jane Austen Abroad," pp. 298-317. "Jane Austen does not travel well, but she travels much." P and P, her "most frequently translated" novel, has encountered various difficulties, including loss of subtlety, distortion of meaning, and shift in tone, in modern Chinese, German, Mexican,

Romanian, Russian, and Swedish versions. And the
different English simplifications or abridgments of
P and P likewise fail to do the original justice.

133 Hardy, Barbara. A Reading of Jane Austen. London:
     Owen, 1975. Part of Hardy's book appears also,
     with the title "The Objects in Mansfield Park,"
     in Jane Austen: Bicentenary Essays, ed. John
     Halperin (New York: Cambridge Univ. Press, 1975),
     pp. 180-96 (see no. 132), and, with the title
     "Properties and Possessions in Jane Austen's
     Novels," in Jane Austen's Achievement, Papers
     Delivered at the Jane Austen Bicentennial
     Conference at the University of Alberta, ed.
     Juliet McMaster (New York: Barnes & Noble, 1976),
     pp. 79-105.

     Rev. by Angus Wilson in Observer, 14 Dec. 1975,
     p. 24; by J. A. V. Chapple in YWES, 56 (1975), 327;
     in Choice, 13 (1976), 1296; by John E. Jordan in ELN,
     14 Supplement (1976), 27; by Laurence Lerner in
     Encounter (London), 47 (July 1976), 66-71; by
     Gabriele Annan in Listener, 22 Jan. 1976, pp. 93-94;
     by Robert Nye in MGW, 8 Feb. 1976, p. 22; by Thomas
     McFarland in SEL, 16 (1976), 715-16; by Hilary
     Spurling in Spectator, 10 Jan. 1976, p. 14; by Nirad
     C. Chaudhuri in TLS, 16 Jan. 1976, p. 55; by A. N.
     Kaul in NCF, 32 (1977), 87-91; by Barry Roth in
     SNNTS, 9 (1977), 233-35; by David Hopkinson in B&B,
     24 (Sept. 1979), 64; by J. F. Burrows in AUMLA, no.
     54 (1980), pp. 251-54; by Pierre Goubert in EA, 33
     (1980), 467-68; by C. C. Barfoot in ES, 61 (1980),
     526-27.

     Genre: JA transformed the novel genre by creating
     "a new and flexible medium" in which to reveal
     together the individual and society, a medium that
     relies on "dramatic, psychological and stylistic"
     powers and enables her "to glide easily from sympathy
     to detachment, from one mind to many minds, from
     solitary scenes to social gatherings." This medium
     partly derives from her concern for nuance, "subdued
     action," "vulnerable characters," and "continuity of
     feeling" between private and public worlds.

     Emotion: JA portrays intense passions, especially
     sexual love, as deep inner realities that always move
     beyond self toward others. She values most the
     blending of emotion and rationality, "the passionate
     mind," and contrasts false and true feeling, shallow
     and profound, the "hardened, perverted, or
     affected" lives of the minor figures and the
     more healthy, natural development of the pro-
     tagonists.

Narrators: "Jane Austen depends on a variety of
viewpoints, a number of internal narrators who carry
much of the narrative responsibility, formally and
informally," who tell and listen and move the story
forward even though silent, who contribute to the
novels' elasticity and density, to their "continuity,
climax and conclusion." She uses narrative, too, to
analyze the human mind, particularly its suscepti-
bility to the tales of others, its imaginative
distortions, and its need to control memory.

Society: Though JA studies groups only through
individual events and personalities, she yet explores
"social limit and social change," imagines microcosms
of the larger society, and generates ideas about
"structures, relationships and roles." She inci-
sively dramatizes the dynamics of groups, illustrating themes like love and sexuality and examining
character and rank, morals and manners. And she
ends each novel with a movement outward, with a
sense of community expanded and renewed.

Symbolism: JA treats "properties and possessions"
symbolically, "always locating description in the
mind of her characters. Places and objects are
animated as they become prominent to people, and are
proportioned by individual viewpoint." Things not
only intimately define "owners and donors" but also
help advance the action, give her world solidity, and
probe social arrangements.

"A Sense of the Author": Whether it be NA's
volubility, S and S's harsh generalizations, or P and
P's sober tones, "the flexible commentary adapts
itself to the particular purposes and needs of individual novels and does not change very much with the
growth of the novelist's art." Usually reticent, she
still voices opinions, brief, occasionally poignant
but usually comic ones, some perhaps having auto-
biographical force. In addition, she shows her preoccupations as a novelist in taking imagination's
dangers as a recurrent subject.

134 Herbstein, Denis. "Double Life for the Famous Miss
        Austen." STimes, 19 Oct. 1975, p. 4.

    (On celebrations honoring the bicentennial of
    JA's birth.)

135 Holloway, David. "Universally Acknowledged . . .
        Jane Austen: Bicentenary Thoughts." DTelegraph,
        22 Aug. 1975, p. 10.

(On JA's life and the bicentennial of her birth.)

136   Howard, Philip. "Jane Austen Oddities Put Together
         for Anniversary." Times, 10 Dec. 1975, p. 18.

         (On the British Library's JA exhibition; see no.
      100.)

137   Howard, Philip. "Villagers of Chawton Fete Its
         Dearest Daughter." Times, 19 July 1975, p. 2.

         (On Chawton's celebrating the bicentennial of
      JA's birth.)

138   "How Hampshire Will Honour Jane's Memory." Hamp-
         shire, 15 (July 1975), 35.

         (On the bicentennial.)

139   Hunt, John Dixon, and Peter Willis, eds. "Jane
         Austen (1775-1817)," in The Genius of the Place:
         The English Landscape Garden, 1620-1820. New
         York: Harper & Row, 1975, pp. 372-75.

         (In addition to printing extracts from P and P
      [on Pemberley] and E [on Donwell Abbey], the editors
      comment on the connection JA and Humphry Repton make
      "between design and social morality," a connection
      that places them "firmly in the traditions of the
      English garden that Pope and Burlington and others
      inaugurated.")

140   Hurley, Joan Mason. Our Own Particular Jane.
         Victoria, British Columbia: Room of One's Own
         Press, 1975.

         Rev. by G. B. Tennyson in NCF, 31 (1976), 77-83;
      by Bruce Bailey in BkIC, 6 (Apr. 1977), 20.

         (A "piece of theatre" based on JA's life,
      letters, and novels.)

141   Irons, Keith. Steventon and the Austens. Steventon,
         Hampshire: Jane Austen Bi-centenary Committee,
         1975.

         (Published at the time of JA's bicentennial, when
      Steventon held a series of celebrations, this

souvenir booklet, which also provides a program of
events, describes her life and the village where she
was born.)

142   Isaacs, Enid. In Jane Austen's Country. (Commemora-
        tion Series, 2.) Canberra: Mulini Press, 1975.

    ("An essay by an addict for addicts" recording an
Australian tourist's "highly subjective impressions
gained during a visit to Jane Austen's country,"
especially Winchester, Chawton, and Bath.)

143   Jackson, Michael. "Jane Austen's View of the
        Clergy." Theology, 78 (1975), 531-38.

    Despite JA's reticence about religion "her ethics
are theological." Much indebted to Shaftesbury,
Butler, and Johnson, she pictures a world founded on
"religious principle, which provides the criteria of
moral judgment, which is then translated into action
in behaviour or manners." Her fictional clergymen,
representing "order and continuity," help bind
society together and, indeed, even "constitute it by
example, pastoral zeal and restraint."

144   Jane Austen Bicentenary, 1775-1975: Loan Exhibition,
        Jane Austen's House, Chawton, 2nd July-31st
        August. Alton, Hampshire: [Jane Austen Society,
        1975].

    (Catalogue of the items at the exhibition,
including, among other things, letters, paintings,
and mementos.)

145   "Jane Austen: Revelation and Ridicule." ChrT, 5
        Dec. 1975, p. 32.

    "The first first-rate woman novelist," JA
combines revelation and ridicule to make us examine
ourselves. Though she ignores the climactic events
of her age, she is not escapist; rather, she captures
"through her clear vision of a narrow sphere of
society those sins that ultimately cause wars and
revolutions."

146   The Jane Austen Society: Report for the Year, 1974.
        Alton, Hampshire: Jane Austen Society, [1975].

    (In addition to the guest speaker's address to
the Society's annual general meeting, abstracted

below, this report includes, among other things, several brief notes.)

Charles Beecher Hogan, "Lovers' Vows and Highbury," pp. 19-27. Both MP and E concern play-acting and temptation, and the heroines, who are alike in "the willingness, even the need, to find out the truth of their innermost natures," face tempta-tion "not to become better but to become wiser." [Hogan's essay appears also in Collected Reports of the Jane Austen Society, 1966-1975 (Folkestone: Dawson, 1977), pp. 227-35.]

147   Julian, Mary. "Jane Austen, Born 16th December, 1775." Lady, 11 Dec. 1975, p. 949.

(A twenty-six-line poem wondering what JA would say "If, by some fortunate celestial blunder, / You could return, and take / A trousered Catherine, Emma or Marianne / For heroine, when you should plan / A novel of today.")

148   Kirkham, Margaret. "The Theatricals in Mansfield Park and 'Frederick' in Lovers' Vows." N&Q, NS 22 (1975), 388-90.

JA once saw "a very funny amateur performance of Lovers' Vows and . . . a good many years later, just after Mansfield Park was finished, she was ready to laugh at the remembrance of the chief male character in it."

149   Laski, Marghanita. "Advice from Aunt Jane." Country Life, 3 July 1975, pp. 24-25.

(Describes JA's comments on the art of writing fiction, contained in letters to her brother James's three children.)

150   Laski, Marghanita. Jane Austen and Her World. Rev. ed. London: Thames and Hudson, 1975.

Rev. in Kirkus, 15 May 1977, pp. 563-64; in Kirkus, 15 June 1977, p. 632; in NY, 1 Aug. 1977, pp. 68-69; by Albert H. Johnston in PW, 23 May 1977, p. 236.

(This edition of the biography, which includes more than one hundred pictures portraying the Austen family, various contemporaries, and different aspects of the life of the period, offers minor changes and

additions to the text and notes of the original,
1969 version.)

151   Lee, James W., ed. "Jane Austen Special Number."
        SNNTS, vol. 7 (Spring 1975).

        Rev. by Joel Weinsheimer in PLL, 12 (1976), 209-
      23; by Barry Roth in SNNTS, 8 (1976), 474-81.

        John Halperin, "The Trouble with Mansfield Park,"
      pp. 6-23. Testifying to its "poverty of conception"
      and "misjudgment of life," MP does not perceive that
      Sir Thomas's house is ethically stagnant and
      emotionally dead, while Portsmouth remains vital and
      dynamic. "What is wrong with Mansfield Park is its
      tone, the angle of its moral perspective--its failure
      to recognize life where it exists, its narrow
      identification of moral existence with decorum and
      placidity, and its identification of impropriety with
      action and noise."

        Gerry Brenner, "Mansfield Park: Reading for
      'Improvement,'" pp. 24-32. MP's central ironies lie
      in JA's pretended choice between the values of "moral
      stability and egoistic animation" and in "her
      sustained, oblique rejection of Fanny." Measuring
      worth by the standard of improvement--the notion of
      remedying problems or bettering oneself--the novel
      generates a pessimistic feeling of imminent social
      disaster because it dramatizes only deterioration,
      the failure of all its people and places to develop
      or have effect or operate in a responsible manner.

        Susan J. Morgan, "Emma Woodhouse and the Charms
      of Imagination," pp. 33-48. (See no. 481.)

        Albert E. Wilhelm, "Three Word Clusters in Emma,"
      pp. 49-60. Three groupings of words in E relate to
      vision, to sickness and medical practice, and to
      ruling and power. These vocabulary clusters,
      complementing and strengthening each other, dramatize
      the heroine's errors and ultimate reformation.

        Jane Nardin, "Charity in Emma," pp. 61-72. E
      treats the theme of charity, distinguishing "acts in
      which the donor shows complete respect for the
      recipient's human dignity and autonomy" from those
      devoid of such respect. Although the protagonist
      begins by assuming, like Mrs. Elton, "that social
      superiority necessarily implies intellectual and
      moral superiority," she grows to resemble Mr.
      Knightley, whose "unobtrusive charity springs
      naturally from close daily contact and formal visits
      of investigation and aid."

David M. Monaghan, "The Decline of the Gentry: A Study of Jane Austen's Attitude to Formality in Persuasion," pp. 73-87. (See no. 480.)

Alice Chandler, "'A Pair of Fine Eyes': Jane Austen's Treatment of Sex," pp. 88-103. The novels are "very much about sex," which JA treats as subtly and realistically as other subjects. Using sexual allusions, puns, riddles, and symbols, she shows herself aware of physical sexuality and "fuses the physical with the emotional and the intellectual to create a sense of total human relationships." Signs of male-female attraction may appear hidden, as in P and P, "but they ring true to the complexities of human emotion and to its intensities."

Lesley H. Willis, "Object Association and Minor Characters in Jane Austen's Novels," pp. 104-19. JA gives substance to her minor characters by associating them with concrete, trivial objects. Especially in P and P and MP she applies this technique to suggest a general moral climate, one defined by materialism and sensuality.

William H. Magee, "The Happy Marriage: The Influence of Charlotte Smith on Jane Austen," pp. 120-32. Though they differ as regards style, subtlety, and the realistic presentation of emotional conflict, Smith nevertheless influenced JA from the juvenilia through Sanditon, both specifically, "in incidental phrasing and situations," and generally, in the theme of courtship and marriage.

Leslie F. Chard II, "Jane Austen and the Obituaries: The Names of Northanger Abbey," pp. 133-36. If obituaries in periodicals of about 1810 were the source for characters' names in NA, as seems likely, then we have further evidence of JA's concept of verisimilitude, as well as proof of a "substantial revision" of the novel at that time, one intended to remove or tone down burlesque elements.

J. Donald Crowley, "Jane Austen Studies: A Portrait of the Lady and Her Critics," pp. 137-60. (Review-essay on nos. 10, 34, 39, 42, and 49; this essay reviews as well a number of critical works first published before 1973.)

152 Litz, A. Walton. "Recollecting Jane Austen." CritI, 1 (1975), 669-82.

Since 1930, in the third phase in the history of JA criticism, some critics have sought close readings of the novels, and others have explored her general

cultural assumptions. "The clear need is for a
critical approach which is open and flexible," which
allows for an accommodation between our sense of the
novels as autonomous literary structures and our
sense of them as historical artifacts.

153   McNutt, Dan J. "Influence on Jane Austen," in The
        Eighteenth-Century Gothic Novel: An Annotated
        Bibliography of Criticism and Selected Texts.
        New York: Garland, 1975, pp. 126-27.

(A brief bibliography of writings describing the
Gothic novel's influence on JA.)

154   Mallinson, Anne. "Hampshire's Jane Was Born 200
        Years Ago." Hampshire, 15 (July 1975), 34 and
        36.

(Biography.)

155   Manley, Seon, and Gogo Lewis. "Jane Austen," the
        introduction to "Novels, Gothic Novels," an
        extract from NA, in Ladies of the Gothics: Tales
        of Romance and Terror by the Gentle Sex. New
        York: Lothrop, Lee, & Shepard, 1975, pp. 148-49.

"Everything from the title to the story is
deliberately, enchantingly gothic," yet NA "is, in
truth, not a gothic novel at all, but a magnificent
satire of the whole genre."

156   Mann, Renate. Jane Austen: Die Rhetorik der Moral.
        (Neue Studien zur Anglistik und Amerikanistik,
        4.) Bern and Frankfurt am Main: Lang, 1975.
        Mann's book, which includes a bibliography of
        writings about JA, is abstracted in EASG (1975),
        no. 52, pp. 99-101.

Rev. by Wolfgang G. Müller in Archiv, 214 (1977),
163-65.

(This book, which considers JA as a unique
transitional figure between the eighteenth- and
nineteenth-century novel, develops the relation of
her morality to her rhetoric. It finds that JA
integrates these two concerns, for her rhetoric
plays a double role, helping both to form a convincing text and to determine meaning. This study also
explores such themes as parental authority, social
reform, time, and chance, as well as such structural
elements as narrative point of view, the happy

ending, and the reader's role in discovering value.)

157 Marsh, Honoria D. Shades from Jane Austen. London:
     Jackman, 1975.

     Rev. in AN&Q, 17 (1978), 12.

     (More than eighty illustrations depicting the
     characters in period dress accompany synopses of the
     six major novels, and a chapter by Peggy Hickman
     presents JA's family in silhouette, a table of the
     family's descent, and a chronology of events in the
     family during JA's lifetime.)

158 Monk, Wendy. "Jane Austen's England." ILN, 263
     (Dec. 1975), 53-55.

     (On JA's preference, in her life and novels, for
     the country rather than the city.)

159 Morgan, Susan. "Intelligence in Pride and Preju-
     dice." ModPhil, 73 (1975), 54-68.

     (See no. 481.)

160 Morrison, Marion. "Jane Austen and Her Gardens."
     Country Life, 11 Dec. 1975, pp. 1701-2.

     "Her novels and letters are full of details to
     interest present-day gardeners. . . . The people she
     created have fine houses, and the houses have fine
     gardens, superb back-cloths for the stage on which
     she brings her groups together."

161 Noel-Bentley, E. R. "Jane Austen and Regina Maria
     Roche." N&Q, NS 22 (1975), 390-91.

     (Cites Roche's The Children of the Abbey as the
     source of the name as well as part of the character
     and situation of Bingley in P and P.)

162 Norris, Rev. W. B. Jane Austen and Steventon.
     [Steventon, Hampshire]: Jane Austen Bi-centenary
     Committee, 1975.

     (This booklet includes an essay on JA's life at
     Steventon and the sermons preached at special
     services in Steventon Church on 27 July 1975 to
     commemorate the bicentennial of her birth.)

163 O'Brien, F. V. Pride and Prejudice: An Inaugural
       Lecture Delivered before the Queen's University
       of Belfast on 23 April 1975. (New Lecture
       Series, 87.) Belfast: Queen's Univ. of Belfast,
       1975.

     (A booklet using comments on medical doctors from
     JA's letters and novels "as a mirror to reflect and
     compare some conditions of the present--in Medicine
     and Dentistry today.")

164 O'Donovan, Patrick. "Jane Austen's World Revisited."
       Observer Mag, 14 Dec. 1975, pp. 36-37 and 39.

     (Biography.)

165 Oldfield, John. "Truth at Last on Jane Austen and
       Lyme." Dorset, no. 43 (Apr.-May 1975), pp. 4-9
       and 11.

     During her one or two visits to Lyme Regis, JA
     probably stayed at Hiscott's and not, as tradition
     has it, at Wings.

166 Perosa, Sergio. "Bicentenario della scrittrice
       Jane Austen: Con molto orgoglio e qualche
       pregiudizio." CdS, 29 Dec. 1975, p. 3.

     Though her work is limited, it develops narrative
     form and leads directly to the larger concerns of
     modern fiction. And E offers a particularly fine
     example of the novel's concern for maintaining an
     equilibrium between psychological and social reality.

166a Pitol, Sergio. "Jane Austen, Orgullo y prejuicio,"
       the introduction to an extract, in Spanish, from
       P and P, in De Jane Austen a Virginia Woolf:
       Seis novelistas en sus textos. (SepSetentas,
       186.) Mexico: Office of the Secretary of Public
       Education, 1975, pp. 9-22.

     Distant from the main events of her time, JA, a
     "pure creator," concentrates on the emotions of her
     characters and on humor. She proves memorable for
     her formal perfection, simple thematic elements,
     satirical capacity, sharp observation, lifelike
     dialogue, irony, and control of diction and narra-
     tive point of view.

167 Plimmer, Charlotte and Denis. "'By a Lady.'" In
       Britain, 30 (Sept. 1975), 9-12.

(On JA's life in Steventon, Chawton, and Winchester.)

168 Proops, Marjorie. Pride, Prejudice, and Proops.
     London: Lemon Tree Press, 1975.

     "The dream of Austen's upper middle-class country
     life was to be the fantasy world in which I lived
     until maturer reality pushed fantasy into the back-
     ground. . . . Looking back at Jane Austen's vanished
     world and considering that which has taken its place
     is a temptation which this contemporary student of
     the female sex finds irresistible. That is my
     reason, if reason I must give, for this piece of
     self-indulgence in the year of my inspiration's
     bicentenary."

169 Pye, Vivienne. "A Persistent Ghost." Lady, 4 Dec.
     1975, pp. 886-87.

     (On JA's association with Kent.)

170 Ram, Atma. "Marriage and Money in Jane Austen's
     Novels." PURBA, 6 (Apr. 1975), 9-18.

     Though recognizing money's significance, JA
     stresses rather the importance of love in marriage.
     In her novels "it is only the minor characters who
     worship Mammon and regard its benedictions as the
     sine qua non of married life."

170a Reynolds, John. "Jane Austen and Her Times."
     Southern Arts (Dec. 1975), p. 16.

     (On Hampshire County Library's bicentennial
     exhibition.)

171 Rodway, Allan. "Regency c. 1800-1830: A. General, B.
     Jane Austen, Peacock; Byron, Shelley," in English
     Comedy: Its Role and Nature from Chaucer to the
     Present Day. Berkeley and Los Angeles: Univ. of
     California Press, 1975, pp. 174-208.

     Though both Peacock and JA opposed romanticism,
     he focused on ideas, she on characters. "In a
     Himalayan world, Jane Austen's often seems to be a
     morality, however refined, of the foothills. Clearly
     her comedy aims at being integrative as well as
     conserving, at reconciling head and heart, pride and
     prejudice, but in so far as it succeeds it does so
     only by fastidious exclusion."

172 Ross, Mary Beth. "The 'Bisexual' World of Jane
        Austen." Aphra, 6 (Winter 1974-75), 2-15. See
        also no. 726.

        JA is neither a "feminine" writer nor limited.
        Her fictional universe transcends "traditional sexual
        stereotypes" because she does not present "maleness
        and femaleness as distinct cultural or biological
        characteristics." And, while she concerns herself
        with the trivial and domestic, these offer, in her
        writings, as deep insight into psychological reality
        and human experience as the epic or romance.

173 Sargeant, Jean. "Jane Austen's Little World."
        STimes, 5 Jan. 1975, p. 43.

        (Describes visiting the places in Hampshire where
        JA lived.)

174 Scholes, Robert. "Dr. Johnson and Jane Austen." PQ,
        54 (1975), 380-90.

        JA shares with Johnson a discriminating ethical
        vocabulary, including words like "elegance," "breed-
        ing," and "politeness," and the idea that "manners
        rest on the moral principle of unselfishness." She
        resembles him, too, in considering love and marriage
        unromantically, as matters of both emotion and
        reason.

175 Sinclair, David. "Creaking Door That Shielded a
        Novelist from the World." Times, 19 July 1975,
        p. 12.

        (About JA's life at Chawton.)

176 Southam, B. C. "Introduction" to Sanditon: An
        Unfinished Novel by Jane Austen, Reproduced in
        Facsimile from the Manuscript in the Possession
        of King's College, Cambridge. Oxford: Clarendon
        Press; London: Scolar Press, 1975, pp. v-xviii.

        Rev. by J. A. V. Chapple in YWES, 56 (1975), 327;
        in Choice, 13 (1976), 64; by Gabriele Annan in
        Listener, 22 Jan. 1976, pp. 93-94; by Hilary Spurling
        in Spectator, 10 Jan. 1976, p. 14; by Alan Bell in
        TLS, 16 Jan. 1976, p. 54; by Marilyn Butler in N&Q,
        NS 24 (1977), 374-76; by F. P. Lock in YES, 7 (1977),
        278-79.

        Manuscript changes "confirm that the new style of

<u>Sanditon</u> was an effect that Jane Austen was working
for consciously." Thus, our uncertainty about "the
character of a completed <u>Sanditon</u>" does not arise
from an unfinished manuscript but from the author's
plan. "<u>Sanditon</u> was destined to have this enigmatic
quality from its beginning."

177 Southam, B. C. <u>Jane</u> <u>Austen</u>. Ed. Ian Scott-Kilvert.
        (Writers & Their <u>Work</u>, 241.) Harlow, Essex:
        Longman for the British Council, 1975. Southam's
        pamphlet, which includes a bibliography of writ-
        ings by and about JA, appears also, with the
        title "Jane Austen (1775-1817)," in <u>William</u>
        <u>Wordsworth</u> <u>to</u> <u>Robert</u> <u>Browning</u>, vol. 4 of <u>British</u>
        <u>Writers</u>, ed. Ian Scott-Kilvert (New York:
        Scribner's, 1981), pp. 101-24.

        Rev. by Laurence Lerner in <u>Encounter</u> (London),
        47 (July 1976), 66-71.

        Immensely readable, totally in command of her
        medium, JA captures the "illusion of the gentry's
        vision," providing "us with a historically accurate
        picture of a society under stress." With a
        "sceptical, testing irony" and "coldly realistic"
        view she deals discriminatingly with the themes of
        marriage, family, self-knowledge, duty, and the
        predicament of women whose world does not grant them
        their full humanity. She satirizes her society not
        polemically but dramatically, as part of the life-
        like quality of her comedy of manners. She treats
        language as behavior and mobilizes her semantic
        energies most powerfully in the consideration of
        love: she demonstrates marriage's moral relationship
        to love and love's uncertain connection to passion or
        romantic feeling. But she "was disturbed by the
        power of sexuality, its threat to the security of
        reason and self-control, its melting attack upon the
        certainties of selfhood and identity."

178 "Sparkling Satirist." <u>MD</u>: <u>Medical</u> <u>Newsmagazine</u>, 19
        (May 1975), 153-57 and 161.

        (Biography.)

179 Spina, Giorgio. <u>Linee</u> <u>classiche</u> <u>della</u> <u>narrativa</u> <u>di</u>
        <u>Jane</u> <u>Austen</u>. Genoa: Tilgher, 1975.

        (This book includes chapters on the novel tradi-
        tion from Defoe to Scott, on JA's letters, minor
        works, and novels, and on her style and major themes.
        It divides the novels into two periods, the later

being more serious and complex, and discusses them in
terms of characterization, plot, irony, and the
influence of romanticism. The book also describes
her style as both indebted to the eighteenth century
and original and shows that she values, among other
things, caution, common sense, and social order.)

180 Suddaby, Elizabeth. "Gunpowder Tea." Letter in TLS,
       19 Sept. 1975, p. 1063. See also letters in TLS,
       A. P. Woolrich, 3 Oct. 1975, p. 1141; William
       Gardener, 24 Oct., p. 1265.

There may be a factual basis for the bad effects
of drinking green tea, mentioned in Sanditon (chap.
10).

181 Thomas, Tony. "Pride and Prejudice," in The Films of
       the Forties. Secaucus, N.J.: Citadel Press,
       1975, pp. 12-15.

(Describes the 1940 film.)

182 Tower, Samuel A. "British Quartet for Jane Austen."
       NYT, 19 Oct. 1975, sec. 2, p. 38.

Four stamps, portraying characters from the
novels, will commemorate the bicentennial of JA's
birth.

183 Vallance, Elizabeth. "Mores the Pity." Guardian,
       17 Dec. 1975, p. 9.

"We'll no doubt go on reading Jane Austen, in the
bicentenary and beyond, not because we readily
identify directly with her characters and the
trivialities of their limited existences, but for the
nostalgia they evoke for more form, more stability,
more elegance and continuity in our own lives."

184 Weinsheimer, Joel, ed. Jane Austen Today. Athens,
       Ga.: Univ. of Georgia Press, 1975.

Rev. by Jane Nardin in Book Forum, 2 (1976), 643-
46; by John Lauber in ELN, 14 (1976), 135-37; by John
E. Jordan in ELN, 14 Supplement (1976), 28; by Avrom
Fleishman in MLQ, 37 (1976), 281-89; by G. B.
Tennyson in NCF, 31 (1976), 77-83; by Joel
Weinsheimer in PLL, 12 (1976), 209-23; by Thomas
McFarland in SEL, 16 (1976), 715; by Barry Roth in
SNNTS, 8 (1976), 474-81; by Nirad C. Chaudhuri in

TLS, 16 Jan. 1976, p. 55; in VQR, 52 (1976), xli-
xlii; by R. D. Stock in ModA, 21 (1977), 104-6; by
JoAnn T. Hackos in SCB, 37 (1977), 49-50; by Stuart
M. Tave in MLR, 73 (1978), 163-66; by Andrew Wright
in SBHT, 19 (1978), 184-87.

Alistair M. Duckworth, "Prospects and Retro-
spects," pp. 1-32. In spite of the large amount of
attention paid JA recently, we remain far from any
critical consensus about her. While her works are
open to many readings, including the "substantive,"
the "relational," and the "symbolic," we should
avoid overemphasizing the "enigmatic nature" of her
art. Our current task is "the search for a criticism
which, while accepting and indeed celebrating a
plurality of significances, can yet argue convinc-
ingly for a measure of 'closure' in the novels."

Karl Kroeber, "Subverting a Hypocrite Lecteur,"
pp. 33-45. As a "classical novel," NA "works with
and through conventions of both language and
behaviour, subverting our preconceptions to free us
from their tyranny." Its "realism expands our awareness of reality," and its conclusion "crystallizes
Jane Austen's novel-long exposure of the
quintessential hypocrisy of novel-readers, a
pretense of not taking novels seriously to conceal a
tendency to take them all too literally."

Joseph Wiesenfarth, "Austen and Apollo," pp. 46-
63. JA uses elements of the Pygmalion and Cinderella
stories to help structure her novels and indicate her
values. While the Cinderella myth, found in P and P
and P, tells a socially radical story and has a
heroine in a "commanding moral position," the
Pygmalion myth, noticeable in MP and E, is
conservative and dominated by a basically male
voice. Since both patterns concern creation and
redemption, they are inherently congenial to
Christianity, another myth JA relies on. [Part of
Wiesenfarth's essay appears also, with the title
"Emma: Point Counter Point," in Jane Austen:
Bicentenary Essays, ed. John Halperin (New York:
Cambridge Univ. Press, 1975), pp. 207-20; see no.
132.]

Juliet McMaster, "Love and Pedagogy," pp. 64-91.
(See no. 351.)

Norman Page, "Orders of Merit," pp. 92-108. One
way to note the differences among the novels is to
consider which novel different periods thought the
best. The nineteenth century recognized P and P "as
the Austen novel" and did not respond as keenly to E
as "post-Jamesian and presentday readers." Modern

criticism has helped MP win "belated recognition,"
but P remains "the most consistently undervalued of
the six novels."

Robert Alan Donovan, "The Mind of Jane Austen,"
pp. 109-27. In contrast to the belief of some
critics, JA the novelist and JA the letter-writer
"are one and the same." Both observe their world
closely, quickly seize on what is ludicrous, espouse
identical ethical values, and think in terms of
"generalized reflections about life." Knowing and
sharing her correspondent's attitudes, however, JA
the letter-writer did not provide the "integrating
view of life" that "controls and disciplines the
substance of the novels."

Joel Weinsheimer, "Jane Austen's Anthropocen-
trism," pp. 128-41. "The central defect of
Jane Austen's novels is that they study man
in a vacuum." Although her basic subject,
"the moral and social relations of men and women,"
is certainly important, she "focuses so exclusively"
on it that she divests her characters of part of
their humanity. Her failure to imagine an
impersonal or nonhuman frame of reference for human
experience "occasions the most damaging criticism
that can be levelled against Jane Austen--that she
is a novelist of manners."

Donald Greene, "The Myth of Limitation," pp.
142-75. Contrary to the assertions of her
detractors, JA is not limited. She does treat,
among other things, strong emotions, death, sex,
hunger, war, and guilt, and the statements she makes
about her narrow range, including the reference to
"two inches of ivory," must be read ironically. What
she accomplishes as a novelist fits exactly "her
dramatic, as opposed to epic, technique of novel-
writing." Observing accurately and presenting
effectively, her novels remain contiguous "with
modern interests," not local manifestations but as
true now as when written.

185 Weinsheimer, Joel C. "In Praise of Mr. Woodhouse:
        Duty and Desire in Emma." ArielE, 6 (Jan. 1975),
        81-95.

Though treated ironically, Mr. Woodhouse is not
"merely an idiot or egotist." JA never permits our
awareness of his "faults to obscure his claims as a
parent and concomitantly as a representative of the
stability of the family, the society, and the moral
order." At the end Emma's decision not to leave him
"epitomizes the novel's central truth, that only

within the community is self-realization possible."

186 Weinstein, Mark A. "An Echo of Mrs. Bennet in
        Waverley." N&Q, NS 22 (1975), 63-64.

     (Locates in Waverley an echo of Mrs. Bennet's
     response upon learning of Elizabeth's engagement to
     Darcy.)

187 Welsh, Alexander, ed. "Jane Austen, 1775-1975."
        NCF, vol. 30 (Dec. 1975).

     Rev. by J. A. V. Chapple in YWES, 56 (1975), 328;
     by Laurence Lerner in Encounter (London), 47 (July
     1976), 66-71; by Barry Roth in SNNTS, 8 (1976), 474-
     81.

     Alexander Welsh, "Foreword," pp. 253-56. We
     study her fiction's limits because she portrays a
     life "one might possess and yet cannot," a life
     involving a seemingly stable society, decipherable
     ambiguities, and a moral experience confined within
     fixed comic boundaries.

     Donald Greene, "New Verses by Jane Austen," pp.
     257-60. (Describes and prints an 1806 "humorous poem
     written by Jane Austen for the amusement of her
     intimate friend Martha Lloyd.")

     Martin Price, "Manners, Morals, and Jane Austen,"
     pp. 261-80. JA creates a comic world based on an
     uncynical awareness of human limits, on a delight in
     incongruity coupled with a belief in "implicit
     purposiveness." She gains density through
     manners--"concrete, complex orderings, both personal
     and institutional," ideally implying emotions and
     beliefs--and moral judgments, which, "at once
     necessary and dangerous . . . exercise our deepest
     passions" yet "terminate our free awareness." She
     values a "sense of the problematic" and "an openness
     to experience that restrains the shaping will."
     [Price's essay appears also, in an enlarged form,
     with the title "Austen: Manners and Morals," in his
     Forms of Life: Character and Moral Imagination in
     the Novel (New Haven: Yale Univ. Press, 1983), pp.
     65-89; see no. 669.]

     Valerie Shaw, "Jane Austen's Subdued Heroines,"
     pp. 281-303. In MP and P, her "muted novels," JA
     broadens and deepens the irony and "ordeal pattern"
     found in her other works, using social and literary
     conventions to challenge convention's power and
     communicate intrinsically private feelings. She here

creates unstable, egotistic societies, which
tragically isolate and pain the protagonists, who
experience "the difficulties of socially mediating
personal value."

Francis R. Hart, "The Spaces of Privacy: Jane
Austen," pp. 305-33. JA's novels "show a formative
concern with the achievement of true privacy and
intimacy on the one hand and the realization of
personal and domestic space on the other." They
articulate distances between people "in sound and
silence, in styles, tones, and levels of speech"
and realize spaces "by the social actions and
rituals" occurring in them. As characters grow,
they discover the need they share with others for
privacy and develop a sense of both physical and
social space.

George Levine, "Translating the Monstrous:
Northanger Abbey," pp. 335-50. NA, which "depends on
the silliness it mocks," does not so much reject
heroism as translate it into another tongue.
"Monstrosity"--impossible, dangerous romantic energy
or aspiration beyond ordinary life's limits--"manages
to squeeze past Jane Austen's ironies into the world"
that denies monstrosity's existence. It lives "at
the formal heart" of all her novels, "parodied but
not dismissed." [Levine's essay appears also, in an
enlarged form, with the title "Northanger Abbey:
From Parody to Novel and the Translated Monster," in
his The Realistic Imagination: English Fiction from
Frankenstein to Lady Chatterley (Chicago: Univ. of
Chicago Press, 1981), pp. 61-80.]

Ruth apRoberts, "Sense and Sensibility, or Growing Up Dichotomous," pp. 351-65. Though we may begin
S and S by accepting the title's polar terms as a
valid test of character, JA refuses us easy generalizations. Because she views learning as a continuing
dialectical process, she "takes her contraries or
antitheses not as ends, but as means, to a kind of
progression or education." We learn finally that
decency means being able to feel for ourselves and
others.

Walter E. Anderson, "Plot, Character, Speech, and
Place in Pride and Prejudice," pp. 367-82. "The
luminosity of Pride and Prejudice resides in its
central love story. In it we may discover the
relatively subordinate formal place of character,
thought, and language to plot. The dramatic action
itself, organized by Elizabeth Bennet's change in
situation and fortune, determines the work's
essential form, power, and interest."

K. K. Collins, "Mrs. Smith and the Morality of

Persuasion," pp. 383-97. Mrs. Smith functions
significantly in P less to advance the plot than
to substantiate the novel's ethical vision and
embody two key themes--"the danger of giving
advice and the elusiveness of evidence." She
"acts according to a principle of conduct
implicit within these themes: one must behave
not only from concern for another's prosperity,
but also with respect to the valid subjectivity of
another's judgments."

Mark Kinkead-Weekes, "This Old Maid: Jane
Austen Replies to Charlotte Brontë and D. H.
Lawrence," pp. 399-419. Charlotte Brontë and
D. H. Lawrence disliked JA partly because of her
satiric temperament and "her perception of life
as primarily social." Yet one can defend her
against their detractions by showing "how much
there is beneath the surface and between the lines,
including a very humane if delicately indirect
concern with the heart and its deceptions" as well
as a concern with "knowing in togetherness."

Andrew Wright, "Jane Austen Adapted," pp.
421-53. While "no one writes Jane Austen so
well as Jane Austen," she has been much adapted
in English--abridged, simplified, continued,
dramatized, and poetically embodied. These
different versions all reflect the "time or
place" of origin and "the internal circumstances
of the countries in which the adaptations make
their appearance." In general "the closer the
rendering" is to the original the better.

1976

188 Abernethy, Peter L., Christian J. W. Kloesel,
       and Jeffrey R. Smitten, comps. "Jane Austen,"
       in English Novel Explication: Supplement I.
       Hamden, Conn.: Shoe String Press, 1976, pp.
       3-9.

     (Bibliography.)

189 Auerbach, Nina. "Austen and Alcott on Matriarchy:
       New Women or New Wives?" Novel, 10 (1976), 6-26.
       Auerbach's essay appears also in Towards a
       Poetics of Fiction: Essays from Novel: A Forum
       on Fiction, 1967-1976, ed. Mark Spilka
       (Bloomington, Ind.: Indiana Univ. Press, 1977),
       pp. 266-86, and, with the title "Waiting
       Together: Two Families," in her Communities of
       Women: An Idea in Fiction (Cambridge, Mass.:

Harvard Univ. Press, 1978), pp. 33-73.

The real center of power in P and P is masculine.
While females abuse power, "the male whom all await
can alone bring substance," endowing existence with
physical, financial, social, and emotional reality.
JA may have derived this sense of a female community's oppressive blankness from her life at
Chawton.

190   Barker, Gerard A. "Ironic Implications in the
          Characterization of Sir Edward Denham." PLL, 12
          (1976), 150-60.

Contrary to much critical opinion, both the flat-
ness and absurdity of Sir Edward Denham's characterization are intentional and would have remained in
a completed Sanditon. He "actually represents a
highly ironic attack on the eighteenth-century
critic-moralist of the novel in his dogmatic insistence on didactic, exemplary fiction devoid of
all 'mixed characters.'"

191   Bateson, F. W., and Harrison T. Meserole. "Jane
          Austen (1775-1817)," in A Guide to English and
          American Literature. 3d ed. New York: Longman,
          1976, p. 166.

(Bibliography.)

192   Batey, Mavis. "Jane Austen at Stoneleigh Abbey."
          Country Life, 30 Dec. 1976, pp. 1974-75.

(Discusses the outing to Sotherton in MP as a
reenactment of the Austen family's visit to
Stoneleigh Abbey in 1806.)

193   Burrows, J. F. "Persuasion and Its 'Sets of
          People.'" SSEng, 2 (1976-77), 3-23.

Though P contrasts the Bath and naval circles, it
also groups its characters more complexly: Sir Walter
represents not the gentry but "certain habits of
mind" common to people in all social ranks; the
sailors, while all firmly individualized, share the
propensities of professional men; and Anne "is more
various and interesting than any 'picture of perfection.'" For JA, finally, "a Christian sense of duty"
transcends other differences between people.

194   Burstall, Christopher, Germaine Greer, Mary McCarthy,

and Arianna Stassinopoulos. "'The Incident Is
Not Closed'--A Conversation about Jane Austen."
Listener, 25 Dec. 1975-1 Jan. 1976, p. 875.

JA is noteworthy for her picture of "the real
state of unregenerate humanity," her "definite
philosophy of life," and her control of tone, which
allows her to keep open "the narrative possibilities
in a description."

194a [Charles, John.] "Jane Austen and Her Contem-
        poraries: Notes for an Exhibition." NRBR, 16
        (1976), 42-55.

(Catalogue of the 1975 exhibition at the University of Alberta commemorating the bicentennial.)

195 Clanchy, V. A. "Jane Austen and the Williams
        Family." Hampshire, 17 (Dec. 1976), 56-58.

(On JA's connection with the family of Philip
Williams.)

196 Daiches, David, and Barbara Hardy. "Jane Austen," in
        The English Novel. Ed. Cedric Watts. (Questions
        in Literature.) London: Sussex, 1976, pp. 13-30.

JA has a profound "sense of daily living and the
ordinariness of life." She knows the abyss is there
but recognizes "that to tell the truth about life we
ought to concentrate more on annoyance than tragedy,
irritation than anger, disturbance than total dislocation." By focusing on the quotidian, she also
shows "the degree of social self-consciousness and
social learning" that people can achieve.

197 Demurova, N. "Predislovie" [Preface] to Gordost' i
        predubiezhdienie: Roman; Abbatstvo Nortenger:
        Roman [Pride and Prejudice: Novel; Northanger
        Abbey: Novel]. Moscow: Hudozhestviennaia
        Litieratura, 1976, pp. 3-20.

A realistic and satiric novelist, JA
proves successful at characterization and plot
because she writes on two planes--negative and
positive, subjective and objective--and these
planes make her work harmonious. In terms of
structure she begins each of her books by
presenting a flawed protagonist, who in the
course of the action achieves self-knowledge,
frees herself from error, and refines her feelings.

198   The Diagram Group. "Cassandra Leigh," in Mothers:
      100 Mothers of the Famous and the Infamous. New
      York: Paddington Press, 1976, pp. 20-21.

      (Biography.)

199   Doubleday, Neal Frank. "Henry & Catherine," in
      Variety of Attempt: British and American Fiction
      in the Early Nineteenth Century. Lincoln, Nebr.:
      Univ. of Nebraska Press, 1976, pp. 19-35.

      JA's satiric target in NA is finally the novel
      form itself. She did not take the genre as seriously
      as did Henry James.

200   Duffy, Joseph M. "The Politics of Love: Marriage and
      the Good Society in Pride and Prejudice." UWR,
      11 (Spring-Summer 1976), 5-26.

      In contrast to others around them Elizabeth and
      Darcy achieve in their marriage an equilibrium
      between the forces of nature and civilization. They
      "establish what is substantially a political order, a
      system of government where feeling and intelligence,
      liberty and restraint will prevail in a state of
      creative movement generated by love. The politics of
      love creates a society adequate for human fulfill-
      ment."

201   Dunn, Richard J., ed. "Jane Austen," in Defoe
      through Hardy, vol. 1 of The English Novel:
      Twentieth-Century Criticism. Chicago: Swallow
      Press, 1976, pp. 1-11.

      (Bibliography.)

202   Fleishman, Avrom. "The State of the Art: Recent Jane
      Austen Criticism." MLQ, 37 (1976), 281-89.

      (Review-essay on nos. 110, 132, and 184.)

203   Gilbert, John. "Introduction" to The Works of Jane
      Austen. New York: Spring, 1976, pp. [vii-viii].

      "Open any of the books at random and you will
      find every page radiating her sweet and gentle
      temperament, her quiet good sense and humour. Life,
      as she found it, surprised, amused and delighted her.
      She had little talent for moralising, no profound
      intellectual pretensions, no deep emotional,

political or religious entanglements."

204 Gold, Joel J. "The Return to Bath: Catherine Morland
        to Anne Elliot." Genre, 9 (1976), 215-29.

        Unlike JA's usual practice, character and setting
     in NA and P do not complement each other. She uses
     the contrast between the heroine and her surroundings
     in the earlier novel as a satiric tool and in the
     later one to reveal Anne's value. After P's "return
     to Bath," JA made new use of a resort setting, for in
     Sanditon place itself "becomes more clearly a focal
     point."

205 Halperin, John, and Janet Kunert. Plots and Charac-
        ters in the Fiction of Jane Austen, the Brontës,
        and George Eliot. (Plots and Characters Series.)
        Hamden, Conn.: Archon, 1976.

        Rev. by J. A. V. Chapple and Owen Knowles in
     YWES, 57 (1976), 280-81; by Koert C. Loomis, Jr., in
     ARBA, 8 (1977), 597; in Choice, 13 (1977), 1570; by
     Gilbert B. Cross in LibJ, 102 (1977), 91; by Charles
     A. Bunge in WLB, 51 (1977), 537; by T. J. Winnifrith
     in MLR, 74 (1979), 663-64.

        (Summarizes the plots of JA's major novels and
     some minor works and catalogues the characters.)

206 Hanson, Christopher. "Jane Austen's Point of View."
        MLPS, 118 (1975-76), 5-21.

        By means of a flexible, uneccentric prose and
     control of novelistic tempo, JA blends successfully
     three different but related methods of communication
     to create "her fictive illusion." She uses direct
     statements, enters into the consciousness of her
     protagonists, and establishes "subtle parallels"
     between the characters "which tacitly comment on
     the nature and value of behaviour and motives."
     The artistic unity thus achieved reflects the harmony
     she "sees as a prime good of society and of the
     individual."

207 Harrison, Bernard. "Muriel Spark and Jane Austen,"
        in The Modern English Novel: The Reader, the
        Writer, and the Work. Ed. Gabriel Josipovici.
        New York: Barnes & Noble, 1976, pp. 225-51.

        Though JA and Spark share certain qual-
     ities, like a preference for what is material

rather than fanciful, they differ significantly in
that JA is more overtly clear. Because JA holds
together fiction and reality "by the tensions and
constraints of simultaneously maintaining the
plausibility of a complex fiction and the coherence
of an organising moral viewpoint, readers feel that
they 'know where they are' with Jane Austen, whereas
with Muriel Spark they don't."

208 Hopkinson, David. "The Naval Career of Jane Austen's
      Brother." HistT, 26 (1976), 576-83.

    (Describes Francis Austen's career and JA's use
in her fiction and letters of her knowledge of naval
affairs.)

209 Hopkinson, Diana. "The Austen Lace." Country Life,
      16 Dec. 1976, pp. 1848 and 1851.

    (Account of three pieces of silk lace, an Austen
family heirloom.)

210 Iwami, Takeo. "Onna no sakka to onna no shujinko:
      Jane Austen to sono sekai" [Jane Austen and her
      world], in Eibungaku no hirointachi [Heroines in
      English literature]. Ed. Yoshinobu Aoyama.
      Tokyo: Hyōronsha, 1976, pp. 157-85.

    Like JA's other novels P and P treats love and
marriage by focusing on the ordinary life of a
female protagonist. In the context of strict
ethical and social codes and in a society that
accorded women only a low status, Elizabeth acts
courageously, confident of the equality of the
sexes.

211 The Jane Austen Society: Report for the Year, 1975.
      Alton, Hampshire: Jane Austen Society, [1976].

    (In addition to the guest speaker's address to
the Society's annual general meeting, abstracted
below, this report includes, among other things,
several brief notes.)

    A. L. Rowse, "The England of Jane Austen," pp.
17-31. JA has a wider social range than is generally
recognized. In addition, she treats realistically
the subtly articulated world of her time, viewing it
with a discriminating mind and without any illusions.
[Rowse's essay appears also in Collected Reports of
the Jane Austen Society, 1966-1975 (Folkestone:

Dawson, 1977), pp. 251-65, and, with the title "Jane Austen as Social Realist," in his Portraits and Views: Literary and Historical (New York: Barnes & Noble, 1979), pp. 3-17.]

212 Kestner, Joseph. "Sanditon or The Brothers: Nature into Art." PLL, 12 (1976), 161-66.

JA's rendering of Plato's Republic, Sanditon opposes two versions of nature and compares them ethically and aesthetically with art. "The creation of a world is the subject of The Brothers, but that world is not Sanditon." Simply stated, the book argues "that one should build a novel out of life."

213 Kestner, Joseph. "Two Centuries After: Jane Austen." Nation, 5 June 1976, pp. 693-95.

Two hundred years after her birth JA "has survived the ultimate test--that of form." Having begun by sabotaging the epistolary, sentimental, and Gothic traditions in fiction, she ended by changing "not only the novel but the art of the novel from passivity to encounter." She brilliantly used "the center or filtering intelligence" and brought "devastating ironic understatement to bear" on such themes as feminism, sex, and marriage.

214 Kulkin, Mary-Ellen. "Jane Austen, 1775-1817: British Novelist," in Her Way: Biographies of Women for Young People. Chicago: American Library Association, 1976, pp. 19-20.

(Biography.)

215 Lee, Hermione. "'Taste' and 'Tenderness' as Moral Values in the Novels of Jane Austen," in Literature of the Romantic Period, 1750-1850. Ed. R. T. Davies and B. G. Beatty. (English Texts and Studies.) New York: Barnes & Noble, 1976, pp. 82-95.

Following eighteenth-century practice, JA presents taste and tenderness as signs of virtue and satirizes affected or excessive manifestations of these qualities. Of all her novels MP asserts the strongest connection between aesthetic sensibilities and moral value. Here, taste and tenderness "sanctify places and relationships with a sense of the past, and are given the force of religious principles."

216 Lewicki, Zbigniew. "Pseudogotycki romans Jane
         Austen." Nowe Książki, 15 Mar. 1976, pp. 65-66.
         Lewicki's essay includes mention of a Polish
         translation of NA.

         Popular in Poland, JA remains enjoyable to read,
     as NA demonstrates. Yet she could only write well
     about women, her men proving dull, unoriginal, and
     sometimes perverse.

217 Lock, F. P. "Camilla, Belinda, and Jane Austen's
         'Only a Novel.'" N&Q, NS 23 (1976), 105-6.

         Maxwell (see no. 85) misreads the passage from
     Belinda that he connects to NA's defense of novels.
     Lady Delacour, far from being hostile to any attack
     on prose fiction, "really is speaking against
     novels." In the passage it is only Edgeworth, not
     her character, who supports Burney's practice in
     Camilla.

218 McMaster, Juliet, ed. Jane Austen's Achievement.
         Papers Delivered at the Jane Austen Bicentennial
         Conference at the University of Alberta. New
         York: Barnes & Noble, 1976.

         Rev. by Barry Roth in SNNTS, 8 (1976), 474-81; by
     Andrew Lincoln in YWES, 57 (1976), 253; by William H.
     Magee in ArielE, 8 (Oct. 1977), 108-10; in Choice, 14
     (1977), 200; by Nina K. Wilson in LibJ, 102 (1977),
     203; by Stuart M. Tave in NCF, 32 (1977), 334-39; by
     F. B. Pinion in RES, NS 28 (1977), 477-78; by Atma
     Ram in RUSE, 10 (1977), 71-75; by John E. Jordan in
     ELN, 16 Supplement (1978), 44; by Marilyn Butler in
     N&Q, NS 25 (1978), 562-63; by Alan Kennedy in ESC, 5
     (1979), 122-24; by Andrew Wright in MLR, 74 (1979),
     423-25.

         B. C. Southam, "Sanditon: The Seventh Novel,"
     pp. 1-26. While closely connected to NA and, through
     the motif of improvement, to the other novels,
     Sanditon signifies a "radical change . . . in Jane
     Austen's art, away from the comedy of character and
     towards the comedy of ideas." Fresh and inventive,
     basing personality on eccentricity, in the manner of
     Congreve and Sheridan, and marked by "detailed social
     and literary reference," it proves the most con-
     centrated work in the canon.

         Lloyd W. Brown, "The Business of Marrying and
     Mothering," pp. 27-43. Clarifying the attitudes
     implied in her novels and reflecting "her essentially
     bleak vision," JA's letters show her de-romanticizing

or demystifying marriage and motherhood without
unequivocally rejecting them. These subjects remain
businesses for her, complete with their "physical
cost to the woman and with role responsibilities that
exact their toll on her individuality." Considered
in this context, the domestic felicity lauded at the
end of the novels functions as "ironic counterpoint
to . . . dominant social realities."

Norman Page, "The Great Tradition Revisited," pp.
44-63. JA influenced, among others, George Eliot,
Henry James, and E. M. Forster, resembling the first
in setting, irony, and language, the second in
themes, situations, and tone, and the third in the
importance accorded moral issues and judgments.
"What is more significant, though less easy to point
to in a text, is a shared notion among these authors
of the purpose of the novel and of its relevance to
the business of living."

A. Walton Litz, "'A Development of Self':
Character and Personality in Jane Austen's Fiction,"
pp. 64-78. JA's fiction provides a sense of the
ego's and the environment's stability, of cohesive-
ness and seeming inevitability, of "a world of Being
rather than a world of Becoming." Only P suggests
"the disturbing possibility of alterations in the
self" and "does not leave us with the composed sense
of 'it is finished.'" Accompanying this development,
P, while still a comedy, "shades constantly toward
the tragic."

Barbara Hardy, "Properties and Possessions in
Jane Austen's Novels," pp. 79-105. (See no. 133.)

George Whalley, "Jane Austen: Poet," pp. 106-33.
"Jane Austen is a poet" in the craftsmanship of her
language and the conduct of her fictional action.
Always precise, economical, and vivid, she has an
"impeccable sense" of the interactions of words,
uses "the isolable pregnant phrase," and imparts an
"electrical vitality" to her style. She creates
worlds which, "though gossamer-fine," are "foot-
thick realities," establishing immediately the
physical and psychic "relations of persons to things,
places, and other persons."

219 "Mól." "W poszukiwaniu męża." Wiadomości (Wrocław),
     1 Jan. 1976, p. 15. The comments by "Mól" on JA
     include mention of a Polish translation of P and
     P.

P and P offers psychological portraits, notably
of the heroine, and in general JA's novels feature

realistic descriptions and humor and center on the
gentry.

220 Monaghan, David. "Jane Austen and the Social
        Critics: Recent Trends." ESC, 2 (1976), 280-87.
        Monaghan's essay includes a bibliography of JA
        social criticism.

    Though recent social criticism of JA has
clarified aspects of her work previously neglected,
much remains to be done in such areas as the role of
women, manners, and politics in the novels. To
examine these subjects completely we will have to go
back to contemporary sources. But "future social
criticism will be of little use unless . . . it also
gives us a fuller appreciation of the beauty of Jane
Austen's art."

221 Monaghan, David. "The Myth of 'Everybody's Dear
        Jane': An Assessment of Jane Austen on Her Two
        Hundredth Birthday." Insight, 5 (Winter 1976),
        2-10.

    (An edited version of a public lecture, this
essay appears also, revised and expanded, with the
title "The Myth of 'Everybody's Dear Jane': A
Reassessment of Jane Austin [sic]," in Atlantis, 3
[Fall 1977], 112-26; see no. 285.)

222 Morgan, Susan. "Polite Lies: The Veiled Heroine of
        Sense and Sensibility." NCF, 31 (1976), 188-205.

    (See no. 481.)

223 Myers, Carol Fairbanks. "Austen, Jane," in Women in
        Literature: Criticism of the Seventies.
        Metuchen, N.J.: Scarecrow Press, 1976, pp. 7-13.

    (Bibliography.)

224 Noel-Bentley, E. R. "A Further Note on Jane Austen
        and 'Thorough Novel Slang.'" N&Q, NS 23 (1976),
        107.

    (Cites another occurrence of the phrase "vortex
of dissipation," to add to those mentioned in no.
26.)

225 Patterson, Emily H. "Family and Pilgrimage Themes

in Austen's <u>Mansfield</u> <u>Park</u>." <u>CLAJ</u>, 20 (1976), 14-18.

Themes pertaining to the family and pilgrimage, familiar to the eighteenth-century novel, persist in JA. In <u>MP</u>, for example, Fanny undergoes two expulsions and pilgrimages but finally finds her true family.

226 Ram, Atma. "The Beginning in the Jane Austen Novel: An Analysis." <u>BP</u>, no. 21 (1976), pp. 57-62.

In each of her opening chapters, which are organic wholes, JA sets the novel's tone, begins to describe characters and storyline, indicates her main interests, such as money and human relationships, and in general "points to the 'impression' of the work."

227 Ram, Atma. "Heroines in <u>Sense</u> <u>and</u> <u>Sensibility</u>." <u>PURBA</u>, 7 (Oct. 1976), 19-23.

(See no. 610.)

228 Rees, Joan. <u>Jane</u> <u>Austen</u>: <u>Woman</u> <u>and</u> <u>Writer</u>. New York: St. Martin's Press, 1976. Rees's book includes a bibliography of writings by and about JA.

Rev. by Michael Hardwick in <u>DQ</u>, 11 (Autumn 1976), 150-51; in <u>Kirkus</u>, 1 Aug. 1976, p. 892; by Nina K. Wilson in <u>LibJ</u>, 101 (1976), 2056; in <u>NY</u>, 18 Oct. 1976, p. 187; by Albert H. Johnston in <u>PW</u>, 2 Aug. 1976, pp. 107-8; by Andrew Lincoln in <u>YWES</u>, 57 (1976), 253-54; by Moira Dearnley in <u>AWR</u>, 26 (Spring 1977), 185-87; by Edward Dickey in <u>BestS</u>, 36 (1977), 359; in <u>Choice</u>, 13 (1977), 1599; by John Halperin in <u>SNNTS</u>, 9 (1977), 98-99.

(Biography.)

229 Reinhold, Heinz. "Jane Austen (1775-1817)," in <u>Der</u> <u>Englische</u> <u>Roman</u> des <u>19</u>. <u>Jahrhunderts</u>. (Studienreihe Englisch, 31.) Düsseldorf: Bagel, 1976, pp. 14-22. Reinhold's book includes a bibliography of writings by and about JA.

Indebted chiefly to the eighteenth century, though showing the influence of romanticism somewhat in her last three novels, and particularly <u>P</u>, JA maintains a classic coolness and distance from her work and stresses the values of clarity, moderation, order, and balance. She adheres strictly to moral norms, handles the themes of love and marriage didactically and satirically, and concentrates on character development. Creating a limited world, she avoids evil and the tragic aspects of life.

230   Roth, Barry. "Celebrating the Bicentennial: Jane Austen and Her Recent Critics." SNNTS, 8 (1976), 474-81.

(Review-essay on nos. 108, 110, 118, 132, 151, 184, 187, and 218.)

231   Ruoff, Gene W., ed. "[Jane Austen Special Issue.]" WC, vol. 7 (Autumn 1976).

Rev. by Andrew Lincoln in YWES, 57 (1976), 254-55; by John E. Jordan in ELN, 15 Supplement (1977), 44-45.

Karl Kroeber, "Jane Austen, Romantic," pp. 291-96. JA's is an "authentic Romantic vision," for her novels encourage "imaginative activity," stressing "possibilities, not predeterminations, of desire, though developing possibilities out of predeter-minations." They are constructively skeptical, built "upon issues of emotionalized perceptions" and "shaped to enable an audience to re-fictionalize itself free from the sterility of established fictions."

Joseph Kestner, "Jane Austen: The Tradition of the English Romantic Novel, 1800-1832," pp. 297-311. The English Romantic novelists, including JA, Edgeworth, and Scott, played an important role in the novel's development. Among other things they defined the legacy of the eighteenth century, de-emphasized plot, and circumscribed locality. They concentrated on the themes of education and law, especially the motif of the entail, and, by developing the novel's dramatic qualities, they directed attention away from the author and toward the reader's role in the narrative process.

L. J. Swingle, "The Perfect Happiness of the Union: Jane Austen's Emma and English Romanticism," pp. 312-19. Like much early nineteenth-century literature E treats "the principle of separation" threatening all human relations. And, "part of that fertile Romantic ground wherein laws are exhibited in order to be broken by exceptions," it offers "a visionary ending": Emma and Mr. Knightley escape from

the world's "tensions, instabilities, and hidden
pressures" to establish, as the novel's conclusion
tells us, a perfectly happy union.

Alison G. Sulloway, "Emma Woodhouse and A
Vindication of the Rights of Woman," pp. 320-32.
Resembling Mary Wollstonecraft, JA "harbored the
subversive--and therefore Romantic--desire that
women be trained to think rationally," a desire that
appears with greatest urgency in E. There, the
heroine, in "frank outbursts, completely devoid of
irony," condemns "the privileges accruing to
masculinity, wealth, caste, [and] property," but Mr.
Knightley, "an utterly traditional man," responds
only with "benevolent feudalism" to her "strangled
yearning to transcend her own fettered condition."

William A. Walling, "The Glorious Anxiety of
Motion: Jane Austen's Persuasion," pp. 333-41.
Emphasizing the importance of creditable exertion,
"the glorious anxiety of motion," in a world "without still point or certain center," P suggests "that
our only recourse amid the accelerations of history
is to commit our deepest energies to an intense
personal relationship, but that an intense personal
relationship is inevitably subject to its own kind of
terrible precariousness."

Gene W. Ruoff, "Anne Elliot's Dowry: Reflections
on the Ending of Persuasion," pp. 342-51. In P
memory helps characterize individuals and supply
dialogue and structure. It functions most significantly, "in the absence of such mnemonic aids
as a stable home and family," to "provide the
continuity essential to the formation of a new
community," one quite distinct from the societies
formed at the conclusions of the earlier novels.

232 Savage, Basil. "Jane Austen Bicentenary Exhibition."
        ChLB, NS no. 14 (1976), pp. 124-25.

        (Describes items at the British Library's exhibi-
        tion; see no. 100.)

233 Shipps, Anthony W. "Pride and Prejudice." N&Q, NS
        23 (1976), 510.

        (Notes two examples of the phrase "pride and
        prejudice" in Gibbon's Decline and Fall.)

234 Smith, Muriel. "Lord St. Ives." N&Q, NS 23 (1976),
        452-53.

(Identifies the reference to Lord St. Ives in P
as JA's implied tribute to two admirals, Nelson and
Exmouth.)

235   Southam, B. C., ed. Jane Austen, Northanger Abbey
        and Persuasion: A Casebook. London: Macmillan
        Press, 1976.

Rev. by Andrew Lincoln in YWES, 57 (1976), 254;
by C. C. Barfoot in ES, 58 (1977), 541; by Nol van
der Loop in DQR, 8 (1978), 145, n. 10; by Frank W.
Bradbrook in N&Q, NS 25 (1978), 257-58.

(In addition to the essays listed below, this
collection reprints several early nineteenth-century
and Victorian comments as well as twentieth-century
studies.)

B. C. Southam, "Introduction," pp. 11-38. Most
critics regard NA as a rather simple, youthful work
and P as mature and autumnal. But we must remember
that JA revised NA in the same year she wrote P and
that she then "hurried on to Sanditon." Consequently, NA proves "the most flawless of the early
novels," and P is no final testament.

Marilyn Butler, "The Anti-Jacobin Position," pp.
106-21. (See no. 110.)

B. C. Southam, "'Regulated Hatred' Revisited,"
pp. 122-27. Henry Tilney's witty remarks about "a
neighbourhood of voluntary spies" and about London
riots have historical substance. They provide an
oblique glimpse of Regency England's darker side,
"an England of unrest, repression and violence" more
terrifying than any Gothic fiction. With profound
irony, then, JA undercuts her hero's posture as an
"ultra-reasonable" man, offering "a supreme instance
of her 'hatred' artistically, disarmingly and
insidiously 'regulated.'"

A. Walton Litz, "Persuasion: Forms of Estrangement," pp. 228-41. (See no. 132.)

236   Southam, B. C., ed. Jane Austen, Sense and
        Sensibility, Pride and Prejudice, and
        Mansfield Park: A Casebook. London: Macmillan
        Press, 1976.

Rev. by C. C. Barfoot in ES, 58 (1977), 541; by
Marilyn Butler in N&Q, NS 24 (1977), 374-76; by Nol
van der Loop in DQR, 8 (1978), 145, n. 10.

(In addition to the essay listed below, this

collection reprints several early nineteenth-century
and Victorian comments as well as twentieth-century
studies.)

B. C. Southam, "Introduction," pp. 9-29. Knowing
what we do of JA's manuscripts and laborious revi-
sions, we can appreciate more fully her conscious and
deliberate conversion of S and S and P and P "from
literary satire to realistic social satire." At the
same time that she accommodated literary elements
within the framework of the comedy of manners, she
developed the novels' ethical concerns and range of
characterization. As in MP, she always makes
didacticism subordinate to the portrayal of human
beings and their relationships.

237   Stern, Irwin. "Jane Austen e Júlio Dinis."
      Colóquio, no. 30 (1976), pp. 61-68.

JA influenced the Portuguese novelist Júlio Dinis
in both style and content. Following her practice,
he portrays realistically the gentry's daily life,
makes family problems a major concern, and views
women as rational beings capable of much more than
the simple duties of mothers and wives.

238   Tomlinson, T. B. "Doubts and Reticence: Sense and
      Sensibility to Persuasion," in The English
      Middle-Class Novel. New York: Barnes & Noble,
      1976, pp. 36-51.

With the exception of MP, which opts for seclu-
sion and reticence, JA's novels are "outward-
looking": they insist, buoyantly, confidently, "that
the public world must and should continue its demands
on the private. And this is particularly the case
since the 'private' world will always, as she herself
has shown, include both threats and challenges that
stem from permanent instabilities built into human
nature itself."

239   Tomlinson, T. B. "Jane Austen's Originality: Emma,"
      in The English Middle-Class Novel. New York:
      Barnes & Noble, 1976, pp. 21-35.

"Jane Austen's originality in Emma is to
formulate, almost for the first time in
English literature, the sense in which the
good qualities in and of a whole society like
that of Highbury may actively depend on the bad,
or at least on impulses that must also result
in foolishness, misjudgement, at times active
cruelty."

240   Trilling, Lionel. "Why We Read Jane Austen." TLS, 5
        Mar. 1976, pp. 250-52. Trilling's essay appears
        also in his The Last Decade: Essays and Reviews,
        1965-75, ed. Diana Trilling (New York: Harcourt
        Brace Jovanovich, 1979), pp. 204-25.

        The ever-increasing attention paid JA is "the
      more significant because . . . young people have a
      salient part in it." Perhaps they wish to study
      her so as "to scrutinize modern life with adverse
      intention," preferring the qualities of her fiction
      to what contemporary life offers. But we may want to
      qualify the humanistic aim of studying the art of a
      past era for relevance to our own; we might
      emphasize, too, the "great range of existential
      differences" stretching between our time and hers.

241   Weinsheimer, Joel. "A Survey of Major Austen
        Studies, 1970-1975." PLL, 12 (1976), 209-23.

        (Review-essay on nos. 10, 23, 30, 34, 39, 42, 49,
      78, 108, 132, 151, and 184; this essay reviews as
      well a number of critical works first published
      before 1973.)

242   Weissman, Judith. "Evil and Blunders: Human Nature
        in Mansfield Park and Emma." W&L, 4 (Spring
        1976), 5-17.

        Proof of the seriousness of JA's concerns and the
      diversity of her fiction, MP and E present "contrast-
      ing philosophical considerations of two views of
      human nature. Human nature in Mansfield Park is
      conceived by a harsh English Protestant, in the
      tradition of Milton and Swift; the characters and
      action of Emma exemplify the Socratic and Enlighten-
      ment idea that there is no evil, only ignorance, for
      here people do not sin, but only blunder."

243   Wherritt, T. Mildred. "For Better or for Worse:
        Marriage Proposals in Jane Austen's Novels."
        MQ, 17 (1976), 229-44.

        JA's failure to portray joyful, successful
      marriage proposal scenes may be viewed "as decorum
      or distance," "as anticlimax or cowardice," "as
      indicative of artistic merit" or "as the result
      of frustrating ineptness." But it seems
      "reasonable to conclude that she did not,
      and therefore probably could not, handle the
      intense emotion implied by a climactic proposal
      scene."

244   White, Edward M. "Freedom Is Restraint: The Ped-
         agogical Problem of Jane Austen." SJS, 2 (Feb.
         1976), 84-90.

      Students have trouble appreciating JA because of
her maturity. She treats "the problem of living
maturely in an immature world" and argues against a
glib romanticism, which defines freedom as an
abolishing of restraints. She insists that "restriction is necessary as a liberating condition of the
human spirit" and employs "a difficult irony based on
intelligent distinctions."

245   Willis, Lesley H. "Eyes and the Imagery of Sight in
         Pride and Prejudice." ESC, 2 (1976), 156-62.

      Imagery pertaining to sight plays an important
role in P and P. Things that are visible, eyes
themselves, and "the act of looking" express the
characters' judgment, feeling, and sexuality.

246   Wood, Margaret. A Person of No Consequence: A Play.
         New York: French, 1976.

      (The characters have their prototypes in JA's
novels.)

247   Zimmerman, Eugenia Noik. "The Proud Princess Gets
         Her Comeuppance: Structures of Patriarchal
         Order." CRCL, 3 (1976), 253-68.

      "A chronicle of the movement to Mrs from Miss,"
E describes the heroine's rebellion against marriage,
the institution assuring male dominance, and her
subsequent punishment and reconciliation to established sources of authority. Although the book
ends with "Patriarchy Triumphant" and "the Proud
Princess . . . transformed into Griselda," the
residence of the Knightleys at Hartfield, "the
original locus of perturbation," creates "an uneasy
synthesis of patriarchal and matriarchal elements."

                        1977

248   Anderson, Patricia D. "Self-Definition in Mansfield
         Park and Joan Didion's Play It As It Lays." JMJ,
         35 (1977), 58-66.

      In contrast to Didion's Play It As It Lays,
MP asserts the possibility of self-definition.

Fanny, for example, can affirm her identity because
she inherits a culture. She is able to change her
situation and commit herself to acting a specific
part in life by giving up any desire to "play games."
She realizes that "what is objectionable to the self-
defining temper about theatricals" is that "they
throw the self out of its proper cooperative role."

249 Auchincloss, Louis. "An Introduction" to Persuasion.
      Westport, Conn.: Limited Editions Club, 1977, pp.
      v-x. Auchincloss's essay appears also, in some-
      what different form, with the title "Jane Austen
      and the Good Life," in his Life, Law, and
      Letters: Essays and Sketches (Boston: Houghton
      Mifflin, 1979), pp. 69-78.

In P, as in JA's other novels, the good life
belongs to very few. It requires, among other
things, money, leisure, and elegance, as well as
restraint from excess, "resignation to the whims of
providence," and the ability to resist compromising
one's principles.

250 Austen, Jane, and Another. The Watsons. London:
      Davies, 1977. An excerpt from this book appears
      in Times, 26 Mar. 1977, p. 6.

Rev. by Ian Stewart in ILN, 265 (July 1977), 107;
by Valentine Cunningham in New Statesman, 15 Apr.
1977, p. 498; by Susan Hill in Times, 21 Apr. 1977,
p. 19; by J. I. M. Stewart in TLS, 8 Apr. 1977, p.
420; by Andrew Lincoln in YWES, 58 (1977), 274; by
Bernard Jones in B&B, 23 (Jan. 1978), 28-30.

(Finishes the fragment.)

251 Batey, Mavis. "In Quest of Jane Austen's 'Mr.
      Repton.'" GardH, 5 (Spring 1977), 19-20.

(Identifies Adlestrop and Stoneleigh Abbey, both
landscaped by Humphry Repton, as the originals of
houses in MP.)

252 Carruth, Jane. "Introduction" to Pride and
      Prejudice. Maidenhead, Berkshire: Purnell,
      1977, pp. [v-vii].

JA's art remains fascinating because of her
characters, who are vivid and memorable and "whose
attitudes and ambitions are perfectly understandable
to present-day readers."

253 Cockshut, A. O. J. "Jane Austen," in Man and Woman:
      A Study of Love and the Novel, 1740-1940.
      London: Collins, 1977, pp. 54-71.

      JA ruthlessly separates feeling and judgment
because she knows how insidious are the elements
deflecting honest dealing. But she does not
therefore advocate complete suppression of the
subjective. Although we can fool ourselves about our
egoism and deepest passions, she believes that the
distinction between our best and worst impulses will
appear gradually, through a long and painful process,
"when it is seen whether the influence led to true or
false judgements of character, to true or false
understanding of events."

254 Collected Reports of the Jane Austen Society, 1966-
      1975. Folkestone: Dawson, 1977.

      (In addition to Elizabeth Jenkins's introduction,
which appeared originally as part of her introduction
to Collected Reports of the Jane Austen Society,
1949-1965 [London: Dawson, 1967], this collection
reprints the Jane Austen Society's reports for the
years 1966-75. Listed below are the guest speakers'
addresses to the Society's annual general meetings,
1972-75.)

      Rosalind Wade, "The Anatomy of Jane Austen," pp.
178-87. (See no. 27.)

      Joan Hassall, "On Illustrating Jane Austen's
Works," pp. 201-8. (See no. 73.)

      Charles Beecher Hogan, "Lovers' Vows and High-
bury," pp. 227-35. (See no. 146.)

      A. L. Rowse, "The England of Jane Austen," pp.
251-65. (See no. 211.)

255 Constantinescu, Ligia Doina. "The Living Pattern of
      Jane Austen's Novels." AnUILit, 23 (1977), 93-
      98.

      JA achieves structural unity through a variety of
techniques, including chapter and plot division,
manipulation of point of view, comparison of the
protagonist and others, and allusions to the passage
of time and the weather. All these devices help
create an ironic order, "which proves to be the
only one that both leads to and makes plausible
the ultimate discovery and reversal of the characters."

256 Crum, Margaret, comp. "Austen, Jane (1775-1817)," in
        English and American Autographs in the
        Bodmeriana: Catalogue. (Bibliotheca Bodmeriana
        Catalogues, 4.) Cologny-Genève: Fondation
        Martin Bodmer, 1977, p. 17.

        (Describes a manuscript of verses by JA and other
     members of her family.)

257 De Rose, Peter L. "Hardship, Recollection, and
        Discipline: Three Lessons in Mansfield Park."
        SNNTS, 9 (1977), 261-78.

        (See no. 454.)

258 De Rose, Peter L. "Sense and Sensibility and
        Persuasion: Variations on a Theme." PAPA, 3
        (Summer 1977), 38-46.

        (See no. 454.)

259 Dry, Helen. "Syntax and Point of View in Jane
        Austen's Emma." SIR, 16 (1977), 87-99.

        "In Emma the use of factives and narrated mono-
     logue constructions is linked to representation of
     Emma's point of view. . . . These linguistic devices
     contribute to the effect that Emma's point of view
     has been adopted because they help to single out Emma
     as the 'speaker,' or source, of the narration."

260 Ebine, Hiroshi. "Mansfield Park no ichi" [A view of
        Mansfield Park], in Eikoku shosetsu kenkyu
        [Studies in English novels]. (No. 12.) Tokyo:
        Shinozaki Shorin, 1977, pp. 70-100.

        Rather than an exception to the canon, as many
     think, MP expresses the same moral attitudes as JA's
     other novels and exemplifies, like S and S, her
     "dark," just as P and P and E exemplify her "light,"
     style. Viewed another way, MP represents the first
     work of JA's mature period and, though imperfect,
     provides evidence of her ambitions as a novelist.

261 Fido, Martin. "A Note on Jane Austen's Use of
        Cross." ES, 58 (1977), 230-31.

        In JA we "observe the semantic shift by which
     'crossness' (obstinate opposition) moved from retain-
     ing that sense of contrariety within itself and not

requiring a stated object of opposition, to a point
at which the subjective bad temper engendered by
opposition became the dominant meaning, and drove out
the recollection that opposition was in fact implied."

262 Fowler, Marian E. "The Feminist Bias of Pride and
        Prejudice." DR, 57 (1977), 47-64.

A "feminist manifesto," P and P rejects the
stereotype of the modest, delicate, elegant woman
advocated by the writers of female courtesy books in
the late eighteenth century. Instead, it argues, as
Mary Wollstonecraft and other radicals did, for a
free, original, and fully rational woman. By choos-
ing Elizabeth as protagonist and Miss Bingley, Miss
De Bourgh, Mary Bennet, and others as satiric
objects, JA clearly upsets her society's norms for
woman's education and role in life.

263 Gilson, David. "Anna Lefroy and 'Mary Hamilton,'" in
        The Warden's Meeting: A Tribute to John Sparrow.
        Oxford: Oxford Univ. Society of Bibliophiles,
        1977, pp. 43-46.

(Discusses the possibility that JA's niece Anna
Lefroy wrote "Mary Hamilton," a short story published
in 1833.)

264 Grawe, Christian. "Nachwort" to Stolz und Vorurteil.
        (Universal-Bibliothek, 9871.) Stuttgart: Reclam,
        1977, pp. 435-60. This edition includes a
        bibliography of writings by and about JA.

Popular in part for its realistic storyline and
characters, P and P concentrates on human interactions, not scenery, hides its social criticism in
irony and a light tone, and makes careful use of
letters. The book's themes include pride and
prejudice, terms having both positive and negative
implications, and the conflict between the individual
and the world around him in relation to marriage.

265 Gregor, Ian. "Does Literary Criticism Date? A
        Review of Three Bicentennial Studies of Jane
        Austen." L&H, no. 5 (1977), pp. 96-104.

(Review-essay on nos. 108, 110, and 132.)

266 Hickman, Peggy. A Jane Austen Household Book, with

Martha Lloyd's Recipes. North Pomfret, Vt.:
David & Charles, 1977.

Rev. by Rosalind Wade in ContempR, 231 (1977),
331-32; by Lavinia Watson in Country Life, 8 Dec.
1977, p. 1790 [and see letter, Peggy Hickman, 26
Jan. 1978, p. 210]; by Hilary Spurling in Observer,
18 Dec. 1977, p. 25; by Patricia Beer in TLS, 18
Nov. 1977, p. 1344; by John Fuller in Encounter
(London), 50 (Jan. 1978), 66; by Albert H. Johnston
in PW, 30 Jan. 1978, p. 113.

(Combines material on domestic matters from JA's
letters and novels, including information on
servants, mealtimes, and the price of food, with "an
hitherto unpublished Austen household recipe book,"
compiled mostly during JA's lifetime and devoted to
cookery, home remedies, perfumes, and household
hints.)

267 Hilton, Isabel. "Is This Jane Austen's Play?"
     STimes, 20 Nov. 1977, p. 2.

(On the discovery and sale of "Sir Charles
Grandison.")

268 Howard, Philip. "Jane Austen Comedy Rescued from
     Oblivion." Times, 1 Dec. 1977, p. 1.

(On the discovery and sale of the play "Sir
Charles Grandison.")

269 Howard, Philip. "Pride and Prejudice against the
     Developers." Times, 7 Feb. 1977, p. 3.

Inhabitants of Chawton are protesting against
plans to redevelop a Tudor cottage in the village.

270 Jackel, David. "Leonora and Lady Susan: A Note on
     Maria Edgeworth and Jane Austen." ESC, 3 (1977),
     278-88.

A comparison of Lady Susan and Edgeworth's
Leonora provides "a framework for the evaluation of
Jane Austen's handling of conventional materials."
While the two works resemble each other in themes and
characters, their differences point to JA's "individual skill," "powers of organization," and "greater
emphasis on consistency, probability, and precision."

271 Jackel, David. "Moral Geography in Jane Austen."

UTQ, 47 (1977), 1-21.

Unlike the novelists preceding her JA uses locations "to assist in developing the relationships
between the characters and to reveal the complex
moral issues which underlie the action." She shapes
P and P, for example, her most sustained treatment of
this technique, around Elizabeth's excursions to
different places and subsequent returns home, where
she reassesses events and people. And the farther
the heroine journeys from Longbourn, the more she
changes her opinions and understands Darcy.

272 "Jane Austen Play Found." NYT, 14 Dec. 1977, p. C21.

(On the sale of "Sir Charles Grandison.")

273 The Jane Austen Society: Report for the Year, 1976.
      Alton, Hampshire: Jane Austen Society, [1977].

(In addition to the guest speaker's address to
the Society's annual general meeting, abstracted
below, this report includes, among other things,
several brief notes.)

Tony Tanner, "In Between--Anne Elliot Marries a
Sailor and Charlotte Heywood Goes to the Seaside,"
pp. 19-30. As in P and Sanditon, JA often pictures
young women without a secure social position, who
are "in between," as it were, bad fathers and
different kinds of potential suitors. These women
are also "in between the various discourses which
they have to engage with but which they refuse to be
taken over by." Thus, in the context of a changing
world they help maintain good sense and enduring
values and guard the language from decay. [Tanner's
essay appears also in Jane Austen in a Social
Context, ed. David Monaghan (Totowa, N.J.: Barnes &
Noble, 1981), pp. 180-94.]

274 "Jane Austen's Proud Prejudice." STimes Mag, 3 July
      1977, pp. 20-21.

(Speaks of the sale of Volume the Second and
gives excerpts from "The History of England.")

275 Jefferson, Douglas. Jane Austen's Emma: A Landmark
      in English Fiction. (Text and Context.) London:
      Chatto & Windus for Sussex Univ. Press, 1977.

Rev. by Eleanor Rogers in HAB, 27 (1976), 503-5;
in Choice, 14 (1977), 1050; by Rachel Blake in TES,

18 Nov. 1977, p. 23; by Andrew Lincoln in <u>YWES</u>, 58
(1977), 273; by Marilyn Butler in <u>NCF</u>, 34 (1980),
434-36.

JA contributed to the realism of the novel by
writing of ordinary life as people usually experience
it. Though allied in some ways to the "more
artificial fiction" of the eighteenth century, she
concentrates, as in <u>E</u>, for example, on presenting
characters simply living their lives in everyday
settings, having "piquancy, tension and mystery"
arise from familiar activities, like the choice of
one's companions and the definition of one's social
duties. She depicts her characters, who are mature,
rounded conceptions and not fixed in any special
category, as members of a community, as, in part,
created by their community: they play changing roles
in it and make changing impressions on it. Just as
she avoids rhetorically conceived or idealized
characterization, she also tends toward a plain,
direct, unobtrusive prose style, yet one still marked
by "the intellectual tradition" of Johnson. In
addition to her other innovations, including the
development of new novelistic themes, such as the
consequences "of meddling with another person's
life," she combines what is simple, straightforward,
and disarming with "the density of implication of the
greatest fiction."

276 Jenkins, Elizabeth. "Jane Austen and the Human
        Condition." <u>EDH</u>, 39 (1977), 57-75.

"The trend of all the novels is to show both that
life affords infinite matter for comic relief and
that it is extremely serious."

277 Johnson, E. D. H. "'The Truer Measure': Setting in
        <u>Emma</u>, <u>Middlemarch</u>, and <u>Howards End</u>," in <u>Romantic</u>
        <u>and Modern: Revaluations of Literary Tradition</u>.
        Ed. George Bornstein. Pittsburgh: Univ. of
        Pittsburgh Press, 1977, pp. 197-205.

As in <u>Middlemarch</u> and <u>Howards End</u>, setting in <u>E</u>,
"instead of seeming primarily a backdrop against
which the narrative unfolds, is instrumental in
forwarding the action." Through her humiliation the
heroine "discovers a truer sense of her relationship
to the surrounding world," and, appropriately, "the
moment of recognition takes place in a scene which
specifically evokes the agency of natural setting."

278 Kendall, D. G. "Jane Austen and 'Co-.'" <u>N&Q</u>, NS 24
        (1977), 277.

The abbreviation "Co-" in Sanditon means
"Co-Heiress."

279 Kennedy, Alan. "Irony and Action in Mansfield Park."
     ESC, 3 (1977), 164-75. Kennedy's essay appears
     also, with the title "Agency and Scene in Jane
     Austen," in his Meaning and Signs in Fiction
     (New York: St. Martin's Press, 1979), pp. 58-69.

     JA treats Fanny Price with "indulgent irony"
     deriving from the "incommensurability which we find
     whenever principles of ultimate or absolute extension
     try to operate in a finite world of fallen men."
     Though she approves of her heroine's morality, JA
     shows that theory is not enough, that Fanny must
     overcome her passivity and learn how to act.

280 Kiriyama, Yukiye. Jane Austen: My Own Reading of Her
     Works. Tokyo: Senjo, [1977].

     (This book, written by one who is "only an
     admirer of Jane Austen" and "no scholar of English
     literature," includes essays originally written for
     university bulletins and the magazines of a literary
     society. The essays, which treat the six major
     novels, discuss, among other topics, "Jane Austen as
     an Unconscious Realist" and the "Supposed Ideal Woman
     in Jane Austen" and analyze the heroines' psychology
     and the author's artistic development.)

281 Llewelyn, Margaret. Jane Austen: A Character Study.
     London: Kimber, 1977.

     Rev. in Economist, 12 Nov. 1977, p. 104; by
     Patricia Beer in TLS, 18 Nov. 1977, p. 1344; by
     Andrew Lincoln in YWES, 58 (1977), 272; by John E.
     Jordan in ELN, 16 Supplement (1978), 44.

     (Discussing such subjects as JA's "love affairs"
     and health and providing information on contemporary
     social customs, this book brings together selections
     from the novels and letters and from biographies and
     other writings about her which "best reveal her
     personality.")

282 Lovell, Terry. "Jane Austen and Gentry Society," in
     Literature, Society, and the Sociology of
     Literature. Proceedings of the Conference Held
     at the University of Essex, July 1976. Ed.
     Francis Barker et al. [Colchester]: Univ. of
     Essex, 1977, pp. 118-32. Lovell's essay appears
     also, with the title "Jane Austen and the Gentry:

A Study in Literature and Ideology," in The
Sociology of Literature: Applied Studies, ed.
Diana Laurenson, Sociological Review Monograph,
26 (Keele, Staffordshire: Univ. of Keele, 1978),
pp. 15-37.

Though her conservative ideology has a material
basis, JA is not, therefore, as others have claimed,
"progressive" or "subversive" but "a realist in terms
of the class and individual interests of her protagonists." However, these protagonists possess
"the moral and intellectual strengths to the lack of
which she had attributed the main threat to gentry
society. The heroines guarantee the renewal of
gentry society by marriages into it."

282a Luijters, Guus. Jane Austen. (Isis-reeks, 7.) The
        Hague: Horus, 1977.

        (Essays on her life and work, including an an-
notated list of Dutch translations.)

283 Malins, Edward. "Humphry Repton at Stoneleigh Abbey,
        Warwickshire." GardH, 5 (Spring 1977), 21-29.

        (Discusses Humphry Repton's improvements for
Stoneleigh Abbey, an estate owned by a member of JA's
family.)

284 Mallalieu, Huon. "Jane Austen Play Sold for
        £17,000." Times, 14 Dec. 1977, p. 16.

        (On the sale of "Sir Charles Grandison.")

285 Monaghan, David. "The Myth of 'Everybody's Dear
        Jane': A Reassessment of Jane Austin [sic]."
        Atlantis, 3 (Fall 1977), 112-26. An earlier
        version of Monaghan's essay appeared, with the
        title "The Myth of 'Everybody's Dear Jane': An
        Assessment of Jane Austen on Her Two Hundredth
        Birthday," in Insight, 5 (Winter 1976), 2-10;
        part of Monaghan's essay appears also in his
        Jane Austen: Structure and Social Vision (Totowa,
        N.J.: Barnes & Noble, 1980), passim, and, with
        the title "Jane Austen and the Position of
        Women," in his ed. of Jane Austen in a Social
        Context (Totowa, N.J.: Barnes & Noble, 1981), pp.
        105-21; see nos. 480 and 547.

        JA "is a much more complex person than the
Janeites would admit," especially as regards her

"cynicism, misanthropy and sexual interests." In
addition, "far from being a sweet, pious spinster who
knew little of the world beyond her Steventon and
Chawton homes, she was a strong-minded woman, who
possessed a keen understanding of the structure of
her society and of the position of her own sex
within it."

286 Monaghan, David. "The Novel and Its Age: A Study of
        Theme and Structure in Pride and Prejudice."
        HAB, 28 (1977), 151-66.

     (See no. 480.)

287 Müller, Wolfgang G. "Gefühlsdarstellung bei
        Jane Austen." Sprachkunst, 8 (1977), 87-
        103.

     JA varies point of view and irony to control our
perception of emotion in a work. While in S and S
we never experience Marianne's inner feelings
directly and thus remain distant from her, the
presentation of Anne's emotional consciousness is P's
major theme. MP uses Fanny's consciousness as a
faultless medium through which we see others, and E,
because of its ironic stance, cuts us off from much
of the heroine's extreme emotion.

288 Nardin, Jane. "Christianity and the Structure
        of Persuasion." Renascence, 30 (1977), 43-
        55.

     "The novel most deeply imbued with Austen's
sincere faith in Christianity," P treats "the
Christian's relationships with his fellow man and
with God." It stresses man's inescapable weaknesses
and consequent need to depend on divine assistance,
as well as judges the characters by their commitment
to usefulness, charity, and Christianity. At the
book's conclusion Wentworth becomes "a Christian
hero, counterpart to Anne, who has always been the
true Christian heroine."

289 Noel-Bentley, Elaine. "An Allusion to Sir Charles
        Grandison in Jane Austen's Letters." N&Q, NS 24
        (1977), 321. See also correction in N&Q, D. J.
        Gilson, NS 25 (1978), 541.

     In her letters JA alludes to Sir Charles
Grandison not twice, as Chapman would have it, but
three times.

290   Norman, Geraldine. "British Library Buys Early Writ-
          ings of Jane Austen." <u>Times</u>, 7 July 1977, p. 4.

      The British Library bought an autograph manu-
script of <u>Volume the Second</u> for ₤40,000.

291   Olsen, Stein Haugom. "Do You Like Emma Woodhouse?"
          <u>CritQ</u>, 19 (Winter 1977), 3-19.

      "Sympathetic identification" proves an in-
adequate, subjective guide to understanding Emma.
To judge her correctly we must relate character to
JA's richly conceived social and moral scheme, a
scheme we need not share to understand. Conceived
thus, Emma must learn to discipline her intellect
"to recognise how people can be expected to behave
because of their position and predicament" and "to
evaluate properly the position a person actually
holds in the social order."

292   Pascal, Roy. "Early Accomplishment," in <u>The Dual
          Voice: Free Indirect Speech and Its Functioning
          in the Nineteenth-Century European Novel</u>.
          Totowa, N.J.: Rowman and Littlefield, 1977, pp.
          37-66.

      The stylistic forms of free indirect speech found
in JA correspond to the overall intention of her
works, to the "concern for the changing patterns of
personal relationships within a small socio-cultural
group, small enough and sufficiently distant from
great issues and events to permit intimacy and
encourage attention to nuances." Though her use of
free indirect speech proves rich and sure, she does
not exploit all the style's resources; she stresses
rational, conscious responses, omitting "that area of
nervous, sentient, emotional reaction that precedes
or eludes verbalisation."

293   Penrith, Mary C. "Plain and Contorted Speech in
          <u>Emma</u>," in <u>An English Miscellany Presented to W.
          S. Mackie</u>. Ed. Brian S. Lee. New York: Oxford
          Univ. Press, 1977, pp. 149-62.

      "Structurally, Emma's linguistic and moral like-
nesses to the residents of Highbury are most heavily
weighted at the beginning of the novel, diminishing
as her affinity to Mr Knightley increases. . . . By
the end of the novel she has come close to a self-
effacing language free of generalizations, elaborate
syntax, excessive negatives, fragmented utterances,
verbless sentences, overworked pronouns, and all the

other features that have come to represent diver-
gencies. What remains is the plain language of
morality."

294 Pinion, F. B. "A Sterne Echo in 'Love and Freind-
        ship.'" N&Q, NS 24 (1977), 320-21.

A passage in "Love and Friendship" echoes a
description in Tristram Shandy.

295 Raizada, Harish. "'Point of View' in Jane Austen's
        Novels." AJES, 2 (1977), 72-89.

JA's handling of point of view, specifically
her deliberate adoption in each novel of "the
central intelligence" or "selective omniscience,"
helps present action and theme, regulate the
reader's opinions, and achieve unity, economy,
and intensity. In NA and E "the narrative
perspective is focused from the beginning to the
end on their heroines," while in S and S, P and P,
MP, and P "the emergence of the view-point
character is delayed."

296 Ram, Atma. "Exactness and Clarity: An Aspect of Jane
        Austen." JKUH, 21 (1977), 128-32.

"There is a strong English-like tendency in Jane
Austen's preference for exactness and clarity" in
dates and times, the weather, and forms of address.
This inclination shows "her strong perception and
firm grasp of reality."

297 Ram, Atma. "Frail and Weak: A Portrait of Fanny
        Price." PURBA, 8 (Apr.-Oct. 1977), 27-34.

(See no. 610.)

298 Ram, Atma. "Jane Austen and Mary Wollstonecraft."
        IJES, 17 (1977), 149-51.

JA and Wollstonecraft resemble each other in
language and theme. Both consider women "rational
creatures" and men's "fellow-beings" and prefer
virtue to elegance as the basis of any educational
system for women.

299 Ram, Atma. "Jane Austen in Our Time." RUSE, 10
        (1977), 71-75.

(Review-essay on nos. 108, 110, and 218.)

300 Rawlins, Ray. "Austen, Jane," in The Guinness Book
      of Autographs. Enfield, Middlesex: Guinness
      Superlatives, 1977, p. 8.

      (Reproduces JA's holograph will.)

301 Schapera, I. Kinship Terminology in Jane Austen's
      Novels. (Royal Anthropological Institute
      Occasional Paper, 33.) London: Royal An-
      thropological Institute of Great Britain and
      Ireland, 1977.

      Rev. in TLS, 14 Oct. 1977, p. 1199.

      JA indicates relationship, among other ways, by
      clear discriminations between relatives and non-
      relatives, between members of the immediate family
      and all other relatives, and, with the exception of
      the word cousin, "between relatives according to
      their sex and generation." The terms a character
      uses often depend on whom he is addressing, and,
      although all terms describing relationship serve
      "as modes of reference," some, like expressions for
      spouses and children, do not function "as modes of
      address." Her system of kinship terminology differs
      from the modern English one "not in the vocabulary
      of relationship terms proper, but in how and when
      those terms and their alternatives" are used.

302 Schwartz, Narda Lacey. "Jane Austen (1775-1817),
      Great Britain," in Articles on Women Writers: A
      Bibliography. Santa Barbara, Calif.: ABC-Clio,
      1977, pp. 9-18.

      (Bibliography.)

303 Sciullo, Luciana. "Miss Bates, personaggio chiave di
      Emma." QLL, 2 (1977), 91-98.

      Like other of JA's minor characters Miss Bates
      has many idiosyncracies and exists to provide both
      information and laughter. In addition, she assumes
      great importance in the novel because, through her
      loquacity, she helps unite Highbury's different
      social groups.

304 Shaw, Patricia. "Las novelas cortas de Jane Austen."
      FMod, 17, nos. 59-61 (1976-77), 125-47.

JA's short works both resemble and differ from her major novels. Though broader in tone, "Love and Friendship" resembles the mature fiction in exploring such subjects as selfishness, vanity, and honesty. And, while Lady Susan, largely because of the perverse nature of its protagonist, stands alone in the canon, Sanditon offers characters much akin to figures in the earlier books.

305 Shipps, Anthony W. "Jane Austen's Minor Works."
         N&Q, NS 24 (1977), 49.

(Offers partial identification of the motto JA uses for "Love and Friendship.")

306 Skilton, David. "Austen, Scott, and the Victorians,"
         in The English Novel: Defoe to the Victorians.
         (Comparative Literature Series.) [New York]:
         Barnes & Noble, 1977, pp. 80-98.

It is impossible to believe JA limited or trivial. She "perfected the techniques of dramatic character-presentation, socially analysed language, and careful narrative control." Above all, she revealed the ethical foundation of ordinary life, showing how everyday events, "no less than great actions, were centered on moral convention, moral judgement and moral choice, so that living in society required a constant alertness of will and intellect to control the self and understand others."

307 Soulsby, Sarah E. "Some Notes on Jane Austen's
         Persuasion." JEn, 4 (1977), 43-50.

Emotionally involved in P's protagonists and lacking her usual ironic energy, JA resembles Anne Elliot in situation and character. And did JA's "'Hampshire gentleman' fail to return except in the virile mirage of Captain Wentworth?" JA here anatomizes "a woman's love . . . with a tremulous attention to detail, with a sympathy which ignores all temptations to ridicule, with a rejoicing at the final triumph after years of suffering."

308 Southall, Raymond. "The Social World of Jane
         Austen," in Literature, the Individual, and
         Society: Critical Essays on the Eighteenth
         and Nineteenth Centuries. London: Lawrence and
         Wishart, 1977, pp. 105-39.

JA, noteworthy for an irrepressible feminine

intelligence composed of grace and felicity as well
as sharp vision and often wicked humor, expresses
"society through character and dialogue" better than
any other English novelist. Anatomizing a world
concerned with income, status, and sexual relations,
she finds manners "necessary but not sufficient," for
they simply give public form to such important values
as family affection, hospitality, and a just
consideration of others' feelings.

309   Stovel, Bruce. "Comic Symmetry in Jane Austen's
       Emma." DR, 57 (1977), 453-65.

       Though manifoldly complex, E offers "a single
comic structure" consisting of three major parts:
"the hidden love of Emma and Mr. Knightley for each
other; the counterpointing of that secret love with
the secret engagement of Frank Churchill and Jane
Fairfax; [and] the use of the other characters to
embody aspects of Emma herself."

310   Teyssandier, Hubert. "Jane Austen," in Les Formes de
       la création romanesque à l'époque de Walter Scott
       et de Jane Austen, 1814-1820. (Études Anglaises,
       64.) Paris: Didier, 1977, pp. 119-93.
       Teyssandier's book includes a bibliography of
       writings about JA.

       JA is an innovator who, in her exceptional
originality, remains attached to the conventions of
contemporary fiction, which she transforms and
deepens without ever entirely renouncing. In the
contrasted tonalities of MP and E, the one solemn
and the other gay, she illustrates the extreme
possibilities of a kind of narrative that allows
for both an anxious moralizing and a joyous irony.

       Though MP presents customary oppositions between
arrogance and modesty, frivolity and wisdom, false
and true systems of education, it transcends the
practice of writers like Maria Edgeworth and Susan
Ferrier by virtue of the author's technical and
intellectual superiority, expressing a personal
vision marked by complexity, exactness, and subtlety.
The book stresses inner conflict rather than external
contingencies, presents mixed, not simplistic,
characters, whose motives often seem obscure, and
charges structure and setting with multiple meanings.
At the novel's conclusion the interior demons to whom
the Park owed its fall leave more profound traces
than the villains of conventional fiction, and the
moral universe, renewed but not transfigured, retains
the imprint of the recent crisis, without being able
to recover its original innocence.

Notably different from its predecessor, for it offers a comic world where tensions resolve themselves with no damage to anyone, E yet provides an example of one type of moralistic fiction, the novel of conversion. While it rejects the sentimental representation of society for a rigorous and precise vision of a hierarchy based on rank and money, the fantasies of its excessively imaginative heroine ironically evoke the novelistic conventions the book itself disavows. E's ethics and aesthetics are one, the passage from pride to humility, from blindness to insight, being inseparable from the association of illusion and the falsehoods of much literature.

311   Todd, Janet M. "Female Friendship in Jane Austen's Novels." JRUL, 39 (1977), 29-43. Part of Todd's essay appears also, with the title "Social Friendship," in her Women's Friendship in Literature (New York: Columbia Univ. Press, 1980), pp. 246-301; see no. 504.

As exemplified by S and S, JA's early novels value "female friendship and the androgynous potential for women it suggests, although she never allows such friendship to be a substitute for marriage." The final works, however, of which MP is representative, reject female friendship for "its socially disruptive implications, its threat to the traditional patriarchy and marriage which she sometimes wishes to modify but never to destroy."

312   Trowbridge, Hoyt. "Mind, Body, and Estate: Jane Austen's System of Values," in From Dryden to Jane Austen: Essays on English Critics and Writers, 1660-1818. Albuquerque, N.Mex.: Univ. of New Mexico Press, 1977, pp. 275-92.

JA uses five basic standards, derived from "the humanistic classical-Christian tradition," to describe her fictional characters. These criteria, arranged in decreasing order of importance, are "intelligence, morality, feeling, beauty, and worldly condition (rank and fortune)." Part of a genuine philosophical system, these values not only help JA differentiate her characters from each other but guide our judgment, define "the range of comic effects," and give the novels seriousness.

313   Uffen, Ellen Serlen. "The Art of Mansfield Park." W&L, 5 (Fall 1977), 29-41. Uffen's essay appears also in Be Good, Sweet Maid: An Anthology of Women & Literature, ed. Janet Todd (New York:

Holmes & Meier, 1981), pp. 21-30. See also no.
742.

MP dramatizes "the confrontation between the
eighteenth and nineteenth centuries and their two
opposing world views," the former representing art
and order, the latter nature and chaos. The new
society formed at the novel's end, which suggests
only "an unnatural future," devoid of vitality,
promises no renewal; rather, this society signifies,
ironically and sadly, "only the death of the old
world and no more."

314 Usaily, M. A. al-. "Jane Austen's Sense and Sensi-
        bility." JEn, 4 (1977), 73-87.

Like her other works S and S illustrates JA's
moral seriousness, skill at characterization, and
fondness for symmetry and understatement. The novel
exemplifies, too, her typical themes, including love,
economics, and illusion, and reveals her modernity,
which, despite the limitations of her art, "is the
effect of her truth," her deep insight into human
nature.

315 Vipont, Elfrida. A Little Bit of Ivory: A Life of
        Jane Austen. London: Hamilton, 1977.

Rev. in Growing Point, 16 (1977), 3138-39; in
JuniorB, 41 (1977), 370; by Jane Aiken Hodge in TLS,
15 July 1977, p. 867; by Andrew Lincoln in YWES, 58
(1977), 272.

(Biography.)

                            1978

316 Auerbach, Nina. "Artists and Mothers: A False
        Alliance." W&L, 6 (Spring 1978), 3-15.
        Auerbach's essay appears also in Be Good, Sweet
        Maid: An Anthology of Women & Literature, ed.
        Janet Todd (New York: Holmes & Meier, 1981), pp.
        9-19.

"It is tempting but misleading to yoke artistic
and biological creativity. In the lives of Jane
Austen and George Eliot, two woman artists made
inescapably aware of the social assumptions equating
womanhood with motherhood, art is a liberation from
that demand, not a metaphoric submission to it. . . .
Austen and Eliot both turned away from motherhood and

embraced a creativity they defined as more spacious,
more adult, more inclusive."

317 Austen-Leigh, Joan. "The Many Faces of Jane Austen."
     <u>Hampshire</u>, 18 (Feb. 1978), 43.

     (On the different artistic representations of JA,
     especially Percy Fitzgerald's 1912 bust of her.)

318 Austen-Leigh, Joan. "Our Aunt, Jane Austen." <u>ILN</u>,
     266 (Christmas no., 1978), 89-90.

     (Biographical account of the Austen-Leighs.)

319 Bander, Elaine. "The Significance of Jane Austen's
     Reference to <u>Camilla</u> in <u>Sanditon</u>: A Note." <u>N&Q</u>,
     NS 25 (1978), 214-16. See also no. 814.

     Charlotte Heywood's chance "notice of <u>Camilla</u>,
     bringing to mind the dangers of overspending at
     watering-places, causes her to alter her behaviour
     in the direction of prudence, and shows us that
     Charlotte reads novels as wisely as she 'reads'
     character. If Sir Edward, in contrast, learns
     immorality from 'our most approved writers,' the
     fault lies not in the books but in Sir Edward."

320 Cecil, David. <u>A Portrait of Jane Austen</u>. London:
     Constable, 1978.

     Rev. by Quentin Bell in <u>B&B</u>, 24 (Dec. 1978), 13-
     15; by Marghanita Laski in <u>Country Life</u>, 16 Nov.
     1978, pp. 1679 and 1681; by John Bayley in <u>Listener</u>,
     26 Oct. 1978, pp. 535-36; by Michael Mason in <u>New
     Statesman</u>, 27 Oct. 1978, pp. 553-54; by Anthony
     Burgess in <u>Observer</u>, 29 Oct. 1978, p. 34; in
     <u>Spectator</u>, 21 Oct. 1978, p. 25; by Claire Tomalin in
     <u>STimes</u>, 29 Oct. 1978, p. 40; by A. O. J. Cockshut in
     <u>THES</u>, 27 Oct. 1978, p. 16; by Derek Hudson in <u>Times</u>,
     23 Oct. 1978, p. 19; by Patricia Beer in <u>TLS</u>, 10 Nov.
     1978, p. 1312; by Bryan Burns in <u>YWES</u>, 59 (1978),
     283; by Laurence Davies in <u>Albion</u>, 11 (1979), 286; by
     Auberon Waugh in <u>B&B</u>, 24 (Jan. 1979), 10; by Brian
     Southam in <u>BBNews</u> (1979), p. 120; by George Danger-
     field in <u>BkW</u>, 1 Apr. 1979, pp. E1 and E3; by Michael
     Dirda in <u>BkW</u>, 2 Dec. 1979, p. 13; by Edward Butscher
     in <u>Booklist</u>, 75 (1979), 1337; in <u>Booklist</u>, 75 (1979),
     1356; in <u>Choice</u>, 16 (1979), 1305; by Sonia Bertolotti
     in <u>Cultura</u>, 17 (1979), 436-39; in <u>Kirkus</u>, 15 Feb.
     1979, p. 230; by Robert E. Kelley in <u>LibJ</u>, 104
     (1979), 1339; by George Dangerfield in <u>MGW</u>, 22 Apr.

1979, p. 18; in NatRev, 30 Mar. 1979, p. 426; in NY,
14 May 1979, p. 176; by Tony Tanner in NYT, 6 May
1979, sec. 7, pp. 7 and 34-36; in The Progressive,
43 (June 1979), 59; by Genevieve Stuttaford in PW, 5
Feb. 1979, p. 88; by J. David Grey in W&L, 7 (Spring
1979), 52-54; by Debbie Kaplan in Arnoldian, 8 (Fall
1980), 40-48; by Douglas Wilson in DQ, 15 (Spring
1980), 113-15; by Merritt Moseley in SR, 88 (1980),
641-47; in ContempR, 238 (1981), 56; by Robert
Folkenflik in NCF, 36 (1981), 95-98; in NYT, 11 Jan.
1981, sec. 7, p. 35; in Observer, 11 Jan. 1981, p.
47; in Observer, 19 July 1981, p. 29; by Edward Neill
in TES, 30 Jan. 1981, p. 22; by Jan Stephens in
Times, 3 Jan. 1981, p. 10; by J. M. Blom in ES, 63
(1982), 144.

(Containing more than fifty illustrations, this
book is "an attempt, with the help of material drawn
from her letters, her novels and other people's
memories of her, to reconstruct and depict her
living personality and to explore its relation to
her art," as well as to place her in the society of
her time. The sections treating the novels "repeat
much of what I said in [my 1935 Leslie Stephen
Lecture on her] and sometimes in the same words.")

321   Cheng, Yung-Hsiao T. "Clergymen in Jane Austen's
       Novels." FJS, no. 11 (1978), pp. 25-40.

       JA adopts "a low-key approach" to the clergymen
in her novels. These characters rarely address
religious issues, and their profession does not much
affect their behavior. "Typical middle-class
gentry," they are, like the people around them,
either "honest and conscientious" (and thus approved
by JA) or "mercenary and selfish" (and consequently
the object of her ridicule).

321a   Cloete, Nettie. "A Background Study of Jane Aus-
       ten." Communiqué (South Africa), 4, no. 1
       (1978), 121-34.

       (Not seen.)

322   Conrad, Peter. "Introduction" to Mansfield Park.
       Ed. Mary Lascelles. New York: Dutton, 1978, pp.
       v-xxvii.

       MP "singles out the novel as the sanctuary of
austere and unforgiving self-knowledge, which the
novelist's omniscience imposes on all characters;
and exposes the drama as the shoddier realm of

evasive and corrupt self-dramatization." Supporting
the contrast between novel and drama with others
between pastoral and epic and between reading and
acting, the book identifies Fanny's "undemonstrative
qualities" and the novel genre's distinctive genius
for privacy, silence, and introversion.

323 Conrad, Peter. "Introduction" to _Pride and Preju-
     dice_. Ed. Mary Lascelles. New York: Dutton,
     1978, pp. v-xxiv.

     "Jane Austen's is an extended, exploratory,
dangerously subversive art, and is neither harmlessly
decorative nor picturesquely provincial." _P and P_,
self-sufficient in its perfection, translates "social
content into aesthetic form": its world's "tedium,
claustrophobia and mercenariness become formulae for
a minute clarity about time, space, quantity and
value; its gossiping ill-will" emerges as a complex
ironic vision, a vision shaping both the novel's
style and subject.

324 Conrad, Peter. "Introduction" to _Sense and Sensi-
     bility_. Ed. Mary Lascelles. New York: Dutton,
     1978, pp. v-xxvii.

     Subtler and more searching than usually per-
ceived, _S and S_ "deals not with the categories of
romantic philosophy but with the transformation of
those categories into ways of feeling and behaving.
It explores the unsettling romantic alteration of the
internal life, and it does so not by setting sense
and sensibility into opposition but by quizzically
suggesting their identity." Like Elinor and Marianne
the title's abstractions depend "on each other as two
halves of the same paradoxical character."

325 Cook, Jackie, and Kay Iseman, eds. "Jane Austen," in
     _Women Writers and the Literary Tradition: Finding
     the Woman in My Head_. (SCAE Occasional Papers,
     17.) Salisbury East, South Australia: Salisbury
     College of Advanced Education, 1978, p. 59.

     (A "wall chart" made during a course given at the
Salisbury College of Advanced Education, outlining
events of JA's life and arranging the characters in _E_
according to social rank.)

326 Creidy, Olga. "The Austen Country: Traveller's
     Notes." _EAA_, no. 2 (1978), pp.
     45-46.

(Biography of JA and description of places in Hampshire important to her.)

327 De Rose, Peter L. "Marriage and Self-Knowledge in
        Emma and _Pride and Prejudice_." _Renascence_, 30
        (1978), 199-216.

     (See no. 454.)

328 Footerman, Sharon. "The First Fanny Price." _N&Q_, NS
        25 (1978), 217-19.

     "The story of Fanny Price, in all its essential
     details, occurs in the second part of George Crabbe's
     poem, _The Parish Register_."

329 Fosbery, M. W. "Jane Austen's Fanny Price." _CQ_, 8
        (1978), 113-28.

     Living largely by complex systems of repression
     and exclusion of all pain and novelty, Fanny Price
     proves defensive, mean, cunning, and "an appalling
     snob." For the sake of Fanny's morally questionable
     virtue and the continuance of "the Edmund-Fanny
     snuggery," JA cultivates her own marked animus
     against Mary Crawford, willing "special conclusions
     onto the material." The author's "severe primness
     in this book seems an attempt to suppress her more
     generous sense of the difficulties of behaviour."

330 Gilson, D. J. "Jane Austen and James Stanier
        Clarke." _BC_, 27 (1978), 109-10, n. 411.

     Though the whereabouts of the Prince Regent's
     librarian's copy of the first edition of _E_ are
     unknown, his copy of the first edition of North-
     anger Abbey _and_ Persuasion has recently been
     discovered.

331 Glock, Waldo S. "Catherine Morland's Gothic Delu-
        sions: A Defense of _Northanger Abbey_." _BRMMLA_,
        32 (1978), 33-46.

     Contrary to much critical opinion, _NA_ proves
     thematically and structurally coherent. Specif-
     ically, Catherine's Gothic delusions in the second
     part of the book constitute an indissoluble part of
     her growth into knowledge, a growth which develops
     by means of opposing "layers of successive experi-
     ences." The novel's basic contrasts, handled

paradoxically and ironically throughout, are between
reason and imagination and romance and ordinary life.

332   Grigson, Jane. "Jane Austen's Family Favourites."
      Observer Mag, 5 Feb. 1978, pp. 32-33.

      (Recipes for white soup, whipt syllabub, and
      other dishes JA mentions.)

333   Grylls, David. "Jane Austen and Dickens," in
      Guardians and Angels: Parents and Children in
      Nineteenth-Century Literature. Boston: Faber
      and Faber, 1978, pp. 111-52.

      Unlike Dickens and other later writers JA treats
      parent-child relationships in a pre-Romantic manner.
      She approves of filial obedience and respect and
      parents who offer "firmly principled guidance."
      Though her letters show her personal responsiveness
      to the young, she does not in her books view them
      emotionally. Rather, as a novelist she adopts a
      utilitarian attitude, using children "as pretext and
      convenience," and remains less interested in what
      they "are than in what they might become."

334   Gyergyai, Albert. "Jane Austen nálunk." Nagyvilág,
      23 (1978), 1380-85.

      JA's works, tremendously popular in Hungary,
      treat well-bred people living in a closed society,
      who permit themselves to pass moral judgments on
      others and remain oblivious to horrors in the out-
      side world. Though the reader alternates between
      pity and contempt for these characters, he yet feels
      drawn to them, as also to JA's handling of plot,
      dialogue, irony, the themes of marriage and the
      education of women, and her peaceful emphasis on the
      everyday.

335   Hopkins, Robert. "General Tilney and Affairs of
      State: The Political Gothic of Northanger Abbey."
      PQ, 57 (1978), 213-24.

      NA's political passages, including references to
      enclosure, riots, and governmental repression, reveal
      "the difference between Gothicism as a false literary
      attitude and Gothicism as a genuine symbol of the
      nightmarish political world of the 1790s and very
      early 1800s." General Tilney, a "flagrantly aggres-
      sive" capitalist and one of the "neighbourhood of
      voluntary spies," is "politicized man writ large, a

pompous ass whose inquisitorial role engendering
fear, distrust, and suspicions is thoroughly
contemptible."

336 Hopkinson, Diana. "Peepshow on Victorian Life:
       Catherine Hubback's Sketchbooks." Country Life,
       30 Mar. 1978, pp. 840-41.

     (Account of the life and drawings of a niece of
     JA, with illustrations from her sketchbooks.)

337 Howells, Coral Ann. "Jane Austen, Northanger Abbey,"
       in Love, Mystery, and Misery: Feeling in Gothic
       Fiction. London: Athlone Press, 1978, pp. 114-
       30.

     Always aware of the complex interplay between
     life and imagination, NA shows the novel form to have
     a paradoxical nature: it draws on the real world for
     its substance but aspires to a more gratifying order
     than actuality affords. In addition, rather than
     condemning the Gothic, NA criticizes "the ir-
     responsibility of those writers who trivialise
     their important insights into human behaviour."

338 Hyland, Peter. "Jane Austen: The Watsons and
       Mansfield Park." N&Q, NS 25 (1978), 216.

     JA used The Watsons "to shape the Portsmouth
     scenes of Mansfield Park."

339 Jane Austen in Southampton: Reproductions of Old
       Prints. N.p.: Hampshire County Library, [1978].

     (Reproduces prints of locations in Southampton
     associated with JA.)

340 Jane Austen 1979 Calendar. Blandford Forum, Dorset:
       Damory, 1978.

     (This calendar includes six drawings--one of JA's
     cottage at Chawton and the others of places mentioned
     in the novels.)

341 The Jane Austen Society: Report for the Year, 1977.
       Alton, Hampshire: Jane Austen Society, [1978].

     (In addition to the guest speaker's address to
     the Society's annual general meeting, indicated

below, this report includes, among other things, a
list of Jane Austen studies for 1977--prepared by
David Gilson--and several brief notes.)

Juliet McMaster, "Jane Austen on the Symptoms of
Love," pp. 25-40. (See no. 351.)

342 "[Jane Austen, Volume the Second.]" BLJ, 4 (1978),
     197.

(On "Add. MS. 59874," "comprising later autograph
copies" of such early compositions as "Lesley Castle"
and "The History of England," recently acquired by
the British Library.)

343 Kawamoto, Shizuko. "Ōsuten to gonin no musumetachi:
     Novel of manners no dento" [Austen and her five
     daughters: The novel of manners tradition].
     EigoS, 123 (1978), 445-48.

The creator of the novel of manners and thus of
much of the English novel tradition, JA had five
significant successors--Elizabeth Gaskell, George
Eliot, Charlotte Brontë, Virginia Woolf, and Margaret
Drabble. The first two followed the pattern JA
established for handling personal and social relationships, and the final three turned away from the
model she offered.

344 Kennard, Jean E. "Jane Austen: The Establishment,"
     in Victims of Convention. Hamden, Conn.: Archon,
     1978, pp. 21-45. Part of Kennard's essay
     appeared originally, with the title "Oates,
     Lessing, and Jong: The Burden of Tradition," in
     Atlantis, 2 (Fall 1976), 14, 16, and 21; see no.
     914.

Each novel presents its heroine with two opposing
sets of values, embodied in two suitors, one of whom
is greedy and selfish, the other virtuous. In moving
toward the suitor of whom JA approves, the heroine
comes to share his "balance of feeling with social
responsibility" and is in that sense an echo of the
man she marries. Since JA's ethic requires that all
good characters limit their personalities, we can
accept the sacrifices her heroines make to the
establishment.

345 Kestner, Joseph. "The Letters of Jane Austen: The
     Writer as Émetteur/Récepteur." PLL, 14 (1978),
     249-68.

JA's letters remain important because of the
historical and sociological information they supply,
their statements about prose fiction, and their
relation to the novels. These letters, in their
"flashes of characterization" and "relentless
accumulation of detail," provide "the unrefined raw
matter of the novels." And in their concern for the
émetteur or sender of a letter and the récepteur
or receiver, we see JA developing her ability to
create dialogue and focus narrative.

346 Killalea, Geraldine. "Introduction" to "Love and
       Freindship" and Other Early Works. London:
       Women's Press, 1978, pp. vii-x. In addition to
       the title piece, this edition includes "Lesley
       Castle," "The History of England," "A Collection
       of Letters," and "The Three Sisters."

       Rev. by Brian Southam in BBNews (1978), p. 497;
       in BkW, 14 May 1978, p. G6; by Deborah Astudillo in
       Booklist, 75 (1978), 24; by David Williams in Punch,
       1 Mar. 1978, p. 375; by Sally A. Lodge in PW, 6 Mar.
       1981, p. 92; by Paul Gray in Time, 13 Apr. 1981, pp.
       104 and 106; in TLS, 27 Mar. 1981, p. 332 [and see
       letter, John Bell, 8 May 1981, p. 517].

       These early works "display aspects of her talent
       which do not appear elsewhere, and which while
       directly relevant to the background of eighteenth-
       century fiction she mocks, are still apposite in the
       twentieth century. Their maturity is astonishing,
       their irony enlightening, and their gaiety con-
       tagious."

347 Kilroy, G. J. F. "Ironic Balance in Persuasion."
       DownR, 96 (1978), 305-13.

       Contrary to much critical opinion, P may be "the
       most firmly structured of all Jane Austen's novels."
       In addition, rather than utterly condemning "pruden-
       tial values, it offers a highly ironic comment on the
       relationship between romance and prudence"; and,
       while relying more on emotion and warmth than her
       other works, it still concentrates as well on her
       more familiar values.

348 Lockwood, Thomas. "Divided Attention in Persuasion."
       NCF, 33 (1978), 309-23.

       A "slight but perpetual division of interest and
       focus . . . between a moral and an emotional self-
       consciousness" characterizes P, making it different

from the other novels and helping to create its "extraordinary beauty and life." Though the awareness of heroine and novelist often coincides, Anne attaches more significance to questions of right and wrong, JA to feeling's role in determining happiness.

349   MacDonagh, Oliver. "Highbury and Chawton: Social
        Convergence in Emma." HistS, 18 (1978), 37-51.

"Jane Austen reproduced in Emma essentially the social organisation and habits which she experienced in Chawton," notably "the same inherent tendencies towards social convergence and personal repression." This glimpse into the early nineteenth century can help us "explain pre-industrial England in the midst of industrialism," "the workings of the workless middle class," and "the nature of intermediate community between town and country."

350   MacDonald, Susan Peck. "Passivity and the Female
        Role in Pride and Prejudice." W&L, 6 (Fall
        1978), 35-46.

P and P explores "the paradox of the active girl constricted and forced to suffer by the passive nature of the female role. . . . [Elizabeth's] illusions of power and her actual power to control her life are in inverse relationship, but by the end of the novel Elizabeth's right way of thinking, combined with suffering, keeping silent, and enduring, have won her the chance to control her life."

351   McMaster, Juliet. Jane Austen on Love. (ELS
        Monograph Series, 13.) Victoria, British
        Columbia: English Literary Studies, Univ. of
        Victoria, 1978.

Rev. by Karl Kroeber in SEL, 19 (1979), 731; by Pierre Goubert in EA, 33 (1980), 215-17; by Marilyn Butler in NCF, 34 (1980), 434-36; by Barry Roth in SNNTS, 12 (1980), 153-60; by G. E. Bentley, Jr., in UTQ, 49 (1980), 423-24; by Sheila Ortiz Taylor in ECS, 14 (1981), 492-94.

"The Symptoms of Love": Like Shakespeare, JA examines love and its conventions in her romantic comedies. An emotion, a subject for debate and playful comment, love affects not only the mind but the body too, revealing itself in certain outward signs, like broken speech patterns and changes in complexion. Because the novelist deals in appearances, "the visible symptoms of love--its

language, as it were--are a fine ready-made set of
terms by which to communicate its reality."

"Surface and Subsurface": JA does not avoid the
presentation of emotion; rather, she presents it
indirectly. While her characters may appear only to
be interacting decorously with one another, "below
the surface are implied the individual's ecstasies
and agonies." The characters are not limited by
social convention but express themselves fully and
deeply through it, meaning "far more than what they
say."

"Love and Pedagogy": JA's novels tell pedagogic
stories, stories concerned both with learning and
teaching. Combining moral and emotional interest,
they involve "courses of instruction," "lectures,
examination, graduation," "pupils apt, and too eager,
and recalcitrant," "teachers discerning, misguided,
perverse." At their resolutions the books celebrate
the love that is fully conscious, the passionate
"integration of head and heart that is represented by
the pupil and teacher coming to loving accord."

"Love and Marriage": JA treats not just the
economic but also the erotic motive for marriage.
Though she suggests rather than describes explicitly
this sexual aspect, the novels abound with examples
of physical magnetism between characters, flirtation,
and seduction. She "doesn't follow her girls beyond
the altar," but "the moral mingling that goes on in
the Austen marriages is a correlative of physical
union."

352   Matthews, Mary W. "Jane Austen: Pride and Preju-
        dice." SocEd, 42 (1978), 346-48.

P and P remains relevant to teen-age students
today because it "speaks to some of the same moral
questions that trouble our own era: the role of
women; the roles of both sexes; personal responsibility; and the relationship between the appearances
of pride and shyness."

353   Midgley, Freda. "A Link with Jane Austen." FDMS, 5
        (Mar. 1978), 21-22.

JA's brother Henry was curate at Farnham and
teacher at the Free School there.

354   Moloney, Jenny. "Some Personal Reflections on Emma,"
        in Women Writers and the Literary Tradition:

Finding the Woman in My Head. Ed. Jackie Cook
and Kay Iseman. (SCAE Occasional Papers, 17.)
Salisbury East, South Australia: Salisbury
College of Advanced Education, 1978, pp. 28-29.

In E, JA "means to make her little country
village look pathetic, its social structure ridiculous, and her protagonist silly and meritless.
I am absolutely sure that when Jane Austen wrote 'I
am going to take a heroine whom no one but myself
will much like,' she had no idea of how much truth
was in her words."

355 Monaghan, David. "Mansfield Park and Evangelicalism:
     A Reassessment." NCF, 33 (1978), 215-30.

Rather than reflecting the influence of the
Evangelicals, MP expresses social and religious
beliefs "completely incompatible" with theirs.
Thus, contrary to Evangelical views, the novel
praises "manners, charm, and the formal social
occasion" and supports orthodox Anglican attitudes
to such issues as residency and vocation. And,
since the Evangelicals deviated from and endangered
the status quo, which MP staunchly defends, "they
can have had no appeal for Jane Austen."

356 Morton, A. Q. "The Inimitable Jane," in Literary
     Detection: How to Prove Authorship and Fraud in
     Literature and Documents. New York: Scribner's,
     1978, pp. 189-91.

If we analyze the 1975 completion of Sanditon
according to stylometry, the science describing and
measuring personal elements in literary and other
utterances, we find that, though Another Lady's
efforts reproduce "with some precision" various
features of JA, "it is easy to see that the imitation is not Jane Austen."

357 Newton, Judith Lowder. "Pride and Prejudice: Power,
     Fantasy, and Subversion in Jane Austen." FemSt,
     4 (Feb. 1978), 27-42. Newton's essay appears
     also, with the title "Pride and Prejudice," in
     her Women, Power, and Subversion: Social
     Strategies in British Fiction, 1778-1860 (Athens,
     Ga.: Univ. of Georgia Press, 1981), pp. 55-85.

P and P "recognizes the shaping influence of
economics" yet "denies its force." Genuine power
here involves not money, autonomy, mobility, all of
which men enjoy and misuse, but "the intelligence,

the wit, and the critical attitudes of Jane Austen,"
whose heroine is basically "an Austen fantasy, a
fantasy of power." Elizabeth's individualism, less
middle-class than feminist, proves a subtle attack on
traditional divisions between the sexes.

358   Norman, Geraldine. "Unfinished Jane Austen Manu-
         script Makes ⨍38,000." Times, 26 July 1978, p.
         16.

      (On the sale of The Watsons.)

359   Olsen, Bruce. "The Empiricism of the Imitator."
         Lang&S, 11 (1978), 181-87.

      As a study of John Coates's 1958 completion of
      The Watsons makes clear, the literary effects evident
      in imitation "have 'grammatical' characteristics,
      consisting of a field of a finite number of classes
      of elements and their functions"; "the field of an
      effect has a bounded, holistic, and synchronic
      character that allows it to be regarded as a global
      concept"; and "an effect is sufficiently inclusive
      of literary phenomena to warrant such designations as
      aesthetic response or literary object."

360   Paris, Bernard J. Character and Conflict in Jane
         Austen's Novels: A Psychological Approach.
         Detroit: Wayne State Univ. Press, 1978.

      Rev. in Choice, 16 (1979), 1174; by Shernaz
      Mollinger in LibJ, 104 (1979), 731; by Stephen Gill
      in TLS, 21 Dec. 1979, p. 167; by Nina Auerbach in
      JEGP, 79 (1980), 452-54; by Barry Roth in SNNTS, 12
      (1980), 153-60; by Merritt Moseley in SR, 88 (1980),
      641-47; by Bryan Burns in YWES, 61 (1980), 283; by
      Sheila Ortiz Taylor in ECS, 14 (1981), 494-97; by
      L. R. Leavis and J. M. Blom in ES, 62 (1981), 313-23;
      by Robert Folkenflik in NCF, 36 (1981), 95-98; by
      George S. Rousseau in Archiv, 219 (1982), 192-95; by
      F. B. Pinion in RES, NS 33 (1982), 484-86; by
      Frederick M. Keener in MLR, 78 (1983), 433-35.

      Introductory: Rather than models of unity and
      balance, JA's novels "are beset by tensions between
      form, theme, and mimesis" because her protagonists
      simultaneously "serve aesthetic, illustrative, and
      mimetic functions." Though the novels harmonize
      "form and theme by moralizing the comic action,"
      their realistic characterization--which we can
      understand best through Karen Horney's psychological
      theories--"fights against theme as well as against
      form."

MP: A narrow, oppressive book, MP celebrates "embeddedness and sterility." While both the plot and treatment of education glorify the heroine, the presentation of her personality shows her to be essentially unhealthy and misinterpreted by JA. Fanny, who is crippled by "a pathogenic environment," develops in a "self-effacing," "self-alienated," and "infantile" manner, becoming "rigid, desperate, compulsive," qualities of which the author approves.

E: Emma as "an imagined human being" does not accord with her dramatic and thematic roles in the novel. Suffering from "narcissistic and perfectionistic trends," induced by excessive approbation early in life, she idealizes first herself, before "her pride is broken," and then Mr. Knightley, after she regresses "to childish dependency." As the heroine substitutes a "compliant for expansive" disposition, JA, who remains "blind to Emma's father problem," offers increasingly unsatisfactory explanations of her character.

P and P: A "fantasy of power" and "expansiveness" and JA's "most complex" book, P and P wrongly supposes the protagonists' marriage "to illustrate the balancing of social and personal values." Actually Elizabeth, a very "defensive" individual, wants Darcy not because she likes, respects, or shares much with him but because he "feeds her pride," satisfying her desire "for glory, for competitive triumph, and for recognition of her worth." Their marriage will prosper as long as they continue "exalting each other."

P: P, which thematically resembles the earlier novels and differs from them in emphasizing the relativity and uncertainty of truth, asks us to admire Anne's "self-effacing" tendencies as noble when in fact they are "compulsive" and "defensive." Beneath her gentleness lies much "repressed resentment," evident especially in her relationship with Wentworth: marrying a successful, "expansive" man lets her escape feeling impotent and "provides her with a vicarious fulfillment of her own aggressive drives."

"The Authorial Personality": "The personality which can be inferred from all of her fiction" contains "perfectionistic, detached, and self-effacing" forces, forces she attempts to keep in equilibrium. In terms of her artistic development she expresses "her moral superiority" in S and S and her "girlish hopes and dreams" in P and P; she "satisfies her self-effacing shoulds" in MP and returns "to her old posture of perfectionistic condescension" in E; finally, she mourns "for what she has missed in life" in P.

361   Paris, Bernard J.   "'Creations inside a Creation':
       The Case of Emma Woodhouse."   PsychoculR, 2
       (1978), 119-38.

       (See no. 360.)

362   Parker, Derek.   "A Letter from Longbourne [sic]."
       Listener, 5 Jan. 1978, pp. 24-25.

       (A letter from Elizabeth Bennet commenting on the
       Christmas 1977 radio programs.)

363   Penrith, Mary.   "Forms of Address and Reference in
       Emma."   UCTSE, no. 8 (1978), pp. 34-45.

       "The variety of forms of address and reference in
       Emma . . . gives some idea of the ways in which
       English of the early nineteenth century compensated
       for the loss of the you-thou contrast."   These forms
       reveal both the real world and the world one desires,
       and, used correctly, they function to protect the
       weak individual and the "society as a whole from the
       power-hungry."

364   Pérez Gállego, Cándido.   "Jane Austen: La inerte
       burguesía," in Temática de la literatura inglesa.
       Zaragoza: Librería General, 1978, pp. 213-38.

       In NA, P and P, MP, and E, JA pictures a limited,
       inert world, criticizing especially the bourgeoisie's
       desire to separate social classes from each other.
       Through her focus in these books on protagonists who
       feel just as uncomfortable in their fantasies as in
       external reality, she creates a dualistic style that
       allows her simultaneously to narrate a story and
       satirize what she narrates.

365   Petit, Jean-Pierre.   "Jane Austen: Pride and Preju-
       dice," in Le Roman anglais au XIXe siècle.   Ed.
       Pierre Coustillas, Jean-Pierre Petit, and Jean
       Raimond.   Paris: Presses Universitaires de
       France, 1978, pp. 127-38.

       P and P shows that it is possible for a writer to
       be a genius without speaking of God, nature, death,
       or romantic passion.   A dynamic novel based on the
       psychological in human relations, it describes a
       process of education that emphasizes problems of

knowledge and judgment. The irony is thoroughgoing,
the style clear and comic, and the dialogue dramatic.

366 Robinson, Lillian S. "On Reading Trash," in Sex,
        Class, and Culture. Bloomington, Ind.: Indiana
        Univ. Press, 1978, pp. 200-222.

A comparison of JA and Georgette Heyer, a writer
of Regency romances, proves valuable not because it
demonstrates the former's superiority but because it
helps explain women's reading habits. "It would
appear that female readers do not seek out trashy
novels in order to escape or to experience life
vicariously, but rather to receive confirmation,
and, eventually, affirmation, that love really is
what motivates and justifies a woman's life."

367 Robinson, Lillian S. "Why Marry Mr. Collins?" in
        Sex, Class, and Culture. Bloomington, Ind.:
        Indiana Univ. Press, 1978, pp. 178-99.

Treating the complexity of women's financial
position and the contradiction "between the ideal of
marriage for love and the social reality of gentry
life," JA shows Charlotte Lucas accepting Mr. Collins
not merely for the sake of money but larger cultural
gain too. The character wishes to define herself
adequately in the only available way, simply to "have
a life--whether or not provision existed for her to
subsist in tolerable material comfort as a spinster."

368 Roditi, Edouard. "Jane Austen and Her Critics."
        VWQ, 3 (1978), 193-98.

Critical responses to JA offer "a remarkably
instructive example, not only of the evolution of
literary taste, but also of the rapid diversifica-
tion of principles of criticism, if not of their
proliferation and deterioration too." And, "in
spite of the vast quantities of Austen criticism of
recent years, much remains to be said about the
very peculiar quality of her wit, her psychology
and her fiction."

369 Rogal, Samuel J. "Meals Abounding: Jane Austen at
        Table." ECLife, 4 (1978), 71-75.

JA uses the act of eating not only as a domestic
ritual helping to structure her works but more
importantly as a way to attack "the waste, the
misunderstanding, the over-indulgence" she observed

in a society valuing "what is shovelled unceremo-
niously into the stomach" rather than "what goes into
the mind." She thus tells us in essence that the
activities in her "narrow world" mean little, if anything.

370   Roth, Barry. "Confessions of a Jane Austen Teacher."
       Focus, 5 (Fall 1978), 25-29.

       Though rewarding, teaching JA may prove difficult
because "she radically reduces to their essences
concerns central to all literature." Among other
things "she makes reading hard by denying us the
comfort of large or easily recognizable actions,"
places great demands on our linguistic resources, and
forces us to pay "close and constant attention" to
communication of every sort. She confronts, com-
prehensively and maturely, without simplifying and
in full awareness, "the given terms of existence."

371   Schwanitz, Dietrich. "Zwei Beispiele zur Erlebten
       Rede und ihrer Entstehungstheorie." GRM, NS 28
       (1978), 349-53.

       Examples from E and Much Ado about Nothing
demonstrate that erlebte Rede can be found in
colloquial and literary speech, both with and without
tense transformation. And the ironic use of erlebte
Rede indicates the author's conscious design.

372   Sedgwick, Fred. "Plain Jane." Letter in Times, 26
       Oct. 1978, p. 19. See also letters in Times,
       Barbara Reynolds, 1 Nov. 1978, p. 17; Douglas
       Hubble, 3 Nov., p. 19; Derek Hudson, 10 Nov.,
       p. 19.

       (Complains that a book reviewer patronizes JA by
referring to her as "Jane.")

373   Séjourné, Philippe. "Les Intentions de Jane Austen
       dans Sense and Sensibility: Héritage et
       innovation," in Hommage à Émile Gasquet (1920-
       1977). (Annales de la Faculté des Lettres et
       Sciences Humaines de Nice, 34.) Paris: Belles
       Lettres, 1978, pp. 149-58.

       S and S derives from the novels of sensibility
written by women between 1750 and 1800, and it also
significantly enriches the tradition. The book
studies some of the same themes as those earlier
works and follows some of the same plotting. It

proves original because JA sets her drama in a
quotidian rather than tragic context, provides acute
psychological analyses, creates complex, evolving
characters, and examines in profound ways relationships between the sexes.

374   Siefert, Susan. "Elizabeth Bennet," in The Dilemma
of the Talented Heroine: A Study in Nineteenth-
Century Fiction. (Monographs in Women's
Studies.) St. Albans, Vt.: Eden Press, 1978, pp.
24-31, 69-73, and 115-22.

Because of a sense of vulnerability, Elizabeth
adopts an image of herself as a detached, discriminating perceiver, an image that is basically correct.
The difficulties she encounters stem partly from
incorrect judgments and partly from the conflict
between her values, based on the need for self-
definition, and the materialism of her society.
In marrying Darcy she reconciles opposing views of
happiness: she both makes a "good marriage" and
achieves individual freedom.

375   Siefert, Susan. "Emma Woodhouse," in The Dilemma
of the Talented Heroine: A Study in Nineteenth-
Century Fiction. (Monographs in Women's
Studies.) St. Albans, Vt.: Eden Press, 1978,
pp. 31-38, 73-80, and 127-32.

Beginning without moral responsibility or self-
awareness, Emma mistakenly believes she can benignly
manipulate others. She chooses the socially acceptable roles of daughter, sister, and friend
because they free her to realize her wish for control
and power. Paradoxically, her aspirations are both
dehumanizing and "an analogue of the human desire to
fulfill oneself."

376   Smith, Ross S. Fanny Bertram: The Structure of
Mansfield Park. (Monograph 1.) [Townsville,
Queensland, Australia]: Dept. of English, James
Cook Univ. of North Queensland, 1978.

JA uses three structural devices to shape MP:
first, through a series of absences from the Park and
returns there, she traces the course of Fanny's
relationship to Sir Thomas, the relationship upon
which narrative and thematic development depends;
second, she devises a coherent, consistent moral
scheme dealing with the virtue of kindness, the vices
of selfishness and ingratitude, and education's
importance for teaching "correct principles that will

ensure sound judgement and provide a sense of duty
and propriety"; and third, she deploys all the
characters about the protagonist, "who functions as
their 'judge and critic.'"

377   Sternberg, Meir. "The Rhetoric of Anticipatory
        Caution: First Impressions in 'First Impressions'
        and the Poetics of Jane Austen," in Expositional
        Modes and Temporal Ordering in Fiction. Bal-
        timore: Johns Hopkins Univ. Press, 1978, pp.
        129-58. Part of Sternberg's essay appeared
        originally, with the title "Temporal Ordering,
        Modes of Expositional Distribution, and Three
        Models of Rhetorical Control in the Narrative
        Text: Faulkner, Balzac, and Austen," in PTL, 1
        (1976), 295-316.

        Like other JA novels P and P illustrates a "model
of dynamic control through expositional manipulation
and temporal ordering in general: the rhetoric of
anticipatory caution. Here the primary effect
itself--and hence our attitude to the protagonist,
whose information or view largely gives rise to
it--is perceptibly qualified from the beginning."
In addition, P and P devises "a correspondence
between the reader's and [Elizabeth's] impression
formation" and stresses, among other things, a
vocabulary pertaining to the "quest for knowledge and
ordeal of knowledge."

378   Tatham, Michael. "Mary Crawford and the Christian
        Heroine." NewB, 59 (1978), 262-68.

        Our view of "Jane Austen's personal commitment
to Christianity must depend upon which of her
heroines appears to speak most nearly for the
author." As has often been noted, Elizabeth Bennet
seems much like her creator, and Mary Crawford
resembles Elizabeth Bennet. Given the identification
of these characters, "Mary Crawford's rejection of
religion" could represent JA's opinion.

379   Taylor, Mary Vaiana. "The Grammar of Conduct: Speech
        Act Theory and the Education of Emma Woodhouse."
        Style, 12 (1978), 357-71.

        "The changing pattern of Emma's speech acts"
embodies in language her social and moral growth.
Before the expedition to Box Hill her "speech acts,"
infelicitous and ambiguous, "break constitutive
rules," but afterward, when she assumes responsibility for what she desires and perceives, these

acts "conform to the rules which establish connections between linguistic events" and the world
outside the individual.

380 Tyler, Ralph. "The Works of Great Writers Available
     Today: Jane Austen." Bookviews, 1 (Feb. 1978),
     24-25. Tyler's comments on JA include
     biographical information and a bibliography
     of writings by her.

     Scrupulously truthful, never mistaken or fuzzy in
     her assumptions about human conduct and emotions, JA
     "has a lovely unpretentious seriousness of her own
     that can teach useful moral lessons to our disordered
     age."

381 Weinsheimer, Joel. "Impedance as Value: Roderick
     Random and Pride and Prejudice." PTL, 3 (1978),
     139-66.

     "In literary judgment . . . value is defined by
     the impedance of interpretive praxis. Pride and
     Prejudice is a better novel than Roderick Random
     because it engages the reader more fully than
     Roderick Random; it gives him something to do. Two
     factors keep us interested in Pride and Prejudice:
     our desire to act--to write or create--combined with
     the opportunities which the text offers for doing
     so."

382 Wilks, Brian. Jane Austen. New York: Hamlyn, 1978.

          Rev. in TES, 20 Oct. 1978, p. 40; by Bryan Burns
     in YWES, 59 (1978), 283-84; in Choice, 17 (1980),
     225.

     (This biography includes more than one hundred
     illustrations depicting the Austen family, various
     contemporaries, and different aspects of the life
     of the period.)

383 Yamawaki, Yuriko. "Jein Ōsuten--Eichi no bungaku"
     [Jane Austen--Intelligent literature], in Eikoku
     joryu sakka ron [Essays on English women
     writers]. Tokyo: Hokuseido Press, 1978, pp.
     33-52.

     Mature and intelligent, JA's novels carefully
     analyze human errors and strictly punish those
     characters who do not improve themselves and achieve
     happiness.

1979

384   Alique, José-Benito. "Emma, o las enseñanzas de una
          edición oportuna." NE, no. 4 (Mar. 1979), pp.
          88-89.

          Unlike the unnecessarily complicated narratives
      of many modern writers E provides a model of
      simplicity, economy, and lucidity. In addition,
      using acute perception and masterly dialogue, it
      attacks both society's caste nature and the
      sentimental spirit.

385   Bompiani, Ginevra. "Postface" to Emma. Paris:
          Bourgois, 1979, pp. 265-70. This edition
          includes a biographical essay on JA by Jacques
          Roubaud, pp. 273-80, an essay appearing also in
          other JA novels published by Bourgois: Orgueil
          et préjugés (1979), Raison et sentiments (1979),
          and Northanger Abbey (1980).

          Like NA and S and S, but more subtly, E
      criticizes novelistic conventions. Its heroine, the
      most French of JA's protagonists, loving intrigue and
      ignoring emotion, rivals her creator by trying to
      arrange human destinies. But the marriages Emma
      plans do not come about because novels and life
      differ.

386   Brown, Julia Prewitt. Jane Austen's Novels: Social
          Change and Literary Form. Cambridge, Mass.:
          Harvard Univ. Press, 1979.

          Rev. in Choice, 16 (1979), 526; by Alistair M.
      Duckworth in Criticism, 21 (1979), 374-76; in Kirkus,
      1 Feb. 1979, p. 158; by Shernaz Mollinger in LibJ,
      104 (1979), 1257; by Tony Tanner in NYT, 6 May 1979,
      sec. 7, pp. 7 and 34-36; by Karl Kroeber in SEL, 19
      (1979), 731-32; by Stephen Gill in TLS, 21 Dec.
      1979, pp. 166-67; in YR, 68 (Summer 1979), xiii-xv;
      by Debbie Kaplan in Arnoldian, 8 (Fall 1980), 40-48;
      by Susanna Roxman in Edda, no. 1 (1980), pp. 55-57;
      by Valerie Wayne Callies in EIC, 30 (1980), 178 and
      181-85; by Joel J. Gold in JEGP, 79 (1980), 585-88;
      by Marilyn Butler in NCF, 34 (1980), 434-36; by John
      E. Jordan in RomMov for 1979 (1980), pp. 64-65; by
      Barry Roth in SNNTS, 12 (1980), 153-60; by Merritt
      Moseley in SR, 88 (1980), 641-47; by Bryan Burns in
      YWES, 61 (1980), 281; by Juliet McMaster in ELN, 18
      (1981), 304-7.

          Introductory: The first English novelist to
      render the significance of "personal, domestic

experience," JA treats marriage, the origin "of
social and moral change" and in general a complex
subject involving the issues of sexuality, emotion,
freedom, and self-definition, and treats it with an
irony accurately reflecting its tensions. To show
that a basic change in human relationships was
occurring at the time, she alternates between two
fictional structures: "the ironic comedies" (NA, P
and P, and E) emphasize a secure social background,
resilience, and enlightenment, and "the works of
satiric realism" (S and S, MP, and P), a sense of
uprootedness, fatigue, and disillusionment.

NA and S and S: NA's "exuberant parody of convention usually takes the form of a comic assault on the
reader. In Sense and Sensibility the language has no
such target but is a deadly mimesis of convention
itself." And, while both novels explore the nature
of feminine identity by concentrating on women
altered by their reading, Catherine escapes suffering, and Marianne undergoes a tragic awakening about
the self's connection to others.

P and P: Because it values both civilized life
and anarchic forces in human nature, P and P
judges the individual according to his capacity to
arbitrate absurdity's energies "by the discrimina-
tions of sense," as well as modify sense's egotism
"by the exigencies of absurdity." The book also
weighs the individual's ability to observe taboos
about mating, for these serve to protect marriage
from contamination, to insure that a person can
affect the moral standards of future generations.

MP: "Deeply pessimistic and enervating,"
dominated by a sense of "infected emptiness" and
"spiritual paralysis," MP ironically exposes
"horrors without resolving them." It pictures a
world in decline, one that struggles unsuccessfully
for regeneration, that resists a high conception of
human values. It ends essentially where it begins,
with a social class and its members suffering from
blindness and ignorance and with the triumph of the
monstrous Fanny and Edmund rendering moral questions
trivial.

E: E concerns a place, Highbury--"a system of
interdependence, a community of people all talking
to one another, affecting, and changing one
another"--and an individual, Emma Woodhouse--who
wishes to rule rather than cooperate, to be single
rather than acknowledge her need for another's
presence. When she awakens to her love for Mr.
Knightley, she recognizes also her link to society
generally as well as the necessity for social

responsibility and compromise.

P: Not about education, for the heroine does not
learn what she needs to, but about disillusion, P,
marked by "debilitating ambiguities and hatreds" and
a "surrender to disgust," differs radically from the
earlier works. It conceives of society as in-
tolerable and impermanent, a meaningless collection of separate places failing to provide a defined
moral context, and of the individual as isolated,
uncertain, and overburdened.

"Jane Austen as a Woman Writer": JA's "deference
to local, civilized history constitutes a conception
of history, not an evasion of it." Barring P, which
focuses more on the deficiencies of women's status,
her exploration of "feminine consciousness" includes
"a generational definition of moral life, a concern
for the actual and immediate quality of social
existence, a belief in human interdependence, and a
value for social cooperation and personal adapta-
bility."

387   Burrows, J. F.   "A Measure of Excellence: Modes of
        Comparison in Pride and Prejudice." SSEng, 5
        (1979-80), 38-59.

        P and P's "measure of excellence" lies partly "in
        the intellectually and emotionally revealing uses to
        which Jane Austen's characters put the forms of
        comparison." But the narrator's comparisons,
        determined by structural concerns, "produce a kind
        of symmetry," a "conciseness and a certain stylish-
        ness" that make the novel seem too tidy. Perhaps
        "the young novelist has hit upon too ready a means
        of marshalling her ideas and too convenient a method
        of transition."

388   Byrde, Penelope. A Frivolous Distinction: Fashion
        and Needlework in the Works of Jane Austen.
        Bath: Bath City Council, [1979].

        ("The references she made to fashion and needle-
        work have been compiled and arranged in six chapters.
        Each chapter includes a general introduction and
        discussion of a topic which is illustrated by quota-
        tions from her works.")

389   Chapman, R. W., coll. and ed. Jane Austen's Letters
        to Her Sister Cassandra and Others. 2d ed.
        1952. Reprint. New York: Oxford Univ. Press,
        1979.

Rev. by G. B. Tennyson in <u>SEL</u>, 20 (1980), 721; in <u>VQR</u>, 56 (1980), xxxix.

(The standard edition, with an amended version of letter 127.)

390 Charlton, Linda. "Fans Lift Their Good Wine to 'the Incomparable Jane.'" <u>NYT</u>, 8 Oct. 1979, p. B2.

(On the first annual general meeting of the Jane Austen Society of North America.)

391 Cockshut, A. O. J. "Austen, Jane," in <u>Novelists and Prose Writers</u>. Ed. James Vinson. (Great Writers of the English Language.) New York: St. Martin's Press, 1979, pp. 59-62. Cockshut's essay, which includes a bibliography of writings by and about JA, appears also in <u>The Novel to 1900</u>, ed. James Vinson, Great Writers Student Library, 8 (New York: St. Martin's Press, 1980), pp. 19-21. See also Cockshut's comments on JA in his "Introduction" to <u>The Novel to 1900</u>, ed. Vinson, pp. 6-8.

Both traditional and original, "easygoing and inexorable," JA is a disturbing novelist, who treats a well-meaning, proper, and corrupt society. To read her carefully proves "a humbling as well as an exhilarating experience."

392 Conrad, Peter. "<u>Emma</u> by Jane Austen." <u>Observer Mag</u>, 1 July 1979, p. 52. Part of Conrad's essay appears also in his "Introduction" to <u>E</u>, ed. Mary Lascelles (New York: Dutton, 1980), pp. v-xxx; see no. 452.

JA's "wisest" and "most disturbing" novel, <u>E</u> is "political" in nature, studying power and "civilisation and its chafing discontents" and worrying "about the problems--central to the novel as a form--of how we survive in society, of what we owe to others, of how far we can permit ourselves to be changed by engaging in relationships." The book concludes that social participation demands "self-suppression, dissembling, compromise."

393 Copeland, Edward. "What's a Competence? Jane Austen, Her Sister Novelists, and the 5%'s." <u>MLS</u>, 9 (Fall 1979), 161-68.

In <u>S and S</u>, JA rigorously explores economic realities so as to define woman's place in society.

She devotes special attention, as do many of her
contemporaries in their fiction, to the idea of a
competence, defined as the money needed to enable
one to live independently of one's own exertion.

394   Cowart, David. "Wise and Foolish Virgins (and
        Matrons) in Mansfield Park." SAB, 44 (May 1979),
        76-82.

        Maria and Julia Bertram, Mary Crawford, and Mrs.
        Norris act foolishly when Sir Thomas leaves for
        Antigua, for they all thirst to be busy, to take
        advantage of the absence by being as active as
        possible in self-indulgent schemes. Only Fanny acts
        wisely: she continues to value decorous behavior and
        quietly awaits the return of the Park's moral
        authority. By thus discriminating between the
        characters early in the book, JA prepares us for the
        judgments she renders at the novel's end.

395   Craddock, Patricia. "The Almanac of Sense and
        Sensibility." N&Q, NS 26 (1979), 222-26.

        The calendar of S and S "most closely resembles
        that of the year of the original epistolary version
        of the novel, 1795. . . . What apprentice qualities
        Sense and Sensibility retains are readily explicable
        by such a retention of its early structure."

396   Crider, Richard. "Emma's Anglican Wedding." C&L, 28
        (Winter 1979), 34-39.

        When Emma speaks of "the building in which N.
        takes M. for better, for worse," she is alluding to
        the wedding ceremony in The Book of Common Prayer.
        JA thus encourages us to consider her heroine's
        marriage as "not only the happy ending of comedy but
        an affirmation of faith."

397   De Rose, Peter L. "Memory in Mansfield Park." N&Q,
        NS 26 (1979), 226-27.

        (See no. 454.)

398   Di Martino, Gabriella. "La lingua e il comportamento
        della classe media nel romanzo di Jane Austen:
        Emma," in Tecniche e forme linguistiche nel
        romanzo inglese del settecento. Naples: Liguori,
        1979, pp. 80-92.

        Using both colloquial and distinctly literary

language, JA creates a flexible prose style, one
which serves as a transition between the writings of
the eighteenth century and the novels of Thackeray.
As passages in E make clear, she carefully chooses
her words, among other reasons, for the sake of
irony, rhythm, and point of view, and she moves
smoothly from direct to indirect speech.

399 Drescher, Horst W., with Rüdiger Ahrens and Karl-
Heinz Stoll. "Austen, Jane," in Lexikon der
englischen Literatur. (Kröners Taschenausgabe,
465.) Stuttgart: Kröner, 1979, pp. 24-25.

(Presents biographical information, speaks of JA
as the most important novelist of her time, and
discusses her treatment of the gentry as characterized by humor, irony, moralizing, and sympathetic
understanding.)

400 Edwards, Ann-Marie. In the Steps of Jane Austen:
Town & Country Walks. London: BBC, 1979.

"Today we can walk in Jane's footsteps and still
capture a great deal of the atmosphere of her world.
The country houses, churches, great estates and
elegant cities she knew have changed surprisingly
little in the course of two centuries. I have found
exploring Jane's England a most rewarding experience."

401 Ehrenpreis, Irvin. "Jane Austen and Heroism." NYRB,
8 Feb. 1979, pp. 37-43. Ehrenpreis's essay
appears also, in an enlarged form, with the title
"Austen: The Heroism of the Quotidian," in his
Acts of Implication: Suggestion and Covert Mean-
ing in the Works of Dryden, Swift, Pope, and
Austen (Berkeley and Los Angeles: Univ. of
California Press, 1980), pp. 112-45.

JA relies "on moral metonymy or synecdoche in a
scheme of ironic parallels and contrasts" for
characterization, novelistic structure, and moral
significance. And subtly and evocatively, by means
of understatement, she reveals her awareness of
sexuality and suggests political, social, and
religious doctrines.

402 Fairbanks, Carol. "Austen, Jane," in More Women in
Literature: Criticism of the Seventies.
Metuchen, N.J.: Scarecrow Press, 1979, pp. 18-26.

(Bibliography.)

403   Fry, Paul H.   "Georgic Comedy: The Fictive Territory
        of Jane Austen's Emma." SNNTS, 11 (1979), 129-
        46.

      "Romance for Jane Austen is not so much an
implausible as an undesirable pattern of expectation.
The plot of Emma acknowledges the accidents of
Romance, and allows them to occur, but only at a safe
distance from the sort of accident that is morally to
be desired. The center of her territory," which we
may call "Georgic Comedy," remains rural at the same
time that it "accommodates itself to a State of
Society."

404   Gay, Penny.   "The Romanticism of Persuasion." SSEng,
        5 (1979-80), 15-30.

      Unique in the canon, P employs metaphor struc-
turally and stresses physical elements in its prose.
In particular P contrasts "warm" and "cold" and
partially replaces dialogue with "eye-contact."   The
novel's emphasis on "body language," on what is
"organic," constitutes a "Romantic acknowledgement
that ordinary speech is insufficient to express the
complex feelings of the isolated ego in its desire
to communicate with another human being."

405   Gilbert, Sandra M., and Susan Gubar.   "Inside the
        House of Fiction: Jane Austen's Tenants of
        Possibility," in The Madwoman in the Attic: The
        Woman Writer and the Nineteenth-Century Literary
        Imagination. New Haven: Yale Univ. Press, 1979,
        pp. 105-83. Part of Gilbert and Gubar's essay
        appears also in vol. 1 of Nineteenth-Century
        Literature Criticism: Excerpts from Criticism of
        the Works of Novelists, Poets, Playwrights, Short
        Story Writers, and Other Creative Writers Who
        Lived between 1800 and 1900, from the First
        Published Critical Appraisals to Current Evalua-
        tions, ed. Laurie Lanzen Harris (Detroit: Gale
        Research, 1981), pp. 65-67.

      "Shut Up in Prose: Gender and Genre in Austen's
Juvenilia," pp. 107-45. In the juvenilia and NA, JA
balances her "commitment to an inherited literary
structure that idealizes feminine submission against
her rebellious imaginative sympathies." She treats
women's miseducation, financial dependence, and
general powerlessness as well as the family's
inadequacy and patriarchy's failures and repressions.
The stories she tells invariably concern women's need
to renounce any claim to stories they themselves
author. It is impossible, she concludes, for women

to escape "the conventions and categories that, in
every sense, belittle them."

    "Jane Austen's Cover Story (and Its Secret
Agents)," pp. 146-83. In the last five completed
novels "Austen's self-division--her fascination with
the imagination and her anxiety that it is unfemi-
nine--is part of her consciousness of the unique
dilemma of all women, who must acquiesce in their
status as objects after an adolescence in which they
experience themselves as free agents." Just as her
fictional women "manage to survive only by seeming to
submit," so JA herself "succeeds in maintaining her
double consciousness in fiction that proclaims its
docility and restraint even as it uncovers the
delights of assertion and rebellion."

406 Glendinning, Victoria. "Introduction" to Three
       Nineteenth-Century Novels. New York: New
       American Library, 1979, pp. v-xii. This volume
       contains Pride and Prejudice, Wuthering Heights,
       and Silas Marner.

    Although costume and idiom change, JA's domestic
comedy remains pertinent. Mercilessly and profoundly, she analyzes "the precise quality of the
feeling between people." She bases P and P, like her
other novels, on the themes of self-discovery and
marriage, depicting the conflict within a young
woman between social pressure and independence of
mind.

407 Grey, Sarah. "Introduction" to Classic Romance
       Omnibus. London: New English Library, 1979, pp.
       7-8. This volume contains Pride and Prejudice,
       Jane Eyre, Wuthering Heights, and Madame Bovary.

    "Arguably the best of all romances," P and P
"invented the English novel of morals, manners and
moods." Perceptively and unsentimentally, it reveals
through a controlled prose style "the emotions and
forces that lay beneath the surface of early
nineteenth-century middle-class life."

408 Hilliard, Raymond F. "Emma: Dancing without Space to
       Turn In," in Probability, Time, and Space in
       Eighteenth-Century Literature. Ed. Paula R.
       Backscheider. New York: AMS Press, 1979, pp.
       275-98.

    In E confinement threatens human vitality.
Dancing symbolizes that vitality, and playfulness

provides its most obvious outlet. In addition, JA
defines the individual by his attitude to his social
situation, that is, the "space" he has "to turn in."
She celebrates true marriage "as an ideal social
relationship in which each participant finds a
'space' where his energies will be contained but
given suitable exercise: the rational and the
playful must balance each other."

409 Hochman, Baruch. "Jane Austen and the Development of
       the Novel." HUSL, 7 (1979), 161-81.

       Like Stendhal, JA contributed to the novel's
development by creating "free-standing, fallible,
conflict-ridden" characters, by placing them in "a
socially and historically concrete world," and by
projecting "a more or less autonomous narrative voice
that is at once involved in the world of the novel
and radically detached from it."

410 "Homage." NY, 5 Nov. 1979, pp. 41-42.

       (On celebrations inaugurating the Jane Austen
Society of North America.)

411 Hopkinson, Diana. "Austens in America." Country
       Life, 16 Aug. 1979, pp. 468-69.

       (Biographical account of the Austen family's
American connections.)

412 The Jane Austen Society: Report for the Year, 1978.
       Alton, Hampshire: Jane Austen Society, [1979].

       (In addition to the guest speaker's address to
the Society's annual general meeting, abstracted
below, this report includes, among other things, a
list of Jane Austen studies for 1978, a supplement
to the list of Jane Austen studies for 1977--both
prepared by David Gilson--and several brief notes.)

       Marilyn Butler, "Disregarded Designs: Jane
Austen's Sense of the Volume," pp. 27-42. Although
four of the novels appeared originally in a three-
volume format, only E "looks like a bold plan for
three volumes rather than for two." The publisher
seems to have rearranged S and S, P and P, and MP,
thereby obscuring aspects of structure, characterization, and theme. The volume divisions in NA, E,
and P also reveal a certain lack of formal clarity.
[Butler's essay appears also in Jane Austen in a

Social Context, ed. David Monaghan (Totowa, N.J.:
Barnes & Noble, 1981), pp. 49-65.]

413   Karrer, Wolfgang, and Eberhard Kreutzer.   "[Jane
        Austen]," in Daten der englischen und
        amerikanischen Literatur von 1700 bis 1890.
        Munich: Deutscher Taschenbuch, 1979, pp. 163-64,
        165-66, 167-68, 172, and 179-80.

(Summarizes the plots of the six major novels
and briefly discusses, among other things, JA's
themes, characterization, and irony.)

414   Kroeber, Karl, Jerome J. McGann, and Robert Langbaum.
        "British Romanticism and British Romantic
        Fiction: A Forum." WC, 10 (1979), 131-46.

Karl Kroeber, pp. 131-35. Even though JA may
seem stylistically conservative, she has, like the
Romantic poets, "thematic originality." The
"innovative tendencies" she shares with writers such
as Wordsworth include the challenges offered "the
repressions and exploitations of traditionally
rationalistic and mechanistic arrangements" and her
"perception of persons as historical entities, of
people as living developmentally, of human-
beingness as growth."

Jerome J. McGann, pp. 136-38. Because "socio-
historical contexts dominate the formation of all
superstructural forms, including, of course, the
forms of art," and the novels, unlike the poetry,
of the early nineteenth century "emphasize rather
than disguise [these] socio-historical contexts," a
study of JA may be helpful "for reading--and
decoding--the transference forms of Romantic
poetry."

Robert Langbaum, pp. 139-46. While showing
"signs of the new sensibility," JA and Scott "do not
fit easily into discussions of Romanticism, because
they were still mainly eighteenth-century in style,
thought, and form." MP, for example, remains
"Neoclassic, because it is committed to a principle
of order and propriety as against disorder,
spontaneity, and passional freedom."

414a Kurrik, Maire Jaanus. "The Novel and the Self's
        Negativity," in Literature and Negation. New
        York: Columbia Univ. Press, 1979, pp. 82-205.

In E, JA criticizes and corrects rather than

changes the self and society, which remain "closed
and narrow." She "can question the subject as a
knower and ironize and negate its self-assurance,
but she does not question the object to be known by
the fully socialized self. This object and the self
that knows it may be in error, but they can never be
portrayed as contingent, unnecessary, and dis-
solvable."

415   Lauber, John. "Jane Austen and the Limits of
        Freedom." ArielE, 10 (Oct. 1979), 77-96.

For JA freedom's value "is potential rather than
intrinsic, depending entirely on the use that is made
of it." Although moral, social, and economic conventions limit it, her heroines enjoy real liberty.
They choose and act freely "in apparently closed
situations," thereby earning their own happiness and
our sympathy and interest.

416   Le Faye, Deirdre. "Jane Austen and Her Hancock
        Relatives." RES, NS 30 (1979), 12-27.

JA's memory of her Hancock relatives helped her
create characters in the juvenilia, MP, and especially S and S, characters who "become fully
coloured and three-dimensional when a genuine living
personality is breathed into them. In turn, the
newly created fictional character gives form and
shape to the spirit within."

416a   Lefroy, J. A. P. "Jane Austen's Irish Friend: Rt.
        Hon. Thomas Langlois Lefroy, 1776-1869." PHSL,
        23, no. 3 (1979), 148-65.

(On the life of Tom Lefroy.)

417   Lemos, Brunilda Reichmann. "Language and Character
        in Jane Austen's Emma." RLet, no. 28 (1979), pp.
        95-105. Lemos's essay includes a Portuguese
        summary.

JA introduces her characters in E systematically,
first presenting them in narrative sections, then
imitating in free indirect speech their typical forms
of expression, and finally dramatizing their interaction with others. And the language of characters
like Harriet Smith, Jane Fairfax, and Mrs. Elton
helps define not only them but, through significant
contrasts, the heroine as well.

418   Litz, A. Walton. "The Achievement of Jane Austen."
        KeyR, 44 (Spring 1979), 2-4 and 8.

        (Much of Litz's essay appeared originally in his
        "Introduction" to his ed. of P and P [New York:
        Random House, 1967], pp. v-xvii.)

419   Lock, F. P. "The Geology of Sense and Sensibility."
        YES, 9 (1979), 246-55.

        "The relationship between 'Elinor and Marianne'
        and Sense and Sensibility, and the extent to which
        the novel as we have it contains fossils of the early
        version, remain unsure and problematical. . . .
        Criticism must resist the temptation to fall back on"
        the lost work to explain what it finds unsatisfying
        in S and S. And none of the speculations advanced
        thus far has been proved; in every case there is
        either "no need to posit an epistolary origin," or
        there are good reasons for doubting such an origin.

420   McKeon, Richard. "Pride and Prejudice: Thought,
        Character, Argument, and Plot." CritI, 5 (1979),
        511-27.

        We may read P and P "as a philosophical novel,"
        "a psychotherapeutic or socioeconomic retributive
        novel," "a novel of manners," and "a novel of plot or
        of narrated civility." Though these interpretations
        are "of the same named-object," they do not oppose or
        contradict each other, and "in combination they may
        serve to disclose qualities of the novel, of ex-
        perience, of nature, life, and thought which might
        otherwise go unnoticed."

421   Mayoux, Jean-Jacques. "Entrée de dame dans le roman
        anglais (Jane Austen rééditée)." QL, 302 (16-31
        May 1979), 13-14.

        As recent French translations of S and S and P
        and P make clear, JA writes of a lazy social class
        whose manners are extremely codified and whose inter-
        actions are artificial and dominated by lies. Dated,
        "totally anti-romantic," and never interested in
        physical contact between people, she believes that
        reason alone allows one to perceive reality cor-
        rectly.

421a Mihalskaia, N. P. "Problema ideala v romane
        Nortengerskoe abbatstvo i esteticheskie

pozitsii Dzhein Osten" [The problem of the ideal in
Northanger Abbey and the aesthetic position of Jane
Austen], in Esteticheskii ideal i hudozhestviennii
obraz [Aesthetic ideal and artistic image]. Moscow:
Moskovskii Pedagogicheskii Institut, 1979, pp. 54-
66.

(Discusses early nineteenth-century literature,
provides plot summary of NA, and argues that JA's
morality and aesthetics help determine the novel's
imagery and the characters' interactions.)

422 Monaghan, David. "Jane Austen and the Feminist
     Critics." Room, 4, no. 3 (1979), 34-39.

"Many feminist critics have misread either Jane
Austen's novels, or her age, or both," often trying
to force her "to conform with currently fashionable
definitions of the woman's situation." To illuminate
her fully we must read the novels more carefully and
take account of late eighteenth-century "conduct
books, the woman's role as arbiter of manners and
morals and its relationship to conservative philosophy, and of attitudes to work, marriage, and
sexuality."

423 Moon, Woo-Sang. "On Mansfield Park." EnglSt, no.
     3 (1979), pp. 51-67.

MP differs from JA's other novels in the breadth
of its narrative point of view, its wide range of
interests, and its great number of different characters. It achieves unity through its basic subject,
the deterioration and regeneration of a highly organized society, attacking selfishness, licentious-
ness, and the failure of religious principle to
influence moral action and valuing fortitude, ab-
stinence, and stability.

424 Persuasion: The Jane Austen Society of North America,
     no. 1 (16 Dec. 1979).

(In addition to the guest speakers' addresses to
the Society's annual general meeting, abstracted
below, this report includes, among other things,
several brief notes.)

Donald Greene, "Pemberley Revisited," pp. 12 and
14. (Identifies Pemberley as Chatsworth.)

A. Walton Litz, "The Picturesque in Pride and
Prejudice," pp. 13, 15, and 20-24. JA found Gilpin's

ideas about the picturesque both helpful in organiz-
ing her responses to nature and pedantically absurd.
In P and P Elizabeth moves from the "surface picturesque," marked by "a playing with emotional
effects for aesthetic ends," to the "moral picturesque," involving a more responsible attitude
to life and art.

425   Petersen, Per Serritslev, ed. "On the First Sentence
          of Pride and Prejudice: A Critical Discussion of
          the Theory and Practice of Literary Interpreta-
          tion." Dolphin, no. 1 (Feb. 1979).

(In addition to the essays abstracted below,
this volume includes sections in which the critics
"comment on each other's interpretations and their
methodological premises.")

Hans Hauge, "The Irony of Meaning," pp. 5-18.
"We are now able to appreciate her imaginative or
'realistic' discourse, which in order to be realistic relies upon the 'naturalness' of metonymy,
but which ironically is the producer of her illusion. What she 'believed' to be a metonymization
of metaphor we can read as a metaphorization of
metonymy."

Kirsten Busck Mellor, "Pride and Prejudice, or
the Intelligent Woman's Guide to Subjection and
Dependence," pp. 19-28. P and P's beginning proves
ironic as regards "male-female roles" but not "the
ultimate unification of men and women." Although JA
shows "the specific predicament of women," she re-
wards with a good marriage those who finally submit
to conventional sexual stereotypes.

Per Serritslev Petersen, "Towards the Meaning of
the First Sentence of Pride and Prejudice," pp. 29-
43. "An analysis of the semantic function of the
TUA ['truth universally acknowledged'] within the
sentence, combined with a semantic/thematic
contextualization of the TUA inside and outside
the novel, leaves no scope for the operation of
irony." In addition, despite "her satirical exposure
of the TUA as such stuff as wish-fulfilment dreams
are made on, Jane Austen will deliver the romantic
goods in the end. . . . Thus the TUA is proved
true."

Michael Skovmand, "The Meaning of the First
Sentence in Pride and Prejudice," pp. 45-56. "The
local irony of the opening sentence is not negated by
the novel as a whole. On the contrary, Jane Austen's
unwavering sense of the dialectical relation between

objective and subjective necessities, the Gestaltung
of which is the authorial position of 'partisan
irony' or ironic solidarity, informs the opening
sentence with multilayered ironies. A non-ironic
reading of the opening sentence means a confusion of
Jane Austen's materialism with determinism."

Torben Vestergaard, "Feudal Sense and Bourgeois
Sensibility in Pride and Prejudice," pp. 57-68. P
and P's initial statement presents two contradictions: first, "we expect a novel (a piece of
fiction), but the first sentence would be more
appropriate as the opening of an essay (fact)"; and
second, "the content of the basic proposition
embedded in the first sentence was an actual social
truth in JA's social context, but in its linguistic/
communicative context it is very hard for us to read
it as anything but ironic."

Knud Sørensen, "A Discredited Generalization
Comes True," pp. 97-101. "In her opening paragraph
Jane Austen wants to do two things: to record a
widely held belief concerning a certain social
problem and at the same time to dissociate herself
from subscribing unconditionally to this belief.
However, by the time the reader has finished the
novel, he may say to himself: You never know;
sometimes the Mrs Bennets are proved right. A
discredited generalization may come true."

426   Phelps, Gilbert. "Emma, Jane Austen," in A Reader's
        Guide to Fifty British Novels, 1600-1900.
        (Reader's Guide Series.) New York: Barnes &
        Noble, 1979, pp. 170-78. Phelps's book appears
        also with the title An Introduction to Fifty
        British Novels, 1600-1900 (London: Pan, 1979).

By emphasizing vivid and pointed detail more than
in her other novels, JA adds to E's richness and
affords "the most effective contrast imaginable to
the insubstantial fancies that haunt Emma's brain."
Different from her usual practice, too, she
makes the heroine quite introverted and uses
physical nature in a manner reminiscent of the
Romantics.

427   Phelps, Gilbert. "Pride and Prejudice, Jane Austen,"
        in A Reader's Guide to Fifty British Novels,
        1600-1900. (Reader's Guide Series.) New York:
        Barnes & Noble, 1979, pp. 160-69. Phelps's book
        appears also with the title An Introduction to
        Fifty British Novels, 1600-1900 (London: Pan,
        1979).

Assured, economical, easily but firmly controlled, P and P marks the end of the experi-
mental, exploratory period in the development of
the novel genre. It values both the formal,
stylized elements found in a ballroom dance and a
deeply realized emotional capacity.

428 Piggott, Patrick. The Innocent Diversion: A Study of
        Music in the Life and Writings of Jane Austen.
        (Clover Hill Editions, 10.) London: Cleverdon,
        1979.

        Rev. by J. R. Banks in CritQ, 22 (Spring 1980),
93-94; by Brigid Brophy in Spectator, 29 Mar. 1980,
pp. 18-19; by Peter Conrad in TLS, 7 Mar. 1980, p.
274.

        (In addition to the commentary on the novels,
abstracted below, this book discusses public and
private music-making in JA's time, including concerts
she attended, and the two music-book collections she
either owned or knew of. There are, as well,
illustrations of her own music master, contemporary
singers, advertisements for concerts, and sheet
music.)

        Because music in Regency England "was an
essential part of a young lady's education," it
proves important in JA's works, which accurately
reflect the period's manners. Although it appears
seldom in the minor works, it comes up frequently in
the major novels, serving, among other things, to
characterize, add comedy, and advance plot. More
particularly, music helps define Catherine Morland's
lack of heroism and Marianne Dashwood's emotional
excesses; it provides "an agreeable, if superficial
diversion" in P and P, where JA takes "a curiously
philistine view of it as a subject for serious
study," and in MP it receives more respect, though
associated only "with the 'bad' characters"; in E,
JA's most varied treatment of the subject, it
stimulates conversation, allowing individuals to
reveal their idiosyncracies and thoughts about each
other, and, finally, in P it takes the form of the
professional concert, the only instance of JA not
limiting her treatment of music to domestic uses.

429 Preston, John. "The Silence of the Novel." MLR, 74
        (1979), 257-67.

        Fanny's role in MP "as a silent watcher and a
listener" helps us understand the language of prose
fiction. Embodying qualities crucial to narrative

art, "she strikingly objectifies the paradox . . .
that the novel depends on silence to become articulate."

430   Ram, Atma. "Emma's Ending: Serious and Consistent."
          RUSE, 12 (1979), 86-92.

      (See no. 610.)

430a Ray, Susmita. "The Happy Endings in Jane Austen's
          Novels." JDEUC, 15, no. 1 (1979-80), 17-25.

      Like Shakespeare and others, JA follows comic
      conventions in having her works end happily, with
      marriage and the triumph of youth and vitality.
      She differs from many of her predecessors, though,
      in exploring internal rather than external obstacles
      to happiness and avoiding artificial devices to
      reach her conclusions, which prove simultaneously
      moral and realistic.

431   Roberts, Warren. Jane Austen and the French Revolu-
          tion. New York: St. Martin's Press, 1979.

      Rev. by Bryan Burns in YWES, 60 (1979), 283; in
      Choice, 18 (1980), 250; by Harold Perkin in History,
      65 (1980), 496; by G. B. Tennyson in SEL, 20 (1980),
      720; by E. Pereira in UES, 18 (Sept. 1980), 46-47; by
      Frank W. Bradbrook in N&Q, NS 28 (1981), 268-69; by
      Thomas Lockwood in NCF, 36 (1981), 99-102; by
      Christopher Kent in ClioI, 11 (1982), 200-201; by
      Henry Kozicki in CLS, 19 (1982), 86-88; by Barry
      Roth in ECS, 15 (1982), 350-56; by Marilyn Butler in
      EHR, 97 (1982), 204-5; by F. B. Pinion in RES, NS 33
      (1982), 92; by John E. Jordan in RomMov for 1981
      (1982), pp. 74-75; by Andrew Wright in YES, 12
      (1982), 294-95.

      Introductory: Contrary to much critical opinion,
      JA "was not just alive in her times but alive to
      them." She experienced the changes wrought by the
      revolutionary age and responded to them in her
      fiction, which records in an indirect way her
      ideological position on politics, war, religion,
      and feminism.

      Politics: In "Catharine, or the Bower" and NA,
      JA alludes to France's troubles in the 1790s and
      resulting English fears and political repression.
      By the time of MP and E she develops Francophobia, a
      view allied to her Toryism and designed to protect
      her country from foreign subversion. While she

begins her career by portraying an essentially stable world, in her final three novels she offers a "Burkean social analysis" to deal with growing threats to the idea of community, becoming increasingly pessimistic about "the gentry's chances of survival."

War: Three phases mark JA's reaction to the English-French military struggle of 1793-1815. First, as her early writings indicate, "she ignored the war, following a code that said she should." Next, according to evidence in the letters, she pretended to be indifferent "but was no longer so." Finally, she became overtly involved, showing the war's impact in MP's structure and most fully in P's patriotism.

Religion: Evangelicalism led JA to heal a personality "deeply divided" between a "compassionate and religious side" and a "cutting and hostile" one, helping her become more reflective, self-aware, and humane. It also influenced the vocabulary, subjects, and characters of her last three books, especially MP, which testifies to social and her own private change and reflects the importance "the Evangelical programme" attached to such issues as clerical pluralism and the abolition of the slave trade.

Feminism: Throughout the canon JA adopts "a feminist position," for she criticizes "the world of female gentility," including boarding schools, courtship practices, and the superficiality of women's values. Yet from MP on, when the antifeminist movement was strong, she retreats to a more conservative stand: she emphasizes the significance of order, continuity, and duty in relation to marriage as well as differences in sexual roles, creating a "more reserved, modest and gentle" kind of heroine and a "more masculine, forceful, and decisive" figure as her hero.

432   Ruoff, Gene W. "The Sense of a Beginning: Mansfield Park and Romantic Narrative." WC, 10 (1979), 174-86.

In contrast to the message conveyed by P and P's classical precision and tautness, the plot of MP argues that "life is continuous, without sharply demarcated beginnings and endings; revelations are not sudden, and genuine turning points are not dramatically vivid." MP's "endogamous plot" resembles attempts by Wordsworth and others of the time "to adapt existing narrative forms to meet the

challenge of presenting an integrated rather than a
fragmented self."

433   Sharma, Atma Ram. "The Feminist Trend in Jane
         Austen." IndSch, 1 (July 1979), 11-22.

        JA rejected both of the views concerning sexual
relationships dominant at the end of the eighteenth
century. To her, woman was neither man's inferior
nor his equal but "had her own important identity.
A woman . . . was a good creature, capable of many
things. Home was her proper and favourite field.
She was an important companion and fellow of man."

434   Sheppard, Roger and Judith, comps. "Austen," in
         Literary Societies for Bookmen: A Collection of
         Societies, Clubs, and Periodicals in England and
         America, Relating to Literature and the Arts.
         Beckenham, Kent: Trigon Press, 1979, p. 9.

        (Lists the address, officers, publications, and
number of members of the Jane Austen Society.)

435   Sherry, James. "Pride and Prejudice: The Limits of
         Society." SEL, 19 (1979), 609-22. See also no.
         761.

        Most fully of all the novels P and P explores
"the dialectic of social participation." By means
of characterization, structure, and point of view
the book defines "the necessary tension between the
impulse, indeed the responsibility, to be open,
engaged and responsive members of a community, and
the need for reserve, distance, and privacy lest
social intercourse become vulgarized and degraded by
familiarity."

436   Sieferman, Sylvia. "Persuasion: The Motive for
         Metaphor." SNNTS, 11 (1979), 283-301. See also
         no. 762.

        P reveals a more complex conception of language
than that of the earlier novels, a newly developed
faith in the indirect and figurative. The protagonists must learn how to put into words "the
right relations between things that are . . . both
alike and different. Thus, the estrangement between
Anne and Wentworth results from his inability to make
and express the right distinctions; their reconciliation comes when Anne gains the courage to speak her
feelings by inventing appropriate metaphors."

437   Swingle, L. J. "The Poets, the Novelists, and the
        English Romantic Situation." WC, 10 (1979),
        218-28.

        As E demonstrates, JA shares much with her
contemporaries, for she, like Wordsworth, Blake,
Mary Shelley, and others, analyzes the quest after
unity, "the persistence of barriers," "the divi-
sionary nature of union itself," and "the behavior
of parties forming, or seeking to maintain, divi-
sionary systems of truth." More specifically, she
creates characters who, as part of their normal
condition, feel and think differently from each
other, "our supposedly common human nature exhibit-
ing a propensity to breed uncommonly different
natures within itself."

438   Tamm, Merike. "Performing Heroinism in Austen's
        Sense and Sensibility and Emma." PLL, 15 (1979),
        396-407. See also no. 775.

        While S and S considers optimistically "the
potentially rewarding role that amateur art might
play in the lives of women with leisure," E "suggests the dangers that exist for idle women with
few outlets other than amateur art." This change in
JA's view during the second decade of the nineteenth
century may reflect her own development from amateur
to professional writer.

439   Tatham, Michael. "Mary Crawford and the Comic
        Heroine." NewB, 60 (1979), 11-26.

        JA's devotion in all her novels to ambiguity and
irony demands that we realize MP's complex division
between Mary Crawford and Fanny Price and the
"duality which runs through the centre of Fanny's
character." Thus, contrary to "a tediously
moralistic reading," Mary proves neither superficial
nor cynical but honest, sensible, caring, and
virtuous; Edmund Bertram appears essentially obtuse
and vacillating; and Fanny is a "comic heroine,"
absurd, pretentious, blind, mockingly indulged by
her creator.

440   Voss-Clesly, Patricia. Tendencies of Character
        Depiction in the Domestic Novels of Burney,
        Edgeworth, and Austen: A Consideration of
        Subjective and Objective World. 3 vols.
        (Romantic Reassessment, 95.) Salzburg:
        Institut für Anglistik und Amerikanistik,
        Universität Salzburg, 1979.

Rev. by G. B. Tennyson in <u>SEL</u>, 20 (1980), 720-21.

(This study demonstrates "the perfection of technique in character depiction in the domestic novels of Burney, Edgeworth and Austen, through a combination of <u>external</u> and <u>internal</u> methods, with increasing emphasis upon and complexity of the latter technique, to develop a <u>subjective</u> <u>world</u> within a <u>framework</u> of external <u>objective</u> orientation." It considers the novel's "fundamental structural framework" and the values adhering in this framework as standards to compare the novelists. It also discusses "the modified application of the epistolary technique in the development of <u>free</u> <u>indirect</u> <u>thought</u>" and the reflection of "the <u>subjective</u> <u>world</u> . . . in pervasive symbolic imagery.")

441   Watters, Tamie. "Incomparable 'Guide' to Britain." <u>CSM</u>, 17 Apr. 1979, p. 21.

Because she helps in understanding its people and manners, "anyone who is planning a journey to Britain--whether inner or actual--should bring along a volume of Jane Austen with his guides and travel books."

442   Weinsheimer, Joel. "Theory of Character: <u>Emma</u>." <u>PoT</u>, 1 (Autumn 1979), 185-211.

"In semiotic criticism, characters dissolve and only text remains. . . . It is no more untenable to argue that <u>Emma</u> contains only text than that it contains people. Nor, I take it, is either position ridiculous: one may talk about 'Emma' as if it were a word in a closed, alienated text, or as if she were alive, a person in an open world that is also our world. It is not ridiculous, but it is inadequate and partial to adopt either mode of expression exclusively."

443   Wilhelm, Cherry. "<u>Persuasion</u>: Time Redeemed." <u>ESA</u>, 22 (1979), 91-98.

<u>P</u> treats time--its passage, its effect on people, and their response to it--and shows love redeeming a world defined by process. "The symbolic wedding of the landed gentry and the navy, the land and the sea, indicates the combination of flexibility and constancy which the novel explores as an ideal state."

444 Yoxall, H. W. "Jane Austen's Post." Letter in
       STelegraph, 25 Mar. 1979, p. 13. See also letter
       in DTelegraph, M. B. Lloyd-Philipps, 9 May 1980,
       p. 18.

     (Uses a passage in E to comment on the English
     postal system.)

                          1980

445 Barfoot, C. C. "Choice against Fate in Sense and
       Sensibility and Pride and Prejudice." DQR, 3
       (1980), 176-98.

     (See no. 572.)

446 Barrett, Hilma. "The Incomparable Jane." Maine Life
       (Nov. 1980), pp. 15-17.

     (On the Jane Austen Society of North America.)

447 Berendsen, Marjet. "Wolf Schmid and the Unreliable
       Narrator in Jane Austen's Emma." Neophil, 64
       (1980), 619-36.

     Wolf Schmid's theory of "the two narrative agents
     of narrator and character" does not significantly
     illuminate E. Though his system, which relies
     primarily on verbal standards, seems objective and
     easy to apply, "the essentially subjective features
     of theme and evaluation are in fact the most im-
     portant, since they inevitably turn the scales in
     those instances when decisive linguistic and sty-
     listic data are lacking."

448 Brewer, Derek. "Mainly on Jane Austen," in Symbolic
       Stories: Traditional Narratives of the Family
       Drama in English Literature. Totowa, N.J.:
       Rowman & Littlefield, 1980, pp. 148-67.

     Variations on the Cinderella theme, JA's novels,
     especially MP, all feature a lonely heroine, dead
     parents, an ambivalent mother-image, an insecure
     home, and a place where the protagonist seeks
     refuge.

449 Brogan, Hugh. "Northanger Abbey." Letter in TLS, 8
       Feb. 1980, p. 145. See also letters in TLS,

H. L. Sartin, 4 Apr. 1980, p. 390; Margaret
Weedon, 26 Nov. 1982, p. 1311.

(Seeks to identify the source of a quotation in
NA.)

450 Butler, Marilyn. "The Woman at the Window: Ann
       Radcliffe in the Novels of Mary Wollstonecraft
       and Jane Austen," in Gender and Literary Voice.
       Ed. Janet Todd. (Women & Literature, NS 1.)
       New York: Holmes & Meier, 1980, pp. 128-48.

       JA rejected the model offered by Radcliffe for
       the subjective treatment of women in fiction,
       deliberately choosing to restrict her emotional
       involvement, to remain moralistic even in rendering
       internal dialogue, and to acquiesce in a hierar-
       chical, paternalistic social scheme. As a result,
       her more external presentation of women lacks "the
       universality, the full human significance, of the
       Radcliffean study of the inner life."

451 Chamberlin, E. R. "Literary Villages, 8: Chawton."
       ILN, 268 (Aug. 1980), 64-65 and 67.

       (Describes Chawton and JA's life and home there.)

452 Conrad, Peter. "Introduction" to Emma. Ed. Mary
       Lascelles. New York: Dutton, 1980, pp. v-xxx.
       Part of Conrad's essay appeared originally, with
       the title "Emma by Jane Austen," in Observer Mag,
       1 July 1979, p. 52; see no. 392.

       JA's version of Rousseau's Social Contract, E
       treats a heroine who abandons the state of nature for
       self-consciousness and conscience, who renounces
       private will for the community's collective good.
       The novel, which classifies characters according to
       their social utility, restricts space to emphasize
       society's self-sufficiency and views units like the
       family as sacred and union with others not as an
       affliction but a privilege, a means to liberation and
       restoration of "a mitigated paradise."

453 Davie, John. "Introduction" to his ed. of Northanger
       Abbey, Lady Susan, The Watsons, and Sanditon.
       New York: Oxford Univ. Press, 1980, pp. vii-xxi.
       The part of Davie's introduction devoted to NA
       appeared originally in 1971.

       Interesting in themselves, Lady Susan, The

Watsons, and Sanditon also offer much information about JA's developing art. In spite of intrinsic limitations in the epistolary form Lady Susan proves noteworthy for its construction and realism. Had The Watsons been completed, it would have compared favorably in plot and characterization with JA's other novels. And Sanditon leaves one "with the sense of a new adventurousness" in her style.

454   De Rose, Peter L. Jane Austen and Samuel Johnson.
       Washington, D.C.: Univ. Press of America, 1980.

       Rev. in JNL, 41 (Mar. 1981), 2-3; by John E. Jordan in RomMov for 1980 (1981), p. 68; by David McCracken in ModPhil, 80 (1982), 196-97.

       JA and Samuel Johnson: JA, whose morality derives "from an orthodox, eighteenth-century English Christianity," affirms ethical principles Johnson developed. Well aware of his work and using it throughout her career, she integrates aesthetically in her novels such Johnsonian ideas as "the importance of self-knowledge and the repudiation of pride, of practical common sense in the face of real and imaginary deception, of rational self-control in the service of moral duty, and of recollection, discipline, and sacrifice in the difficult education for life."

       NA: The burlesque aspects of NA do not merely parody literary form but expose fully the dangers of imagination, including its tendency to deceive. And the novel's "comic-realistic episodes" teach us, through their empirical emphasis, to avoid withdrawing into illusion and to see the world as it actually is.

       MP: In MP "the alleged conflict between Jane Austen's art and her morality is more apparent than real." The characters she creates accord perfectly with what she teaches: "that recollection of principle is the basis of moral judgment, that discipline brings theoretical principle into practice, and that unavoidable hardship, suffering, and sacrifice strengthen moral character."

       E and P and P: Both Emma Woodhouse and Elizabeth Bennet suffer from pride but come to regret their errors and know themselves "through habitual reflection and self-examination and even the vigilant guidance of a sympathetic friend." This educational pattern, culminating in marriage, which represents genuine change, reflects eighteenth-century moral concerns, particularly Johnson's "methods of recognizing and avoiding self-deception."

S and S and P: P constitutes "an artistically successful exploration of the same theme which [S and S] narrowly and unrealistically explores--the subordination of feeling to reason and moral principle." While the earlier book portrays characters lacking psychological complexity, the later offers "a genuinely convincing and attractive heroine in a novel of restrained emotional intensity."

455   Donaldson, Norman and Betty. "Austen, Jane (1775-
       1817)," in How Did They Die? New York: St.
       Martin's Press, 1980, p. 18.

       (Biography.)

456   Drew, Philip. "Jane Austen and Bishop Butler."
       NCF, 35 (1980), 127-49.

       "While Jane Austen works within the broad tradition of ethical judgment which Shaftesbury and Butler have in common, where they differ she is closer to Butler than to Shaftesbury," notably to Butler's view that in determining moral value the principles motivating an action are more important than the outcome. And "it is her analysis of different ways of evaluating conduct which constitutes her claim to be regarded as a moralist even more than her acute particularizing of individual actions."

457   Dunbar, Janet. "A Card of White Lace." Times, 13
       Dec. 1980, p. 6. See also letter in Times, David
       Croom-Johnson, 18 Dec. 1980, p. 15.

       (Describes the trial of JA's aunt Mrs. Jane Leigh Perrot.)

458   Ephron, Nora. "A Few Words about Elizabeth Bennet."
       Dial, 1 (Oct. 1980), 36-39.

       Not only do we lack Mr. Darcys today, "there are probably no more Elizabeth Bennets either. What's more, there were probably none in the first place. Which is wonderful. It means that those of us who would love to be like her can never feel too bad that we aren't; no one is. That's what makes Lizzy so lovable: She doesn't exist."

459   Fowler, Marian. "'Substance and Shadow': Conventions

of the Marriage Market in <u>Northanger</u> <u>Abbey</u>."
<u>ESC</u>, 6 (1980), 277-91.

As a study of eighteenth-century courtesy books,
periodicals, diaries, and letters reveals, <u>NA</u> severely criticizes social abuses. It "shows how
preoccupation with money corrupts character, en-
courages parental tyranny and inhibits the free,
independent courtship of two young people in love.
<u>Northanger</u> <u>Abbey</u> is a work of moral earnestness and
strong didacticism in which Jane Austen decisively
rejects her society's mercenary bias in matrimonial
affairs."

460 Giuffre, Giulia. "The Ethical Mode of <u>Pride</u> <u>and</u>
        <u>Prejudice</u>." <u>SSEng</u>, 6 (1980-81), 17-29.

All aspects of <u>P</u> <u>and</u> <u>P</u>, including characterization, theme, language, and style, simultaneously
entertain and teach. "Perhaps more successfully
than any major novelist of the Eighteenth Century,
Jane Austen was able to combine the stuff of the
novel, everyday life, with the matter of the sermon.
But she does so with such skill that any seams remain
invisible."

461 Grawe, Christian. "Nachwort" to <u>Emma</u>. (Universal-
        Bibliothek, 7633.) Stuttgart: Reclam, 1980, pp.
        541-60.

<u>E</u>, the masterpiece of JA's mature period, has the
reader identify with typical social experiences and
pictures a heroine deeply flawed by her snobbery,
manipulation of others, and lies. And the climax of
the author's critical and ironic distance from the
action comes during Mrs. Elton's chatter while pick-
ing strawberries.

461a Greene, Mildred. "'A Chimera of Her Own Creating':
        Love and Fantasy in Novels from Madame de
        Lafayette [sic] to Jane Austen." <u>SVEC</u>, 193
        (1980), 1940-42.

Using Karen Horney's concept of "the perfec-
tionist type of character" to analyze Anne Elliot,
the Princesse de Clèves, and Clarissa Harlowe reveals that, of the three, only Anne exerts herself
"beyond her limited circle of weak father, superficial sister, and mother surrogate, to transform her
fantasy lover, Wentworth, into a genuine one."

462 Grey, J. David. "A Spurious Jane." Letter in

Country Life, 20 Mar. 1980, p. 846. See also the
editorial comment in Country Life, 20 Mar. 1980,
p. 846.

(On a portrait mistakenly thought to be of JA.)

463   Hagstrum, Jean H. "The Aftermath of Sensibility:
       Sterne, Goethe, and Austen," in Sex and Sensi-
       bility: Ideal and Erotic Love from Milton to
       Mozart. Chicago: Univ. of Chicago Press, 1980,
       pp. 247-77.

       JA does not offer any simple contrast of reason
       and feeling in S and S but rather transcends her
       title's implied antithesis. "Under the pressure of
       life and experience" Elinor and Marianne, who embody
       the abstractions of the title, interact dynamically
       with each other and achieve finally an equilibrium
       in which "sense becomes sensibility, and sensibility
       becomes sense."

464   Hardman, Phillipa. "Jane Austen and the Periodical
       Works of Henry Mackenzie." SN, 52 (1980), 323-
       31.

       JA may have used literary conventions found in
       The Mirror and The Lounger, such as the character
       sketch, the brief life history, and the confessional
       letter, to create character, situation, and theme in
       S and S, P and P, and E. But as always when she
       draws on some "literary model, she uses her borrow-
       ings to comment both on the convention" and her own
       novelistic demands for probability and nature.

465   Harris, Jocelyn. "'All the Impassioned, & Most
       Exceptional [sic] Parts of Richardson': Jane
       Austen's Juvenilia," in The Interpretative Power:
       Essays on Literature in Honour of Margaret
       Dalziel. Ed. C. A. Gibson. [Dunedin, New
       Zealand]: Dept. of English, Univ. of Otago, 1980,
       pp. 59-68.

       Though JA loved Sir Charles Grandison, she tests
       it by laughter in the juvenilia, exaggerating,
       transposing, inverting, and placing Richardson's work
       in incongruous contexts in order "to detect its
       extravagances of emotion, its falsities of tone, and
       its impossibilities of expression." She thus trains
       herself for the major novels, which continuously
       correct human experience by wit.

466   Harris, Jocelyn. "'As If They Had Been Living

Friends': <u>Sir Charles Grandison</u> into <u>Mansfield Park</u>." <u>BRH</u>, 83 (1980), 360-405.

In writing <u>MP</u>, JA borrowed significantly from <u>Sir Charles Grandison</u>, especially as regards plot, characterization, structure, setting, and theme. The two works share, among other things, similar attitudes to marriage, education, friendship, memory, self-knowledge, family relations, and the conflict between wit and wisdom. Both reflect, too, the idea of the novel form as "an active agent of moral philosophy operating on a fictional world that extends into the real world."

467   Ireland, K. R. "Future Recollections of Immortality: Temporal Articulation in Jane Austen's <u>Persuasion</u>." <u>Novel</u>, 13 (1980), 204-20.

JA's handling of time in <u>P</u> helps us understand the book's emotional intensity and underlying gravity as well as the careful, subtle nature of her art. Time functions here, among other ways, to indicate a character's psychology and his fate. In addition, the "strategic use of external analepse" highlights the past's force, and "narrative climax and temporal expansiveness coincide."

468   Ives, Sidney. <u>The Trial of Mrs. Leigh Perrot</u> . . . <u>to Which Are Added, Some Circumstances Attendant on That Interesting Trial</u>. Boston: Club of Odd Volumes, 1980.

(Describes the imprisonment and trial of JA's aunt and speculates that JA used the Scadding household, the lower-middle-class milieu where Mrs. Leigh Perrot was detained, as the basis for her portrait of the Prices in <u>MP</u>.)

469   The <u>Jane Austen Society: Report for the Year, 1979</u>. Alton, Hampshire: Jane Austen Society, [1980].

(In addition to the guest speaker's address to the Society's annual general meeting, abstracted below, this report includes, among other things, a list of Jane Austen studies for 1979, a supplement to the list of Jane Austen studies for 1978--both prepared by David Gilson--and several brief notes.)

Lord David Cecil, "Jane Austen--A Summing Up," pp. 19-24. JA makes her limited range work to her advantage and reconciles reality with fantasy. Comic, moral, and ironic, she endures because she portrays basic human nature and relies on "universal

standards of value," notably virtue, good sense, and
taste.

470   Jones, Myrddin. "Feelings of Youth and Nature in
        Mansfield Park." English, 29 (1980), 221-32.

        JA demonstrates the difficulty of arriving at
clear judgments by allowing us to imagine more than
one outcome to the relationship between Fanny Price
and Henry Crawford. "This uncertainty involves, too,
the recognition of a gap--of knowledge and of
maturity, but not of principle--between Fanny's
understanding and that of the narrator."

471   Kaplan, Debbie. "Jane Austen in History: Recent
        Scholarship." Arnoldian, 8 (Fall 1980), 40-48.

        (Review-essay on nos. 320 and 386.)

472   Karr, Phyllis Ann. Lady Susan: Based on the Unfin-
        ished Novel by Jane Austen. New York: Everest
        House, 1980.

        (Adaptation.)

473   Kearney, John. "Emma and Mr Knightly [sic]: Jane
        Austen's Concern in Emma with Marriage as an
        Alliance of Equal Partners." UCTSE, no. 10
        (1980), pp. 31-48.

        In E the heroine and Mr. Knightley make the ideal
marriage. Intellectual and spiritual equals at the
end of the novel, they form a union "attained only
after much misunderstanding and pain, and founded on
mutual generous sacrifice."

474   Lardner, James. "TV Preview: Pride and Prejudice."
        WPost, 25 Oct. 1980, p. F5.

        (On the BBC adaptation.)

475   Leimberg, Inge. "'Humble Independence': Das Thema
        und seine dichterische Verwirklichung in Jane
        Austens Emma." GRM, NS 30 (1980), 395-422.

        E examines the theme of independence in terms of
society, economics, and morality. All the characters
represent aspects of this theme or of the related
issues of dependence and interference. The

protagonist, who experiences difficulties because
she stands alone and supposedly independent while
actually dependent, becomes truly free when she
renounces her imaginary independence.

476 Lenta, Margaret. "Form and Content: A Study of the
        Epistolary Novel." UCTSE, no. 10 (1980), pp. 14-
        30.

        JA's experiments with the novel of letters, from
the juvenilia through P and P, led her to discover
that she could offer "the advantages of the mode
without its limitations." Transcending the possibilities of the epistolary form, she developed
techniques to deepen our intimacy with the protagonist and her process of moral education and
self-discovery.

477 MacDonald, Susan Peck. "Jane Austen and the Tradi-
        tion of the Absent Mother," in The Lost
        Tradition: Mothers and Daughters in Literature.
        Ed. Cathy N. Davidson and E. M. Broner. New
        York: Ungar, 1980, pp. 58-69.

        Like other women novelists from Fanny Burney to
George Eliot, JA separates the heroine, either
psychologically or physically, from her mother so
that, lacking maternal nurturing, the daughter "can
develop her own strength and autonomy." But,
paradoxically, because motherhood remains a potent
ideal, the daughter still must "recreate a version
of her mother without simply copying her mother."

478 Marais, Trudi. "Northanger Abbey in the '80s."
        Crux, 14 (Oct. 1980), 42-43.

        (Presents and studies the errors in meaning,
language, and style made by secondary-school
students in answering an examination question on
NA.)

479 Merrett, Robert James. "The Concept of Mind in
        Emma." ESC, 6 (1980), 39-55.

        A work of complex "moral dialectic," E stresses
the interdependence of the conflicts between fancy
and intelligence, egoism and altruism, and empiricism
and rationalism. By novel's end the heroine learns
to observe, imagine, and think "in a connected way,"
as Mr. Knightley does, "because she has acquired an
expanded awareness of time, because she regards

physical and mental experience as complementary, and
because she exercises a balanced perspective upon
herself and her relationship to others."

480 Monaghan, David. Jane Austen: Structure and Social
     Vision. Totowa, N.J.: Barnes & Noble, 1980.
     Part of Monaghan's book appeared earlier, with
     the title "The Myth of 'Everybody's Dear Jane':
     A Reassessment of Jane Austin [sic]," in
     Atlantis, 3 (Fall 1977), 112-26; see no. 285.

     Rev. by Bryan Burns in YWES, 60 (1979), 282-83;
     in Choice, 17 (1980), 540; by G. B. Tennyson in SEL,
     20 (1980), 720; by Zachary Leader in TLS, 25 July
     1980, p. 855; by J. Chalker in BBNews (1981), p.
     438; by C. C. Barfoot in ES, 62 (1981), 540; by
     Alistair Duckworth in ModPhil, 79 (1981), 96-101; by
     Thomas Lockwood in NCF, 36 (1981), 99-102; by Richard
     Wilson in THES, 15 May 1981, p. 15; by Jean Wilson in
     TLS, 17 Apr. 1981, p. 446; by Barry Roth in ECS, 15
     (1982), 350-56; by Vivien Jones in N&Q, NS 29 (1982),
     360-61; by Deborah Kaplan in Novel, 15 (1982), 267-
     70; by F. B. Pinion in RES, NS 33 (1982), 484-86; by
     Frederick M. Keener in MLR, 78 (1983), 433-35.

     Introductory: A study of the canon's formal
     social occasions like balls and visits shows how JA
     integrates novelistic structure and social vision.
     Using such occasions to test the individual and his
     community, she develops steadily in the course of her
     career toward a fuller realization of the fictional
     possibilities of social rituals and from confidence
     to a loss of faith in the existing order of things.

     NA: Like the later novels, though less subtly,
     NA explores the relationship between the individual's
     manners and society's health and uses formal social
     occasions to connect form and theme. Three major
     patterns--the exclusiveness of the Thorpe and Tilney
     families, the motif of prior invitations, and invita-
     tions to dance and to visit the Abbey--point to the
     novel's moral hierarchy and the heroine's potential
     for growth, growth based on the making of proper
     distinctions.

     S and S: The structure of S and S helps
     reinforce the book's conclusions: it vindicates
     Elinor's judgments, exposes Marianne's deficiencies,
     and reveals Colonel Brandon's value. Yet the ideal
     community established at Barton and Delaford remains
     unconvincing because JA does not adequately realize
     the male characters, dramatize the courtship of the
     sisters, or demonstrate that the major figures
     sufficiently grasp the positive implications of
     manners.

P and P: P and P follows a general plan of "approach-rejection-acceptance" and divides readily into sections controlled by various social rituals--"dancing for the problems of courtship, the visit for the broadening of social horizons, and marriage for the resolution of conflicts." Truly blending content and form, the novel ends when the aristocracy, gentry, and middle class unite in the awareness of "a shared ideal of concern for others."

MP: MP develops the equation between moral influence and attractive manners, for it traces Fanny's movement from isolated, impotent passivity to active involvement with others and finally, when she becomes the focus of attention, to a stillness indicative of steadfast principles. Only by realizing the importance of social participation and charm can she affect the lives around her and help regenerate Mansfield.

E: Emma acts humanely toward natives of Highbury but disregards the feelings of those she considers outsiders. Such inconsistency imposes limits on her development and keeps her world static. Following the expedition to Box Hill, though, where she learns she cannot compartmentalize her world, she begins to treat all people responsibly and "seek stimulation in a generous engagement with the familiar and in a readiness to accept change."

P: "Persuasion is fractured into two rather contradictory halves": the first shows, through the breakdown of the gentry's manners, the death of the old order, and the second, which lacks a suitable "elegiac note," rationalizes that formality may be unnecessary, "even synonymous with hypocrisy and alienation," and that "openness and spontaneity . . . are adequate to any situation." JA thus equivocates, denying both the first part's darker implications and values affirmed consistently throughout her career.

481   Morgan, Susan. In the Meantime: Character and Perception in Jane Austen's Fiction. Chicago: Univ. of Chicago Press, 1980.

Rev. in Choice, 17 (1980), 222; by Avrom Fleishman in JEGP, 79 (1980), 588-90; by G. B. Tennyson in SEL, 20 (1980), 720; by Merritt Moseley in SR, 88 (1980), 641-47; by Zachary Leader in TLS, 25 July 1980, p. 855; by Bryan Burns in YWES, 61 (1980), 282-83; by Juliet McMaster in ELN, 18 (1981), 304-7; by L. R. Leavis and J. M. Blom in ES, 62 (1981), 313-23; by Alistair Duckworth in ModPhil, 79 (1981), 96-101; by Robert Folkenflik in NCF, 36 (1981), 95-98; by John E. Jordan in RomMov for 1980

(1981), pp. 69-70; by Mona Scheuermann in SAB, 46
(Jan. 1981), 94-97; by Gene W. Ruoff in WC, 12
(1981), 169-72; by Palma Lower in Austenilia, 1
(1982), [3]; by Barry Roth in ECS, 15 (1982), 350-56;
by Robert Lance Snyder in SNNTS, 14 (1982), 207-11;
by Frederick M. Keener in MLR, 78 (1983), 433-35.

Introductory: Epistemologically and ethically,
JA's subject is perception, the mind's relation to
its objects. She presents vision as problematic,
temporal, and creative because truth and people
change. To explore these ideas she writes "novels of
crisis" (E, NA, and P and P), which concern a morally
blind heroine experiencing an epiphany about her
errors, and "novels of passage" (S and S, MP, and P),
which, instead of offering any sudden revelation,
conceive of the heroine's "perceptual activities" as
"ongoing."

E: E "is about the powers of the individual mind,
the powers of sympathy and imagination, and about how
these powers can find their proper objects in the
world outside the mind." When the protagonist
recognizes her own limits and the separate existence
of others, life--partly represented by Jane Fairfax,
who remains of great value though mysterious and
beyond Emma's control--becomes more interesting, the
real world larger, and love possible.

NA: NA, which explores the imaginative nature of
perception, offers the "idea of character as limited
and therefore able to change" and "the problem of
interpretation" as fiction's subject. Using the
Bildungsroman format, the novel considers education
not a mimetic process but "an expression of self" and
shows Catherine learning that truth proves elusive
and multiple, judgment never complete, people
fallible, and preconceived structures restricting.

P and P: Expressing "the theme of perception as
involvement . . . in terms of intelligence," P and P
examines "the possibilities and responsibility of
free and lively thought." It follows the heroine's
movement from moral disengagement and mental de-
fensiveness, in which she resembles her father and
Charlotte Lucas, to unreductive, flexible, emotionally committed methods of understanding people
and experience. Only when she gives up her supposed
"objectivity" and suspends judgment can her mind grow
and become serious.

S and S: In S and S, a novel not of crisis but
continuity, seeing, always imperfect, "becomes a
matter of time." Faced with an unstable world
composed of mixed characters and defined by ignorance

and deception, Marianne simplistically seeks certainty in romantic codes. But Elinor, braver and
more imaginative, uses decorum--a polite fiction
promising truth, an avowal that knowledge evolves
slowly, "a way of behaving which sustains the
potential in experience for active and changing"
human relations.

MP: Rather than an exception to the canon or a
defense of conservatism, MP, describing a child's
growth, treats "perceiving in time." It shows
"character not only in the process of judging but
also in the process of changing." And Fanny
develops, unlike Mary, Henry, or Edmund, who
complacently impose pre-existing forms on their
lives, because, though flawed, she takes seriously
the reality outside her; struggling against selfishness and toward awareness, she pays generous attention to others.

P: Through the theme of persuasion, which implies
involvement, time, and alteration, JA's final novel
focuses "on how the very process of understanding can
itself shape character." While Wentworth and Mrs.
Smith, denying an individual's continuity and active
personal relationships, use revelations to understand
others, Anne, open to experience, trusts to memory,
hope, and "the risks of responsible judgment."
Persuasion thus becomes "a moral imperative. For it
is a receptiveness to others which depends upon feeling."

482 Morrow, Patrick D. "Sublime or Sensible: The
        Mysteries of Udolpho and Northanger Abbey," in
        Tradition, Undercut, and Discovery: Eight Essays
        on British Literature. (Costerus, NS 28.)
        Amsterdam: Rodopi, 1980, pp. 93-117.

Though alike in ending with the heroine's
marriage, NA and The Mysteries of Udolpho differ
otherwise. JA's novel, essentially a satire of
Radcliffe's, replaces "the sublime with sense," a
self-indulgent Gothicism with a responsible morality,
and shallow characterization with complex portraits.
In addition, it values the life enriched by overcoming illusions and "finding individual freedom
within the context of society."

483 Moseley, Merritt. "In Pursuit of Jane Austen."
        SR, 88 (1980), 641-47.

(Review-essay on nos. 320, 360, 386, and
481.)

484   Myer, Valerie Grosvenor. Jane Austen. (Authors in
       Their Age.) London: Blackie, 1980.

       Rev. by Edwina Burness in TES, 15 Aug. 1980, p.
       20; by Bryan Burns in YWES, 61 (1980), 281.

       (This introduction to JA provides biographical
       material about her and background information on the
       England of her time. Using in part evidence found in
       the novels, it treats, among other subjects, the
       gentry, manners, economics, education, and religion.)

485   Nabokov, Vladimir. "Mansfield Park (1814)," in
       Lectures on Literature. Ed. Fredson Bowers.
       New York: Harcourt Brace Jovanovich, 1980, pp.
       8-61. An excerpt from Nabokov's essay appears,
       with the title "Jane Austen: Mansfield Park," in
       Esquire, 94 (Sept. 1980), 67.

       MP "is the work of a lady and the game of a
       child. But from that workbasket comes exquisite
       needlework art, and there is a streak of marvelous
       genius in that child." The book combines practical
       sense with fairy tale and has a subdued imagery and
       an epigrammatic rhythm to its witty style. Though
       the reliance on letter-writing toward the end
       constitutes a formal weakness, the book's overall
       structure proves solid, based on the close linking
       of different themes.

486   Nath, Prem. "Dr. Johnson and Jane Austen." N&Q,
       NS 27 (1980), 55-56.

       P and P's opening sentence "has its origin in
       Johnson's Rambler No. 115."

487   O'Connor, John J. "TV Weekend: Pride and Prejudice,
       Sensitive Father Figure." NYT, 24 Oct. 1980, p.
       C32.

       (On the BBC adaptation.)

488   Person, Leland S., Jr. "Playing House: Jane Austen's
       Fabulous Space." PQ, 59 (1980), 62-75.

       Each of the heroines, attempting "to conform
       available space to the outline of her private
       desires," "imagines herself and an ideal husband-
       lover isolated within a kind of play house and safe
       from intrusions." The subject of "spatial fantasiz-
       ing," pertinent to JA's own life and apparent already

in the juvenilia, first flowers in P and P, where
marriage enables Elizabeth to restructure her family,
and continues through P, where Anne ends by excluding her family from the society around her.

489 Persuasions: The Jane Austen Society of North
        America, no. 2 (16 Dec. 1980).

        (In addition to summaries of the guest speakers'
    addresses to the Society's annual general meeting,
    abstracted below, this report includes, among other
    things, several brief notes.)

        Nina Auerbach, "Jane Austen's Dangerous Charm:
    Feeling As One Ought about Fanny Price," pp. 9-11.
    (See no. 680.)

        David Spring, "The Social Context of Mansfield
    Park," p. 14. Knowledge of the cultural context
    shows that, contrary to some interpretations, the
    Bertrams' "temporary and minor financial embarrass-
    ment" does not constitute "a crisis, economic, social
    and spiritual, in the history of English landed
    society."

        Avrom Fleishman, "How Many Beliefs Had Lady
    Jane?" p. 19. "In reading Mansfield Park we never
    get to hear the author speak of her beliefs, for the
    simple reason that she is unlikely to have had
    any--in the sense of formulable positions on
    politics, religion and even ethics."

        Gene Koppel, "The Theme of Contingency in
    Mansfield Park," p. 20. (See no. 597.)

490 Plard, Henri. "Postface" to Persuasion. Paris:
        Bourgois, 1980, pp. 239-54.

        In P, JA, "the most sensible and discreet of
    English novelists," treats realistically the themes
    of love and marriage as well as misunderstanding and
    blindness. Though more given to observation than
    introspection, she here boldly provides, for the
    first time in the canon, an inside, tender view of
    her heroine. She creates, too, a formally perfect
    narrative structure, which "is a model of economy
    and elegance."

491 Polhemus, Robert M. "Austen's Emma (1816): The
        Comedy of Union," in Comic Faith: The Great
        Tradition from Austen to Joyce. Chicago: Univ.
        of Chicago Press, 1980, pp. 24-59.

"Through 'union,' a word connoting physical
intimacy, human solidarity, and contractual association, the self, in Emma, makes a commitment to the
future. In Austen's fiction, comic concern for one
individual woman includes comic concern for the
society. Her comedy of union turns out to be the
witty celebration of potent individualism embracing
the world."

492   Ram, Atma. "Jane Austen's Appeal to Indian Readers."
       IndSch, 2 (July 1980), 35-42. Ram's essay, which
       includes a bibliography of Indian editions,
       translations, and criticism of the novels,
       appeared originally, without the bibliography and
       with the title "Jane Austen in India," in The
       Jane Austen Society: Report for the Year, 1978
       (Alton, Hampshire: Jane Austen Society, [1979]),
       pp. 5-8.

       (See no. 610.)

493   Romano, John. "Background: Pride and Prejudice."
       TV Guide, 25 Oct. 1980, pp. 33 and 35.

       Highly witty and entertaining, P and P treats
       "the awesome difficulty of really loving in a world
       where it is hard even to know one another," takes
       account of significant historical changes affecting
       the middle class, and shows a remarkable under-
       standing of human psychology.

494   Rossdale, P. S. A. "What Caused the Quarrel between
       Mr. Collins and Mr. Bennet? Observations on the
       Entail of Longbourn." N&Q, NS 27 (1980), 503-4.

       If Mr. Bennet and Mr. Collins "were born with the
       same surname (being paternal relatives) the inference
       is that the document constituting the entail of
       Longbourn contained a provision requiring the use of
       the surname 'Bennet.'"

495   Roth, Barry. "One for the Money, Two for the Show:
       Three New Austen Studies." SNNTS, 12 (1980),
       153-60.

       (Review-essay on nos. 351, 360, and 386.)

496   Seymour-Smith, Martin, ed. "Austen, Jane," in Novels
       and Novelists: A Guide to the World of Fiction.
       New York: St. Martin's Press, 1980, p. 93.

(On her life and some qualities of her novels.)

497   Sharma, Atma Ram. "Jane Austen's Presentation of
      Women Characters." JDEUC, 16, no. 1 (1980-81),
      69-79.

      (See no. 610.)

498   Smithers, David Waldron. "Where Was Jane Austen's
      Rosings? The Case for Chevening." Country Life,
      30 Oct. 1980, pp. 1568 and 1571. Smithers's
      essay appears also, in an enlarged form, with the
      title "Chevening," in his Jane Austen in Kent
      (Westerham, Kent: Hurtwood, 1981), pp. 37-56; see
      no. 560.

      JA may have based Hunsford in P and P on
      Chevening.

499   Southam, Brian, ed. Jane Austen's "Sir Charles
      Grandison." New York: Oxford Univ. Press,
      1980. See also no. 513.

      Rev. by Rosalind Wade in ContempR, 239 (1981),
      48; by Jeremy Barnard in CritQ, 23 (Autumn 1981), 90-
      91; by Patricia Beer in Listener, 16 Apr. 1981, p.
      514; by Stuart M. Sperry in SEL, 21 (1981), 716; by
      Gerard Kilroy in Spectator, 28 Mar. 1981, pp. 26-27;
      by Richard Wilson in THES, 15 May 1981, p. 15; by
      Pat Rogers in TLS, 3 Apr. 1981, p. 369 [and see
      letter, D. C. Measham, 17 Apr. 1981, p. 437]; by Park
      Honan in N&Q, NS 30 (1983), 173-74; by Margaret Anne
      Doody in NCF, 38 (1983), 220-24.

      (In addition to the introduction, abstracted
      below, this volume includes a foreword by Lord David
      Cecil; it also presents a reading text of the play,
      transcribes and describes the manuscript, comments on
      changes and corrections to the manuscript, and offers
      notes on specific details of Richardson's novel that
      JA works into her text.)

      "Introduction," pp. 1-34. Undeniably by JA, this
      play was "a piece of home entertainment, dashed off
      to amuse the family, begun in the early 1790s, put
      aside for some years and then finished about 1800."
      Though uneven and juvenile, it does shed light on
      JA's reading of Richardson and her use of dramatic
      and satiric techniques in the novels.

500   Spiteri, Gérard. "Prenez le thé avec Jane Austen!"

NL, 14-21 Feb. 1980, p. 31.

While merely conversing and drinking tea, JA's
characters reveal part of their souls. And their
creator, despite the serenity, reserve, and measured
quality of her fiction and the seeming transparence
of her portrait of social life, has her eyes fixed
on an invisible spectacle that leaves her vaguely
anxious.

501   Spring, David. "Jane Austen's Last Days in
       Winchester." N&Q, NS 27 (1980), 79-80.

(Uses an account by her brother Charles to
describe the chronology of her final illness.)

502   Tanselle, G. Thomas. "Jane Austen, Emma, 1816: A
       Cancel?" BC, 29 (1980), 114, query 329.

Three copies of the first edition of E "have now
been discovered to contain a supplied leaf, which may
be a cancel."

503   Todd, Janet. "The Biographical Context," in Women's
       Friendship in Literature. New York: Columbia
       Univ. Press, 1980, pp. 359-402.

"Perhaps then, Austen somewhere blamed her
powerful tie with Cassandra for her own single
state and made her heroines avoid the female friendship that might deny them marriage."

504   Todd, Janet. "Social Friendship," in Women's
       Friendship in Literature. New York: Columbia
       Univ. Press, 1980, pp. 246-301. Part of Todd's
       essay appeared originally, with the title "Female
       Friendship in Jane Austen's Novels," in JRUL, 39
       (1977), 29-43; see no. 311.

"Jane Austen's Mansfield Park (1814)," pp. 246-
74. Throughout MP Fanny defines herself by a male
concept of womanhood that stresses diffidence,
propriety, and silence. She abjures female friendship because it threatens the familial marriage she
so desires and, with JA's evident approval, remains
neurotic, undeveloped socially, intellectually,
morally, or sensually.

"Jane Austen's Emma (1816)," pp. 274-301. E
seeks to define women's social friendship, "picturing
its abuse as well as its use, admitting its necessary
limits in an ordinary world of marriage and sub-

ordinate women, and indicating its potential to help
a young girl discover herself and a world beyond the
family." Although Emma properly outgrows Mrs.
Weston and Harriet, she never really establishes a
satisfying friendship with her equal, Jane Fairfax,
for JA laughingly "chops off the relationship at its
inception."

505 Unger, Arthur. "Television Previews: BBC's Ladylike
     Peek at 18th-Century English Family Life." CSM,
     23 Oct. 1980, p. 18.

     (On the adaptation of P and P.)

506 Usuda, Akira. "Jein Ōsuten ni okeru chino no mondai
     ni tsuite" [About Jane Austen's treatment of
     intelligence], in Suga Yasuo, Ogoshi Kazugo: Ryo
     kyoju taikan kinen ronbunshu [Yasuo Suga,
     Kazugo Ogoshi: Collected essays commemorating the
     retirement of both professors]. Kyoto:
     Apollonsha, 1980, pp. 370-80.

     JA believes that people need intelligence in
order to live well, because it controls the emotions
and helps develop self-awareness, and that all who
make the effort can become more intelligent. She
accordingly judges her characters in reference to
this key quality, ranking Elizabeth Bennet and Fanny
Price among her wisest figures and Mr. Rushworth and
Dick Musgrove among her most foolish.

507 Walton, James. "Mansfield Park: The Circle Squared,"
     in Studies in Nineteenth-Century Literature.
     (Romantic Reassessment, 87:2.) Salzburg:
     Institut für Anglistik und Amerikanistik,
     Universität Salzburg, 1980, pp. 44-108.

     In MP Fanny's is the supreme consciousness, "the
Good Mind." She develops "within herself, in all
humility, an idea of natural harmony that is neither
immanent in external things nor sustained by the
imagination of her culture." She overcomes "the
agents of disintegration" and serves as "the creative
source of the values [Mansfield Park] represents."

508 Weiss, Fredric. "The Era of Gothic Parody," in The
     Antic Spectre: Satire in Early Gothic Novels.
     (Gothic Studies and Dissertations.) New York:
     Arno Press, 1980, pp. 193-223. Weiss's study
     appeared originally, with the title "Satiric Ele-
     ments in Early Gothic Novels," as his Ph.D.
     diss., Univ. of Pa., 1975.

Emphasizing social rather than literary satire,
NA attacks the "archetypal Gothic reader" more than
the Gothic novel itself. Indeed, JA's work implicitly serves as tribute to the Gothic tradition
because it adopts the same structure and themes as
The Mysteries of Udolpho and issues warnings about
passions, temptations, moderation, and common sense
similar to those of Radcliffe and Lewis.

509   Wilt, Judith. "Jane Austen: The Anxieties of Common
      Life," in Ghosts of the Gothic: Austen, Eliot, &
      Lawrence. Princeton, N.J.: Princeton Univ.
      Press, 1980, pp. 121-72.

JA neither subverted nor converted the Gothic
machinery that constituted part of her novelistic
inheritance; rather, she genuinely transformed it.
As evident in NA and E, she especially reworked five
key machines, all "energized by dread": "The Mysteries of Udolpho itself, the programmatic Gothic setting, the isolated and tyrannical villain, the ruined
church, and the overimaginative heroine." She
"interposited" these five into the common life portrayed in her work not to mock at them but to raise
them to their true importance. "The result is not to
make romance ridiculous but to make common anxiety
'serious' or 'high.'"

510   Woolf, David. "Pride and Prejudice," in An Aspect of
      Fiction: Its Logical Structure and Interpreta-
      tion. (Speculum Artium, 7.) Ravenna: Longo,
      [1980], pp. 23-30.

Because it tells a story intended to illustrate a
principle, in this case "that an uncritical over-
indulgence in a virtue is apt to degrade the virtue
until it approaches the nature of a vice," P and P
constitutes an example of "moralized fiction." It is
thus not "open-ended" but rather "provides its own
context and any interpretation of it must be true to
that context."

1981

511   Aers, David. "Community and Morality: Towards Read-
      ing Jane Austen," in Romanticism and Ideology:
      Studies in English Writing, 1765-1830, by David
      Aers, Jonathan Cook, and David Punter. Boston:
      Routledge & Kegan Paul, 1981, pp. 118-36.

Rather than a great moralist or social and

psychological realist, JA is a conservative polem-
icist "utterly committed" to "market values and
practices" that clash "incoherently" with the "neo-
feudal ideology" she also espouses. As a result,
she remains severely limited: "instead of her art
opening out gentry/middle-class reality and assumptions to a genuinely exploratory fiction which takes
alternative forms of life and aspiration seriously,
Jane Austen systematically closes up her imagination
against critical alternatives."

512 Armstrong, Nancy. "Inside Greimas's Square: Lit-
        erary Characters and Cultural Constraints," in
        The Sign in Music and Literature. Ed. Wendy
        Steiner. (Dan Danciger Publication Series.)
        Austin, Tex.: Univ. of Texas Press, 1981, pp. 52-
        66.

P and P demonstrates the utility of A. J.
Greimas's cultural model, which comprehends personal
desire, economic necessity, and social stability, as
well as the difficulties accompanying "the reduction
of all semiotic experience to three specific codes."
The novel, whose heroine "incorporates all conflicting female roles and lends them coherence by means of
the mediating concepts of 'manners' and 'judgment,'"
formulates and reformulates opposing terms "to pro-
duce a single mode of interpreting human behavior,
one that adequately and accurately represents human
worth."

513 Austen, Jane. Sir Charles Grandison, or the Happy
        Man. 3 vols. Burford, Oxfordshire: David Astor
        at Jubilee Books, 1981. See also no. 499.

(Volume one of this limited edition is a foreword
by David Cecil; volume two is the text of JA's play,
edited from the original manuscript by Brian Southam;
and volume three is the original manuscript in
facsimile.)

514 Bodenheimer, Rosemarie. "Looking at the Landscape in
        Jane Austen." SEL, 21 (1981), 605-23.

JA's handling of characters in landscape develops
from "satire of picturesque talk" (in NA and S and S)
to an emphasis "on the metaphorical resources of
pictorial values" (in P and P and E) and finally to
a "celebration of natural process" (in MP and especially P). S and S and MP also use description
of nature as a projection of character, and P,
retreating in part to earlier satiric habits,

indicates "the strains and limits in Austen's
romantic tendencies."

515 Boles, Carolyn G. "Jane Austen and the Reader:
     Rhetorical Techniques in Northanger Abbey, Pride
     and Prejudice, and Emma." ESRS, vol. 30 (Summer
     1981). Boles's essay includes a bibliography of
     writings about JA.

     JA relies on many rhetorical devices to involve
the reader in her novels, including "matters of
style, characterization, narrative method, and the
narrator-reader relationship." Her style, based
largely on the use of irony and conceptual terminology, helps the reader refine and expand his
perception and understanding of the characters as
well as the author's standards of evaluation. Her
methods of characterization emphasize the non-
physical aspects of human nature, the real rather
than the ideal, and the importance of an individual's
thoughts, manners of speech, and word choices. Her
flexible narrative method balances dramatic scenes
with commentary, thereby combining subjective and
objective elements, sympathy and judgment. Finally,
"by means of the narrator-reader relationship, she
creates a sense of community" that strengthens the
reader's awareness of a shared ethical viewpoint.

516 Booss, Claire. "Introduction" to Jane Austen: Her
     Complete Novels. New York: Avenel, 1981, pp.
     [vii-viii].

     Noteworthy for her prose style, perceptiveness,
and sense of humor, JA treats love, imagination,
economics, and morality. "There is an apparent
innocence in her portrayal of human foibles that is
devastating: folly, self-deception, self-servingness,
priggishness, vulgarity, and deceit are captured
with deadly aim."

517 Brüggemeier, Luise-Marie. The Journey of the Self:
     Studien zum Reisemotiv im Roman Jane Austens.
     (Europäische Hochschulschriften, 14:91.)
     Frankfurt am Main and Bern: Lang, 1981.
     Brüggemeier's book includes a bibliography of
     writings about JA.

     (Arguing that her use of "the journey of the
self" served as a pattern for nineteenth-century
English fiction, this study considers the travel
motif essential to all of JA's novels. It examines
her abiding concern for marriage as the goal of the

movement through life, the happy ending to the
individual's traveling. More particularly, it shows
that P and P, by a synthesis of different narrative
modes, represents Elizabeth's inner and outer journey
and that MP treats Fanny's alienation from the
community as exile. This study also discusses the
impact of a specifically feminine perspective upon
the novels. In this context it denies that JA's
writings contain picaresque elements, which typified
the work of male authors in the eighteenth century,
and it sees E as the first conclusive character study
of a woman and P as a picture of a woman's experience
with all its social, emotional, and spiritual implications.)

518 Butler, Marilyn. "Novels for the Gentry: Austen and
        Scott," in Romantics, Rebels, and Reactionaries:
        English Literature and Its Background, 1760-1830.
        New York: Oxford Univ. Press, 1981, pp. 94-112.

    "The gentry's greatest artist," JA tends "to
rebuke individual self-assertion" and to write
"defensively--fearing subversion, advocating the
values which in times past justified" the gentry's
rule. She subtly and profoundly takes part in
contemporary controversies, for her early novels
reflect their origin "in the period of most violent
counter-revolution," and the later ones "contain a
far more specific critique of the gentry in its
performance of its function."

519 "Chinese Buy Austen, Brontë." NYT, 3 Jan. 1981, p.
        19.

    P and P was "among the most popular translations"
sold in China last year.

520 Cooke, Alistair. "Jane Austen: Pride and Prejudice,"
        in Masterpieces: A Decade of Masterpiece Theatre.
        New York: Knopf, 1981, pp. 55-61.

    "This adaptation demonstrated a fine ear for the
spare, exquisite language of the original and a ready
talent for taking Jane's maliciously cheerful view of
social pretension. The result was as true a rendering of the essential Austen as we are likely to get.
Viewers who disliked this Pride and Prejudice do not
like Jane Austen."

521 Corse, Larry B. and Sandra, comps. "Austen, Jane,"
        in Articles on American and British Literature:

An _Index to Selected Periodicals, 1950-1977._
Chicago and Athens, Ohio: Swallow Press, 1981,
pp. 305-8.

(Bibliography.)

522   Cottom, Daniel. "The Novels of Jane Austen: Attach-
         ments and Supplantments." _Novel_, 14 (1981), 152-
         67.

         In JA's novels society's instability renders all
human connection and communication, including family
and love relationships, essentially impersonal in
nature, matters "of chance and circumstance." Human
desire emerges, then, not "from the realm of individual expression and spontaneous affinity" but "from
the complex, contradictory, equivocal, unsympathetic
forces of society," and individuals gather together
because of "money, pedigree, and power" rather than
for the sake of "emotion or destiny or common experience."

523   Crespo Allue, María José. _La problemática de las_
         versiones españolas de Persuasión de Jane Austen:
         Crítica de su traducción. 2 vols. Valladolid:
         Office of the Secretary of Publications, Univ.
         of Valladolid, 1981. Crespo Allue's book in-
         cludes a bibliography of writings about JA and
         of Spanish translations of _P_.

         (This book, written as a doctoral dissertation,
discusses literary translation in general, analyzes _P_
in particular, including style and characterization,
and compares two Spanish versions of the novel.)

524   Ebine, Hiroshi. "_Emma_ no plot" [The plot of _Emma_].
         EigoS, 126 (1981), 554-58.

         Partly because of its skillful plot, _E_ proves
JA's masterpiece. Like Fielding in _Tom Jones_, but
more successfully, she adapts to the novel form an
eighteenth-century conception of comedy that focuses
on ordinary life, demands a careful observation of
society, and involves irony.

525   _Five Letters from Jane Austen to Her Sister Cas-_
         sandra, 1813. Brisbane: Locks' Press, 1981.
         The introduction describing the letters is by
         David Gilson, and the text of the letters is due
         to F. P. Lock.

(Prints for the first time from the original
manuscripts the complete text of five letters of JA,
numbers 75-79 inclusive in Chapman's standard edition.)

526 Fujita, Seiji. Hyoden Jein Ōsuten [A critical
        biography of Jane Austen]． Tokyo: Hokuseido
        Press, 1981.

     (Biography.)

526a Gilson, David John. "Face Value." Letter in ABMR,
        8 (1981), 145 and 147.

     (On fake first editions of S and S, P and P,
     and MP.)

527 Grawe, Christian. "Nachwort" to Kloster Northanger.
        (Universal-Bibliothek, 7728.) Stuttgart: Reclam,
        1981, pp. 275-93.

     NA's publication so long after the vogue for
     works like The Mysteries of Udolpho had passed helps
     clarify JA's criticism of Gothic fiction and
     emphasize her affinity with the nineteenth-century
     realistic novel. She here parodies the whole range
     of terror created by Radcliffe, uncovers the
     improbable nature of Catherine's fantasies, and
     focuses as well on the importance of language.

528 Harris, Laurie Lanzen, ed. "Jane Austen, 1775-1817,"
        in vol. 1 of Nineteenth-Century Literature
        Criticism: Excerpts from Criticism of the Works
        of Novelists, Poets, Playwrights, Short Story
        Writers, and Other Creative Writers Who Lived
        between 1800 and 1900, from the First Published
        Critical Appraisals to Current Evaluations.
        Detroit: Gale Research, 1981, pp. 29-68.

     (Reprints critical statements about JA from 1812
     to 1979, provides an additional bibliography of
     writings about her, and comments briefly on her
     style, form, and general accomplishment.)

529 Izubuchi, Keiko. "Jane Austen (1775-1817)." EigoS,
        127 (1981), 310-11.

     JA writes from the point of view of an insider
     about women who know that the only way not to be an

outsider in their world resides in marriage. And she
believes that education, of decisive importance in
the raising of children, should not just add to one's
accomplishments but improve morality.

530 "[Jane Austen]," in A Catalogue of Books by and about
the Brontë Family, Jane Austen, and Other
Literary Ladies of the Nineteenth Century.
(Catalogue 24.) Stroud, Gloucestershire:
Hodgkins, [1981], nos. 1-77 and passim.

(Lists rare and out-of-print books for sale by
and about JA.)

531 The Jane Austen Society: Report for the Year, 1980.
Alton, Hampshire: Jane Austen Society, [1981].

(In addition to the guest speaker's address to
the Society's annual general meeting, abstracted
below, this report includes, among other things,
several brief notes.)

Elizabeth Jenkins, "Some Notes on Background,"
pp. 12-28. JA's works reflect contemporary interest
in such subjects as mechanical improvements, landscape, the picturesque, the Gothic, and the East.
"The structure of the novels is of a technical
brilliance that is unsurpassed, but the miracle is
the creation of life."

532 Jein Ōsuten: Shosetsu no kenkyu [Jane Austen: A study
of the novels]. Ed. Members of "The Study of
Literature" at Tsudajuku University. Tokyo:
Aratake, 1981.

(This collection of eighteen essays has three
parts: the first studies the six novels, focusing on
such subjects as language, love, freedom, and
society; the second compares JA to Shakespeare,
Fielding, and Natsume Sōseki; and the third examines
recent books about her.)

533 Johnston, Laurie, and Robert McG. Thomas, Jr. "Jane
Austen Is a Victim of a Nonfictional Mix-up."
NYT, 7 May 1981, p. A28.

The jacket portrait on a recent collection of her
minor works is not of JA.

534 Klieneberger, H. R. "The Novel in the Age of

Romanticism," in The Novel in England and Germany: A Comparative Study. London: Wolff, 1981, pp. 7-58.

While JA, Goethe, and Jean Paul all treat the conflict between spontaneous feeling and social restraint, JA handles it "with a psychological and social realism which was not available to her German contemporaries." Possessing a "subtlety and maturity of moral discernment" unknown in their work, she not only states "a theoretical resolution of the conflict," as they do, but lets it "be enacted by the characters of her novels."

535 Klinkenborg, Verlyn, Herbert Cahoon, and Charles Ryskamp. "Jane Austen, 1775-1817," in British Literary Manuscripts: Series II, from 1800 to 1914. New York: Pierpont Morgan Library with Dover, 1981, pls. 16 and 17. This book includes a complete checklist of JA manuscripts in the Morgan Library.

(Reproduces and describes pages from the autograph manuscript of Lady Susan and of a letter of 21 May 1801, both owned by the Morgan Library.)

536 Kloesel, Christian J. W., and Jeffrey R. Smitten, comps. "Jane Austen," in English Novel Explication: Supplement II. Hamden, Conn.: Shoe String Press, 1981, pp. 4-12.

(Bibliography.)

537 Lauritzen, Monica. Jane Austen's Emma on Television: A Study of a BBC Classic Serial. (Gothenburg Studies in English, 48.) Göteborg: Acta Universitatis Gothoburgensis, 1981.

Rev. by C. C. Barfoot in ES, 63 (1982), 542.

Partly because of the fact that JA's novel lends itself to dramatization, the BBC Classic Serial adaptation of E (1972) proved "both faithful and effective" in regard to such matters as plot and setting. As might be expected of the transition from prose narrative to drama and that from novel to television, the serial had directness and emotional power yet did not attain the original's subtlety and analytical precision. This difference affected both characterization and theme. In general, though viewing the serial cannot supersede reading the novel, the television production, with both strengths

and weaknesses, "may stimulate and enrich the reading, and also attract new readers, who might otherwise never have found their way to Jane Austen's
masterpiece."

538   Leavis, L. R., and J. M. Blom. "A Return to Jane
       Austen's Novels." ES, 62 (1981), 313-23.

Many recent studies, including Bernard J. Paris's
Character and Conflict in Jane Austen's Novels: A
Psychological Approach (1978) and Susan Morgan's In
the Meantime: Character and Perception in Jane
Austen's Fiction (1980), prove "detrimental . . . to
an appreciation of Jane Austen's essential distinction," for they gloss over her "complexity and
realism" and show no understanding of her "moral and
social values." In contrast to such critics' thin,
reductive arguments, JA actually expresses a robust,
healthy, tough attitude to life, one able to
accommodate diverse elements, including emotion,
and full of "high spirits" and "creative enjoyment."

539   Lellis, George, and H. Philip Bolton. "Pride but No
       Prejudice," in The English Novel and the Movies.
       Ed. Michael Klein and Gillian Parker. New York:
       Ungar, 1981, pp. 44-51.

Although it wisely "borrows from Austen qualities
of her narrative and theatrical manner that suit the
film medium," the movie P and P basically represents
"another case of Hollywood reducing a great novel to
the external action of melodrama." The movie
"successfully evokes Darcy's pride, for which
external equivalents are easy to find, but only
partly evokes Lizzy's prejudice," which is subtle,
internalized, and difficult to visualize.

540   Lenta, Margaret. "Jane Austen's Feminism: An
       Original Response to Convention." CritQ, 23
       (Autumn 1981), 27-36.

Transcending the "limitations imposed on her
sex," JA "does not create a woman's world; she
presents the real world" as seen by women. She
proves a feminist to the extent that she stresses,
particularly in E, her heroines' self-determination,
moral independence, and originality, qualities
"public opinion of the day would probably have denied
them."

541   Lenta, Margaret. "Jane Fairfax and Jane Eyre:

Educating Women." <u>ArielE</u>, 12 (Oct. 1981), 27-41.

Both JA and Charlotte Brontë use the figure of the governess to examine women's special problems. They agree that the life of the woman forced to seek work entails deprivation, repression, and subjugation and that marriage constitutes the happiest conclusion to such an existence. They differ in that the former emphasizes economic constraints and considers society ultimately benevolent and the latter stresses the denial of emotional outlets and the world's tendency to oppress the helpless.

542   Levine, George. "The Pattern: <u>Frankenstein</u> and Austen to Conrad," in <u>The</u> <u>Realistic</u> <u>Imagination</u>: <u>English</u> <u>Fiction</u> <u>from</u> <u>Frankenstein</u> <u>to</u> <u>Lady</u> <u>Chatterley</u>. Chicago: Univ. of Chicago Press, 1981, pp. 23-57.

Though she "sought primarily to make words conformable to reality, and particularly to the reality of social action," JA perceives "monstrous, unnameable possibilities" that threaten the order the books describe and her voice implies. She suggests that the unaccountable or inconceivable "is not merely the absurdity of hyperactive sensibility or false feeling, but a continuing possibility and, indeed, the condition for many of the heroines' ultimate successes."

543   McClain, Yoko. "Natsume Sōseki and Jane Austen." <u>Selecta</u>, 2 (1981), 1-5.

Natsume Sōseki, the twentieth-century Japanese scholar and novelist, admired JA, particularly her naturalness and simplicity, and his novel <u>Meian</u> resembles <u>P</u> <u>and</u> <u>P</u>, among other ways, in its domestic setting, ethical concerns, portrayal of complex characters through dialogue, and dramatic irony.

544   McMaster, Juliet. "<u>Pride</u> <u>and</u> <u>Prejudice</u>: 'Acting by Design,'" in <u>The</u> <u>Novel</u> <u>from</u> <u>Sterne</u> <u>to</u> <u>James</u>: <u>Essays</u> <u>on</u> <u>the</u> <u>Relation</u> <u>of</u> <u>Literature</u> <u>to</u> <u>Life</u>, by Juliet and Rowland McMaster. Totowa, N.J.: Barnes & Noble, 1981, pp. 19-36.

Like many of the characters in <u>P</u> <u>and</u> <u>P</u> the heroine distorts "reality by subordinating feeling to calculation." Inheriting much of her style from her father, a style based on detachment and wit, Elizabeth acts by design, willfully makes mistakes, "to project an image of herself that is distinct from

the real self." As her clever misunderstandings
provide us with aesthetic pleasure, so are they
also subject to our clear moral assessment.

545 Les Mères peuvent le faire lire à leurs filles: The
     Prefaces to the First French Translations of
     Jane Austen's Sense and Sensibility and Emma.
     Leiden: Ter Lugt Press, 1981.

     (This book, which includes an introduction by R.
     Breugelmans, typographically reprints "the first (and
     only?) communications on Jane Austen written in a
     foreign language during her lifetime"--the preface by
     Isabelle, baronne de Montolieu, to Raison et
     sensibilité and the anonymous preface to La Nouvelle
     Emma.)

546 Miller, D. A. "The Danger of Narrative in Jane
     Austen," in Narrative and Its Discontents:
     Problems of Closure in the Traditional Novel.
     Princeton, N.J.: Princeton Univ. Press, 1981,
     pp. 3-106.

     JA's art disowns "at an ideological level what it
     embraces at a constructional one." For her what
     motivates a novel's narratability coincides with
     lapses from her moral standards (ignorance, am-
     biguity, mystery, obsession, incoherence), and
     what motivates a novel's closure depends on her most
     significant official values (insight, clear communi-
     cation, common sense, "proper names, categories,
     feelings, and relationships"). The task of closure
     thus consists of an ethically inspired "passage
     between two orders of discourse, two separable
     textual styles. One of them (polyvalent, flirta-
     tious, quintessentially poetic) keeps meaning and
     desire in a state of suspense; the other (univocal,
     earnest, basically cognitive) fixes meaning and
     lodges desire in a safe haven; and the passage from
     one to the other involves a voiding, a strategic
     omission--so to speak, a good riddance."

547 Monaghan, David, ed. Jane Austen in a Social
     Context. Totowa, N.J.: Barnes & Noble, 1981.

     Rev. by Bryan Burns in YWES, 61 (1980), 281-82;
     in Choice, 18 (1981), 1261; by Stuart M. Sperry in
     SEL, 21 (1981), 716; by Palma Lower in Austenilia, 1
     (1982), [3]; by C. C. Barfoot in ES, 63 (1982), 542;
     by Deborah Kaplan in Novel, 15 (1982), 267-70; by
     Joel J. Gold in ModPhil, 80 (1983), 313-16; by
     Margaret Anne Doody in NCF, 38 (1983), 220-24; by

John E. Jordan in RomMov for 1982 (1983), pp. 74-75.

David Monaghan, "Introduction: Jane Austen as a Social Novelist," pp. 1-8. Because JA firmly bases her aesthetics "in contemporary ideology," we must reconstruct her social context to see more clearly "the macrocosmic significance of the tiny events" she describes. "The final synthesis towards which Jane Austen criticism is aiming" will emerge when we recognize the many different elements of her social consciousness and view her work as in the main affirmative of her society but also in some ways subversive.

Nina Auerbach, "Jane Austen and Romantic Imprisonment," pp. 9-27. "Jane Austen shares the Romantic sense of pervasive and inescapable imprisonment," for her novels present "one long, and always doomed, fight for escape." Featuring "shadowed epithalamia" and the movement "from clarity to obscurity," she offers a "double vision," according to which the familiar world appears both secure and confining; sense simultaneously assuages and verifies our terrors; and men serve as ambiguous "redeemer/jailer" figures.

Ann Banfield, "The Influence of Place: Jane Austen and the Novel of Social Consciousness," pp. 28-48. In MP, JA fuses the Richardsonian novel of consciousness with the Gothic novel's emphasis on place to create a "radically new conception," one which embodies her critical response to the new industrial society. Wishing to transcend class differences, she offers in Fanny the perspective of the outsider, who, because she has experienced oppression and all the book's places, can bring to the Park and the novel the broadening sympathy derived from full social awareness.

Marilyn Butler, "Disregarded Designs: Jane Austen's Sense of the Volume," pp. 49-65. (See no. 412.)

Jan S. Fergus, "Sex and Social Life in Jane Austen's Novels," pp. 66-85. "There is no escaping sexuality in Austen's novels": she relentlessly dramatizes, with "freedom, wit and good sense," the interplay in everyday life of the full human personality and sexuality. She explores, among other things, physical attraction, sexual antagonism, infatuation, flirtation, the mentor relationship, and the connection between sexuality and social conventions. Much unlike her

contemporaries she provides "resolutions in which
sexuality is as tested and satisfied as is morality
or any other aspect of character."

Christopher Kent, "'Real Solemn History' and
Social History," pp. 86-104. "Not about history" but
"themselves the very evidence of social history,"
JA's novels treat the great events of her time by
being accurate representations of contemporary life.
Her fictional world adopts "a consumer's perspective"
on the Industrial and French Revolutions, dramatizing
the effect on gentry life in southern England of the
demand or consumption aspects of new technology and
marketing strategies as well as of a militia needed
to keep order at home.

David Monaghan, "Jane Austen and the Position of
Women," pp. 105-21. While she considers the sexes as
equals, in contrast to prevailing stereotypes held by
her society, JA remains content with the contemporary
"restriction of women to domestic and polite functions" because she believes these functions to be as
crucially important as any others. But when manners
and the family decline in significance, as they do in
P, she redefines woman's role to include endeavor in
fields once limited to men. [Part of Monaghan's
essay appeared earlier, with the title "The Myth of
'Everybody's Dear Jane': A Reassessment of Jane
Austin" (sic), in Atlantis, 3 (Fall 1977), 112-26;
see no. 285.]

Jane Nardin, "Jane Austen and the Problem of
Leisure," pp. 122-42. In her final three novels JA
replaces her early assumptions about leisure's educative value, derived from eighteenth-century novelistic conventions, with ideas that reflect Samuel
Johnson's emphasis on "the possibility of achieving
fulfilment through sustained, socially useful
labour." Challenging such premises of her initial
works as the belief in self-discipline as "the only
possible protection against idleness and ennui," she
develops the idea of professional commitment and
"questions of ambition and earning money."

Leroy W. Smith, "Mansfield Park: The Revolt of
the 'Feminine' Woman," pp. 143-58. (See no. 676.)

Patricia Meyer Spacks, "Muted Discord: Generational Conflict in Jane Austen," pp. 159-79.
"Constructing plots which turn on moral conflicts
between accurate young and muddled old, yet basing
those plots on mores which assume the authority of
society's elders, Austen expands her readers' perceptions. Her mode of fictional embodiment enlarges the
meaning of generational conflict, placing it in the

context of a poetics as well as a morality of personal growth," growth that occurs through the action of the imagination. [Spacks's essay appears also, with the titles "The Generations: Imagination and Growth (Walter Scott, Jane Austen)" and "The Generations: Submerged Conflict (Walter Scott, Jane Austen)," in her The Adolescent Idea: Myths of Youth and the Adult Imagination (New York: Basic Books, 1981), pp. 146-90.]

Tony Tanner, "In Between--Anne Elliot Marries a Sailor and Charlotte Heywood Goes to the Seaside," pp. 180-94. (See no. 273.)

548 Odmark, John. An Understanding of Jane Austen's Novels: Character, Value, and Ironic Perspective. Totowa, N.J.: Barnes & Noble, 1981. Odmark's book includes a bibliography of writings about JA.

Rev. by Valerie Shaw in BBNews (1981), p. 689; in Choice, 19 (1981), 382; by Robert Folkenflik in TLS, 13 Nov. 1981, p. 1338; by C. C. Barfoot in ES, 63 (1982), 542; by Frances Ferguson in SEL, 22 (1982), 725; by Park Honan in N&Q, NS 30 (1983), 254-55; by Margaret Anne Doody in NCF, 38 (1983), 220-24.

Irony: Irony, not arbitrary but rather "based on a particular Weltanschauung with a fixed set of values," constitutes the structuring principle that shapes all of JA's novels, a principle she handles with increasing mastery in the course of her career. She uses it, among other things, to study the problem of knowledge and the nature of reality, shifting point of view and introducing symbolic episodes so as to alter our relation to character and circumstance.

As part of the process leading the reader to a thorough grasp of her ideas, JA "exploits the possibilities of inside views and dramatic scenes in order to delineate the nature of human interactions in her fictional world and to place her characters and their conduct within a moral frame of reference." She focuses especially on communication's difficulties and tends to have conflicts arise in the dramatic scenes and "be clarified in the inside views."

Conclusions: The formal conclusion to each novel, marriage, resolves the narrative's ethical problems. Yet because these problems differ from book to book, as does the relation between reader and narrator, JA varies the way she creates her endings. While

typically revealing more of herself at such times
than at others, she emphasizes, in P and P, for
example, the individual's behavior, in MP the
story's moral import, and in E the complex workings
of the protagonist's mind.

Language: JA indicates her ideological premises
and assists precise judgment through the careful
handling of language, drawing particularly upon three
different groupings of words, which, in order of
ascending importance, pertain to economic, social,
and moral norms. Whereas the first set of values
serves as "the basis of negative action," and the
second suggests the significance of manners as an
index of character, the third, founded on Christianity, points to a person's duty to others.

549   Olshin, Toby A. "Jane Austen: A Romantic, Sys-
           tematic, or Realistic Approach to Medicine?"
           in vol. 10 of Studies in Eighteenth-Century
           Culture. Ed. Harry C. Payne. Madison, Wis.:
           Univ. of Wisconsin Press for the American
           Society for Eighteenth-Century Studies, 1981,
           pp. 313-26.

As incidents involving illness in each of the
novels suggest, JA saw the contemporary medical
profession as impotent and the two basic approaches
to diagnosis and therapy as useless. She viewed "the
very general dietary and bathing cures as laughable,
and the trust in existing systems of disease
classification as misplaced. She was--in her
attitude toward these views, neither romantic nor
rationalistic, but rather wryly, acceptingly, and
ironically--correct."

550   Patteson, Richard F. "Truth, Certitude, and
           Stability in Jane Austen's Fiction." PQ, 60
           (1981), 455-69.

"Ambiguities, anxieties, and inconsistencies" in
the novels reveal that to JA "real stability--the
epistemological stability of assured, objective
truth--does not exist." Though the characters seek
a single version of reality because they do not
relish a fluid, basically unknowable world, they
cannot find any certainty beyond individual interpretation. And "the multiplicity of narrative
voice makes the reader's search for determinacy even
more difficult than the characters'."

551   Persuasions: The Jane Austen Society of North
           America, no. 3 (16 Dec. 1981).

(In addition to the guest speaker's address to the Society's annual general meeting, abstracted below, this report includes, among other things, several brief notes.)

Ian Watt, "Jane Austen and the Traditions of Comic Aggression: Sense and Sensibility," pp. 14-15 and 24-28. "Based on her psychological and moral realism," JA's greatest literary originality consists in her having her protagonists assume "many of the aggressive functions which stage comedy has traditionally allotted to other actors--to the witty helpers, blocking characters, and villains." Her novels, including S and S, thus show "the 'good' characters as well as the others" involved in three major kinds of comic aggression--the social, the interpersonal, and the internal.

552   Phelan, James. "Determinate and Indeterminate Value in the Linguistic System: J. Hillis Miller and the Language of Persuasion," in Worlds from Words: A Theory of Language in Fiction. Chicago: Univ. of Chicago Press, 1981, pp. 117-52.

Rejecting a deconstructionist interpretation of P, we find that JA accomplishes "an extraordinarily difficult task of determinate communication," one dependent on both linguistic and non-linguistic factors. The novel helps show that, "though fictional worlds emerge from words, and though sometimes the particular words an author chooses are extremely important for creating a fictional world effectively, those worlds finally are not worlds of words, but worlds of characters, actions, emotions, and thoughts."

553   Pigrome, Stella. "'Jane!'" ChLB, NS no. 36 (1981), pp. 70-81.

JA varies forms of address to indicate, among other things, the demands of formality and the significance of certain relationships. She thus reserves Christian names for family occasions, creates husbands and wives who "might have no Christian names at all, for all we learn of them," and uses "Sir" and "Madam" or "ma'am" as the universal mode of reference, one current even with one's closest relatives.

554   Ram, Atma. "The Inadequacy in Catherine Morland." Triveni, 50 (Apr.-June 1981), 17-20.

(See no. 610.)

555   Raphael, Frederic, and Kenneth McLeish. "Austen,
       Jane," in The List of Books. New York: Harmony,
       1981, p. 54.

       "The determination of orthodox criticism to find
       in Jane Austen the virtue of moral sensitivity tends
       to make furtive the view that her books maintain
       their vitality because they are about what interests
       readers: love and money."

556   Ratcliffe, Michael. "Drama on Television." Drama,
       no. 140 (1981), pp. 43-46.

       (On the BBC adaptation of S and S.)

557   Rumrich, John Peter. "The Importance of Being
       Frank." ELWIU, 8 (1981), 97-104.

       Frank Churchill, "harbinger of change" and "comic
       catalyst," acts "on behalf of love and marriage, and,
       in general, for succession from the dying old to the
       living new." He both plays a key structural role in
       the novel and transcends "mechanical function": he
       becomes associated with mystery and wonder, does not
       fit prearranged categories, and reflects the author's
       "living solution to the story of Emma."

558   Schmidt, Kari Anne Rand. "Male and Female Language
       in Jane Austen's Novels," in Papers from the
       First Nordic Conference for English Studies,
       Oslo, 17-19 September, 1980. Ed. Stig Johansson
       and Bjørn Tysdahl. Oslo: Institute of English
       Studies, Univ. of Oslo, 1981, pp. 198-210.

       "There are basic differences between male and
       female language in Jane Austen's dialogue. These
       differences . . . apply to the distribution of such
       features as predicative and attributive adjective
       constructions, comparatives and superlatives, and
       adjectives in clusters. Furthermore, the language of
       the female characters is subject to norms to a much
       greater extent than that of the male characters."

559   Singh, Sushila. Jane Austen: Her Concept of Social
       Life. Ram Nagar, New Delhi: Chand, 1981.
       Singh's book includes a bibliography of writings
       about JA.

       Introductory: Though aware of contemporary
       political, social, and literary upheaval, JA
       deliberately excludes momentous events from her
       novels because she wishes to support "the idea of

stability as much in the life of the individual as in the larger society." She abhors all threats to order and values everyday, domestic experience, "which she considered to be based on the principle of sanity."

Love and Marriage: JA treats love and marriage soberly, rationally, realistically. She mistrusts strong passion and romantic illusion, for they disturb human tranquillity and place personal satisfaction above social claims, and focuses on the adjustments husband and wife must make to each other, believing a happy family life vital to the security of society as a whole.

The Feminine World: Depicting "a feminine world," a profound world though seemingly concerned with trivialities, JA examines women's genuine social significance, which entails achieving harmonious personal relationships. If educated properly, she believes, women can help create "a domestic paradise with a sure guarantee of stability and security" for the entire family.

Domestic Life: JA sees in the domestic sphere "all that goes on in real life." She "assigns certain duties to every member of the family and believes that if they all realize their responsibilities, there will be no clash." Because of her unreserved faith in social codes, she can describe hardship and difficulty in the home and still picture existence as "fairly bright and cheerful."

Social Classes: JA restricts herself to the gentry, a self-contained, privileged, complacent group not responsive to external influences. Though the gentry exists apart from the aristocracy and others, the relation among the different levels of society "is one of mutual help and not of conflict." And, because all classes accept given conditions, her works "reflect no urge for social change."

Technique: "Rigorously selective," JA's social vision helps her create compact, balanced, coherent novels. Her "great virtue is the completeness of her imaginary world, tiny though it is. Her strict sense of proportion, in content as well as in form, gives us a sure sense of serenity and assurance."

560 Smithers, David Waldron. _Jane Austen in Kent_. Westerham, Kent: Hurtwood, 1981. Part of Smithers's book appeared originally, with the title "Where Was Jane Austen's Rosings? The Case for Chevening," in _Country Life_, 30 Oct. 1980, pp. 1568 and 1571; see no. 498.

Rev. by Elizabeth Jenkins in Spectator, 13 Mar.
1982, pp. 24-25; by Brian Southam in TLS, 23 Apr.
1982, p. 470.

"Learning that Jane passed through my village in
a post-chaise going by the house where I was born,
led me to explore whatever evidence I could find
about her Kentish expeditions." In general, Kent,
where her family had its origins and she came often,
influenced her work, especially the early novels, by
enlarging "her experience of people, of society and
of the intimate relationships of families living
close enough for regular visiting which was the
continuing basis on which her imagination thrived."

561   [Southam, Brian C.] "Jane Austen, 1775-1817," in The
        Shorter New Cambridge Bibliography of English
        Literature. Ed. George Watson. New York:
        Cambridge Univ. Press, 1981, cols. 881-84.

(This condensation of the section on JA found in
the third volume of The New Cambridge Bibliography of
English Literature, 1969, adds a few new entries.)

562   Spence, Jon. "The Abiding Possibilities of Nature in
        Persuasion." SEL, 21 (1981), 625-36. See also
        no. 763.

"Persuasion images a world dominated by the abiding possibilities of nature, which can be destructive
as well as beneficial." "Mysterious," "haphazard and
incomprehensible," "beyond the control of the human
will or human reason," nature serves paradoxically
both to make Anne happy and to deny her "the certainty and security celebrated at the conclusions
of Jane Austen's other novels." In such a context
"love determines one's response to intimations of
death."

563   Swanson, Janice Bowman. "Toward a Rhetoric of Self:
        The Art of Persuasion." NCF, 36 (1981), 1-21.
        See also no. 836.

"The freeing of Anne's voice" in P "represents an
escape from Lady Russell's powers of speaking into a
persuasive mode of the heroine's own definition and
making." This birth charges "the central concept of
'persuasion' with both psychological and rhetorical
meaning and [shifts] the very grounds of persuasion
from outer compulsion to inner assurance and con-
viction, from influence exerted to insight ex-
pressed."

564 Tatham, Michael. "A Need for Tenderness." <u>NewB</u>, 62
       (1981), 465-72.

       JA values tenderness of heart more than she does
  the gentry's social and economic arrangements. In <u>E</u>,
  for example, the heroine's growing ability to feel
  for others "transforms her understanding of human
  relationships and effectively destroys the importance
  of such limited social criteria as 'elegance.'" Such
  a development creates "a small area of difference
  <u>within</u> society, and this is the most we are entitled
  to hope for from a writer of such strict moral
  realism."

565 Webb, Igor. "⌈<u>Pride</u> <u>and</u> <u>Prejudice</u> and <u>Mansfield</u>
       <u>Park</u>⌉," in <u>From</u> <u>Custom</u> <u>to</u> <u>Capital</u>: <u>The</u> <u>English</u>
       <u>Novel</u> <u>and</u> <u>the</u> <u>Industrial</u> <u>Revolution</u>. Ithaca,
       N.Y.: Cornell Univ. Press, 1981, pp. 49-72, 101-
       23, 158-77, and passim.

       <u>P</u> <u>and</u> <u>P</u> treats the qualities the individual needs
  to achieve fulfillment, stressing the personal choice
  involved in courtship as a means of maintaining the
  gentry's position. <u>MP</u>, in contrast, explores more
  the social circumstances that nurture a full life
  and, moving "beyond courtship," questions the idea
  "that individualism might be a means to invigorate
  community."

       "The great representative novel of the major
  transition between the system, real and wished for,
  of the early eighteenth century and the new
  industrial and agricultural capitalism," <u>P</u> <u>and</u> <u>P</u>
  reconciles many ideological conflicts, including that
  between trade and land and the one between the lesser
  and greater gentry. These "reconciliations obscure
  and overcome the failures of the novel's paternalistic society and thereby apotheosize it." While the
  protagonists do substantially improve themselves, "it
  is the unchanged past embodied in Pemberley that
  actually triumphs."

       In <u>MP</u>, written "under greater strain" and "in a
  more defensive posture," "the primacy of the landed
  estate becomes unpleasant dogma." The Park's virtue
  as an institution remains obscure, as does Fanny's
  character: "she represents Jane Austen's effort to
  push back the forces of social change into the old
  norms." Through Fanny, JA argues for "a system
  rooted in land and tradition, glossing over its
  actual basis in capital and empire. The novel
  demonstrates, in its particular use of memory, the
  kind of forgetfulness that an affirmation of landed
  capitalism necessitated in 1812-13."

566   Wilt, Judith. "Jane Austen's Men: Inside/Outside
      'the Mystery,'" in Men by Women. Ed. Janet Todd.
      (Women & Literature, NS 2.) New York: Holmes &
      Meier, 1981, pp. 59-76.

      The "Handsome Strangers" in JA's novels, the
      charming young idlers like John Willoughby and Frank
      Churchill, threaten anarchy because, not trying to
      become somebody and find work, they "shake the very
      foundations of masculine ego, challenge the funda-
      mental, painfully aborning, rite of the male
      Mystery." And, while rootless and adaptable, they
      prove selfish and materialistic, living "the
      planned life over the spontaneous. They are at
      heart, oddly, antipassion."

567   Wolff, Robert Lee, comp. "Austen, Jane (1775-1817),"
      in A-C, vol. 1 of Nineteenth-Century Fiction: A
      Bibliographical Catalogue Based on the Collection
      Formed by Robert Lee Wolff. (Garland Reference
      Library of the Humanities, 261.) New York:
      Garland, 1981, p. 40.

      (Describes the collection's five JA novels.)

                            1982

568   Adams, Timothy Dow. "To Know the Dancer from the
      Dance: Dance as a Metaphor of Marriage in Four
      Novels of Jane Austen." SNNTS, 14 (1982), 55-65.

      NA, P and P, MP, and E, whose intricate pattern-
      ing resembles a formal dance, consider "dancing as a
      metaphor for marriage and marriage proposals." All
      four novels depict "a sort of courtship dance,"
      stressing "the terrible importance of getting a
      partner both for the dance and for life." The
      heroines must judge potential partners carefully,
      even though hampered somewhat in their selection by
      dancing conventions.

569   Ashe, Rosalind. "Northanger Abbey," in Literary
      Houses. New York: Facts on File, 1982, pp. 90-
      101.

      (Using NA's "atmosphere, scattered hints and
      flavour" as well as original drawings, including
      floor plans, this book explores the Abbey as a
      house.)

570   Austen-Leigh, Joan. "Jane Austen's Housewife."

Country Life, 28 Oct. 1982, p. 1323.

(On the sewing bag JA made for Mary Lloyd in
1792 and the verses placed in it, "the first scrap
of writing we have of Jane's addressed to another.")

571 Bander, Elaine. "A Possible Source for Jane Austen's
     Names." N&Q, NS 29 (1982), 206.

     Following her preference for giving characters
     "socially authentic names," JA may have derived the
     names "Crawford" and "Dalrymple" from the subscrip-
     tion list for Camilla.

572 Barfoot, C. C. The Thread of Connection: Aspects of
     Fate in the Novels of Jane Austen and Others.
     (Costerus, NS 32.) Amsterdam: Rodopi, 1982.

     Rev. by Dieter Mehl in Archiv, 219 (1982), 478;
     in Choice, 19 (1982), 1555; by L. R. Leavis in ES,
     63 (1982), 189-92; by Frances Ferguson in SEL, 22
     (1982), 725; by Margaret Anne Doody in NCF, 38
     (1983), 220-24.

     (In addition to the sections on JA, abstracted
     below, this book includes chapters on "The Fate of
     the Novel" and "The Novelist's Fate" and five ap-
     pendixes, including one on "The Figures for 'Fate'
     in Jane Austen's Novels" and another on "'Fate' in
     the Novels of Some of Jane Austen's Contemporaries
     and Predecessors.")

     NA, S and S, and P and P: While NA "cannot take
     the idea of fate seriously at all," S and S and even
     more clearly P and P explore JA's distrust of fate
     and commitment to choice, which requires self-command
     and discrimination and can lead to true felicity.
     Choice in S and S "involves both the rights of the
     individual and of the community," and in P and P,
     vital to the free, responsible spirit, it triumphs
     with great comic energy over chance and design.

     MP: In MP, which juxtaposes choice based on
     genuine feeling and fate motivated by cynical calcu-
     lation, notions of destiny pose serious threats to
     morality and vocation. "Although some doubt is
     thrown upon human reasoning and planning and upon the
     ability of mortals to ensure the best and proper out-
     come for their choices, and while providence is
     regarded as an actively involved and instructive
     agent of good," the characters still best secure
     their well-being by choosing wisely.

     E: Trying to arrange the destiny of others, Emma

blindly imagines that she has none herself but discovers it finally in what proves natural and congru-
ous and learns as well to contemplate woman's overall
lot. Though fate remains an ominous term, interfering with the ability to control one's life, JA seems
increasingly willing to admit it as a conception
"that people in general, and novelists in particular,
cannot do without."

P: Most concerned of all the novels with time and
alteration, P defines fate as "the dependence of
happiness on situation and circumstances." Living as
one ought, Anne realizes, means exerting and trusting
in God, or, put another way, submitting to nature,
one's own and that of external conditions. "Constancy of love and affection is the only thing that
it is required should remain unchanged" in a universe
where mutability dominates.

573 [Blackley, Emma.] "Introduction" to Pride and Preju-
       dice, Northanger Abbey, Persuasion, Emma.
       (Treasury of World Masterpieces.) London:
       Octopus, 1982, pp. 9-12.

     (A biographical sketch including remarks about
JA's comic achievement.)

574 Bradbrook, M. C. "Reticence in the Later Novels of
       Jane Austen," in Women and Literature, 1779-1982,
       vol. 2 of The Collected Papers of Muriel Brad-
       brook. Totowa, N.J.: Barnes & Noble, 1982, pp.
       24-48.

     In the later novels JA relies less on irony and
increasingly on reticence, "the power to inhibit
response, or to regulate it." Reticence allows her
to develop character, to reveal character in style,
and to mark the growth of love. Thus, MP studies the
heroine's control, derived from reticence, E
varieties of "reticence or frankness, malice or
candour," and P the strong relationship between
Anne and Wentworth, which "flows under or through
ordinary intercourse."

575 Brown, Carole O. "Dwindling into a Wife: A Jane
       Austen Heroine Grows Up." IJWS, 5 (1982), 460-
       69.

     As a study of its narrative point of view, plot,
imagery, and characters makes clear, P and P does not
prove lighter or more spirited than the other novels
but merely illustrates a different stage in the same

process JA always describes. Like the rest of the
canon it tells the ultimately pessimistic story "of
the turning--and taming--of a girl into a woman"
noteworthy for her passivity and submission, her
acceptance of loss and limit.

576 Brownstein, Rachel M. "Getting Married: Jane
         Austen," in <u>Becoming a Heroine: Reading about
         Women in Novels</u>. New York: Viking Press, 1982,
         pp. 79-134.

     Treating "the play between consciousness and con-
     vention," JA rewrites Richardson and romance when she
     describes "a young woman's struggle to define herself
     by reflecting on and revising, doubting and reaffirm-
     ing, the truth of the heroine's old story" that the
     individual can indeed control her life and achieve
     happiness. In addition, a JA protagonist must, among
     other things, be "precise and particular" and differ
     from other women while learning she resembles them
     too.

577 Brückmann, Patricia. "Sir Walter Elliot's Bath
         Address." <u>ModPhil</u>, 80 (1982), 56-60.

     Camden Place proves an appropriate Bath address
     for Sir Walter not only because of its lofty and
     dignified situation "but because he is extravagant,
     showy, unlikely to note architectural flaws, or to
     think much on the view."

578 Bruns, Gerald L. "The Interpretation of Character in
         Jane Austen," in <u>Inventions: Writing, Textuality,
         and Understanding in Literary History</u>. New
         Haven: Yale Univ. Press, 1982, pp. 111-24.

     In part "a hermeneutical allegory," <u>P and P</u>
     offers "a world of hidden meanings which require to
     be recovered by interpretation," a constructive
     rather than investigative activity. JA here teaches
     that "social life is not simply a province of
     psychology or a place of behavior; it is a domain
     of human understanding" presupposing that we become
     what we know and that we fix or determine character.

579 Davidson, Arnold E. "Pride and Prejudice in Margaret
         Drabble's <u>A Summer Bird-Cage</u>." <u>ArQ</u>, 38 (1982),
         303-10.

     A modern rendering of <u>P and P</u>, <u>A Summer Bird-
     Cage</u>, which tells of two Bennett sisters, resembles

the earlier work in describing a protagonist sepa-
rated by pride from the man she loves and learning
to view herself more accurately. Drabble's novel
also differs from JA's, for it represents in part a
refutation of P and P's opening sentence and defends
pride and prejudice.

580   De Rose, Peter L., and S. W. McGuire. A Concordance
        to the Works of Jane Austen. 3 vols. (Garland
        Reference Library of the Humanities, 357.) New
        York: Garland, 1982.

        Rev. in Choice, 20 (1983), 1573; by John E.
Jordan in RomMov for 1982 (1983), pp. 72-73; by John
E. Jordan in SEL, 23 (1983), 689.

        (The first two volumes of this concordance
alphabetically list over 16,300 words found in the
six major novels, Lady Susan, The Watsons, and
Sanditon, noting the frequency of their occurrence,
providing a context for each appearance, and identi-
fying the source by title, volume, chapter, page, and
paragraph number; they also include miscellaneous
entries, like the ampersand sign and numerals. The
third volume consists of three appendixes, entitled
"Alphabetical List of All Words and Their Frequency
Counts," "Auxiliary Concordance of Commonly-Used
Adverbs, Conjunctions, Prepositions, Pronouns, Verbs,
etc.," and "Frequency Order of All Words.")

581   Figes, Eva. "The Supremacy of Sense," in Sex and
        Subterfuge: Women Novelists to 1850. London:
        Macmillan Press, 1982, pp. 76-112.

        JA firmly endorses "prudence and propriety,"
"English sense as opposed to foreign sensibility,"
valuing unselfishness and restraint and excluding
forces destructive of social cohesion such as sexual
passion. While she expresses this conservatism in
her first three novels with a "fierce underlying
cynicism," in her final works, "after a decade of
loss and uncertainty" at the start of the nineteenth
century, she drops all parody and ambiguity and
welcomes the security limitations represent.

582   Gibbon, Frank. "The Antiguan Connection: Some New
        Light on Mansfield Park." CQ, 11 (1982), 298-
        305.

        The Nibbs family, owners of an estate in Antigua
for which JA's father once acted as trustee, not only
provided her "with the type of background Sir Thomas

would be likely to have had, but also suggested some of the events and characterization of the novel."

583 Gilbar, Steven. "[Jane Austen]," in Good Books: A Book Lover's Companion. New Haven and New York: Ticknor & Fields, 1982, pp. 171, 188, and 392.

(Brief descriptions of S and S, P and P, and E.)

583a Gillespie, Jane. Ladysmead. New York: St. Martin's Press, 1982.

("A novel in the Jane Austen tradition" that includes characters from MP.)

584 Gilson, David. A Bibliography of Jane Austen. (Soho Bibliographies, 21.) Oxford: Clarendon Press, 1982.

Rev. by Anthony Payne in BWA, 1 (Nov. 1982), 18-19; by Pat Rogers in TLS, 12 Nov. 1982, p. 1242; by Stuart Bennett in ABMR, 10 (1983), 140; by Myrna J. McCallister in ARBA, 14 (1983), 572-73; by Sidney Ives in BC, 32 (1983), 358-60; by David McKitterick in BC, 32 (1983), 399-402 and 405-6; in Choice, 20 (1983), 690; by A. J. Shelston in CritQ, 25 (Winter 1983), 92; by George Watson in EIC, 33 (1983), 153-58; by G. E. Bentley, Jr., in Library, 6th ser., 5 (1983), 305-8; by John E. Jordan in RomMov for 1982 (1983), pp. 73-74; by Jo Modert in SLPD, 14 Aug. 1983, p. 4E; by Barry Roth in SNNTS, 15 (1983), 387-89; by Joseph Kestner in WC, 14 (1983), 148; by J. D. Fleeman in N&Q, NS 31 (1984), 138-40.

(This bibliography, based in part on Sir Geoffrey Keynes's "pioneering bibliography of 1929" but extensively altering and adding to that work, includes sections on the original editions of the novels, the first American editions, translations, the editions published by Richard Bentley, and later editions and selections. There are also sections on editions of the minor works and letters, on dramatizations, continuations, and completions, on books owned by JA, on miscellaneous items, and on biography and criticism, as well as plates and facsimiles of title-pages, spine labels, and the like and a note by Nicolas Barker on typographical identifications.)

584a Gooch, Bryan N. S., and David S. Thatcher. "Austen, Jane, 1775-1817," in vol. 1 of Musical Settings of British Romantic Literature: A Catalogue.

(Garland Reference Library of the Humanities,
326.) New York: Garland, 1982, pp. 2-3.

(Lists the musical settings of NA, P and P, and
Three Evening Prayers.)

585 Goubert, Pierre. "Jane Austen, Gilpin, et la beauté
        pittoresque." BSEAA, no. 14 (June 1982), pp. 91-
        106.

    Like Gilpin, JA has a taste for the natural in
landscape and uses the estate as emblem of its owner,
but, different from him, she stresses also the
countryside's utility and prefers English to Italian
scenery. As her career develops, and she frees
herself from the constraints of the picturesque,
nature comes to function not just as an agreeable
spectacle but also as part of a character's
psychology, growing less intellectual and more
emotional and romantic.

586 Grawe, Christian. "Nachwort" to Verstand und Gefühl.
        (Universal-Bibliothek, 7836.) Stuttgart: Reclam,
        1982, pp. 413-30.

    In S and S, which remains flawed because the
author identifies more with Elinor than with
Marianne, JA develops her technique of telling the
story from the heroine's point of view. In addition,
she here criticizes the irresponsibility of sentimental fiction, seeks a harmony between head and
heart, and courageously reveals social sins.

587 Grey, J. David. "Introduction" to Pride and Preju-
        dice. New York: Washington Square Press, 1982,
        pp. ix-xxviii.

    JA's appeal rests, as P and P demonstrates, on
her precision, sense of humor, prose style, and
plotting. Her themes in this novel, which features
"one of the most human heroines in all of literature," include friendship, family relations, money,
pride, and prejudice.

588 Halperin, John. "Unengaged Laughter: Jane Austen's
        Juvenilia." SAQ, 81 (1982), 286-99.

    Precocious, not brilliant, and only intermit-
tently entertaining, the juvenilia remain important
primarily because they show JA defining her artistic
preference for irony, detachment, and hostility.

These early pieces move from literary satire to
social comedy, anticipating many of her future concerns, and <u>Lady Susan</u>, of about the same period as
the late juvenilia, foreshadows the psychological
richness of the mature fiction.

589 Hassler, Donald M. "Irony and the Uses of Death from
     Wordsworth to Le Guin," in <u>Comic Tones in Science
     Fiction: The Art of Compromise with Nature</u>.
     (Contributions to the Study of Science Fiction
     and Fantasy, 2.) Westport, Conn.: Greenwood
     Press, 1982, pp. 49-67.

     Thematically and structurally, both JA and
     science-fiction writer Ursula Le Guin see awareness
     of death, limitation, and separation as a precondi-
     tion for love.

590 Hertz, Alan. "Dancing, <u>Romeo and Juliet</u>, and <u>Pride
     and Prejudice</u>." <u>N&Q</u>, NS 29 (1982), 206-8.

     With great artistic economy an allusion to <u>Romeo
     and Juliet</u> early in <u>P and P</u> (chap. 3) helps direct
     the reader's sympathies, develop the themes of love
     and civility, and characterize Darcy, Bingley, and
     Meryton society.

591 Holyoake, Gregory. "Jane in Kent. Part 1--Good-
     nestone and Rowling." <u>Bygone Kent</u>, 3 (1982),
     301-8.

     (On JA's association with Kent.)

592 Holyoake, Gregory. "Jane in Kent. Part II--God-
     mersham." <u>Bygone Kent</u>, 3 (1982), 349-56.

     (On JA's association with Kent.)

593 Izubuchi, Keiko. "Kenkyu no genkyo to kadai: Jein
     Ōsuten" [Present studies and problems: Jane
     Austen]. <u>EigoS</u>, 128 (1982), 154-55.

     (Review of Japanese writings about JA.)

594 "[Jane Austen]," in <u>A Catalogue of Books by and about
     the Brontë Family, Jane Austen, and Other
     Literary Ladies of the Nineteenth Century</u>.
     (Catalogue 28.) Stroud, Gloucestershire:
     Hodgkins, [1982], nos. 1-138 and passim.

(Lists rare and out-of-print books for sale by and about JA.)

595   The Jane Austen Society: Report for the Year, 1981.
      Alton, Hampshire: Jane Austen Society, [1982].

      (In addition to the guest speaker's address to
      the Society's annual general meeting, abstracted
      below, this report includes, among other things, a
      list of Jane Austen studies for 1981, a supplement
      to the list of Jane Austen studies for 1980--both
      prepared by David Gilson--and several brief notes.)

      Laurence Lerner, "Kissing," pp. 23-34. JA does
      not allow her successful lovers to touch each other.
      She admits only indirectly a physical basis for
      passion, overlooking the body almost entirely during
      "those moments when we might most expect it to be
      present, the moments when the lovers declare"
      themselves. She does, though, permit illicit feel-
      ing a freer expression.

596   Kelly, Gary. "Reading Aloud in Mansfield Park."
      NCF, 37 (1982), 29-49.

      MP explores "the relationship between moral
      character and public utterance through the theme of
      reading aloud," studying silent and vocal eloquence,
      contrasting different texts and performances, and
      challenging us to read properly too. It also treats
      reading aloud in relation to ordination, which
      signifies both order and orders and entails the
      individual's initiation into his social and religious
      heritage, the transformation of his life.

597   Koppel, Gene. "The Role of Contingency in Mansfield
      Park: The Necessity of an Ambiguous Conclusion."
      SoRA, 15 (1982), 306-13. A summary of Koppel's
      essay appeared, with the title "The Theme of
      Contingency in Mansfield Park," in Persuasions:
      The Jane Austen Society of North America, no. 2
      (16 Dec. 1980), p. 20.

      Of vital importance in MP, contingency, the idea
      that everything depends on circumstances, affects
      structure and meaning, plot and characterization.
      This theme emphasizes JA's interest in responsibility
      and education and forces us to examine our precon-
      ceptions about literature and life, as well as choose
      whether a world evolving independently implies the
      existence of a God. And, because it precludes a
      feeling of inevitability at the conclusion, it makes

unlikely any comforting critical agreement about this
"problem novel."

598 Kubal, David. "Jane Austen's Midsummer's Dream," in
       The Consoling Intelligence: Responses to Literary
       Modernism. Baton Rouge, La.: Louisiana State
       Univ. Press, 1982, pp. 33-51.

E resembles A Midsummer Night's Dream in that the
heroine, like the young lovers of Shakespeare's
comedy, rebels against society's repressiveness,
escaping to a dream world filled with confusion and
destructive possibilities. And the concluding
marriages in both works, which balance reason and
emotion, restraint and liberty, constitute only a
temporary, magical harmony because "there will always
be 'Box Hills' of the self and nature--Puck cannot be
restrained for long."

599 Lane, Maggie. The Jane Austen Quiz and Puzzle Book.
       Bristol: Abson, 1982.

(Crosswords, name games, word search puzzles, and
quizzes on the novels.)

600 Lee, David. "Modality, Perspective, and the Concept
       of Objective Narrative." JLS, 11 (1982), 104-11.

E's opening chapter involves "a complex process
of hypothesis development and exploration . . .
incompatible with the concept of 'objective narrative,'" a concept which may lack validity. Rather
than assigning the reader "a relatively passive
role," JA asks for creative interpretation, for
participation "in the construction and ongoing
evaluation of a model whose function it is to
explain the discrepancy between two contrasting
perspectives."

600a Leimberg, Inge. "Jane Austen und das Diktat der
        Wirklichkeit: Anmerkungen zu einer
        literatursoziologischen These und ihrer
        Durchführung." Archiv, 219 (1982), 313-
        23.

Critics of JA differ as to the relationship
between fiction and reality in her work, some
believing that the novels create a second nature
and others that they directly mirror contemporary
life. It remains true, though, that artistic
expression does not exist independently of the

external world, nor does it have a set relationship
with that world.

601 Macey, Samuel L. "Clocks and Chronology in the
        Novels from Defoe to Austen." ECLife, 7 (Jan.
        1982), 96-104. Part of Macey's essay appears
        also, with the title "Austen: Gaining a Suffi-
        cient Competence with an Insufficient Dowry," in
        his Money and the Novel: Mercenary Motivation in
        Defoe and His Immediate Successors (Victoria,
        British Columbia: Sono Nis Press, 1983), pp.
        146-64; see no. 657.

JA opposes the clockwork efficiency of a General
Tilney and Mr. Collins as well as the improvidence of
a Willoughby and Wickham, advocating a synthesis of
sense and sensibility such as Elinor and Marianne are
able to demonstrate.

602 McGrory, Mary. "Pages: I Prefer Jane Austen's."
        WPost, 11 July 1982, p. C2.

(On MP and Washington politics.)

603 Mason, Philip. "Elegance and Principle," in The
        English Gentleman: The Rise and Fall of an Ideal.
        New York: Morrow, 1982, pp. 70-80.

Based partly on models derived from Chaucer and
Castiglione and illustrating eighteenth-century
ideas, JA's gentlemen prove elegant, tasteful,
principled, warm, faithful, and considerate of
others.

604 Molan, Ann. "Persuasion in Persuasion." CR, no. 24
        (1982), pp. 16-29.

JA in P "penetrates the intrinsic doubleness of
persuasion, its ability to destroy and fashion, its
ineradicable presence in all human dealings, and the
riskiness of deciding one's lot by something un-
certifiable." Interested more in the process by
which the heroine secures her happiness than in the
enunciation of general moral principles, JA concentrates on Anne's movement from "a false persuasion of
self-abnegation or denial" to a belief in fulfillment
and the venturing of her hopes.

605 Moore, Susan. "The Heroine of Mansfield Park." ES,
        63 (1982), 139-44.

In MP, JA consistently presents the Crawfords as
morally weak, cynical, callous, and narrow and Fanny
as generous, strong, and courageous. For readers to
be attracted to the former rather than to the latter
"is to be deceived by appearances, to mistake the
superficially pleasing for something more, to honour
conventional notions of attractiveness, and to prefer
seeming to real virtue."

606 Myer, Valerie Grosvenor. "Caro Sposo at the Ball:
       Jane West and Jane Austen's Emma." N&Q, NS 29
       (1982), 208.

A passage in West's Letters to a Young Lady
contains the same "cluster of associations (the
dance, the smug married woman, the neglected spinster
and the caro sposo)" that appears during the ball at
the Crown in E.

607 Parke, Catherine. "Vision and Revision: A Model for
       Reading the Eighteenth-Century Novel of Educa-
       tion." ECS, 16 (1982-83), 162-74.

Reversing the pattern of Evelina and the novel of
education in general, E presents a heroine moving
from her name, "the functional counterpart of the
third-person pronoun," into the first-person
singular, "whose characteristic function is to note
the world in language." In the course of this movement Emma must unlearn "her specious social identity"
and travel "backward into the regions of vision and
of the clarified 'I.'"

608 Persuasions: The Jane Austen Society of North
       America, no. 4 (16 Dec. 1982).

(In addition to the guest speakers' addresses to
the Society's annual general meeting, abstracted
below, this report includes, among other things,
several brief notes.)

John Hart, "Jane Austen's Sailors: Gentlemen in
the Military Capacity," pp. 18-20. Gentility in MP
and P "is not simply a given of one's profession,"
and in P "the naval officers represent a cohesive set
of values, whether merging with the gentry, co-
existing as an enclave, or founding a new social
order."

Juliet McMaster, "Hospitality," pp. 26-33. JA
considers the ideal relationship between host and
guest as "a contract of mutual agreeableness; and

like all the intricate social contracts in the novels
it is one that epitomises the delicate balance that
must be maintained between the will of the individual and the needs of the community."

Enid G. Hildebrand, "Jane Austen and the Law,"
pp. 34-41. "It is the knowledge of the laws linking
the Englishman to his property, of the intricacies of
wills and settlement, the tolerance of man's failings
that give the universal reality to the works, and do
not date them with the faded chintz of another day."

609 Prescott, Stephanie, ed. <u>Austenilia</u>, vol. 1 (1982).

(First and only issue of the newsletter of the
Jane Austen Society of North America.)

610 Ram, Atma. <u>Heroines in Jane Austen: A Study in
     Character</u>. New Delhi: Kalyani, 1982. Ram's
     book includes a bibliography of writings about
     JA and a bibliography of Indian editions,
     translations, and criticism of the novels.

"Jane Austen's Appeal to Indian Readers": As
evidenced by the number of printings and translations
of her novels in India, JA appeals to readers there
for several reasons. The attention she pays domestic
humor, the small details of ordinary social intercourse, and rural settings makes her novels meaningful to many Indians. And her treatment of marriage,
sexual roles, and relationships within a family
accords with traditional Indian views.

Catherine Morland: Almost the opposite of the
usual thoughtful, quick-witted JA heroine, Catherine
"is somewhat poorly drawn," for she develops in two
inconsistent directions. She both parodies the
typical Gothic protagonist and grows in her own
right: "in the first case common-sense is to be shut
out, and in the second allowed in."

Elinor and Marianne Dashwood: "Jane Austen
proposes to herself a very complex task in ⌈S and S⌉:
to develop a character embodying sense towards
sensibility and one with sensibility towards mature
sense." She succeeds better with Marianne, who
shares the author's taste for such things as balls,
walks, and village life.

Elizabeth Bennet: Elizabeth's negative view of
Darcy, "created by her prejudice against him in the
beginning, maintained by the common report, and
strengthened by George Wickham's account," changes

when she visits Pemberley, symbol of the entire process used to establish "a true Darcy image."

Fanny Price: Though her moral sense provides her
with "some growth and confidence," "Fanny as a character does not come to life as she is not thoroughly
analysed. . . . The most outstanding women are
physically active in one way or the other. Because
of the added drawback of her frail health, Fanny
Price gives the impression of being only a girl."

Emma Woodhouse: E's conclusion is neither ironic
nor unhappy but "serious and consistent" with the
rest of the novel. The heroine's revelation about
her ignorance remains "partial: she my [sic] again,
and probably will, commit such mistakes. But a truly
perfect wife would be boring to live with; so would
be a truly perfect husband. An ideal wife should be
intelligent but certainly less smart than her husband."

Miss Bates: Never really insufferable like Mrs.
Elton, Miss Bates proves entertaining, pitiable,
and well-meaning. She represents part of JA's
study of female folly, demonstrating that "to speak
much on trivial topics is not so hateful a thing in
women."

Anne Elliot: Though Anne may appear at times to
express contradictory attitudes to Lady Russell and
the issue of persuasion, the heroine always follows
the precept that "the parents have a right to oppose
even as lovers have a right to affirm." And, rather
than reward filial disobedience, as many contemporary
novelists tended to do, JA "follows a realistic and
more honourable path: she makes the objecting parents
see the desirability of the union."

"Jane Austen's Presentation of Women Characters":
JA presents her fictional women dramatically, psychologically, and overall in a lifelike manner, offering increasingly penetrating portraits as her career
develops. She studies these women, especially the
heroines, in contrast to other characters and by
means of small but nevertheless significant details.
"In doing big things, usually all people are alike.
However, in doing small things, persons, particularly
women, are really themselves."

"Jane Austen and Shakespeare": As examples from
MP indicate, JA echoes Shakespeare more than commonly
thought.

611 Scott, P. J. M. Jane Austen: A Reassessment.

(Critical Studies Series.) Totowa, N.J.:
Barnes & Noble, 1982.

Rev. in Choice, 20 (1983), 988; by C. C. Barfoot
in ES, 64 (1983), 539-40; by Angela Leighton in TLS,
15 Apr. 1983, p. 384; by Park Honan in N&Q, NS 31
(1984), 140.

Lady Susan, Sanditon, and NA: A powerful, subtle
piece, Lady Susan explores, through the energy of
its heroine and the insipidity of the rest of its
characters, the plight of vital women in a torpid
environment. Sanditon, in addition to satirizing
"hypochondria and other ruling ideas," dramatizes
"phenomena which do not yield a secure interpretation." And NA remains interesting not for its
trivial opposition of fiction to life but "a sense
of spiritual death in the face of all existence."

P and P and E: These works offer different
aspects of JA's nature, the former exemplifying her
moral responsibility, the latter her moral failure.
P and P, a tonic fantasy, "affords as one unitary
experience the dark side of social living and a
compensating buoyancy which can be derived athwart
its current," and E, contrary to received opinion,
proves nasty and dishonest, "an unreal daydream,"
because it endorses egoism and does not punish the
heroine enough "for her generally delinquent attitudes."

S and S: Though it ends in the comic mode, S and
S stands as "one of the great tragic novels," enact-
ing the destructive possibilities of both sense and
sensibility and denying the world's ability to fulfill the deserving. In the portrait of Willoughby
JA shows "an ideal reciprocity" out of reach and in
those of Edward Ferrars and Colonel Brandon, whose
insufficiencies she deliberately emphasizes, the
most that sensitive, intelligent women can realistically expect.

MP: "A flawless masterpiece," MP realizes that
deprivation, which strengthens human identity, also
cramps personality and that, more largely, "there are
no perfect ambits or achieved sanctuaries of the
spirit." Accordingly, the book asks us to view the
episode of the theatricals with mixed feelings, the
failure of Fanny and Henry Crawford's relationship as
evidence that reality frustrates the best prospects,
and the "scamped" ending as indicating the "patched
up" nature of the heroine's marriage.

P: Like The Winter's Tale, P confronts and transcends life's defeating elements, such as the ravages

of society and time, comparing different concepts of
selfhood and valuing a high order of awareness and
discrimination, qualities that give existence meaning. As in her earlier novels, JA here creates
extraordinarily lifelike characters through their
speech and finds most of them myopic and selfish.

612   Southam, Brian. "Austen, Jane, 1775-1817," in Makers
        of Nineteenth-Century Culture, 1800-1914. Ed.
        Justin Wintle. Boston: Routledge & Kegan Paul,
        1982, pp. 17-18.

"A supreme artist of the novel," who transformed
the genre, JA wrote unromantic romantic comedies
noteworthy for their sardonic, intellectual social
criticism, especially about woman's lot, and for
their lifelike characterization.

613   Spear, Hilda D., comp. "Austen, Jane (1775-1817),"
        in From Blake to Byron, vol. 5 of The New Pelican
        Guide to English Literature. Ed. Boris Ford.
        New York: Penguin, 1982, p. 391.

(Updates the bibliography found in the original
edition.)

614   Steele, Pamela. "In Sickness and in Health: Jane
        Austen's Metaphor." SNNTS, 14 (1982), 152-60.

Using sickness and health as metaphors, JA links
"unbounded energy . . . with deficiency in character
or understanding, fever with learning, and debility
with wisdom and a tender conscience." She has illness and accident function not only to advance plot
but to illustrate the same theme underlying her
attitude to general human conduct: "if we do not
behave ourselves properly something bad is bound to
happen."

615   Stehle, Claudia. "Jane Austens Persuasion: Neue
        Formen," in Individualität und Romanform:
        Theoretische Überlegungen mit Beispielen aus dem
        18. Jahrhundert. (Neue Studien zur Anglistik und
        Amerikanistik, 24.) Frankfurt am Main and Bern:
        Lang, 1982, pp. 141-71. Stehle's book was
        written as a doctoral dissertation.

P, which demonstrates the changes JA made in
novelistic narrative technique and in the portrayal
of women, treats the conflict between private needs
and public values. The book shows that good manners

no longer indicate inner morality and that one must
rely above all on intuition in assessing others.

616 Stewart, Ralph. "Fairfax, Churchill, and Jane
        Austen's Emma." HSL, 14 (1982), 96-100.

        Jane Fairfax and Frank Churchill have the sur-
     names of famous English generals, whom they resemble
     in personality and circumstance: Jane, for instance,
     like Thomas Fairfax, becomes "drawn into intrigue
     against the dictates of conscience" and appears
     "halfhearted, ineffectual, and rather colorless," and
     Frank, like John Churchill, proves a skillful diplo-
     mat in arbitrating between dissimilar relatives and
     strikes others as "remarkably handsome, charming, and
     lucky--or, to a hostile view, effeminate, Frenchi-
     fied, and deceitful."

617 Stout, Janis P. "Jane Austen's Proposal Scenes and
        the Limitations of Language." SNNTS, 14 (1982),
        316-26.

        JA subdues intensely emotional moments, including
     proposal scenes, not out of personal fear, ignorance,
     or incapacity but because of conscious theories of
     her form and medium. She thus avoids full, direct
     presentation of particulars at these times in order
     to retain her focus on general themes and not break
     decorum. Moreover, she doubts language's adequacy to
     strong feeling and the integrity of individuals "able
     to remain fluent, flowery, or verbose" in situations
     demanding such feeling.

618 Taylor, Elisabeth Russell. "The Essence of Austen."
        Observer, 28 Nov. 1982, p. 44.

        (On Hampshire.)

619 Uglow, Jennifer S., comp. and ed. "Austen, Jane," in
        The International Dictionary of Women's Biogra-
        phy. New York: Continuum, 1982, pp. 30 and 32.
        Uglow's book appears also with the title The
        Macmillan Dictionary of Women's Biography
        ([London]: Macmillan Reference Books, 1982).

        (Biography.)

620 Ward, Philip. "Jane Austen (1775-1817)," in A Life-
        time's Reading. New York: Oleander Press, 1982,
        pp. 149-50.

"Her command of irony, her stylish ear for conversation betraying every nuance of character, and
her gift for gradually unravelling a plot organ-
ically, by means of the clash of character with
character: every technique of the psychological
novelist is already fully operative in Pride and
Prejudice, a consummation never surpassed in all
her subsequent novels."

621   White, Pamela. "Jane Austen, 1775-1817," in Arnold-
        Gissing, pt. 1 of vol. 4 (1800-1900) of Index of
        English Literary Manuscripts. Comp. Barbara
        Rosenbaum and Pamela White. London: Mansell,
        1982, pp. 21-31.

      (Survey of JA's literary manuscripts, fol-
lowed by a list describing and locating them and
providing information about their first publication.)

622   Yamamoto, Toshiharu. "Ōsuten ni okeru 'manners'"
        [Manners in Austen's novels]. EigoS, 127 (1982),
        618-22.

      JA's novels study manners, especially the
element of ease in behavior, using them to
characterize individuals and develop themes like
morality and the conflict between appearance and
reality.

                        1983

623   Anastaplo, George. "Jane Austen (1775-1817)," in
        The Artist as Thinker: From Shakespeare to Joyce.
        Chicago and Athens, Ohio: Swallow Press, 1983,
        pp. 86-99.

      Noteworthy for their "quiet worldliness" and
measured depiction of household life, JA's novels
suggest the possibility of "a good life based on
rational principles," a life requiring deliberation,
self-knowledge, and discipline. She views life as a
comedy, "but it does seem important to her that the
comedy not be frivolous, that the play be well
acted."

624   Barry, Naomi. "Discovering Jane Austen." Gourmet,
        43 (Mar. 1983), 18-23 and 128-36.

      (On a visit to Chawton Cottage.)

624a   Battaglia, Beatrice. La zitella illetterata:
       Parodia e ironia nei romanzi di Jane Austen.
       (Il Portico: Biblioteca di lettere e arti,
       77.) Ravenna: Longo, 1983.

       (This book studies the parodic vein underlying
       the conventional surface of the novels. It argues
       that JA rewrites such traditional narrative forms
       as the "contrast novel" (in S and S), the "didactic
       novel" (in MP), and the "quixotic novel" (in E) and
       that she relies on the ambiguous, subtle play of
       parody and irony and aims to flout authority and do
       away with dogmatism.)

625   Bronson, Larry L. "Loiterer, The," in British
       Literary Magazines: The Romantic Age, 1789-
       1836. Ed. Alvin Sullivan. (Historical Guides
       to the World's Periodicals and Newspapers.)
       Westport, Conn.: Greenwood Press, 1983, pp. 284-
       87.

       (Profiles the serial edited by James Austen and
       discusses the similarity of some of its interests to
       JA's, particularly the attack on "excessive senti-
       mentality in literature and its evil consequences
       for human behavior.")

626   Burke, Karen. "Foreword" to Pride and Prejudice.
       (Chatham River Press Classics.) New York:
       Chatham River Press, 1983, pp. v-vii.

       (Describes the novel's style as ironic and witty,
       its subjects as love and marriage, and its charac-
       ters, for whom the author feels genuine affection, as
       original.)

627   Burrows, J. F. "'Nothing Out of the Ordinary Way':
       Differentiation of Character in the Twelve Most
       Common Words of Northanger Abbey, Mansfield Park,
       and Emma." BJECS, 6 (1983), 17-41.

       "Jane Austen's verbal universe is much more
       generally energetic than has ever been shown," not
       even the smallest part of it proving "inert." As
       revealed by a study of the "incidence in dialogue of
       the twelve most common words" in NA, MP, and
       E--"the," "to," "and," "of," "a/an," "her," "I,"
       "was," "in," "it," "she," and "not"--JA quietly
       and profoundly embeds the differentiation of
       characters "in the plain stuff of the language"
       and subtly varies their idiolect "as their cir-
       cumstances change."

628 Citati, Pietro. "L'occhio di Jane sulla tazza di
       te': Rileggendo due famosi romanzi della Austen."
       CdS, 23 Aug. 1983, p. 3.

     Good reading for a convalescent because not up-
     setting or overstimulating, JA portrays a closed,
     limited world noteworthy for its equilibrium and the
     slow movement of time, values decorum more than any-
     thing else, and paradoxically combines an absolute
     acceptance of existence with an equally absolute
     nihilism, whereby she sees the world as composed of
     nothing but vain surfaces.

629 Crook, Nora. "Gowland's Lotion." Letter in TLS, 7
       Oct. 1983, p. 1089.

     In P, Mrs. Clay's "use of the discredited
     Gowland's [may be] intended to reinforce her connec-
     tion with the unacceptable face of Bath," perhaps
     even including syphilis.

630 Delorme, Mary. "Happy Ever After." Letter in Times,
       9 July 1983, p. 7.

     JA demonstrates that romantic fiction need not be
     "soppy."

631 Ermarth, Elizabeth Deeds. "Jane Austen's Critique of
       Distance," in Realism and Consensus in the
       English Novel. Princeton, N.J.: Princeton
       Univ. Press, 1983, pp. 144-77.

     Between E and P "the balance shifts from a narra-
     tive of correction, one that challenges and reaffirms
     a social order, to a narrative of corroboration and
     consensus, one that validates the heroine's reliance
     on memory and her radical separation" from an un-
     stable, confused society. And, while E devalues
     linear time and mobility and condemns detachment, P
     establishes the importance of temporal continuity
     and flux and "dramatizes the opportunity of the fully
     realistic narrator."

632 Fergus, Jan. Jane Austen and the Didactic Novel:
       Northanger Abbey, Sense and Sensibility, and
       Pride and Prejudice. Totowa, N.J.: Barnes &
       Noble, 1983.

     Rev. in Choice, 20 (1983), 1595-96; by John E.
     Jordan in SEL, 23 (1983), 703; by Nicholas Spoliar in
     TLS, 19 Aug. 1983, p. 884.

NA: Different from the other works, NA lacks
their ethical interests and didactic purpose and remains "simply comic." JA does not here choose to
trace the protagonist's growth or portray full personal relationships but concentrates instead on
demonstrating both the absurdity and force of
literary convention, specifically sentimental fiction's concern for distress and the Gothic novel's
for suspense, and showing off her budding powers to
her readers.

S and S: In S and S, for the first time in her
career, JA "elicits and manipulates the responses of
judgment and sympathy, with a moral intention,"
namely, to develop and educate her audience's reactions. By constructing elaborate comparisons among
the characters, she studies sensitive behavior's
nature and costs and the value of regulating the
passions according to social rather than literary
codes.

P and P, Cecilia, and Sir Charles Grandison:
Cecilia and Sir Charles Grandison anticipate and
partly share P and P's aims. Burney resembles JA,
among other ways, by examining pride's effects on
different minds, setting feeling and judgment at
odds, and depicting emotional flux, and Richardson
does so through his thematic and technical handling
of first impressions, including the desire to control
and improve our responses to his work.

P and P: Climaxing the initial stage in her
development, P and P reveals JA's mastery of structural devices like parallels, contrasts, and irony
and her simultaneously playful and complex adaptation of the comedy of manners to the novel form,
notably such elements as wit and dialogue. The
book's techniques allow her to expose, both in the
readers and Elizabeth and Darcy, "complacency or
pride of judgment," as well as instruct and refine
the emotions, perceptions, and moral sense.

The Later Novels: Especially in MP and E, demands
and power continue to intensify, and the increasingly
complicated effects derive mostly from JA's limiting
the number of topics appearing in her fictional
conversations and allowing these topics to be often
repeated. More particularly, MP concentrates on
judgment as it relates to feeling, E on concealed
love and intimacy, and P on recovery from loss.

633   Frazer, June M. "Stylistic Categories of
        Narrative in Jane Austen." Style, 17 (1983),
        16-26.

Four stylistic features--sentence type, coordination type, verb type, and average sentence length--distinguish passages in JA's novels spoken in the narrator's voice from those representing a character's inner thoughts. Thus, the narrator's utterances, for example, tend to consist of declarative sentences, without questions or exclamations; to use serial conjunctions more than contrastive ones; to avoid verb forms reflecting condition and doubt; and to rely on longer sentences.

634 Ganner-Rauth, Heidi. "To Be Continued? Sequels and Continuations of Nineteenth-Century Novels and Novel Fragments." ES, 64 (1983), 129-43.

Unlike the 1958 completion of The Watsons by John Coates, the 1977 version by Another does not "acquire an originality of its own" and imitates rather superficially JA's style and language. And the 1975 completion of Sanditon by Another Lady, while it somewhat successfully imitates style, presents characters lacking depth and fails to exhaust the fragment's potentialities.

635 Gibbon, Frank. "Jane Austen and a Bleached Stain: The Case of Lady Bolton." N&Q, NS 30 (1983), 217.

(On bleaching "the stain of illegitimacy" in E and in a family JA knew.)

636 Grant, John E. "Shows of Mourning in the Text of Jane Austen's Persuasion." ModPhil, 80 (1983), 283-86.

(Suggests emendations of a passage in P concerned with the mourning for Mr. Elliot's dead wife.)

637 Grawe, Christian. "Nachwort" to Überredung. (Universal-Bibliothek, 7972.) Stuttgart: Reclam, 1983, pp. 302-20.

About the unexpected reawakening of the soul, P requires an older protagonist than usual for JA because it deals with the more mature topic of romantic love rather than with the wisdom of life. The novel, which implies much about the author's biography, has a melancholy tone, features grotesque characters and situations, and reflects its theme in the fall weather.

638 Green, Benny. "Television: Monky Business." _Punch_,
      16 Nov. 1983, p. 80.

      (On the BBC adaptation of _MP_.)

639 Grove, Robin. "Jane Austen's Free Enquiry: _Mansfield
      Park_." _CR_, no. 25 (1983), pp. 132-50.

      Rather than affirming absolutes, JA shows in _MP_
      and elsewhere "a willingness to unmake the very
      solidities" she establishes, to subvert the "models
      and morals" she proposes. She reveals herself as "a
      confident open spirit," "iconoclastic, radical,
      free," her style proving skeptical, her ironies far-
      ranging, her characters unpredictable, and her end-
      ings unsettling. And she makes the reader "one of
      the interested parties to the process of judgment:
      one of those whose beliefs and predilections will
      colour the judgments formed."

640 Hayball, Jane. "Austen, Jane," in _The Europa
      Biographical Dictionary of British Women:
      Over 1,000 Notable Women from Britain's Past_.
      Ed. Anne Crawford et al. London: Europa,
      1983, pp. 22-23.

      (On her life and some qualities of her novels.)

641 Hutcheson, John. "Subdued Feminism: Jane Austen,
      Charlotte Brontë, and George Eliot." _IJWS_, 6
      (1983), 230-57.

      JA, Charlotte Brontë, and George Eliot "contrib-
      uted to what can be called a feminist literary
      heritage" but themselves achieved only a subdued,
      not a full, feminism. They treat the tensions be-
      tween individualism and social conservatism affect-
      ing woman's lot, tensions JA resolved through irony
      and the others found increasingly difficult to
      reconcile.

642 James, Selma. "[Jane Austen]," in _The Ladies and the
      Mammies: Jane Austen & Jean Rhys_. Bristol:
      Falling Wall Press, 1983, pp. 11-56.

      JA, who helped to start feminist fiction, treats
      the tragic division between the sexes, money's in-
      fluence over personality and human relationships, and
      women's dependent position within the family and
      marriage.

643   The Jane Austen Society: Report for the Year, 1982.
      Alton, Hampshire: Jane Austen Society, [1983].

      (In addition to the guest speaker's address to
      the Society's annual general meeting, abstracted
      below, this report includes, among other things, a
      list of Jane Austen studies for 1982, a supplement
      to the list of Jane Austen studies for 1981--both
      prepared by David Gilson--and several brief notes.)

      Christopher Ricks, "Jane Austen and the Business
      of Mothering," pp. 27-44. Although, contrary to the
      views of some feminists, JA certainly did love
      children, she yet pays little specific attention to
      them in her fiction, using them basically as little
      more than a means of moving the plot and enhancing
      comic effects. She allows them only this subordinate
      role in order to preserve the privacy of the parent-
      child relationship and admonish a world fast becoming
      baby-fixated to retain a sense of proportion.

643a Johnson, Claudia L. "The 'Operations of Time, and
      the Changes of the Human Mind': Jane Austen
      and Dr. Johnson Again." MLQ, 44 (1983), 23-38.
      See also no. 818.

      A survey of references to Johnson in JA's novels
      shows she did actively borrow from him, particularly
      ideas about the mind's behavior, including "the
      importance of attention and concentration, the
      danger of fixation and obsession; the need to live
      'in idea' and to possess animating hopes, the aware-
      ness that hopes can become excessively absorbing and
      are generally disappointed anyway," and "the cow-
      ardice of prudence or the presumption of confidence
      in face of the unknown future."

644   Johnson, Claudia L. "The 'Twilight of Probability':
      Uncertainty and Hope in Sense and Sensibility."
      PQ, 62 (1983), 171-86. See also no. 818.

      "Opaque and sceptical," indebted specifically to
      Locke and Johnson and generally to the eighteenth-
      century philosophical tradition treating the "prob-
      lems of knowing and assent," S and S "dramatizes the
      danger of accepting even the most compelling of
      probabilities as certainties, and urges the need to
      govern what we allow ourselves to hope and to be-
      lieve." These epistemological concerns, of greater
      importance than the title's abstractions for under-
      standing the novel, help determine, among other
      things, plot, characterization, and diction.

645   Johnson, Judy Van Sickle. "The Bodily Frame: Learn-
           ing Romance in **Persuasion**." <u>NCF</u>, 38 (1983),
           43-61.

       Her "most unreservedly physical novel," <u>P</u> sus-
tains "the credibility of a renewed emotional attachment" not through words but through signs related to
the body. By focusing on the protagonists' "eyes,
cheeks, entrances and exits, their 'mouths, hands,
and feet,' their positions in carriages and on sofas,
in enclosures and open spaces," the novel dramatizes
both the depth of their love for each other and their
sexual desire.

646   Johnson, Paul. "Miss Austen Approves. . . ."
           <u>DTelegraph</u>, 9 July 1983, p. 8.

       <u>MP</u>, which offends critics by being morally reac-
tionary rather than progressive, insists that traditional values must finally triumph if adhered to
tenaciously and offers in Fanny a successful study
of a truly good woman.

647   Kaplan, Deborah. "Achieving Authority: Jane Austen's
           First Published Novel." <u>NCF</u>, 37 (1983), 531-51.

       <u>S and S</u> contemplates and adjusts the idea of
authority. It distinguishes tropes of masculine
authority, which are culturally sanctioned, from
those of feminine authority, which are illegitimate,
yet identifies both kinds of metaphors as narcissistic and fallacious. It offers in their place the
concept of revision--the modification and correction
of assertion--which proved "sufficient to justify for
Austen a writing career within a patrilineal and
patriarchal social context."

648   Keener, Frederick M. "The Philosophical Tale, Jane
           Austen, and the Novel," in <u>The Chain of
           Becoming--The Philosophical Tale, the Novel,
           and a Neglected Realism of the Enlightenment:
           Swift, Montesquieu, Voltaire, Johnson, and
           Austen</u>. New York: Columbia Univ. Press, 1983,
           pp. 241-307.

       "Self-Assessment in <u>Les Liaisons dangereuses</u> and
<u>Northanger Abbey</u>," pp. 243-74. More than Laclos in
<u>Les Liaisons dangereuses</u>, JA in <u>NA</u> adheres to the
formal and thematic concerns of the philosophical
tale, notably the attention characteristically paid
"realism of psychological self-assessment." In the
tradition of <u>Rasselas</u> and <u>Candide</u>, <u>NA</u> emphasizes the

protagonist's internal capacity to judge the self and
others, shows the characters, the narrator, and the
reader all standing "in some degree of dramatic
conflict with each other," and studies self-love and
the association of ideas.

"'Delicious Consciousness' in Persuasion, via
Mansfield Park," pp. 275-307. In P, JA "consolidates
her original development of the theme and pattern of
the philosophical tale," focusing on the connection
between self-knowledge and self-love. More successfully than in MP, she here explores the importance of
the chain of ideas depending from initial associations and uses the vocabulary of eighteenth-century
psychology "to describe perception, conflict, and
resolution within a single mind," the heroine's,
which the novel's narrative strategy helps define as
independent and powerful.

649 Keith-Lucas, Bryan. "Francis and Francis Motley
     Austen, Clerks of the Peace for Kent," in Studies
     in Modern Kentish History Presented to Felix Hull
     and Elizabeth Melling on the Occasion of the
     Fiftieth Anniversary of the Kent Archives Office.
     Ed. Alec Detsicas and Nigel Yates. Maidstone,
     Kent: Kent Archaeological Society, 1983, pp. 87-
     102.

     (On JA's great-uncle and his son.)

650 Kemp, Peter. "Commentary: Disparate Educations."
     TLS, 30 Dec. 1983, p. 1458.

     (On the BBC adaptation of MP.)

651 Kirkham, Margaret. Jane Austen: Feminism and Fic-
     tion. Totowa, N.J.: Barnes & Noble, 1983. Part
     of Kirkham's book appears also, with the title
     "The Austen Portraits and the Received Biog-
     raphy," in Jane Austen: New Perspectives, ed.
     Janet Todd, Women & Literature, NS 3 (New York:
     Holmes & Meier, 1983), pp. 29-38; see no. 680.

     Rev. by Valerie Shaw in BBNews (1983), p. 387; in
     Choice, 20 (1983), 1138; by John E. Jordan in SEL, 23
     (1983), 703; by Angela Leighton in TLS, 15 Apr. 1983,
     p. 384.

     Feminism and the Novel: Much resembling Mary
     Wollstonecraft, JA adheres to Enlightenment femi-
     nism's central convictions, notably the belief in
     the sexes' moral equality and women's status as

accountable beings. In addition, she lived at a time
when the novel was helping to reassess woman's nature
and the relationship between the sexes, when the
emergence of women as authors encouraged both feminism and apprehension about female emancipation, and
when, finally, a reaction against feminism late in
the eighteenth century made open discussion of
liberal views nearly impossible.

Biography and Reputation: The controversy over
feminism occasioned by Godwin's Memoirs of his wife
affected JA's development as a writer, the publication of her works, and her early reputation. The
received biography suppresses the true breadth of her
interests and her professionalism, together with the
significance of the years spent in Bath, and the
coincidence of Scott's rise as a novelist with the
issuing of MP helped prevent the feminist nature of
her accomplishment from being understood.

Allusion and Irony: In the course of her career
JA makes increasingly radical and subtle criticisms
of life and literature. In the early fiction she
modifies different literary models, though not with
complete success, trying to free them of antifeminist bias, and later she enlarges her comedy's
scope and widens her allusive irony's range, satirizing especially August von Kotzebue's treatment of
women.

MP: MP's protagonist, only superficially like
Rousseau's Sophie and other sentimental heroines, in
fact possesses a strong, clear, rational mind, and
the book's title, which refers to a famous legal
judgment, implicitly compares women's condition to
that of slaves. In general the novel, shaped in the
manner of a play, reverses characters and circumstances in Lovers' Vows and uses Shakespeare's King
Lear and Henry VIII to assist in defining nature,
reason, and good government.

E: The ideas for E evolved gradually, from about
the period of The Watsons until the revival in 1814
of JA's interest in burlesque. In this novel, keeping close to the plot of Kotzebue's The Birthday,
she corrects romantic misconceptions about devoted
daughters and the chivalric tradition. She also sub-
verts the stereotypes, found in Barrett's The
Heroine, of governesses as ignorant fools, young
women as natural imbeciles, heroes as guardians, and
illegitimacy as glorious.

P and Sanditon: These works show JA presenting
new female characters and experiences. The former,
uneven because lacking "a proper allusive-ironic

focus," insists even more pointedly than the earlier novels on women's moral intelligence and independence, reversing completely the roles of the heroine-as-pupil and hero-as-teacher. The latter, her most unreserved attack on Richardson's anti-feminism, mocks the violence and degradation of sentimental literature, the notion of women as hypochondriacs, and their transformation into useful but mindless creatures.

"The Critical Tradition": Assessments of JA have rarely considered her feminism. Of her early critics, Scott proved less intelligent in this regard than Whately and not so impartial and sympathetic overall as usually believed. The unfounded idea that she admired but refused to meet Madame de Staël can only have estranged writers like George Eliot from her. Subsequently, Virginia Woolf ignored JA's real context, and in recent years JA's supposed conservatism has alienated feminist and leftist critics.

652   Kolson, Ann. "'Janeites' Are Prejudiced--and Proud of It." HartC, 26 Oct. 1983, p. D3.

(On the fifth annual meeting of the Jane Austen Society of North America.)

653   Leavis, Q. D. "Jane Austen: Novelist of a Changing Society," in The Englishness of the English Novel, vol. 1 of Collected Essays. Ed. G. Singh. New York: Cambridge Univ. Press, 1983, pp. 26-60.

JA's novels reflect social changes that imply a psychological and moral revolution. Though formed by eighteenth-century culture, including the principles of decorum and restraint and general authoritarian, even "tyrannical," views, in the course of her career she examined her assumptions and came to sympathize with the newer style of life dominant in the Regency period, a style characterized by warmth, spontaneity, informality, privacy, and freedom.

654   Le Faye, Deirdre. "'The Business of Mothering': Two Austenian Dialogues." BC, 32 (1983), 296-314.

(Transcribes and discusses two brief dialogues on the raising of children, possibly by Mary Lloyd, James Austen's second wife, and perhaps also owing something to JA.)

655   Lenta, Margaret. "Androgyny and Authority in

Mansfield Park." SNNTS, 15 (1983), 169-82.

Like the other novels MP demonstrates JA's belief
in the "androgynous" nature of authority, in the idea
that power should derive from merit, not sex. The
book concerns Fanny's deserved promotion from low to
high status, a promotion based on her own abilities
rather than her husband's position, and the consequent transformation of the faulty patriarchal regime
threatening Mansfield into a system that allows all
with sound moral judgment to share influence.

656   Loveridge, Mark. "Francis Hutcheson and Mr. Weston's
       Conundrum in Emma." N&Q, NS 30 (1983), 214-16.

On a few occasions in E, JA "sardonically makes
characters repeat or echo phrases from the Moral
Sense writers," notably Hutcheson and Shaftesbury.

657   Macey, Samuel L. "Austen: Gaining a Sufficient
       Competence with an Insufficient Dowry," in Money
       and the Novel: Mercenary Motivation in Defoe and
       His Immediate Successors. Victoria, British
       Columbia: Sono Nis Press, 1983, pp. 146-64. Part
       of Macey's essay appeared originally, with the
       title "Clocks and Chronology in the Novels from
       Defoe to Austen," in ECLife, 7 (Jan. 1982), 96-
       104; see no. 601.

In the tradition of Defoe, Richardson, and Fielding, JA writes novels concerned with money, emphasizing a middle way between extremes of prudence and
improvidence as well as the necessity of accommodat-
ing worthy tradespeople in rural society. She also
uses the need to make solvent marriages as a major
structuring device, presents variations on the
Cinderella story, has ideas about ideal incomes for
her protagonists, and bases many ironies on financial
matters.

658   McGrory, Mary. "Literature: Fanatic for Miss Jane."
       WPost, 16 Oct. 1983, pp. B1 and B5.

(On the fifth annual meeting of the Jane Austen
Society of North America.)

659   Marshall, Mary Gaither, ed. Jane Austen's Sanditon:
       A Continuation by Her Niece, Together with
       "Reminiscences of Aunt Jane" by Anna Austen
       Lefroy. Chicago: Chiron Press, 1983.

(In addition to the introductions, abstracted

below, this book includes a description and transcription of the manuscript of Sanditon: A Continuation, a transcription of the manuscript of
"Reminiscences of Aunt Jane," and summaries of the
two other continuations of JA's fragment--Somehow
Lengthened: A Development of Sanditon by Alice
Cobbett [1932] and Sanditon by JA and Another Lady
[1975].)

"Introduction to Sanditon: A Continuation," pp.
xi-xlvii. Written sometime after 1830 and published
now for the first time, Sanditon: A Continuation dou-
bles the length of but does not complete JA's novel.
It expands the characters found in the original,
especially Clara Brereton, and introduces new ones,
unfolds the plot slowly, and of the three continuations of Sanditon may be "the closest in language,
style, and development to what Jane Austen herself
would have written."

"Introduction to the 'Reminiscences,'" pp. 145-
52. Dating from about 1867 and published only now in
its entirety, the "Reminiscences" has three parts:
the author's notes about her ownership of JA's
Sanditon manuscript, her recollections of JA, which
prove limited but help bring their subject to life,
and different drafts of her recollections.

660 Milligan, Ian. "The Novel and the Story," in The
    Novel in English: An Introduction. New York:
    St. Martin's Press, 1983, pp. 72-98.

JA gives P and P its distinctive shape, among
other ways, by dividing the novel into three cumula-
tive sections, by beginning with one kind of equilibrium and ending with a new one, and by establishing
links among the characters, whom she classifies
according to such standards as self-awareness, wit,
and the ability to marry well. She works largely by
contrast, studying in particular different forms of
knowledge and judgment, and uses dialogue to clarify
and advance relationships.

661 Moler, Kenneth L. "The Balm of Sisterly Consola-
    tion: Pride and Prejudice and Sir Charles
    Grandison." N&Q, NS 30 (1983), 216-17.

A speech by Mary Bennet echoes language in Sir
Charles Grandison.

662 Moler, Kenneth L. "The 'Olive Branch' Metaphor
    in Pride and Prejudice." N&Q, NS 30 (1983),
    214.

The image Mr. Collins uses occurs also in Sir
Charles Grandison.

663   Moler, Kenneth L.   "'Only Connect': Emotional
        Strength and Health in Mansfield Park." ES,
        64 (1983), 144-52.

Exploring the theme of "human interdependence,"
MP characterizes the Crawfords and most of the
Bertrams as shrinking from, having limited capac-
ities for, or egocentrically perverting personal
relationships and Edmund and especially Fanny as
being able to feel deeply and generously for
others. Reading Fanny's story in terms of the
"'connection' theme lends strong support to the
views of critics who find her alleged moral worth
justified by the 'facts' of the novel."

664   Newman, Karen.   "Can This Marriage Be Saved: Jane
        Austen Makes Sense of an Ending." ELH, 50
        (1983), 693-710.

"The marriages that end her novels can only be
saved by reading them not as statements of romantic
harmony or escape, but in the context in which she
placed them. Far from acquiescing to women's traditional role in culture, Austen's parodic conclusions
measure the distance between novelistic conventions
with their culturally coded sentiments and the social
realities of patriarchal power."

665   Norman, Geraldine.   "Jane Austen's 'Mansfield Park'
        for Sale." Times, 13 Apr. 1983, p. 12.

(On the proposed sale of Godmersham, once the
home of JA's brother Edward and reputedly the model
for Mansfield Park.)

666   Norman, Geraldine.   "Sale Records Tumble at
        Godmersham Park." Times, 7 June 1983, p. 16.

(On the sale of the house that once belonged to
JA's brother Edward.)

667   Persuasions: The Jane Austen Society of North
        America, no. 5 (16 Dec. 1983).

(In addition to the guest speakers' addresses to
the Society's annual general meeting, abstracted
below, this report includes, among other things,
several brief notes.)

Wayne C. Booth, "Emma, _Emma_, and the Question of Feminism," pp. 29-40. Considered conventionally or formally, _E_ embraces sexist beliefs concerning women's dependence, inferiority, and need for marriage to provide fulfillment. Yet the novel also imaginatively resists these preoccupations, treating them as "fairy-tales or fantasies" and teaching us "what it means to keep our wits about us, and how we must maintain a steady vision about the follies and meannesses in our world."

Judith Wilt, "The Powers of the Instrument, or Jane, Frank, and the Pianoforte," pp. 41-47. Derived in part from the portrayal of the heroine in Gothic novels and ancestor of characters in Charlotte Brontë and George Eliot, Jane Fairfax proves noteworthy for her reserve, "pale eroticism, sensitive illness," and aesthetic talent. Life for her, as for other intelligent women in JA, becomes an artistic performance, to which she brings "the elegance, the taste, the execution, that demonstrate the power of her instrument."

Mary Poovey, "'The True English Style,'" pp. 48-51. In _E_, JA's failure to "resolve the contradiction between the promises of romance and the realities of marriage" represents not a criticism of her insight or novelistic skill but a comment "about the way things were in her society for women and about how one crucial contradiction provided both vital complications for fictional plots and debilitating complications for actual women."

668 Poovey, Mary. "_Persuasion_ and the Promises of Love," in _The Representation of Women in Fiction_. Selected Papers from the English Institute, 1981, NS 7. Ed. Carolyn G. Heilbrun and Margaret R. Higonnet. Baltimore: Johns Hopkins Univ. Press, 1983, pp. 152-79. Poovey's essay appears also, in an enlarged form, with the title "'The True English Style,'" in her _The Proper Lady and the Woman Writer: Ideology as Style in the Works of Mary Wollstonecraft, Mary Shelley, and Jane Austen_ (Chicago: Univ. of Chicago Press, 1984), pp. 208-40; see no. 689.

_P_ explores the ambiguities of individualism and patriarchal values, both the novel's structure and content dramatizing the triumph of personal desires over public forms. But the aesthetic resolution, based as it is on the idea of romantic love, involves ideological contradictions, which point especially to the illusory nature of female power, of women's ability to assert their own needs and improve society.

669   Price, Martin. "Austen: Manners and Morals," in
      Forms of Life: Character and Moral Imagination in
      the Novel. New Haven: Yale Univ. Press, 1983,
      pp. 65-89. Part of Price's essay appeared
      originally, with the title "Manners, Morals, and
      Jane Austen," in NCF, 30 (1975), 261-80; see no.
      187.

      Unlike other of JA's heroines Elinor Dashwood and
      Fanny Price do not themselves change but instead
      become more valued by others. Both suppress their
      feelings, Elinor to be serviceable, "Fanny through
      self-distrust as well. Each is denied the kind of
      presence which easy manners supply, but there is an
      unobserved intensity, an undemonstrative delicacy,
      that is at work in them."

670   Reinstein, P. Gila. "Moral Priorities in Sense and
      Sensibility." Renascence, 35 (1983), 269-83.

      S and S does not oppose sense and sensibility so
      much as selfishness and selflessness, portraying the
      differences between the two through the characters'
      actions and speech patterns. The novel concludes
      that both sense and sensibility prove mixed quali-
      ties, able to promote either private satisfaction
      or a more general welfare, and advocates moderation,
      the combination of judgment and prudence with emotion
      and enthusiasm.

671   Robinson, Philip. "Introduction" to his ed. of Pride
      and Prejudice. (Longman Study Texts.) Harlow,
      Essex: Longman, 1983, pp. vii-xxxv.

      (Comments on JA's life, provides information
      about money, class, and social conventions in the
      early nineteenth century, discusses the influence
      of Richardson and Fielding on her, and speaks of her
      skillful novelistic construction and balanced, subtle
      characterization.)

672   Scully, Michael A. "Sense as Psychotherapist."
      NatRev, 18 Mar. 1983, p. 329.

      "Long after literary pedants have numbered every
      cobblestone in England, Jane Austen's novels will
      still be expanding the 'human resources,' and sooth-
      ing the souls, of ordinary cultivated readers."

673   Shepherd, Patricia M. Come into the Garden,
      Cassandra. Ed. Joan Austen-Leigh. Vancouver,

British Columbia: Jane Austen Society of North
America, 1983.

("Some light-hearted but loving lines on a
favourite author.")

674 Shoben, Edward Joseph, Jr. "Impulse and Virtue in
Jane Austen: Sense and Sensibility in Two
Centuries." HudR, 35 (1982-83), 521-39.

We read JA because she provides a "perspective
on, a correction to, and a protection against the
fads, the momentary forces, and the temptations of
our own time." For her, as S and S demonstrates,
"the mentally healthy person is one who acknowledges
the reality of the moral realm and who grapples in
a principled fashion with moral dilemmas. If we
remember that human selves are also and ineluctably
cultural beings," then she will always deserve our
serious attention.

675 Smith, Jack. "Despite a Lack of Singles Bars, the
Time of the Regency Had Its Share of Romance."
LAT, 15 Nov. 1983, sec. 5, p. 1.

Although JA lacks "graphic, explicit, audible sex
scenes," her novels "are almost as saturated with sex
as those of today's liberated female novelists; but
of necessity, given the hypocrisy of the times, it is
implicit, offstage; we do not hear the cries, murmurs
and wows of the bedchamber, but only the resulting
gossip."

676 Smith, LeRoy W. Jane Austen and the Drama of Woman.
New York: St. Martin's Press, 1983. Smith's book
includes a bibliography of writings about JA.

Early Writings: Like the mature fiction, Lady
Susan and NA (as well as The Watsons and parts of the
juvenilia) center on the "drama of woman," that is,
women's difficulties in a patriarchal society. While
Lady Susan offers a "fantasy of successful combat,"
of a heroine adopting masculine roles to avoid
domination and assert her will, NA presents a
"fantasy of successful accommodation," of a heroine
appreciated for her merits achieving happiness within
a sexually repressive order.

S and S: S and S focuses on the female's social
and sexual vulnerability in a world controlled by
egoistic, powerful males. It argues that unre-
strained feeling increases one's chances to be

oppressed and that pursuit of self-interest means
collaboration with dehumanizing forces. It favors
"a judicious adjustment" to given conditions as the
only way to survive with integrity, an adjustment
demanding awareness of external threats as well as
prudence and self-understanding.

P and P: Emphasizing the dangers courtship poses
to personal fulfillment, P and P rejects the stereotype of masculine superiority and feminine inferiority and reconciles love, sex, and marriage. The
protagonists, who "demand that they be judged as
individuals, both discover how difficult it is to
shake off conventional modes of thought in judging
others, and both come to realise that correct judgement depends upon a knowledge of both oneself and
the other," a view opposed to prevailing assumptions.

MP: MP depicts woman's victimization by a male-
controlled society. "Fanny Price is a 'heroine of
principle'; the main concern of the novel is her
welfare; the patriarchal society at the Park is the
'enemy'; the contention springs from the latter's
attempt to dictate Fanny's marriage choice; and
Fanny's ordeal and triumph provide the dramatic
centre of the novel."

E: Emma, fleeing from womanhood to avoid dependence, resists love and marriage but discovers that
her "masculine" behavior isolates her and increases
her vulnerability and blindness. And, when Mr.
Knightley similarly overcomes paternalistic attitudes, learning of his limitations and the mutuality
of the sexes, the two create a relationship founded
on openness and equality.

P: P, which "blows up" patriarchy, concentrates
on "the obstacles to intimacy caused by sexual
stereotyping" and moves toward "a concept of
androgynous being." More particularly, it studies
Wentworth's change from a "bipolar" to a "dualistic"
conception of human nature as he comes to realize
that both he and Anne equally share "male" and
"female" traits.

676a Smithers, Sir David Waldron. "Godmersham Park."
      WLH, 3 (Autumn 1983), 2-7.

      (On the Austen family's connection to the Park
      and the 1983 sale.)

677 Spacks, Patricia Meyer. "Afterword" to Sense and

Sensibility. New York: Bantam, 1983, pp. 332-43.
Part of Spacks's "Afterword" to this edition,
which includes a bibliography of writings by and
about JA, appeared originally, with the title
"The Difference It Makes," in Soundings, 64
(1981), 343-44 and 353-57; see no. 1020.

S and S, a profound, realistic comedy noteworthy
for a vital and complex prose style, takes as its
major subject the relationship between outer and
inner worlds, between economic and psychic realities.
Treating, too, the significant social differences
between the sexes, which severely narrowed women's
possibilities, the novel affirms the value of both
sense and sensibility; it acknowledges things as they
are but triumphs over them by seeing them clearly and
revealing their costs and limits.

678   Stapleton, Michael. "Austen, Jane," in The Cambridge
      Guide to English Literature. New York: Cambridge
      Univ. Press; Feltham, Middlesex: Newnes, 1983,
      pp. 38-39.

      (In addition to the article on JA, this book
includes separate articles on the six novels and
Sanditon, providing information about their composition and original publication, describing their
plot, and assessing their relative merit.)

      "Jane Austen's novels are an object lesson to
aspiring writers, though it must necessarily be borne
in mind that neither her wit nor her intelligence can
be emulated. But her precision and economy, her
knowledge of the world she wrote about, and her
wisdom in using that world alone for her subject--all
these factors help to account for her success."

679   Starr, Martha H., and Elizabeth W. Hill, eds. Jane
      Austen Calendar/Diary, 1984. New York: Harcourt
      Brace Jovanovich, 1983.

      (Includes quotations from the novels and letters,
maps of Bath, Chawton, and Steventon, and photographs of places in England associated with JA, as
well as specifies dates important to her.)

680   Todd, Janet, ed. Jane Austen: New Perspectives.
      (Women & Literature, NS 3.) New York: Holmes
      & Meier, 1983.

      Joan Austen-Leigh, "The Austen Leighs and Jane
Austen, or 'I Have Always Maintained the Importance

of Aunts,'" pp. 11-28. "It is to our branch of the family, the Austen-Leighs, that the maintenance of Jane's importance has chiefly fallen."

Margaret Kirkham, "The Austen Portraits and the Received Biography," pp. 29-38. As a comparison of Cassandra's drawing of her sister and its 1870 adaptation suggests, "the received 'life' of Jane Austen, together with general ignorance about the development of feminist ideas from the beginning of the eighteenth century, has obscured her importance as a feminist moralist of the age of Enlightenment. The family biographers created, as far as they could, a portrait of a conventional, domesticated spinster." [Part of Kirkham's essay appears also, with the title "The Feminist Controversy and the Received Biography," in her _Jane Austen: Feminism and Fiction_ (Totowa, N.J.: Barnes & Noble, 1983), pp. 53-60; see no. 651.]

Alistair M. Duckworth, "Jane Austen and the Conflict of Interpretations," pp. 39-52. JA has received "diverse and contradictory" readings because, having many contextual origins, she does not "achieve 'univocal' certainties." Future research, which may not easily distinguish "between 'reading' Jane Austen (being receptive, objective, attentive to rhetorical signals and to informing historical contexts) and 'writing' Jane Austen (being productive, subjective, suspicious of rhetoric, anachronistic)," will find new perspectives on her, to which we should remain open.

David Spring, "Interpreters of Jane Austen's Social World: Literary Critics and Historians," pp. 53-72. Some confusion has marked interpretation of JA's society. Strictly speaking, she pictured the rural elite, what she called "neighborhood," a world consisting of the aristocracy, gentry, and nonlanded families. These groups shared a common view of their country; the first two had no "dying feudal tradition" in the early nineteenth century but proved strong, progressive agrarian capitalists, and the third, more aptly called pseudo-gentry than bourgeois, sought not to displace but emulate the gentry.

Jane Nardin, "Children and Their Families in Jane Austen's Novels," pp. 73-87. In ways that alter little throughout the novels children often develop problems because they resemble a flawed parent and lack the influence of a good model. As part of their maturation, the heroines "learn to evaluate themselves and their families critically," frequently relying on a male outside the original home to guide

them, and "become the true adults that their parents
rarely were."

David Monaghan, "The Complexity of Jane Austen's
Novels," pp. 88-97. JA's complexity derives from the
dialectical relationship between her main plots,
which function ideologically, as expressions of conservative philosophy, and archetypally, as versions
of myths and fairy tales, and her subplots, which
transcend ideology and complicate archetype. Together, the two kinds of plot embody "a rich world
vision" noteworthy for its "antithetical portraits of
human nature and experience" that "capture the tensions of real living."

Edward Copeland, "The Burden of Grandison: Jane
Austen and Her Contemporaries," pp. 98-106. Where
Sir Charles Grandison pictures a carefully ordered
society that helps the novelist anchor plot and
imagery, form and character, those who followed
Richardson in domestic fiction, including JA,
perceive an incoherent new world, shown in part by
"the wreckage of families," and narrow their focus
from "gentility" to "respectability" and from a
"grand, public scale" to "a smaller grouping of
perhaps the wife, the old grandfather, a child or
two, and a cat."

Janet Todd, "Who's Afraid of Jane Austen?" pp.
107-27. Virginia Woolf responds to JA ambivalently
and uneasily: she praises as well as faults "the
mother of writers" for her impersonality, non-
polemical stance, sureness of class, artistic perfection, and critical awareness. Because JA fails to
accord with Woolf's ideas about women, women authors,
and Woolf herself, she threatens the later novelist,
representing "the context that limits and proves
limits."

Angela Leighton, "Sense and Silences: Reading
Jane Austen Again," pp. 128-41. Although JA allows
Elinor's "self-censored story" to be told in S and S,
she censors Marianne's part of the narrative because,
composed of silences signifying emotions beyond
speech, beyond control, it opposes JA's conservative
and limiting art. The irrelevance of Marianne's
voice illustrates both the protest and chastisement
of "the feminine": by the end she "escapes from the
marginalized language of Sensibility only to be
tamed and punished by the public language of Sense."

Zelda Boyd, "The Language of Supposing: Modal
Auxiliaries in Sense and Sensibility," pp. 142-54.
JA bases S and S and the other novels on modals, the
vocabulary of hypothesis, inference, and supposition.

She relies on words like "must," "ought," and "could"
to provide comedy, as when characters willfully shape
worlds objectifying their desires, to define the
imperfect nature of human knowledge, its foundation
in probability rather than certainty, and to reflect
a process by which language allows people to live
comfortably together in society.

Katrin R. Burlin, "'Pictures of Perfection' at
Pemberley: Art in Pride and Prejudice," pp. 155-70.
P and P, as Pemberley's pictures reveal, "laughs at
perfection," exposes the illusion that life partakes
of the aesthetic. Though the estate may seem ideal,
it constitutes an art gallery--composed of minia-
tures, the full-scale painting of Darcy, and a
"conversation-piece"--where the reader views portraits of fallible individuals.

Martha Satz, "An Epistemological Understanding of
Pride and Prejudice: Humility and Objectivity," pp.
171-86. P and P considers the processes by which we
acquire knowledge faulty, inevitably distorted, and
prejudiced, at the same time that it contends that
the human mind can grasp objective truth. The novel
bridges the gap between these opposing perspectives
by validating Elizabeth's epistemologically modest
stance, which, because it accepts limitations, avoids
rigidity, and weighs possibilities, can finally
arrive at certainty. [See also no. 835.]

Mark M. Hennelly, Jr., "Pride and Prejudice: The
Eyes Have It," pp. 187-207. Probably influenced by
empiricism, romanticism, the rise of the novel, and
the motif of the "lady-in-watching" in English
fiction, JA pays much attention to eyes in P and P:
they help reveal character, advance plot, develop
such themes as love and pride, and contribute to the
handling of point of view.

Nina Auerbach, "Jane Austen's Dangerous Charm:
Feeling As One Ought about Fanny Price," pp. 208-23.
MP's "mobility and malleability" darkly realize "an
essentially Romantic vision, of which Fanny Price
represents both the horror and the best hope. Only
[here] does Jane Austen force us to experience the
discomfort of a Romantic universe presided over by
the potent charm of a charmless heroine who was not
made to be loved" and who, unaccommodating, baleful,
perverse, anti-human, stands with Frankenstein's
creature, Grendel, and Dracula as a sinister outsider, a monstrous predator. [A summary of
Auerbach's essay appeared in Persuasions: The Jane
Austen Society of North America, no. 2 (16 Dec.
1980), pp. 9-11.]

Marylea Meyersohn, "What Fanny Knew: A Quiet
Auditor of the Whole," pp. 224-30. Fanny's character stems not from fatigue or inertia but deferral,
passivity, silence, a silence equated with chastity
and eloquence, the opposite of the eroticism marking
the Crawfords' "language performance." When she does
talk, as she does increasingly toward the end in the
process of gaining status, she talks, unlike many
others, to good purpose. But most importantly, she
knows how to listen.

Margaret Kirkham, "Feminist Irony and the Price-
less Heroine of <u>Mansfield Park</u>," pp. 231-47. (See no.
651.)

Avrom Fleishman, "Two Faces of Emma," pp. 248-56.
Emma has two faces: we can psychoanalyze her, finding
her, among other things, "a case study in <u>projective
neurosis</u>, <u>repressed homosexuality</u>, and associated
<u>phobic delusions</u>," or we can regard her from a
literary perspective, seeing her as an imaginative,
lively, competent individual noteworthy for her comic
perceptions. The first viewpoint tends to belittle
the character and magnify the observer, and the
second, based on love, to confirm a suspicion of our
limitations.

Joel Weinsheimer, "<u>Emma</u> and Its Critics: The
Value of Tact," pp. 257-72. As a passage from Kant
demonstrates, both <u>E</u>'s characters and critics need
tact, "a capacity to apply rules aptly, without any
superior rule that dictates their application."
Considered thus, "tact is not merely the reticence
that lets pass what should remain concealed but also
the bluntness that opens up what should be disclosed.
Tact is not merely the knowledge of general possibility but the wisdom that can employ it in particular and actual situations."

Jocelyn Harris, "Anne Elliot, the Wife of Bath,
and Other Friends," pp. 273-93. JA alludes in <u>P</u> to
Richardson, Shakespeare, and especially Chaucer, from
whose <u>Wife of Bath's Tale</u> she could have derived the
story of the Loathly Lady becoming beautiful and the
conception of "gentillesse" as inherent virtue
instead of noble descent or riches. And the Wife's
<u>Prologue</u> may have offered ideas about "maistrie," or
sovereignty in marriage, as well as the defense of
women's constancy based on the authority of experience rather than of books.

681   Tucker, George Holbert. <u>A Goodly Heritage</u>: <u>A History
      of Jane Austen's Family</u>. Manchester: Carcanet

New Press in association with Mid Northumberland
Arts Group, 1983.

Rev. by Joan Grigsby in Hampshire, 23 (Oct.
1983), 63-64; by Elizabeth Jenkins in Spectator,
6 Aug. 1983, pp. 20-21; by Anna Shapiro in NYT,
20 May 1984, sec. 7, p. 31.

(A biography of JA's family, this book includes
chapters on the Austen and Leigh background, her
brothers and sister, and her nephews and nieces.)

682 Wallace, Robert K. Jane Austen and Mozart: Classical
     Equilibrium in Fiction and Music. Athens, Ga.:
     Univ. of Georgia Press, 1983. Wallace's book
     includes appendixes on "Jane Austen at the Key-
     board" and "Persuasion and Jane Austen's Love
     Songs."

Rev. by Brigid Brophy in TLS, 24 Feb. 1984, p.
187.

General Stylistic Achievement: The "classical
equilibrium" JA and Mozart achieve in their separate
art forms comprises comparable aesthetic, social, and
spiritual components. Aesthetically, they both
stress balance, harmony, proportion, and symmetry,
restraint rather than vehemence of expression,
clarity, the use of ambiguity as a means to ultimate
unity, a playful and not a sentimental or scornful
kind of wit, and the use of conventional language.
Socially, they emphasize the individual's ability to
live fully "within the confines established by the
many," as well as an indoor, "deathless" world, a
sense of home, sanity, growth of fictional character
or musical theme without transformation, and happy
endings. Finally, as regards spirit, they tend "to
preserve the fabric" of tradition instead of burst-
ing its form, to merge feeling and manners, and,
while possessing subversive streaks, to prefer
accommodation to struggle.

P and P and Piano Concerto No. 9 (K. 271): Light,
bright, and sparkling, yet possessing emotional
depth, both of these works feature a three-part,
home-away-home, happy-sad-happy, fast-slow-fast
format, a "balanced opposition between the stately
and the impertinent," and comparable "protagonists":
Elizabeth in the one and the solo piano in the other
prove equally brilliant and witty, mature as they
assimilate grief, deepening and refining their innate
qualities, and by the conclusion achieve "an expansive and elastic freedom" within their respective
worlds.

E and Piano Concerto No. 25 (K. 503): E and K.
503, "two seasoned masterpieces," differ from the
earlier works in being spacious, grave, and densely
textured, in investigating more subtle forms of
feeling, and in making seemingly neutral material
dramatic and complex. They move from a "grandiose
ambiguity of stability and tension," with the opposing forces far apart, through the individual's
growing appreciation of "the other" to a cordial
interdependence, in which Emma and the solo voice
realize their best possibilities by losing themselves in commonplace experience.

P and Piano Concerto No. 27 (K. 595): Comparably
personal, poignant, and autumnal, P and K. 595
concentrate less on "action" than the presentation
of extreme emotion in a moderate and reserved
manner, following Anne and the solo as they progress
"from resigned melancholy to lonely hope to profound joy." These compositions prove more Romantic
than their predecessors, for they tend to avoid the
stability of a physical home or home key and, pointing toward social change, probe "a world of self-
communion."

683   Zelicovici, Dvora. "The Inefficacy of Lovers' Vows."
       ELH, 50 (1983), 531-40.

       Contrary to much critical opinion, Lovers' Vows
does not threaten Mansfield Park but instead shares
the same standards of behavior as JA's novel, including the concern for duty and self-restraint. The
real threat stems from high society's false values,
which prevent characters like Maria, Mary, and Henry
from learning the ethical lessons of Kotzebue's play.
Art, JA ironically implies, "can have no moral
efficacy for such people."

                              1984

684   Austen-Leigh, Joan, Lorraine Hanaway, and Gene
       Koppel, eds. Persuasions: Occasional Papers.
       (No. 1.) [Tucson, Ariz.]: Jane Austen Society
       of North America, 1984.

       Tad Mosel, "Jane Austen's Two Inches of Ivory,"
pp. 1-8. (On JA's life and some characteristics of
her novels.)

       J. David Grey, "Henry Austen: Jane Austen's
'Perpetual Sunshine,'" pp. 9-12. (On the life of
JA's brother.)

685   Cheetham, Paul. "Introduction" to his ed. of Emma.
      (Longman Study Texts.) Harlow, Essex: Longman,
      1984, pp. viii-xxxiii.

      (On E's limited scope, its treatment of love,
      marriage, class distinctions, and the conflict be-
      tween reason and imagination, its subtle shifting
      of narrative viewpoint, and its good-natured but
      pointed comedy.)

686   Gilson, David. "Jane Austen's Verses." BC, 33
      (1984), 25-37.

      (Records "the existence and whereabouts of manu-
      scripts of some of the verses" and notes "any
      substantial differences between manuscript and
      printed texts.")

687   "[Jane Austen]," in A Catalogue of Books by and about
      the Brontë Family, Jane Austen, and Other
      Literary Ladies of the Nineteenth Century.
      (Catalogue 30.) Stroud, Gloucestershire:
      Hodgkins, [1984], nos. 1-131 and passim.

      (Lists rare and out-of-print books for sale by
      and about JA.)

688   Poovey, Mary. "Ideological Contradictions and the
      Consolations of Form: The Case of Jane Austen,"
      in The Proper Lady and the Woman Writer: Ideology
      as Style in the Works of Mary Wollstonecraft,
      Mary Shelley, and Jane Austen. (Women in Culture
      and Society.) Chicago: Univ. of Chicago Press,
      1984, pp. 172-207. Poovey's book includes a
      bibliography of writings about JA.

      JA gradually develops artistic strategies balanc-
      ing the demands of anarchic passion and social in-
      stitutions. In Lady Susan she reveals desire's
      destructive potential as well as propriety's dis-
      tortion of constructive energy; in S and S,
      ambivalent about romance and realism, she recog-
      nizes her world's limitations yet prefers not to
      liberate female feeling but correct its excesses;
      and in P and P she defuses the conflict between
      sensibility and sense, endorsing "both the indi-
      vidualistic perspective inherent in the bourgeois
      value system and the authoritarian hierarchy retained
      from traditional, paternalistic society."

689   Poovey, Mary. "'The True English Style,'" in The

Proper Lady and the Woman Writer: Ideology as
Style in the Works of Mary Wollstonecraft, Mary
Shelley, and Jane Austen. (Women in Culture
and Society.) Chicago: Univ. of Chicago Press,
1984, pp. 208-40. Part of Poovey's essay
appeared originally, with the title "Persuasion
and the Promises of Love," in The Representation
of Women in Fiction, Selected Papers from the
English Institute, 1981, NS 7, ed. Carolyn G.
Heilbrun and Margaret R. Higonnet (Baltimore:
Johns Hopkins Univ. Press, 1983), pp. 152-79;
see no. 668.

Though as aware as ever of unchecked individualism's potential for chaos, JA in her later novels
increasingly criticizes the social conventions shaping women's desire. Exploring the connection between
ideology and psychology and arguing for both public
reform and personal education, she creates heroines
noteworthy for their principled feelings, such as
Fanny Price and Anne Elliot, who help dramatize the
regeneration of society "from within its own values"
and the congruence of romantic passion and morality.

690 Smith, Grahame. "Persuasion," in The Novel & Soci-
     ety: Defoe to George Eliot. London: Batsford
     Academic and Educational, 1984, pp. 116-46.

The creative tensions of P between conflicting
sets of value, including the public and the private,
the Augustan and the Romantic, help define JA's
special position in the English novel tradition.
"At the cross-roads of eighteenth and nineteenth-
century fiction," she stresses the human qualities
of social groups, balances restraint against self-
expression, and extends the older concept of
gentlemanliness into the newer idea of professionalism. She proves original as a writer while
representing objective reality.

691 Williams, Merryn. "Jane Austen," in Women in the
     English Novel, 1800-1900. New York: St. Martin's
     Press, 1984, pp. 44-52.

"A free spirit," JA typically values lively women
who feel a warm, though not obsessive, interest in
sex, preserve their integrity as they deal with money
and marriage, do their duty, and have "sisterly
affection" and "delicacy of mind." And she prefers
men who treat women not as objects of flattery but
as intellectual equals.

II. Doctoral Dissertations

1973

692 Acabal, Perla G. "Jane Austen's Moral Vision: Form
        and Function." DAI, 33 (1973), 6297A-98A (Ind.
        Univ.).

        Though portraying realistically the harsh econom-
     ic conditions of her age, JA espouses a morality "of
     the purest kind," which transcends personal and so-
     cial limitations. She uses the educational process
     to give the novels shape and to measure individual
     worth, "and the education consists mainly of an ad-
     justment to an ideal functional union of the rational
     and the emotional faculties sustaining the emotional
     intelligence."

693 Ames, Carol. "Love Triangles in Fiction: The Under-
        lying Fantasies." DAI, 34 (1973), 717A (State
        Univ. of N.Y., Buffalo).

        MP presents two possible outcomes for love trian-
     gles. While Fanny and Edmund perhaps approach "ideal
     love," Henry Crawford finds triangular relationships
     so much a part of his "sense of identity that he
     repeatedly duplicates the situation."

694 Chabot, Charles Barry. "The Vicissitudes of Desire:
        Jane Austen and the Concept of Style." DAI, 33
        (1973), 4403A (State Univ. of N.Y., Buffalo).

        (See no. 113.)

695 Clayton, David Merle. "The Transformations of the
        Object: Some Aspects of the Novel as a Problem in
        English Literature." DAI, 33 (1973), 5116A
        (Univ. of Calif., San Diego).

        If we consider "the novel as the vehicle of a
     myth of bourgeois society, one in which a subject
     seeks an object," E illustrates "the function of
     this myth in reconciling social conflict--in this
     case that between Emma's real status and the false
     maternal role she has assumed."

696 Constantine, Annette Vincze. "Wit in Jane Austen's
       Novels: An Expression of the Conflict between
       Duty and Desire." DAI, 34 (1973), 721A-22A
       (Univ. of Ill., Urbana-Champaign).

       Wit in JA indicates "much disguised hostility"
       toward society, hostility kept from becoming total
       condemnation "by the introduction of a kind of erotic
       'deus ex machina': Wentworth, Knightley, or Darcy.
       Without them, the heroines are in a bleak, unsympa-
       thetic, demanding environment. Even with them, the
       criticism remains."

697 Garland, Barbara Carolyn. "Comic Form in Nineteenth-
       Century English Fiction." DAI, 33 (1973), 4412A
       (Ind. Univ.).

       Of four different kinds of comic construction
       within the nineteenth-century English novel, "all de-
       riving from the idealized form of the hero as victor-
       victim," P, like Pickwick Papers, displays "a
       transitional comic form which has affinities with
       both the structure of the hero as victor and that
       of the hero as victor-victim."

698 Glucksman, Stuart. "The Happy Ending in Jane
       Austen." DAI, 34 (1973), 2559A-60A (State
       Univ. of N.Y., Stony Brook).

       S and S, MP, and E "address the issues of clo-
       sure raised in all Jane Austen's work: the opera-
       tions of conventions, the functions of protagonists
       and narrators, and the quality of happiness." While
       S and S's ending fails, owing to changes in char-
       acterization and focus, and MP's largely succeeds,
       except "when the narrator's partiality for Fanny
       seems compromised by 'objectivity,'" E's proves
       most satisfying because it excludes speculation
       about the future and does not alter the heroine's
       personality.

699 Hirst, Clinton Sheppard. "Jane Austen's Mansfield
       Park." DAI, 34 (1973), 1858A (Univ. of Notre
       Dame).

       MP's aesthetic problems, which concern character-
       ization, theme, and narrative point of view, "can
       best be described as manifold failures of the novel
       to embody the concept behind it." Yet the book "re-
       mains readable and rewarding," though flawed, because
       what it "so imperfectly" treats proves "so basic to
       human interests."

700 Irvine, Ian Mackay. "Figurative Representation in
      the Novels of Jane Austen: A Study of Style."
      <u>DAI</u>, 33 (1973), 6913A (Univ. of Pa.).

      "Anticipating a world of dissociations and dis-
      continuities at all levels through the progressive
      deterioration of links between form and meaning, Jane
      Austen's style works upon the reader to a moral end
      by leading him to share her consciousness of the se-
      mantic content of objective forms." She thus acti-
      vates figurative properties in ordinary structures,
      including language, literary convention, and the
      physical universe.

701 Katz, Judith Nina. "Rooms of Their Own: Forms and
      Images of Liberation in Five Novels." <u>DAI</u>, 34
      (1973), 1283A (Pa. State Univ.).

      Like <u>Evelina</u>, <u>P and P</u> depicts its heroine as hav-
      ing no choice but to enter a world defined by the
      "rooms and houses" of a society noted for "vulgarity,
      ignorance and cruelty." But through her wit she
      "resists enslavement."

702 Krier, William John. "A Pattern of Limitations: The
      Heroine's Novel of the Mind." <u>DAI</u>, 34 (1973),
      277A-78A (Ind. Univ.).

      In <u>E</u>, JA separates "her heroine's mind from the
      world" and "uses this separation to choose her hero-
      ine's mind as a more interesting subject for her fic-
      tion than the world."

703 Meyer, Joan L. "André Gide, Reader and Critic of
      the Nineteenth-Century English Novel." <u>DAI</u>,
      34 (1973), 3418A (Univ. of Conn.).

      Gide considered JA "too detached" from her
      novels.

704 Morgan, Susan. "The Changing Novel: Richardson,
      Austen, and Scott." Ph.D. diss., 1973 (Univ. of
      Chicago).

      (See no. 481.)

705 Nelson, Carolyn Christensen. "Patterns in the
      <u>Bildungsroman</u> As Illustrated by Six English
      Novels from 1814 to 1860." <u>DAI</u>, 33 (1973),
      3597A-98A (Univ. of Wis.).

Like Waverley and unlike later nineteenth-century
novels in the Bildungsroman tradition, MP, which depicts the individual's education "as a social initiation," ends "with the protagonist assuming his place
in the established society."

706 Oliver, Barbara Christine. "Eighteenth-Century
      Theory of the Beautiful, the Sublime, and the
      Picturesque, and Its Influence upon English Fic-
      tion from Henry Fielding to Walter Scott." Ph.D.
      diss., 1973 (Univ. of Newcastle upon Tyne).

      In MP, JA sets ideals of beauty, truth, and
social order against the realities of human limitation. Human beings, she finds, are too imperfect
and too much in a state of continuous change ever
to be adequately measured by any literary convention
or absolute philosophical system.

707 Pickering, Jean Eldred. "Comic Structure in the
      Novels of Jane Austen." DAI, 33 (1973), 6881A
      (Stanford Univ.).

      Form fits vision in NA, P and P, and E but
not in the other three novels, where the mis-
alignment indicates "a confusion of authorial
intention." Even in works in which JA's "literary experience was no longer a major source of
content," particularly MP and P, "she retained the
comic structure which she had first employed in
burlesque."

708 Post, Alfred Philip, III. "Jane Austen and the
      Loiterer: A Study of Jane Austen's Literary
      Heritage." DAI, 34 (1973), 333A (Univ. of
      N.C., Chapel Hill).

      Not "a direct source" for her, The Loiterer
served rather "as an influence, or as a mirror reflecting the literary tastes and attitudes of the
Austen family." Significant parallels between the
periodical and JA show that her "themes and techniques pervade her early literary environment, that
she was exposed early to those themes and techniques
that she continued to explore and re-explore throughout her life."

709 Ram, Atma. "Women Characters in the Novels of Jane
      Austen." Ph.D. diss., 1973 (Panjab Univ.).

      (See no. 610.)

710 Speakman, James Stewart. "Wit, Humor, and Sensibil-
      ity in Evelina, Belinda, and Northanger Abbey."
      DAI, 34 (1973), 791A-92A (Univ. of Calif.,
      Davis).

      More successfully than Evelina and Belinda, NA
      integrates wit, humor, and sensibility. "Writing a
      parody and a realistic comedy of manners, [JA] de-
      pends upon an omniscient second-self narrator who is
      witty, satirical and sympathetic, characters who are
      comic and sympathetic, characters who are satirical
      objects and incidents which are both comic and real-
      istic."

711 Stamper, Donald Rexford. "Success and Openness in
      English Fiction from Richardson through Jane
      Austen." DAI, 34 (1973), 2656A-57A (Univ. of
      Ark.).

      Unlike the protagonists of eighteenth-century
      fiction JA's heroines harmoniously balance internal
      and external standards of success. The "openness" or
      "unresolved conflict" at the end of her novels "re-
      sults when the quality of vision necessary for this
      harmony is compared with the vision that provided the
      basis for these characters' earlier actions."

712 Teyssandier, Hubert. "Les Formes de la création
      romanesque à l'époque de Walter Scott et de Jane
      Austen, 1814-20." 3 vols. Ph.D. diss., 1973
      (Univ. of Paris III).

      (See no. 310.)

713 Vopat, James Bernard. "The Denial of Innocence: The
      Theme of Social Responsibility in the Early
      British Novel." DAI, 33 (1973), 4437A (Univ. of
      Wash.).

      Like Robinson Crusoe, Pamela, Tom Jones, and
      Evelina, E treats "the passage from innocence to
      experience," affirming the need for self-awareness,
      "a mature social consciousness," and "rational
      values" and emphasizing the paradox that control
      "assures ultimate liberty." It also resembles those
      earlier novels in its "pervasive optimism," which
      "expresses the confidence that life, after all, can
      be managed, and, in fact, be lived as a celebration
      of order."

714 Waidner, Maralee Layman. "From Reason to Romance: A

Progression from an Emphasis on Neoclassic Ra-
tionality to Romantic Intuition in Three English
Woman Novelists." DAI, 34 (1973), 1259A-60A
(Univ. of Tulsa).

More than Charlotte and Emily Brontë, JA consults
reason "to ascertain or justify 'feeling,'" tends
toward a "social orientation" rather than a personal
one, relies on humor instead of "lyric," and characterizes individuals generically, not particularly.

1974

715 Arthurs, Alberta. "Arrangements with the Earth: Jane
     Austen's Landscapes." DAI, 34 (1974), 4185A-86A
     (Bryn Mawr College).

     JA, who inherits eighteenth-century novelistic
visions of landscape as both ethical and emotional,
uses natural settings as a source of structure, characterization, theme, and symbolism. In her career
she develops from parody of the traditions to more
various and original handling of them and becomes
less certain of the beauty and order of "man's arrangements with the earth."

716 Bhagwut, Diileep G. "Jane Austen devant la critique
     française: Étude de la réaction suscitée par
     l'oeùvre de Jane Austen en France entre 1815 et
     1972." Ph.D. diss., 1974-75 (Univ. of Paris-
     Sorbonne).

     JA alone among the great English novelists has
been neglected by the French. Though she has enjoyed
very brief periods of popularity, the Classical
rather than Romantic nature of her art and its typically English cast, notably its comic sense, have
never profoundly affected the imagination of French
readers.

717 Citino, David John. "From Pemberley to Eccles
     Street: Families and Heroes in the Fiction of
     Jane Austen, Charles Dickens, and James Joyce."
     DAI, 35 (1974), 1090A-91A (Ohio State Univ.).

     Like novels by Dickens and Joyce P and P and
E depict protagonists battling their families
and being "eventually checkmated: placed in an
untenable position in which each choice of a
route to escape and victory turns out to be no
choice at all."

718 Eisner, Seth Alan. "Jane Austen's Characters: Man-
     ners of Being." <u>DAI</u>, 34 (1974), 7747A (Univ. of
     Pa.).

     Each JA character constitutes "a special nexus in
the system of interpersonal relations" composing society, which conditions all. And "what a character,
standing within the fictional world of a novel, perceives as another's 'manners,' the reader, standing
outside that world, perceives as <u>style</u>. Style is the
enactment of selfhood in an Austen novel."

719 Higbie, Robert Griggs. "Characterization in the
     English Novel: Richardson, Jane Austen, and
     Dickens." <u>DAI</u>, 34 (1974), 4263A-64A (Ind.
     Univ.).

     An example of a "conscious" character, one who
can be aware of and "resolve the forces causing tension," Elizabeth Bennet embodies JA's view of character "as an interaction between natural impulses and
acquired self-control. Elizabeth learns to balance
feeling and restraint by seeing the imbalance in
others and by discovering that her selfish emotions
have made her misjudge others, not understanding
their private feelings."

720 Kormali, Sema Günisik. "The Treatment of Marriage in
     Representative Novels of Jane Austen and Henry
     James." <u>DAI</u>, 35 (1974), 2228A-29A (Tex. Tech
     Univ.).

     In JA "the conflict of interests and philosophies
between the heroine and the hero epitomizes the conflict between the moral and social values of a
visionary or romantic life view and those of a
realistic or conventional life view." And the protagonists' final union symbolizes the author's
"urge for a society that synthesizes reason and
emotions, individual freedom and social order."

721 Lynch, Catherine Mary. "The Reader as Guest: Jane
     Austen's Audience." <u>DAI</u>, 35 (1974), 1627A-28A
     (Univ. of Pittsburgh).

     Whether one considers the reader as "a certain
unique individual reading, at a particular time, a
given book," as "the idea in the author's mind to
which the book is written," or as "an abstraction
the critic creates by some sort of synthesis of all
or some of the available information about the book
or its author," JA establishes a unique relation-

ship "with her reader(s) by the metaphor 'guest.'"

722 Mann, Renate. "Jane Austen: Die Rhetorik der Moral."
     Ph.D. diss., 1974 (Univ. of Cologne).

     (See no. 156.)

723 Margulies, Jay Warren. "The Marriage Market: A Study
     of Variations of the Marriage Plot Convention in
     Novels by Austen, Thackeray, Eliot, James, and
     Hardy." Ph.D. diss., 1974 (Univ. of Calif.,
     Berkeley).

     Especially in E, JA uses a plot originated by
     Richardson and Fielding in which three suitors--"the
     rake," "the clergyman," and "the gentleman"--pursue
     the heroine. The third of these male types, who
     embodies the society's "highest moral and rational
     values," eventually emerges as her best possible
     choice.

724 Perebinossoff, Philippe Roger. "Home Entertainments
     and Theatre: Metaphors of Decadence and Blurred
     Reality." DAI, 34 (1974), 7774A (Univ. of Ill.,
     Urbana-Champaign).

     As in MP, "the play within a play convention
     often reenforces the themes of loss of identity and
     chaos."

725 Riley, Michael David. "Reduction and Redemption: The
     Meaning of Mansfield Park." DAI, 34 (1974),
     5926A (Ohio Univ.).

     Presenting everything as "conditional, qualified,
     complex, and frequently ambivalent," MP deliberately
     and thoroughly questions "the essential nature of the
     moral life," including our assumptions about deter-
     minism, knowledge, will, and chance. Though the
     novel insists on man's limitations and impotence, on
     the strength of error and misery, it yet affirms the
     possibility of redemption through faith, a faith
     that, among other things, gives to ethical "intention
     a value that its actual effect might seem to null-
     ify."

726 Roth, Mary Beth. "Tiresias Their Muse: Studies in
     Sexual Stereotype in the English Novel." DAI, 34
     (1974), 6604A-5A (Syracuse Univ.). See also no.
     172.

JA differs from Dickens, Meredith, Hardy, Lawrence, and Joyce in portraying the sexes as morally and psychologically similar.

727 Stewart, Kay Lanette. "The Rhetoric of the Confession: Essays in Theory and Analysis." DAI, 34 (1974), 5997A (Univ. of Oreg.).

P and P, as a novel, has a "detached" narrative stance and a "process-directed" structure.

728 Ward, John Chapman. "The Tradition of the Hypocrite in Eighteenth-Century English Literature." DAI, 34 (1974), 5128A (Univ. of Va.).

JA portrays "the figure of the hypocrite" differently from most writers of comedy in eighteenth-century English literature. She "sees the hypocrite not as a type but as a personality."

729 Weinsheimer, Joel Clyde. "Three Assays of Jane Austen's Novels." DAI, 34 (1974), 6002A-3A (Ohio Univ.).

(See nos. 93 and 185; the other essay in this dissertation, "Chance and the Hierarchy of Marriages in Pride and Prejudice," appeared originally in ELH, 39 [1972], 404-19.)

1975

730 Bedick, David B. "The Changing Role of Anxiety in the Novel." DAI, 36 (1975), 3682A (N.Y. Univ.).

MP offers "a mild Nineteenth-Century treatment" of the theme of anxiety felt by characters in response to an abrasive setting.

731 Brown, Julia Prewitt. "The Bonds of Irony: A Study of Jane Austen's Novels." DAI, 36 (1975), 1517A-18A (Columbia Univ.).

(See no. 386.)

732 Deller, Hans-Alois. "'3 or 4 Families in a Country Village'? Der Raum bei Jane Austen." Ph.D. diss., 1975 (Univ. of the Ruhr).

In her novels JA emphasizes idea and dialogue and
reduces spatial background to a minimum. When she
indicates places, she does so to characterize individuals and provide information about social rank.
And her allusions to actual locations serve as reference points for the fictional settings.

733   De Rose, Peter Louis. "Jane Austen and Samuel
      Johnson." DAI, 35 (1975), 6662A (Ind. Univ.).

      (See no. 454.)

734   Dylla, Sandra Marie. "Jane Austen and George Eliot:
      The Influence of Their Social Worlds on Their
      Women Characters." DAI, 36 (1975), 899A (Univ.
      of Wis., Milwaukee).

      The social world JA creates in her novels, in-
      cluding class structure and consciousness, educa-
      tional and economic systems, courtship and marriage,
      affects the way she develops her fictional women,
      especially as regards financial security, self-
      respect, self-knowledge, and personal relationships.

735   Fergus, Jan Stockton. "Jane Austen's Early Novels:
      The Educating of Judgment and Sympathy." DAI, 36
      (1975), 2218A (City Univ. of N.Y.).

      (See no. 632.)

736   Goubert, Pierre. "Jane Austen: Étude psychologique
      de la romancière." Ph.D. diss., 1975 (Univ. of
      Caen). This study is abstracted in EA, 28
      (1975), 370.

      (See no. 126.)

737   Greenstein, Susan Mitchell. "The Negative Principle
      and the Virtuous Character: Undercutting in the
      Work of Richardson, Austen, and James." DAI, 35
      (1975), 4521A (Ind. Univ.).

      As virtuous heroines, Fanny Price and Anne Elliot
      derive from Clarissa Harlowe. In MP, JA "encounters
      the challenge to artistic integrity offered by the
      ambiguities of severe situational undercutting,"
      which questions "the rituals of social intercourse,"
      and in P "the difficulties presented by this method
      of creating a virtuous heroine are resolved without
      calling attention to them."

738 Lachman, Michele Schurgin. "Jane Austen: Studies in
       Language and Values." DAI, 36 (1975), 2848A-49A
       (Brandeis Univ.).

       In JA's novels, which treat ethical decisions and
       language, specifically its relation to knowledge of
       others, "the narrative affects the reader's percep-
       tion of the dialogue and serves as a standard of
       evaluation."

739 Newman, Ronald Bruce. "Life Style in the Novels of
       Jane Austen." DAI, 35 (1975), 7262A-63A (Univ.
       of Mich.).

       JA represents manners "as matrices of the true,
       the good, and the beautiful, as complexes of social
       and moral values that are fundamentally rational and
       structurally aesthetic." Believing in the interde-
       pendence and unity of substance and form, she
       progresses steadily in the course of her career
       toward a perfect "correlation between the interior
       unity of her characters' style of life and the
       organicism of her style of writing."

740 Podis, JoAnne Med. "'The Way They Should Go': Family
       Relationships in the Novels of Jane Austen."
       DAI, 35 (1975), 6153A-54A (Case Western Reserve
       Univ.).

       Largely through unsuccessful relationships JA
       pictures the family's importance in the individual's
       moral development. And, though she emphasizes nega-
       tive examples, she concludes the novels with mar-
       riages promising the establishment "of family circles
       which do preserve and transmit the moral heritage."

741 Scannell, Michael. "The Treatment of Emotion in Jane
       Austen and Charlotte Brontë." Ph.D. diss., 1975
       (Univ. of Oxford).

       Like Charlotte Brontë, JA wrote in order to ex-
       plore and share personal experience, including such
       subjects as the abilities of women and such emotions
       as love. To treat these concerns in a more serious
       and authentic manner than her contemporaries, JA
       developed her own idiom, which combines elements of
       Johnson and the school of sensibility.

742 Serlen, Ellen. "The Rage of Caliban: Realism and
       Romance in the Nineteenth-Century Novel." DAI,
       36 (1975), 911A (State Univ. of N.Y., Stony

Brook). See also no. 313.

MP, which yearns for an ideal unobtainable in actuality, "encompasses a fictional world divided between the 'perfection' of Mansfield and its inhabitants and the encroaching harsh reality of nineteenth-century English city life."

743 Siefert, Susan Elizabeth. "The Dilemma of the Talented Woman: A Study in Nineteenth-Century Fiction." DAI, 36 (1975), 285A-86A (Marquette Univ.).

(See nos. 374 and 375.)

744 Smith, Louise Zandberg. "The Transforming Eye: Response to Landscape as a Measure of Social Sensibility in Late Eighteenth-Century Fiction." DAI, 35 (1975), 4558A-59A (Univ. of Va.).

Like The Monk, P rejects the "correspondence of aesthetic and social responses" that many late eighteenth-century novels rely on. P frees the protagonists "from particular estates and infuses into them through imagination the vitality and stability of unconfined nature."

745 Stoller, Annette Linda. "Jane Austen's Rhetorical Art: A Revaluation." DAI, 35 (1975), 7271A (Brown Univ.).

To persuade her readers to accept her radical views about women, JA constructs "strategies of narration with elements borrowed from ancient and neoclassical theories of rhetoric." She follows especially Blair, whose Lectures on Rhetoric and Belles Lettres influenced, among other things, her "emphasis on perspicuity and unity" and whose sermons showed "how the virtues of the heart . . . can be nourished and utilized in secular life."

746 Taylor, Roselle. "The Narrative Technique of Jane Austen: A Study in the Use of Point of View." DAI, 36 (1975), 912A (Univ. of Tex., Austin).

Anticipating the practice and theory of the twentieth-century novel, JA develops in the course of her career "a narrative technique which strives to remove the narrator from the surface of the novel and to present the story through the dramatized consciousness of the central character." With little interruption to her basic progress she thus moves from <u>NA</u>'s "conventional use of third-person narrative omniscience" to <u>P</u>'s focus on Anne as "controlling consciousness."

1976

747 Bell, David Hartman. "Connected Parts: Social Harmony in Jane Austen's Novels." <u>DAI</u>, 36 (1976), 6697A (Univ. of Calif., Irvine).

Examining "part-whole relationships from a decidedly eighteenth-century point of view," JA, like Pope, gradually loses "faith in the possibility of social harmony." While in <u>P</u> and <u>P</u> she creates a community successfully combining two key ordering principles--"natural subordination and <u>concordia discors</u>"--in the novels that follow she concentrates increasingly on fragmentation, lack of connection, and "threats to social coherence."

748 Burlin, Katrin Ristkok. "Jane Austen: 'The Labours of Art.'" <u>DAI</u>, 37 (1976), 1560A (Princeton Univ.). See also no. 132.

By creating characters who invent their own fictions and play with different kinds of literature, JA treats "the Johnsonian theme of the tyranny of fiction-making, which in turn permits her to explore the consequences of her own art and the responsibility of the artist." Her novels, conceived in this manner as "essays on writing," thus explore "the possibilities of genre, experimenting until the last with the <u>best</u> form."

749 Cohen, Sue Winters. "Threat and Resistance: Society vs. the Individual in the Novels of Jane Austen." <u>DAI</u>, 36 (1976), 7433A (Ohio State Univ.).

The novels both affirm and criticize society, offering protagonists who believe in traditional values like generosity and justice but live in a world that tries to turn them from their ideals. The heroines struggle to preserve or discover their best selves "in spite of the intense pressure to conform to immorality," and marriage signifies the success of resistance and "the possibility of a true society."

750 Curry, Steven Scott. "The Literature of Loss: A

Study of Nineteenth-Century English and American
Fiction." DAI, 37 (1976), 1529A-30A (Univ. of
Calif., Davis).

Like The Scarlet Letter, E treats "the character
of the feminine spirit and the ineffectual but nonetheless obstructive role of the patriarchal social
order."

751   Dry, Helen. "Syntactic Reflexes of Point of View in
        Jane Austen's Emma." DAI, 37 (1976), 263A (Univ.
        of Tex., Austin).

        (See no. 259.)

752   Dvorak, Evelyn Fearing. "Technique as Moral Purpose:
        Parody and Romance in the Development of Jane
        Austen's Narrative Method." DAI, 37 (1976),
        2194A-95A (Ind. Univ.).

        In progressing from parody to realism, JA merges
        "Richardson's use of eye-witness or 'participating'
        narrators with Fielding's use of reliable, omniscient
        'authorial' narrators." This combination of differ-
        ent ways to establish "the 'authority' of narrators
        in relation to the values of the implied author" and
        incorporate the romance's ethics and aesthetics into
        realistic fiction helps JA make her created world
        appear authentic, present her characters' subjective
        experience, and express her moral vision.

753   Fairclough, Peter Frederick. "Humour in the Novel,
        1800-1850: The Moral Vision and the Autonomous
        Imagination." Ph.D. diss., 1976 (Univ. of
        Warwick).

        Like Peacock and Byron, JA questioned the
        eighteenth-century tradition of amiable humor. For
        her the individualism implicit in the concept of the
        humorous character threatened social order.

754   Francone, Carol Burr. "Women in Rebellion: A Study
        of the Conflict between Self-Fulfillment and
        Self-Sacrifice in Emma, Jane Eyre, and The Mill
        on the Floss." DAI, 36 (1976), 4507A (Case
        Western Reserve Univ.).

        Because JA in E, like Charlotte Brontë in Jane
        Eyre and George Eliot in The Mill on the Floss, "re-
        jected the false image of women presented in the bulk
        of fiction in favor of the image" based on her own

intelligence and experience, her heroine reflects "the real nature of womanhood and the real problems of women in a patriarchal society."

755 Gandesbery, Jean Johnson. "Versions of the Mother in the Novels of Jane Austen and George Eliot." DAI, 37 (1976), 3640A-41A (Univ. of Calif., Davis).

Unlike most nineteenth-century English novelists JA and George Eliot picture maternal figures--whether "social-climbing," "destructive," "lazy, stupid," or "ideal"--as "agents of control, not just paternal foils. Part of the basis for Austen and Eliot's concentration upon maternal significance resides in the necessity for the female artist to discover her own identity as a woman, never completely independent of male authority but always critical and skeptical of its implications and demands."

756 Hass, Robert Louis. "Reason's Children: Economic Ideology and the Themes of Fiction, 1720-1880." DAI, 36 (1976), 8033A-34A (Stanford Univ.).

MP and Moll Flanders represent "typical instances of the novelist's way of imagining economic man through the metaphors of orphaning, theft, and in-heritance."

757 Hilliard, Raymond Francis. "Role-playing and the Development of Jane Austen's Psychological Realism." DAI, 37 (1976), 2895A-96A (Univ. of Rochester).

"The first English novelist to perfect the tech-nique of delineating radical internal changes in a character's perception of himself," JA becomes in-creasingly insightful about role-playing as she develops her psychological realism. She structures each novel so that the heroine, discovering the truth about others who "play rather than fill social roles," may come to know herself and her own roles better.

758 Hutton, Alice H. "The Satiric Novels of Jane Austen." DAI, 37 (1976), 2197A (Univ. of South Fla.).

JA's satiric vision and techniques mature throughout her career. She begins by attacking, in NA and S and S, the follies of sentimental

fiction and turns in her later novels to "the vices
as well as the follies of both literature and life."
She develops, too, in her treatment of satiric "plot,
characterization, and thought and diction," P and P
and E representing her finest handling of all these
elements.

759   Levin, Jane Aries. "Marriage in the Novels of Jane
      Austen." DAI, 37 (1976), 335A (Yale Univ.).

      Marriage serves as a fitting comic ending to JA's
      novels; it fulfills "our wish for love and order
      without falsifying our sense of reality" because "the
      moral exertions needed to achieve the ability to make
      a proper marriage assure that its happiness is fully
      earned, and allow the concluding marriages to cele-
      brate an order that is satisfying but hardly simple."

760   Mills, Russell. "Settings in Fiction: A Study of
      Five English Novels." DAI, 36 (1976), 7442A-43A
      (Ind. Univ.).

      Concerned in MP with the relation between the
      individual and society, JA focuses on "public ob-
      jects. . . . Her country houses are reflections, of-
      ten sharply ironic, of their owner's personalities."

761   Sherry, James John. "The Limits of Detachment and
      Involvement: A Dialectical Reading of Jane
      Austen's Novels." DAI, 37 (1976), 340A (Johns
      Hopkins Univ.). See also no. 435.

      Each of the novels dialectically explores "the
      limits of detachment and involvement": in NA and S
      and S "this dialectic is bound up with the problem
      of convention"; in P and P and E the dialectic "is
      given a more specifically social formulation"; and
      in MP and P "the dialogue between detachment and
      involvement modulates into a concern for the re-
      spective values of past and present, traditional and
      new."

762   Sieferman, Sylvia Lynn. "Language and Structure in
      Jane Austen's Novels." DAI, 36 (1976), 6120A-
      21A (Stanford Univ.). See also no. 436.

      P and P, E, and P explore how the individual uses
      words for comprehension, expression, and self-
      definition, the first novel studying descriptive and
      the second prescriptive language and the third not
      simply opposing these two kinds of language but

joining emotion and imagination "with descriptive
language in a new way." While P and P and P affirm
language's adequacy "to carry the full weight of
human understanding and feeling," E concludes that
words do not necessarily achieve truth.

763 Spence, Jon Hunter. "From Prudence to Romance: Some
     Aspects of Jane Austen's Evolving Views of Nature
     and Society." Ph.D. diss., 1976 (Univ. of
     London). See also no. 562.

JA's major theme in her first four completed
novels is man's relationship to social forms, that
is, to a world of man's own creating. In E and P she
adds to this concern a growing awareness of the power
and mystery of physical nature, which she sees as a
haphazard force shaping human destiny.

764 Sprinker, John Michael. "'Questions of Air and
     Form': Fictional Paradigms in Jane Austen,
     George Meredith, and Henry James." DAI, 37
     (1976), 1535A (Princeton Univ.).

By fitting her novels to the pattern of romantic
comedy, JA implicitly affirms that fiction has meaning, and by creating well-ordered societies, she
implies that the individual can achieve social integration. Such integration derives from an educational process involving language.

765 Stwertka, Eva Maria. "Created Images of Author and
     Reader in Seven English Novels from 1747 to
     1953." DAI, 36 (1976), 7446A-47A (St. John's
     Univ.).

Like Our Mutual Friend and Middlemarch, E assumes
"a conservationist and civilizing function." It
"unequivocally draws the reader into its centripetal
dynamics by giving instruction in the countless acts
of discrimination and judgment which preserve a well-
centered world from entropy."

766 Wingard, Sara Burke. "The Journey as Initiation and
     Revelation in the Works of Jane Austen." DAI, 36
     (1976), 5330A (Univ. of Ga.).

JA uses travel as "a complex and flexible means
of initiation and revelation for both her characters
and her readers. Through her explorations of the
psychological ramifications of a journey in time and
space, she bridges the gap between the eighteenth

century's emphasis on the external and spectacular
events of a journey and the modern emphasis on the
interior investigation of the mind and heart."

1977

767 Bauska, Kathy Anderson. "The Feminine Dream of Hap-
     piness: A Study of the Woman's Search for Intel-
     ligent Love and Recognition in Selected English
     Novels from Clarissa to Emma." DAI, 38 (1977),
     1403A (Univ. of Wash.).

     E presents the themes of community, intelligent
     love, and the male's protective guidance--themes
     begun in the English novel by Richardson--as attrac-
     tive but visionary, for the story takes place "in a
     safely pastoral (and therefore artificial) land-
     scape." And P, which "prefigures a change in the
     feminine dream of the future," concerns loneliness,
     social fragmentation, and the difficulties a woman
     faces in having her worth acknowledged.

768 Carter, Barbara Sue. "Jane Austen: The Moral Impera-
     tive." DAI, 38 (1977), 801A (Univ. of Md.).

     JA's novels describe "a moral imperative, a di-
     rection one should take to come to successful terms
     with life." According to this imperative, one must
     face reality, care for one's family, achieve self-
     knowledge, raise children soundly, use conscience as
     a guide, act responsibly and compassionately to those
     less fortunate, and obey social codes.

769 Fulton, Karen Uitvlugt. "Illusions of Innocence: The
     Character of Evil in Jane Austen's Novels." DAI,
     37 (1977), 4366A (Case Western Reserve Univ.).

     "There are only illusions of innocence in
     Austen's world," which emphasizes "the evil of our
     thoughts, words, and actions" and where luck plays
     as important a part in achieving happiness as
     virtue. In this world the heroine confronts evil,
     which partly stems from herself, and shapes her life
     accordingly, defining "for herself what is accepted,
     what is tolerated, and what is destructive to her."

770 Held, Leonard Edgar. "The Reader in Northanger Ab-
     bey." DAI, 38 (1977), 805A (Univ. of N.Mex.).

     Though potentially disruptive, the narrator's

"elusive and inconsistent" commentary in NA coalesces "the reader's own composition" of the novel and strengthens one's connection to the work. In addition, the novel's structure forces "the reader into the emotional center of Catherine's various encounters" and leads to a better understanding, among other things, of her imagination, Henry's rationality, and the ending's "false optimism."

771   Law, Dale Raymond. "Education to Perfection in the Novels of Jane Austen." DAI, 38 (1977), 3517A-18A (Univ. of Wis., Madison).

JA's novels "show her active and sustained interest in controversies over education and the status of woman." S and S parallels Wollstonecraft's Vindication and, like Locke, considers nurture a more important educator than nature. MP, in contrast, which resembles Rousseau's Émile, "substitutes a sort of determinism, with 'nature' supreme and education the object of heavy irony." Finally, P "reconciles nature and nurture in Anne Elliot, the heroine raised to a higher level of perfection than any other."

772   Livingston, Judith Hochstein. "The Impact of Africa upon Major British Literary Figures, 1787-1902." Ph.D. diss., 1977 (Univ. of Wis., Madison). This study is abstracted in DAI, 38 (1978), 4847A.

JA knew of the slave trade and the abolitionist movement, referring indirectly to these issues in E, P, and, most prominently, MP, where she suggests that the gentry should adopt more humane social attitudes.

773   Martin, Susanna. "The Eighteenth-Century Novel Heroine--A Changing Ideal: A Study of Novel Heroines from Aphra Behn to Jane Austen." Ph.D. diss., 1977 (Univ. of Vienna).

JA reflects the shift in the eighteenth-century English novel from the creation of sensual, high-spirited heroines, who form part of elegant society, to an emphasis on colder, more languishing figures, who dedicate themselves to the home. In addition, she seeks, like other women writers of the period, to better women's education and abolish conventional prejudices against educated women.

774   Robbins, Susan Pepper. "The Included Letter in Jane Austen's Fiction." DAI, 37 (1977), 4375A (Univ. of Va.).

JA rejected the novel of letters for the novel
that includes letters because the former assumes society's stability and uniformity, and she wished to
explore "the ambiguous relationship of the private
life to public norms" and the family's changing
nature. "From Sense and Sensibility where the
letter is rejected as evidence to Persuasion where
it is used as gesture, we see Austen's redefinition
of the device of the letter in the structure of
fiction."

775 Tamm, Merike. "Inter-Art Relations and the Novels of
     Jane Austen." DAI, 37 (1977), 5149A-50A (Univ.
     of Wis., Madison). See also no. 438.

"Inter-art study" contributes to our understanding of JA, among other ways, by distinguishing literary realism from realism found in the visual arts,
by showing "how activities involving various arts can
be used in defining the themes and creating the
structure of novels" (as in S and S and E), and by
explaining her own views on relationships among the
arts "and what she saw as the reasons for pursuing
activities involving the arts."

776 Taylor, Nancy McKeon. "Conscious Construction: The
     Concept of Plot in Five Novels by Women." DAI,
     38 (1977), 2115A (Loyola Univ. of Chicago).

In E, "by concealing the traditional plot, Jane
Austen focuses our attention on a major plot which
confronts the social and literary expectations upon
which the minor or traditional plot is based.
Through the major plot, she explores the effect of
private consciousness on a world (and a novel)
oriented toward an external system of roles and
behavior. At the end, the innovative plot is sur-
rendered to the traditional plot."

777 Weiser, Irwin Howard. "Alternatives to the Myth of
     the Family: A Study of Parent-Child Relationships
     in Selected Nineteenth-Century English Novels."
     DAI, 37 (1977), 7147A-48A (Ind. Univ.).

JA uses and modifies "eighteenth-century fictional conventions dealing with the family, such
as tyrannical fathers and interfering relatives,"
and accepts the values of the myth of the family
as "a source of happiness, stability, and moral
propriety," though not necessarily the actual
existence of such families.

778 Youngren, Virginia Rotan. "Moral Life in Solitude:
     A Study of Selected Novels of Jane Austen, Char-
     lotte Brontë, Elizabeth Gaskell, and George El-
     iot." DAI, 38 (1977), 814A-15A (Rutgers Univ.,
     New Brunswick).

     JA, Charlotte Brontë, Elizabeth Gaskell, and
     George Eliot all maintain a "feminine and domestic"
     point of view, one which "emphasizes the value of
     introspection and a private moral perspective and is
     articulated by an essentially private writing voice."
     They consider life's circumstances "more a burden and
     a challenge than a 'fate'" and virtue "complex and
     uncertain."

1978

779 Anderson, Mary Lynn. "Lexical Cohesion in Emma: An
     Approach to the Semantic Analysis of Style."
     DAI, 38 (1978), 4837A (George Peabody College for
     Teachers).

     Study of two forms of lexical cohesion in E--the
     reiterative and the collocational--helps in analyzing
     style and in pointing to relationships among differ-
     ent aspects of the novel. "Ultimately, however,
     there is a cohesion in Emma which cannot be iden-
     tified grammatically or statistically, but must be
     appreciated intuitively."

780 Armstrong, Nancy Bowes. "Character and Closure in
     Selected Nineteenth-Century Novels." DAI, 38
     (1978), 6736A (Univ. of Wis., Madison).

     Like Jane Eyre, P and P results from "increas-
     ingly optimistic individualism, most perfectly mani-
     fested in the Bildungsroman form where the individual
     is thought to be capable of 'self-fulfillment.'"

781 Flynn, Thomas Peter. "The Growth of Community in
     Jane Austen's Mansfield Park." DAI, 38 (1978),
     7343A-44A (Ohio Univ.).

     Opposed to materialism and selfishness, "the
     charitable community [established at the end] of
     Mansfield Park demonstrates that in Austen's work
     the characters band together to form such groups
     because they have learned that only by coordinat-
     ing their life with others who act on Christian
     principles can men establish an orderly environment

in which they can most fully be themselves."

782   Graeber, George. "Comic, Thematic, and Mimetic Im-
        pulses in Jane Austen's Persuasion." DAI, 38
        (1978), 6141A (Mich. State Univ.).

        P has a "fully developed comic structure" cele-
        brating life's renewal, "clearly articulated themes"
        related to persuasion and duty, and "rich mimetic
        characterization," notably that of the heroine, whom
        we may conceive according to psychologist Karen
        Horney's views as a proud, "compulsive," and "defen-
        sive" "perfectionist." Yet P does not adequately
        integrate these "thematic, mimetic, and structural
        impulses" and proves most powerful in its "mimetic
        portraiture."

783   Grossman, Miriam. "Jane Austen: The Testing of Wit."
        DAI, 39 (1978), 295A-96A (Columbia Univ.).

        JA tests wit throughout her career, progressing
        from scattered early comments to a "sustained philo-
        sophical and moral inquiry." In P and P, MP, and E
        she defines "wit as a central, broadly human activ-
        ity, involving at its best . . . both manner and
        intellect" but recognizes as well "that too often, in
        practice, wit abdicates its intellectual function and
        deteriorates into mere manner." And in P she argues
        that "wit is no longer defensible, or even neces-
        sary."

784   Hunt, Linda Sussman. "Ideology, Culture, and the
        Female Novel Tradition: Studies in Jane Austen,
        Charlotte Brontë, and George Eliot as Nineteenth-
        Century Women Writers." DAI, 39 (1978), 897A-98A
        (Univ. of Calif., Berkeley).

        JA's literary achievement derives partly from her
        complex relationship to the tradition of women's fic-
        tion: she struggled "to reconcile the ideal of femi-
        ninity which prevailed in her day with her commitment
        to the real in art."

785   Miller, David Albert. "Narrative and Its Discon-
        tents: Jane Austen, George Eliot, Stendhal."
        DAI, 39 (1978), 1534A-35A (Yale Univ.).

        (See no. 546.)

786   Rosenbaum, Jane Elaine. "On Trial and Found Wanting:

The Heroine and Her Society in Jane Austen's Novels." <u>DAI</u>, 38 (1978), 5501A (Univ. of Pittsburgh).

Contrary to much critical opinion, JA's novels do not endorse but ridicule "the eighteenth century's prevailing ideas" about social issues. <u>P</u> <u>and</u> <u>P</u>, for example, describes a heroine embracing "the superficial principles of a society which she has, with our blessing, initially denigrated"; <u>MP</u> seriously qualifies the moral righteousness of its protagonists; and both <u>E</u> and <u>P</u> question accepted values and forms.

787 Timson, Beth Snavely. "'In My Father's House': The Structure of Inheritance in Modern British and American Fiction." <u>DAI</u>, 39 (1978), 2934A (Vanderbilt Univ.).

Though different otherwise, <u>MP</u> and <u>Wuthering Heights</u> resemble each other structurally, for both follow the pattern of inheriting a house, a pattern that seems particularly English rather than American.

1979

788 August, Richard Kenneth. "A Critical Study of Wallace Stevens' <u>Notes</u> <u>toward</u> <u>a</u> <u>Supreme</u> <u>Fiction</u>; <u>The</u> <u>Two</u> <u>Noble</u> <u>Kinsmen</u>: A Modern Edition; Family Politics in Jane Austen's Novels." <u>DAI</u>, 39 (1979), 4264A (Rutgers Univ., New Brunswick).

JA's treatment of the family develops in the course of her career. Early (in <u>S</u> <u>and</u> <u>S</u> and <u>P</u> <u>and</u> <u>P</u>) she explores the family's strong bonds; later (in <u>The</u> <u>Watsons</u> and <u>MP</u>) she discusses disintegrating family connections; and finally (in <u>E</u>, <u>P</u>, and <u>Sanditon</u>) she proceeds to the heroine's separation from the family. JA also focuses in the last novels on illness and hypochondria to show the family's decay and the protagonist's health.

789 Burt, Della A. "The Widening Arc and the Closed Circle: A Study of Problematic Novel Endings." Ph.D. diss., 1979 (Ind. Univ.). This study is abstracted in <u>DAI</u>, 40 (1980), 4011A.

Though excessively didactic, <u>MP</u>'s conclusion does accord with the novel's moral structure. Moreover, "the ending shows a tendency towards openness because the narrator implies that the peace [Fanny and Edmund] now enjoy cannot be continuous without

renewed and successful struggle. Yet we get a sense
of completeness because we have been assured throughout that while they may not be able to change the
world, they have the moral stamina to meet the challenge."

790 Devor, Alice Noyes. "Jane Austen--Student and
     Teacher: A Study of Jane Austen's Use of Educa-
     tional Ideas in Her Novels." DAI, 39 (1979),
     4267A (Univ. of Kans.).

     JA uses her life-long educational interests func-
     tionally "in the narration and in the delineation of
     characters in her novels," both criticizing women's
     generally poor education and revealing her regard for
     education that develops good reading habits and the
     ability to reason. Early in her career she communi-
     cates her ideas about education through direct com-
     mentary and later less obtrusively, and she tends
     throughout the novels to make morally worthy indi-
     viduals well-educated.

791 Freedman, Francine Susan. "'Ceremonies of Life':
     Manners in the Novels of Jane Austen." DAI, 39
     (1979), 7355A (Tufts Univ.).

     "The detailed code of behavior so obvious in the
     novels has a purpose and a meaning far beyond the
     mere reflection of contemporary custom. Furthermore
     . . . those who find her insistence on propriety
     trivial have failed to understand the ethical and
     psychological bases of manners in the novels, or
     what they reveal about Austen's main themes: the
     nature of moral life, social order, and self-
     knowledge."

792 Goode, Alice. "Mothers and Daughters and the Novel."
     DAI, 40 (1979), 1447A (State Univ. of N.Y., Stony
     Brook).

     "Jane Austen, and her successors as well, portray
     the power of mothers as grotesque when they try to
     fulfill their responsibilities, and land their daugh-
     ters in the arms of security and respectability."

793 Hawkes, Daniel. "Jane Austen: Heroines and Hori-
     zons." DAI, 39 (1979), 4272A-73A (Rutgers Univ.,
     New Brunswick).

     "Austen's works are not defenses against 'in-

volvement' but a criticism of the limited possibilities, particularly for women, within a genteel society increasingly permeated by bourgeois values.
Far from being against internality, Austen tries to
develop within her chief female figures a kind of
subjectivity that avoids usurping or manipulating
others."

794   Horwitz, Barbara Joan.   "Jane Austen and the Writers
     on Women's Education." DAI, 40 (1979), 1482A
     (State Univ. of N.Y., Stony Brook).

     JA resembles late eighteenth-century writers on
women's education in discussing pedagogical goals and
methods but differs in insisting on self-knowledge as
education's aim and refusing "to be dogmatic about
human behavior," especially in regard to sexual
stereotyping. As a result, her novels lack "the
didacticism and tendentiousness that mark" other
works of the period.

795   Jones, Elizabeth Falk.   "Ends and Means of Fictions:
     Hard Times and Mansfield Park." DAI, 39 (1979),
     6776A-77A (State Univ. of N.Y., Stony Brook).

     Rather than a didactic fiction about education,
MP constitutes "a comic plot of situation," and as
such "the primary function of values is as a means of
eliciting appropriate responses to the agents and
events of the action." When we read MP thus, we can
grasp the working of the novel's different parts and
explain "the pleasurable yet serious effect of the
whole."

795a   Jones, Hannah Hinson.   "Jane Austen and Eight Minor
     Contemporaries: A Study in the Novel, 1800-
     1820." Ph.D. diss., 1979 (Univ. of Newcastle
     upon Tyne).

     Although JA shared much with novelists popular
in the early nineteenth century, including Mary
Brunton, Elizabeth Hamilton, and Amelia Opie, her
work impressed the reading public less than theirs
because it seemed lacking in excitement, emotion,
"elevation of virtue," and novelty.

796   Kaplan, Deborah Ellen.   "Structures of Status:
     Eighteenth-Century Social Experience as Form
     in Courtesy Books and Jane Austen's Nov-
     els." DAI, 39 (1979), 7357A (Brandeis
     Univ.).

As regards "status experience of persons of mid-
dling and upper ranks in England in the eighteenth
century," both JA's novels and courtesy books depend
on social context for their structures but, because
they belong to different genres, express such structures differently. In JA's novels these structures,
termed "witnessing, evaluating, and knowing," function not only as the characters' typical behaviors
but have as well "a symbolic dimension, an existence"
in the characters' minds.

797 Noonan, Paula Elizabeth. "Women and Love: Feminine
      Perspectives on Love and Sexuality in the Fiction
      of 19th- and 20th-Century Women Writers." DAI,
      40 (1979), 252A (Univ. of Denver).

"At least since Jane Austen" women writers "describe a particularly feminine ambivalence toward
ideals of love which, until the nineteenth century,
have been defined primarily by men. Symptoms of this
ambivalence appear first in the increasingly critical
feelings of women in fiction about their sexual relationships."

798 Packer, P. A. "The Portrayal of the Anglican Clergy-
      man in Some Nineteenth-Century Fiction." Ph.D.
      diss., 1979 (Univ. of Durham).

Reflecting her middle-class background and in
keeping with her general consideration of society,
JA portrays her clergymen as men rather than priests:
"personally varied" and observed sharply and accurately, they "scale no heights of sanctity and reach
no depths of degradation but they come alive across
the years as many later, more detailed and decidedly
clerical portraits do not."

799 Rothmel, Steven Zachary. "Similarities in the Nov-
      elistic Techniques of Jane Austen and Henry
      James." DAI, 39 (1979), 6148A-49A (Univ. of
      Utah).

JA and James, devising "similar techniques for
efficiently conveying the richness and the complexity of life," dramatize a story whenever possible, minimize their own presence, reveal their
characters, who are fully human, through speech and
thought processes, and create meaningful settings
for the action. Through such innovation and adaptation of different narrative methods "these craftsmen
meld the novel's parts into a cohesive appealing
whole."

800   Seidel, Kathleen Gilles. "How Novels End: A Study of
      Henry Fielding and Jane Austen." DAI, 39 (1979),
      5506A-7A (Johns Hopkins Univ.).

      "Rather similar," the conclusions of JA's and
      Fielding's novels perform four functions: "the
      closural," including changes in narrative stance
      and sentence patterns, "the terminating," involving
      signals that the work will soon end, "the summative,"
      which ties up loose ends, and "the narrative," which
      continues the story. In addition, JA's endings show
      her valuing clarity and certainty and attempting to
      conceal a work's fictionality.

801   Thurin, Susan Molly Schoenbauer. "Marriageability: A
      Study of the Factors Entering the Marriage Choice
      in Eight English Novels." DAI, 40 (1979), 2080A
      (Univ. of Wis., Milwaukee).

      Like eighteenth-century novels P and P connects
      marriageability "to the development of democratic
      values and individualism," and unlike later
      nineteenth-century novels, though it challenges
      society, it finally supports traditional beliefs.
      In addition, "the pre- and post-Austen novels
      reverse the presentation of ideal and flawed mar-
      riages in the major and minor characters."

                              1980

802   Butler, Mary Elizabeth. "The Rhetoric of Self-
      Consciousness and of Self-Knowledge in Moll
      Flanders, Evelina, Anna St. Ives, and Emma."
      DAI, 40 (1980), 5061A-62A (Stanford Univ.).

      Unlike the protagonists of some other novels Emma
      progresses safely from a solipsistic state to ac-
      knowledgment of her connection to others and thus
      learns "from their experience of themselves and of
      the world."

803   Carson, Sydney Sylvia Rosenbaum. "Indefiniteness in
      the Novel: Jane Austen, Virginia Woolf, Gertrude
      Stein." DAI, 40 (1980), 4011A (Univ. of Calif.,
      Berkeley).

      JA, Woolf, and Stein share many concerns. Among
      other things they take as their basic subject "con-
      sciousness with all its indefinite dimensions," value
      "vulnerability and receptivity," not "manipulation
      and power," and perceive reality as complex, even

contradictory. In addition, they believe regeneration derives from acknowledging "the endless and
infinitely rich possibilities of not only one's own
unique and secret inner life but also an equally
awesome inner life in others."

804   Clayton, John Bunyan, IV. "Romanticism and the
      English Novel: Visionary Experience in Narra-
      tive." DAI, 40 (1980), 5063A (Univ. of Va.).

      "Jane Austen persistently undercuts the romantic
      impulse toward visionary experience in Mansfield
      Park. Fanny Price, though physically passive, has a
      wandering spirit which can create lyric interludes
      in the midst of narrative. Yet these still moments
      threaten to isolate her from others."

805   Darma, Budi. "Character and Moral Judgment in Jane
      Austen's Novels." DAI, 41 (1980), 259A (Ind.
      Univ.).

      To enunciate her morality and entertain simulta-
      neously JA manipulates point of view and creates
      fallible characters. In NA, for example, she treats
      us as needing instruction, and in P and P and E she
      invites us to judge the protagonist "through the nar-
      rator's voice." And she uses her characters to
      reveal that only those who develop "good moral
      qualities, despite their weaknesses at the begin-
      ning, are able to act as moral agents."

806   Dunbar, Jean Catherine. "Words in a Line: Process as
      Novelistic Concept and Technique." DAI, 41
      (1980), 1574A-75A (Univ. of Va.).

      Like Gertrude Stein's career JA's "development
      reveals a gradual acceptance of fluctuating percep-
      tion." Her "acknowledgement that the perceptible
      world embodies the ideal makes language, with its
      (for her) absolute meanings, a path to reality.
      Thus, Jane Austen's moral sense is her aesthetic
      sense."

807   Durgun, Lynn Kathryn Hogan. "Jane Austen's Art of
      Adjustment: Symbolic Presentation in Four Nov-
      els." DAI, 41 (1980), 2611A (Syracuse Univ.).

      As evidenced by, among other things, the handling
      of Pemberley in P and P, the theme of improvement in
      MP, the treatment of carriages in E, and the idea of
      time in P, symbolism in these novels "is of the most

skillfully integrated sort, a simultaneous expansion
and concentration of meaning." JA here "amplifies
meaning without disturbing the verisimilitude of the
characters or the progress of the narrative in passages of verbal and thematic resonance."

808 Jacobs, Maureen Sheehan. "Beyond the Castle: The
     Development of the Paradigmatic Female Story."
     DAI, 41 (1980), 679A-80A (American Univ.).

     Of the two means of reshaping the Gothic novel's
"paradigmatic female story," JA in NA represents the
humorous mode, Charlotte Brontë in Jane Eyre the
angry one.

809 Kubitschek, Martha Dehn. "Self and Society in the
     Novel: The Victorian Synthesis." DAI, 40 (1980),
     5452A (Univ. of Ill., Urbana-Champaign).

     Unlike Charlotte Brontë, who stresses "the per-
sonal suffering from social injustices," JA emphasizes "the necessity of personal adjustments to the
surrounding society."

810 Milech, Barbara Hoehl. "Narrative Transactions: Jane
     Austen's Novels and the Reader's Role in the
     Construction of Narrative Meaning." DAI, 41
     (1980), 263A-64A (Ind. Univ.).

     JA dramatizes "the paradox of the realization of
the free self in and through community." In addition, a text's meaning "is contingent upon, mediated
by, the reader's activity." Thus, "the reader's
affective experience of a narrative is both the means
and the product of her or his reconstruction of the
text's implicit attitude or meaning."

811 Olive, Barbara Ann. "The Eighteenth-Century Family
     and Puritan Domestic Literature: A Study of the
     Origin and Development of Fictional Domestic
     Themes." DAI, 40 (1980), 4610A (Southern Ill.
     Univ., Carbondale).

     JA's novels, like Richardson's and Fielding's,
reveal the influence of "Puritan domestic conduct
manuals" as well as a shift to a more worldly version of courtesy literature. Her novels thus, while
developing the significance of domestic relationships, portray the family as losing some of its
traditional functions and partly replace "attention
to familial duty based in religion . . . by a

preoccupation with more secular concerns of courtship
and marriage."

812   Pettigrew, Joan A. "Sentimentalism as a Mythology:
       Samuel Richardson, Henry Fielding, Laurence
       Sterne, and Jane Austen." DAI, 40 (1980), 5877A-
       78A (Brown Univ.).

       Unlike Fielding, JA considers moral discernment
       more significant than benevolence. "Her characters
       frequently disregard sentimental strictures about
       benevolent behavior when such activity stands in the
       way of their judgments," and happiness results not
       from merely being benevolent but from perceiving,
       classifying, and assessing "affections according to
       sentimental dogma."

813   Wright, Richard Joseph. "The Siege of Reason: A
       Study of Jane Austen, George Meredith, and E. M.
       Forster." DAI, 40 (1980), 4065A (Univ. of
       Calif., Berkeley).

       Sharing "a creative sensibility," JA, Meredith,
       and Forster all shape their fiction by "the tension
       between comic and romantic elements": they use both
       irony, particularly in novels deflating romantic
       idealism, and "romantic technique," namely, "compa-
       rable patterns of imagery for similar symbolic
       purposes."

                           1981

814   Bander, Elaine. "Jane Austen's Readers." DAI, 42
       (1981), 1642A (McGill Univ.). See also no. 319.

       "Readers in the novels illuminate her assumptions
       about readers of the novels." In NA, S and S, and P
       and P good readers, among other things, "trust their
       own educated judgments rather than rely upon external
       monitors," and in MP, E, and P "readers are invited
       to judge without monitor or narrator to direct them."

815   Bennett, Paula. "Family Relationships in the Novels
       of Jane Austen." DAI, 41 (1981), 4717A (Univ. of
       Wash.).

       JA's view of the family corresponds to the ideals
       of social reformers like Locke and Defoe and empha-
       sizes, among other things, a balanced distribution of
       power and freedom in the home, love and respect as

the basis for marriage, and the significance of one's relationship with siblings. "Her perception of character development and the influence of parents on their children also reflects the rise of science and Newton's discovery of universal laws of cause and effect."

816 Cohen, Paula Marantz. "Heroinism: The Woman as the Vehicle for Values in the Nineteenth-Century English Novel from Jane Austen to Henry James." DAI, 42 (1981), 222A (Columbia Univ.).

In the early novels, which picture a world with clearly defined limits, JA's heroine "has no imagination to speak of," and in the later ones, where society has lost established boundaries, she uses her imagination to reestablish order. But throughout the canon the heroine's imaginative faculty causes tension "since it must work against itself in order to place her back within a traditional self-effacing role."

817 Haberhern, Margot Anne. "Imitation with a Twist: The Literature of Exhaustion and Beyond." DAI, 41 (1981), 4705A (Fla. State Univ.).

Like The Fall, The Sot-Weed Factor, and The French Lieutenant's Woman, NA exemplifies the ironic imitation of a literary model: it combines "authorial presence and the fact of the fiction . . . with references to prior works," creates a protagonist who inverts the figure of the hero, traces the protagonist's departure from home and journey to an unknown world, and includes mythic elements.

818 Johnson, Claudia L. "Using the Mind Well: The Moral Life in Jane Austen's Novels and the Heritage of Johnson and Locke." DAI, 41 (1981), 4720A-21A (Princeton Univ.). See also nos. 643a and 644.

From Johnson and Locke, JA "inherited a dynamic conception of the mind and a belief that moral agency as well as sanity depend on disciplining mental activities properly. Within the genre of comedy and the confines of domestic life, Austen investigates the moral dimensions of assent, wishing, wit, memory, anticipation and other activities."

819 Kantrov, Ilene M. "'A Deep and Enlightened Piety': The Religious Background of Jane Austen's Fiction." DAI, 41 (1981), 4042A (Tufts Univ.).

A Christian novelist, JA reflects contemporary religious doctrine. She espouses a morality founded on faith, makes the church's terminology an integral part of her language, and creates characters whose behavior exemplifies religious norms and errors frequently cited in the sermons of the day. In addition, she believes in original sin and constantly examines the virtues of humility and charity and the defects of pride and selfishness.

820 McKenzie, Lee Smith. "Jane Austen, Henry James, and the Family Romance." DAI, 41 (1981), 4404A (Univ. of Okla.).

JA and James resemble each other, among other ways, in their ironic voice, concern for novel form, use of manners to arrive at truth, focus on family relationships, and preference for the Cinderella story. And in one variation of this fairy tale, in which the heroine marries a brother or father figure rather than the prince, both writers depict society's fragmentation and the retreat from modern anxieties "into the intimacy of the childhood family."

821 Miller, Katharine Fraser. "The Archetype in the Drawing Room: Fairy Tale Structures in the Novels of Jane Austen." DAI, 41 (1981), 5109A (Brown Univ.).

JA's novels mirror the structural patterns of fairy tales, challenging the protagonist "to overcome the internal and/or external obstacles to her triumph of moral and emotional selfhood." Characters like Elinor Dashwood and Fanny Price "exemplify the passive 'princess' mode of heroineship," which involves unjust persecution and endurance, and others like Elizabeth Bennet and Emma Woodhouse "embody the self-deluding 'peasant girl's' education in reason and self-control."

822 Nash, Susan Antoinette. "'Wanting a Situation': Governesses and Victorian Novels." DAI, 41 (1981), 4045A (Rutgers Univ., New Brunswick).

"Three novels written in 1814--Ellen, the Teacher, Mansfield Park, and O'Donnel--display the unity and diversity of governess fiction, and their heroines foreshadow the major directions it is to take as the century progresses."

823 Odmark, John. "An Understanding of Jane Austen's

Novels." Ph.D. diss., 1981 (Univ. of Regensburg). (See no. 548.)

824 Smith, Mack L., Jr. "Figures in the Carpet: The Ekphrastic Tradition in the Realistic Novel." DAI, 42 (1981), 693A (Rice Univ.).

Like Tolstoy, Joyce, and other novelists JA introduces different works of art within her own writing to "create the format of a debate on artistic representation." Thus, in E the heroine and Mr. Knightley's discussion about the agreement of Frank Churchill's letters with a defined, objective reality serves as "an analogue of the author's transformation of life through the medium of language."

825 Walters, Karla Krampert. "Ladies of Leisure: Idle Womanhood in the Victorian Novel." DAI, 41 (1981), 4724A (Univ. of Oreg.).

By the beginning of the nineteenth century, as MP witnesses, "romantic and Puritan notions of individualism operated to create a fictional feminine ideal in which leisure must be balanced with a moral impetus of duty."

826 Weissman, Cheryl Ann. "Character and Pattern in Jane Austen's Fiction." DAI, 41 (1981), 5099A (Cornell Univ.).

In the course of her career as JA develops her narrative technique, but especially in P and Sanditon, "heightened symmetry and patterning in the diction express an increasingly unstable, unstructured world. Furthermore, by emphasizing patterns of repetition in fictional events and referring to human conduct quantitatively, Austen augments rather than diminishes the suggestion of depth and even mystery in her characters."

1982

827 Jeffords, Susan Elizabeth. "Notes of Discord: Language and Power in the English and American Novel." DAI, 42 (1982), 4819A (Univ. of Pa.).

As a study of MP and other novels reveals, documents appearing in fiction, including letters and books, "function to indicate the nature of textual

representation as it changes over time. The issues
of power, control, and meaning become significant as
the control over documents within novels indicates
the perceived ability of novels to represent and
interpret adequately the perceived reality of a
particular time period."

828   Kreuzer, Paul Geoffrey. "The Development of Jane
      Austen's Techniques of Narration." DAI, 43
      (1982), 173A (Syracuse Univ.).

      As she progresses from the juvenilia to P and P,
      JA defines her chosen form, "the novel of ordinary
      life," experimenting "with such techniques as parody,
      direct address, irony, comparative juxtaposition, and
      presentation of character consciousness." At first
      she uses the narrator obtrusively, to explain her
      art, and later less obviously, to move the story for-
      ward.

829   Lee, Elisabeth McDonald. "Significance of Stone: An
      Analysis of the Operation of the Metaphor in
      Victorian Literature." DAI, 42 (1982), 4833A-
      34A (Univ. of Colo., Boulder).

      As evidence of "the range and complexity of the
      metaphor of stone" in nineteenth-century English lit-
      erature, stone in JA's novels "is essentially a back-
      ground concern, one which implies a degree of
      stability in the existing social order."

830   Lescinski, Joan M. "An Examination of Marriage in
      Six Novels by Jane Austen and Henry James." DAI,
      43 (1982), 452A (Brown Univ.).

      Both JA and James "stress the failed marriage
      over the successful one" in their novels and require
      in a good marriage "intellectual qualities such as
      equality of intelligence, the ability to learn and
      to change one's behavior as a result of that learn-
      ing, and respect for the personal integrity of the
      spouse."

831   McKinstry, Susan Jaret. "Rational Creatures: The
      Process of Fictionalizing in Jane Austen's Nov-
      els." DAI, 43 (1982), 1981A (Univ. of Mich.).

      JA's protagonists "become not only social crea-
      tures but rational 'imaginists' who, by learning an
      active process of 'reading' through perception and
      then 'writing' through imagination, fictionalize
      stories for themselves that fall within social and

novelistic conventions while fulfilling individual
fictions." The novels thus "explore fictionaliz-
ing as thematic (perception as fiction), ideological (social convention as fiction), and
phenomenological (knowledge as fiction) ways of
ordering the world."

832 Mulcahy, Kevin Patrick. "Individualism and the Fam-
    ily in the Novels of Defoe, Richardson, and
    Austen." DAI, 43 (1982), 173A-74A (Rutgers
    Univ., New Brunswick).

    Unlike Defoe in Roxana or Richardson in Clarissa,
    JA, especially in MP, rises above "the pattern of
    destructive antagonism between individual and family
    to a new mode of reconciliation. Without denying the
    tensions that exist between her heroines and their
    families, Austen demonstrates that an imaginative
    moral intelligence, on both sides, can make possible
    a free and fulfilling life for the individual within
    the family."

833 Neary, John Michael. "Stories of Marriage: The
    Epithalamial Imaginations of Jane Austen, Charles
    Dickens, and James Joyce." DAI, 42 (1982), 4009A
    (Univ. of Calif., Irvine).

    Though otherwise dissimilar, JA, Dickens, and
    Joyce all root their art "in the imperfect, uncom-
    pleted world of everyday" and depict "a dynamic
    process--a process of linkage." Put another way,
    their "books tell stories; and the stories concern
    some sort of marriage, metaphorical or actual."

834 Raj, Hans. "The Parent-Child Relations in Jane
    Austen's Novels." Ph.D. diss., 1982 (Himachal
    Pradesh Univ.).

    While she describes unhappy parent-child rela-
    tionships, JA "suggests through her heroines the
    adoption of a harmonious synthesis of good points of
    both the Evangelical and the Romantic ideologies for
    a more purposeful and sound family life." She ac-
    cordingly characterizes her heroines as social,
    sensible, and moral and shows them to be capable of
    deep feeling.

835 Satz, Martha G. "Deities and Translucent Volley-
    balls: An Epistemological Approach to Pride and
    Prejudice and 'Die Marquise von O. . . .'" DAI,
    43 (1982), 795A (Univ of Tex., Dallas). See also
    no. 680.

Though P and P and "Die Marquise von O . . ." respectively embody "epistemological optimism at its apex and epistemological pessimism at its nadir," they prove more epistemologically complicated than originally apparent. In addition, P and P, a profoundly structuralist work, suffers toward its conclusion because JA tries "to wed two incompatible epistemological positions."

836 Swanson, Janice M. Bowman. "Speaking in a Mother
     Tongue: Female Friendship in the British Novel."
     DAI, 43 (1982), 174A (Univ. of Calif., Santa
     Barbara). See also no. 563.

P studies "the art of persuasion, a skill in speaking which has been stifled in Anne Elliot by the powerfully persuasive Lady Russell," whose maternalism "controls rather than fosters the self."

1983

837 Fahnestock, Mary Lane. "The Reception of Jane Austen
     in Germany: A Miniaturist in the Land of Poets
     and Philosophers." DAI, 43 (1983), 3588A (Ind.
     Univ.).

JA's reception in Germany entails four periods, the first (1811-61) including little but two translations of her novels, the second (1862-1910) involving acknowledgment of her but also antagonism, the third (1911-45) favoring appreciation, and the fourth (after World War II) bringing her "a modicum of real popularity." In general German readers have found her art "too prosaic and too shallow intellectually to be very interesting, and have read her more for the sake of English social and cultural history than for pleasure."

838 Fazio, Ruth Morton. "'A Person of Some Consequence':
     The Influence of Mothers and Mother-Figures on
     Jane Austen's Heroines." DAI, 44 (1983), 492A
     (Case Western Reserve Univ.).

JA's novels treat the relationship between daughters and mothers or mother-figures and show the kind of mothering the heroines receive affecting their identity and interactions with men.

839 Gupta, Linda Roberta. "Fathers and Daughters in
     Women's Novels." DAI, 44 (1983), 1783A
     (American Univ.).

P and P and other nineteenth- and twentieth-century novels by women "view conflict with the father, or father-figure, as an inevitable and essential element in their heroines' progress toward maturity" and "as a metaphor for the struggles of women in a patriarchal society."

840   Lawson, Tom Oliver. "Samuel Richardson's Sir Charles Grandison and Its Influence on Jane Austen's Persuasion and George Eliot's The Mill on the Floss." DAI, 43 (1983), 3325A (Univ. of Ark.).

In its characters, plot, symbols, themes, and especially techniques P shows the influence of Sir Charles Grandison.

841   Levy, Elaine Barbara. "The Unconscious and Existentialism: A Dialectic in Modern Fiction." DAI, 43 (1983), 2659A (N.Y. Univ.).

Because they picture "a rational world in which the self and culture coexist in a mutually harmonious relationship," JA's novels differ significantly from modern fiction, which assumes the individual's dissatisfaction with society and consequent search for meaning.

842   Messick, Judith Hassan. "Reading As If for Life: The Female Quixote." DAI, 44 (1983), 166A-67A (Univ. of Calif., Santa Barbara).

In their "conjunctions of female and male psychology, the novels [in the tradition of the female Quixote] show antithetical lines of quixotic response. Jane Austen's novels of courtship are prototypical: Marianne creates fictions to intensify passion, to free her from the bonds of social expectation; Emma creates fictions for other people, controlling erotic feelings by the displacements and constraints of art."

843   Molzahn, Laura Jeanne. "The Novel as Speech Act: A Linguistic/Psychological Perspective on the Novel." DAI, 44 (1983), 761A (Northwestern Univ.).

As P and P helps illustrate, every novelist "performs the speech act of novelizing," which establishes values and creates sympathies, and the best novelists use irony and try to eliminate the genre's "naturally self-aggrandizing tendency."

844   Sibley, Gay Palmer. "The Cross-Pollination of
       'Taste' and Evolutionary Theory in the Develop-
       ment of the British Novel." DAI, 43 (1983),
       2999A-3000A (Univ. of Oreg.).

       A study of P and P and other English novels of
the nineteenth century helps show the development
from comfortable narrative assumptions about aesthetic sensibility, which support class distinctions,
to a "rhetoric of taste," which, providing "for alternative interpretations" on aesthetic matters, both
preserves those assumptions and reflects democratic
change.

845   Whealler, Susan Cornelia. "The Use of Distance in
       Jane Austen's Novels." DAI, 43 (1983), 2686A
       (Purdue Univ.).

       JA uses distance, "defined as the spatial, emo-
tional, intellectual, social and moral relationships
between characters, reader, narrators, and implied
author of the novels," for such purposes as structuring her work, controlling our responses, and giving
scenes visual and dramatic impact. In addition, by
having most of the characters fail to respond to different kinds of art aesthetically, she reveals their
"distance from the owner or creator of the art."

846   Williams, M. J. "Jane Austen: The Novels of Six Fic-
       tional Methods." DAI, 44C (1983), 26 (Univ. of
       York).

       Though significantly similar, the six novels also
prove "individual and separate," each arranging and
exploring its material differently: NA examines "the
workings of novels," MP "a pattern that is at once
necessary and limited," and P "its own organising
principle as a novel"; S and S represents "novel as
formal argument," P and P "novel as informal argument," and E novel as "active mystery."

1984

846a   Annable, Mary Mahar. "'Not . . . for Such Dull
        Elves': Rhetorical Strategies for Reader In-
        volvement in Pride and Prejudice and Mansfield
        Park." DAI, 44 (1984), 2769A-70A (Case Western
        Reserve Univ.).

        In P and P and MP, JA uses irony, free indirect
speech, and abstract terms as well as manipulates

fictional conventions to create "indeterminacy, the powerful impetus for reader involvement in the formulation of meaning." And the crucial differences in her handling of these strategies account for "the consistently great disparity in the responses of readers to these two novels.

847   Searle, Catherine Riordan.   "Prose Style in the Works of Jane Austen."   DAI, 44 (1984), 2155A (Fordham Univ.).

The six novels center on judgment, as revealed in the plot, in outdoor settings, in the recurring pattern of acceptance and rejection, which charts the protagonists' psychological development, and in sentence structure, which relies on parallelism and antithesis and helps shape the reader's responses.

III. Mentions

1973

848   Allen, Walter. "The Virtues of the Epistolary Novel." <u>TLS</u>, 26 Jan. 1973, p. 98.

After early experiments JA may have abandoned the epistolary novel form because she believed that Richardson had accomplished all that could be attempted in that mode.

849   Banfield, Ann. "Narrative Style and the Grammar of Direct and Indirect Speech." <u>FLang</u>, 10 (1973), 36.

"Austen's narrator appears only in chapters which summarize the aftermath of events dramatically rendered in the body of the novel (i.e., by direct speech or the free indirect style), as in the last chapter of <u>Mansfield Park</u>."

850   Borinski, Ludwig. "Anthony Trollope: <u>Phineas Finn</u>, the <u>Irish Member</u>," in <u>Der englische Roman im 19. Jahrhundert: Interpretationen zu Ehren von Horst Oppel</u>. Ed. Paul Goetsch, Heinz Kosok, and Kurt Otten. Berlin: Schmidt, 1973, pp. 200-203 and 206.

Trollope's <u>Phineas Finn</u> resembles JA's novels in its characterization, dialogue, and sense of dramatic development and differs in its colorful descriptions and the attention paid the working class.

851   Brophy, Brigid. <u>Prancing Novelist: A Defence of Fiction in the Form of a Critical Biography in Praise of Ronald Firbank</u>. New York: Barnes & Noble, 1973, p. 17 and passim.

JA worked out "her own non-naturalistic mode of fiction" by creating <u>NA</u>: "the creating consisted of destroying, by satire, the gothick romances whose more than illusionistic, whose almost hallucinatory daydream or day-nightmare narratives had obviously (to judge from her betrayingly deep knowledge of them) served her as extensions of her own young fantasy-life."

852   Craig, David. "Scott's Shortcomings as an Artist," in Scott Bicentenary Essays. Selected Papers Read at the Sir Walter Scott Bicentenary Conference. Ed. Alan Bell. New York: Barnes & Noble, 1973, pp. 105-6.

In P, JA showed that she "could create a prose sensitive enough, in touch enough with the speaking voice, to enact a person's inner life."

853   Hardwick, Michael. A Literary Atlas & Gazetteer of the British Isles. Detroit: Gale Research, 1973, passim.

(Surveys JA's association with different English localities.)

854   Haworth, Helen E. "'A Milk-White Lamb That Bleats'? Some Stereotypes of Women in Romantic Literature." HAB, 24 (1973), 291-92.

JA's heroines increasingly fit the general Romantic stereotype of women as obedient and dependent. "The spirited but partly wrong Elizabeth progresses (or degenerates?) into the spirited but largely wrong Emma, and then into the unspirited, submissive, but right Anne. And all three, of course, are seen entirely in their domestic roles as daughters, sisters, and future wives and mothers."

855   Heilbrun, Carolyn G. Toward a Recognition of Androgyny. New York: Knopf, 1973, pp. 74-78.

Absolutely androgynous, JA's genius represented men and women as "equally responsible, both morally and socially, for their actions; nor are the qualities of humanity which mark the admirable characters in Jane Austen's world distinguished by sex." Her heroes and heroines end by discovering "the spectrum of masculine and feminine impulses within themselves."

856   Kincaid, James R. "'Be Ye Lukewarm!': The Nineteenth-Century Novel and Social Action." BMMLA, 6 (Spring 1973), 89-90.

Though quite "dedicated to realizing the princi-

pal internal values in the external social forms and
particularly in marriage," JA "manifests a peculiar
ambivalence about the possibility of merging the
moral and the social self. There is always a conflict, very often unresolved, between the demands
of the private self--the free life of the imagina-
tion--and the demands of one's social and physical
surroundings."

857 Moers, Ellen. "Money, the Job, and Little Women."
     Commentary (New York), 55 (Jan. 1973), 57-61.
     Moers's comments on JA appear also, with the
     title "Denaro, lavoro, e piccole donne: Il
     realismo femminile," in Comunità, 30, no. 176
     (1976), 179-92, and, with the title "Money, the
     Job, and Little Women: Female Realism," in her
     Literary Women (Garden City, N.Y.: Doubleday,
     1976), pp. 67-78.

     Money "may be the first obviously feminine thing
     about [JA's] novels, for money and its making were
     characteristically female rather than male subjects
     in English fiction." JA's concern with the connec-
     tion of money and marriage and with the professions
     of her heroes reflects her realistic attention to the
     economic problems of young women.

858 Page, Norman. Speech in the English Novel. (English
     Language Series, 8.) London: Longman, 1973, pp.
     29-30.

     JA often conflates "into a single speech what
     must probably be supposed to have been uttered as
     several separate speeches." She thereby gains "in
     speed and concentration of effect" and avoids "the
     tendency to diffuseness inherent in the use of direct
     speech."

859 Pearce, T. S. George Eliot. (Literature in Per-
     spective.) Totowa, N.J.: Rowman and Littlefield,
     1973, pp. 55-57.

     JA resembles George Eliot in treating egotism and
     the complexities of the individual's inner life but
     differs in being "less grand, for the most part much
     less serious," and deficient in "the power to express
     the stronger emotions so that their strength is
     realised by the reader."

860 Pittock, Joan. "Scott and the Novel of Manners: The
     Case of St. Ronan's Well." DUJ, 35 (1973), 1-3
     and 5.

St. Ronan's Well, Scott's only novel of manners,
differs from JA's works: where she structures action
by "an exchange of familiar observations or significant dialogue," he "spends the greater part of his
time in narrating events, which . . . are too
cluttered anyway to be treated in the leisurely
fashion necessary to social satire, polite wit and
irony."

861   Roberts, Mark. The Tradition of Romantic Morality.
      New York: Barnes & Noble, 1973, p. 31.

      JA often sees things from an eighteenth- rather
than a nineteenth-century point of view. Her conception of happiness, for example, is "a 'low-key' af-
fair largely because the potentialities of human life
are felt to be so limited: one hopes for this kind of
happiness because any other kind of happiness seems
to be ruled out by the nature of the world in which
one lives."

862   Steeves, Edna L.   "Pre-Feminism in Some Eighteenth-
      Century Novels." TQ, 16 (Autumn 1973), 52-53.
      Steeves's comments on JA appear also in Feminist
      Criticism: Essays on Theory, Poetry, and Prose,
      ed. Cheryl L. Brown and Karen Olson (Metuchen,
      N.J.: Scarecrow Press, 1978), p. 227.

      JA, Fanny Burney, and Maria Edgeworth "can see
or imagine no other" career for women than marriage.
"In their novels they create personalities in a traditional social situation, but never examine the
situation itself closely. [They] were not bold
women; they are not critical of institutions, nor
even of men in their character as men."

863   Swinden, Patrick.   Unofficial Selves: Character in
      the Novel from Dickens to the Present Day. New
      York: Barnes & Noble, 1973, pp. 50-52.

      "In such a way--by virtue of the use she makes of
Emma's consciousness creating hypothetical situations
that we take, at least with one half of our mind, as
real--Jane Austen substantiates and deepens the reality of her characters, rendering them surprising,
unfathomable and lifelike."

864   Thomas, Eugene.   "Johnson's Continued Popularity."
      JNL, 33 (Mar. 1973), 6-7.

      (Comparison of the popularity of different

English writers, including JA, as based on the number
of items listed in the Annual Bibliography of English
Language and Literature for the years 1964-69.)

865 Williams, George G. Guide to Literary London. New
        York: Hastings House, 1973, passim.

    (Surveys JA's association with different London
    locations.)

866 Williams, Raymond. The Country and the City. New
        York: Oxford Univ. Press, 1973, pp. 112-19 and
        passim.

    The society JA describes is not single or settled
    but "an active, complicated, sharply speculative
    process." Though she writes of social contradiction
    and confusion, she is able paradoxically to achieve a
    unity of tone, a steady and confident way to see and
    judge, because she assumes that social improvement is
    or should be moral improvement.

867 Wilson, Angus. "Morality under the Microscope." New
        Statesman, 26 Oct. 1973, p. 602.

    Strongly influenced by Richardson, JA "mainly
    drew on the insufficiencies of Grandison and created
    the deadening moralities of Mr Knightley and Edmund
    Bertram, while unintelligently ridiculing the more
    superficial aspects of Clarissa in Sanditon."

                            1974

868 Allen, Walter. "Narrative Distance, Tone, and Char-
        acter," in The Theory of the Novel: New Essays.
        Ed. John Halperin. New York: Oxford Univ. Press,
        1974, pp. 333-34.

    In the English novel JA proves "the master of
    narrative distance." Her "immense authority" stems
    from the creation of a fictional world "in which the
    aesthetic order exactly mirrors the moral order."

869 Bayley, John. "Character and Consciousness." NLH, 5
        (1974), 230-31.

    "The extreme importance to Jane Austen of Miss
    Bates, or of Sir Thomas Bertram, is to show that the
    social contract is insufferable, but invaluable: that

we are entitled to mock at the same moment in which
we are reassured by the wrongness of our mockery."

870   Booth, Wayne C. A Rhetoric of Irony. Chicago: Univ.
       of Chicago Press, 1974, pp. 64-66 and passim.

       As Lady Susan shows, JA's irony clearly invites
       the reader's mentally and "morally active engage-
       ment."

871   Colby, Vineta. Yesterday's Woman: Domestic Realism
       in the English Novel. Princeton, N.J.: Princeton
       Univ. Press, 1974, pp. 15-17 and passim.

       "Much as we think we know her world--landscapes,
       interiors, and the habits and activities of her char-
       acters--we discover that she gave scant space to
       physical description of any kind." She had a fond-
       ness for typology and generalization that derives
       from the eighteenth century.

872   Doody, Margaret Anne. A Natural Passion: A Study of
       the Novels of Samuel Richardson. Oxford: Clar-
       endon Press, 1974, p. 358 and passim.

       It is from Richardson that JA learned, among
       other things, how "to use the details of drawing-
       room life and the trivial events of a ball" to re-
       veal character and sustain the storyline.

873   Karl, Frederick R. The Adversary Literature--The
       English Novel in the Eighteenth Century: A Study
       in Genre. New York: Farrar, Straus, and Giroux,
       1974, p. 53 and passim. Karl's book appears
       also with the title A Reader's Guide to the
       Eighteenth-Century English Novel (New York: Noon-
       day Press, 1974) and with the title A Reader's
       Guide to the Development of the English Novel in
       the Eighteenth Century (London: Thames and Hud-
       son, 1975).

       JA sensed the novel's dangerous ability to expose
       a community's flaws and offer alternatives, which,
       because of her conservatism, she felt bound to re-
       ject. Her art "resulted from just this dialectic;
       that is, from her structuring a society in shaky
       balance only after she had examined the minute
       threats to its existence."

874   Keith, W. J. The Rural Tradition: A Study of the

Non-fiction Prose Writers of the English Country-
side. Toronto: Univ. of Toronto Press, 1974, pp.
102-3. Keith's book appears also with the title
The Rural Tradition: William Cobbett, Gilbert
White, and Other Non-fiction Prose Writers of the
English Countryside (Brighton, Sussex: Harvester
Press, 1975).

The connection between JA and Mary Russell Mit-
ford "is not so much in their presentation of country
manners as in shrewd understanding linked with verbal
dexterity."

875 Low, Donald A. "Introduction" to his ed. of Robert
     Burns: The Critical Heritage. Boston: Routledge
     & Kegan Paul, 1974, p. 39.

JA introduces into Sanditon (chap. 7) "a passage
of dialogue parodying dishonest bluster about Burns,"
subtly reinforcing "a conservative view of genius by
exposing an incoherent rhapsodist . . . to delicate
raillery."

876 Mayo, Robert D. "Introduction" to George Moore's
     Grasville Abbey: A Romance. 3 vols. (Gothic
     Novels, 2.) New York: Arno Press, 1974. I,
     xix-xx.

Henry Tilney's satiric description of what
Catherine can expect as a guest at his father's
house derives partly from Moore's Gothic novel.
"Grasville Abbey is therefore an important member
of the Northanger canon, though never mentioned by
name."

877 Miles, Rosalind. The Fiction of Sex: Themes and
     Functions of Sex Difference in the Modern
     Novel. New York: Barnes & Noble, 1974, pp.
     58-61.

JA often leads us to reject romance themes in
favor of moral and human concerns. She "asserts the
supremacy of individual need over social and conventional requirements."

878 "MLA Membership Survey: England versus France." MLA
     Newsletter, 6 (Mar. 1974), 1-2.

According to a Modern Language Association membership survey, JA was the twenty-third most frequently cited author in English literature.

879   Richter, David H.   Fable's End: Completeness and Clo-
            sure in Rhetorical Fiction.   Chicago: Univ. of
            Chicago Press, 1974, pp. 10-11.

       To enhance our pleasure in the final reunion of
Anne and Wentworth, JA represents in the course of
P her heroine's "changing states of consciousness.
. . . This representation of consciousness, then,
is not an end in itself, but a means subordinate to
the end, a method used to increase the power of a
plot of action."

880   Steinbrink, Jeffrey.   "Novels of Circumstance and
            Novels of Character: Emerson's View of Fiction."
            ESQ, 20 (1974), 103 and 107.

       Emerson's antipathy to JA derives from his con-
viction that of all forms of literature the novel is
"most closely tethered to the circumstances of conformity which render it pathologically sterile and
repetitive."

881   Wolff, Cynthia Griffin.   "The Problem of Eighteenth-
            Century Secular Heroism."   MLS, 4 (Fall 1974),
            39-41.

       "If Austen permits herself the language of
heroism--even jokingly--as a valid means of constru-
ing Emma's character, then she can convey" to the
reader a sense of Emma's pride, as well as "the vitality, the independence, the aggressive intelligence that no language of heroism could manage."

882   Yeazell, Ruth.   "Fictional Heroines and Feminist
            Critics."   Novel, 8 (1974), 34 and 37.

       "To a jaundiced eye, Emma may seem to marry the
wise and strong father she never had, but the marriage is most significant as a social ritual which
metaphorically ratifies a transformation in Emma
herself," a transformation from ignorance to knowledge and from selfishness to love of another.

                              1975

883   Alter, Robert.   "History and Imagination in the
            Nineteenth-Century Novel."   GaR, 29 (1975), 45.

       As in most novels, the major concern in E is "the
disparity between the structures of the imagination

and things as they are, novelistic plot consisting in
the multifarious effects of that disparity on the
protagonist" and the other characters.

884   Athas, Daphne. "Goddesses, Heroines, and Women
       Writers." StAR, 3 (Fall-Winter 1975), 10.

       Although JA's characters may suffer, they "do not
derive value from suffering. Rather they would be
devalued if they messed around in it as George Eliot's do. Thus we may say that the dominant syn-
drome of her characters is Persephone-Athena with a
little bit of Artemis thrown in."

885   Auerbach, Nina. "Incarnations of the Orphan." ELH,
       42 (1975), 419, n. 8.

       "Both Jane Fairfax and Frank Churchill seem to be
semi-picaresque orphans playing manipulative games
with a fixed social medium. Harriet Smith seems to
be Jane Austen's version of the Romantic orphan-
waif."

886   Barbu, Zev, and David Daiches. "The Rise of the Nov-
       el in England," in Hopes, vol. 1 of The Modern
       World. Ed. David Daiches and Anthony Thorlby.
       (Literature and Western Civilization.) London:
       Aldus, 1975, pp. 457-60.

       "What we see in Jane Austen is the highest de-
velopment of what we might call the Addisonian reconciliation between style and virtue." She advocates a
bourgeois morality and treats social mobility and
economic reality.

887   Blythe, Ronald. "The Dangerous Idyll: Sweet Auburn
       to Akenfield." EDH, 38 (1975), 25-26.

       JA's "interpretation of Augustanism is to present
the park as Paradise. It is unnatural or unwise to
wish to leave, or to leave, Paradise."

888   Brantlinger, Patrick. "Romances, Novels, and Psycho-
       analysis." Criticism, 17 (1975), 27.

       As distinct from landscapes in James Hogg or
Emily Brontë, which read like transcendental poetry,
landscapes in JA tend to resemble travelogues or essays on the picturesque and not to point beyond
themselves.

889 Davis, Terence. The Gothick Taste. Rutherford,
     N.J.: Fairleigh Dickinson Univ. Press, 1975, p.
     17.

     Like George Eliot and others JA reflects archi-
     tecture's influence on literature with her "refer-
     ences to fashions in buildings and satirical comments
     upon them."

890 Dorosz, Wiktoria. Subjective Vision and Human Rela-
     tionships in the Novels of Rosamond Lehmann.
     (Studia Anglistica Upsaliensia, 23.) Uppsala:
     Acta Universitatis Upsaliensis, 1975, pp. 16-20.
     Dorosz's book was written as a doctoral disser-
     tation.

     JA and Rosamond Lehmann resemble each other in
     "the shared yin character of their work," including
     the concern for "a small intimately known world where
     the emotional and moral problems of individuals are
     of paramount importance." Yet because they do not
     have the same kind of organization and style, they
     produce altogether different effects.

891 Ebbatson, J. R. "The Schlegels' Family Tree." ELT,
     18 (1975), 195 and 197.

     JA's contrast in S and S of two sisters with op-
     posing temperaments influenced Forster in creating
     the Schlegels in Howards End.

892 Faulkner, Peter. Humanism in the English Novel.
     London: Elek/Pemberton, 1975, pp. 36-38.

     "There was a considerable division in [JA] be-
     tween her conscious religious principles and the more
     humanistic assumptions guiding her characteristic
     comedy towards earthly felicity." In her novels,
     noteworthy for "the elusiveness of their religious
     commitment," characters make crucial moral decisions
     "with reference to no higher power than conscience,
     and with no suggestion" of the relevance of faith or
     prayer.

893 Fleishman, Avrom. "[Comment in] a Panel Discussion,"
     in Forms of Modern British Fiction. Ed. Alan
     Warren Friedman. (Symposia in the Arts and the
     Humanities, 2.) Austin, Tex: Univ. of Texas
     Press, 1975, p. 226.

     NA "might qualify as having the same dryness,

coldness, meticulousness" as Robbe-Grillet makes use of. Like his novels, too, it works out "a set of propositions with ironic discoveries of the implications of convention and of form."

894   Hardy, Barbara. _Tellers_ and _Listeners_: _The_ _Narrative_ _Imagination_. London: Athlone Press, 1975, pp. 8-9 and passim.

"When Jane Austen wrote _Emma_ she seems to have been writing about the strengths and weaknesses of human imagination from a sensibility alerted by professional experience."

895   Lansbury, Coral. _Elizabeth_ _Gaskell_: _The_ _Novel_ _of_ _So-_ _cial_ _Crisis_. New York: Barnes & Noble, 1975, p. 91.

The theatricals in _MP_ are wrong simply because, "if Sir Thomas had been lost at sea or died in the Indies (no word had reached the family to the contrary), then it would have been harrowing for his children to discover later that a merry comedy had been played out when their father was dead."

896   McIntosh, Carey. "Quantities of Qualities: Nominal Style and the Novel," in vol. 4 of _Studies_ _in_ _Eighteenth-Century_ _Culture_. Ed. Harold E. Pagliaro. Madison, Wis.: Univ. of Wisconsin Press for the American Society for Eighteenth-Century Studies, 1975, pp. 149 and 151.

JA proves as effective in what she omits or glosses over as in what she says directly. In her world "self-control and the capacity to harness socio-psycho-moral abstractions (including 'desires') within a nominal syntax are by no means incompatible with passion."

897   Okamoto, Seikei. _Igirisu_ _kindai_ _shosetsu_ _no_ _keisei_ [The growth of the modern English novel]. Tokyo: Kirihara Shoten, 1975, pp. 368-73.

JA's greatness derives from her unique ability to describe a character's personality skillfully by means of simple words and refined humor.

898   Schulz, Gerhard. "The Lonely Hero, or the Germans and the Novel." _AUMLA_, no. 43 (1975), pp. 14-16.

While Goethe has a wider range than JA, she tells
a story more economically and creates fuller characters. Unlike him, too, she makes money a key subject
and treats the merger of different social classes.
And, although she writes about education, in contrast to the writers of the German Bildungsroman she
values compromise and avoids "lonely and exceptional
heroes."

899 Spacks, Patricia Meyer. The Female Imagination. New
     York: Knopf, 1975, pp. 115-29 and passim.

JA's protagonists are paradigms "of adolescent
potential fulfilled." The optimism of the novels
"depends on a notion of individual development which
makes ridiculous the common level of social assumption about marriage, about personal possibility.
Despite the novels' dependence on a firm social
structure, they raise quietly revolutionary questions about the usual effects of this structure on
individuals."

900 Steiner, George. After Babel: Aspects of Language
     and Translation. New York: Oxford Univ. Press,
     1975, pp. 8-11.

Though apparently clear and open, JA makes "assured reading" difficult by being "radically linguistic," by "encoding" reality "in a distinctive idiom."
She relies much on the unspoken, on diction resting
"on a specific scale of social and heuristic nuances"
and "a complex field of semantic and ethical values."

901 Stewart, Garrett. "Teaching Prose Fiction: Some 'In-
     structive' Styles." CE, 37 (1975), 384-90.

JA's style appears serene, assured, rational, and
unembellished while relying on significant metaphors
for much of its impact. One such metaphor in P and
P, concerning portraits, affects the novel's dialogue, characterization, and themes.

                              1976

902 Bayley, John. The Uses of Division: Unity and Dis-
     harmony in Literature. New York: Viking Press,
     1976, pp. 22 and 24-26.

Partly revolutionary, JA describes "the tension
between the growing claims of the individual and

those of society. . . . She is the vessel both of
serene authority and of joyous anarchy: in the exercise of her art she is both Rameau and Diderot,
honest soul and wilful geist."

903   Bersani, Leo. A Future for Astyanax: Character and
       Desire in Literature. Boston: Little, Brown,
       1976, pp. 74-77 and 79-82.

       In accord with "her sense of the social dan-
gers of movement," JA proposes in MP "an ethic of
stillness": as "moral heroine," Fanny "is a
stable, nondesiring center of judgment," and the
Crawfords represent a "version of the evils of
agitation."

904   Brown, Jane K. "Die Wahlverwandtschaften and the
       English Novel of Manners." CL, 28 (1976), 98-
       105.

       MP and Goethe's Die Wahlverwandtschaften resemble
each other in setting, structure, characters, and
theme, both treating, among other things, manners,
marriage, and the improvement of the estate. But
they differ in that JA shows the importance of good
manners in holding society together, while Goethe
stresses the failure of any kind of manners to maintain social cohesion.

905   Calder, Jenni. Women and Marriage in Victorian Fic-
       tion. New York: Oxford Univ. Press, 1976, pp.
       22-23 and passim.

       JA suggests that there are "two kinds of men,
fathers and sons, the sons indicative of the perils
of society while the fathers hold moral law together. Within such a pattern it is obviously of some
importance that Jane Austen's heroines marry fathers
rather than sons."

906   Copeland, Edward W. "Money in the Novels of Fanny
       Burney." SNNTS, 8 (1976), 36.

       Unlike Burney and other women novelists of the
late eighteenth century, who "turned to the exter-
nalizing conventions of melodrama" to portray the
economic problems of women, JA "internalized 'Female
Difficulties' in her heroines."

907   Coxe, Louis. Enabling Acts: Selected Essays in Crit-

icism. Columbia, Mo.: Univ. of Missouri Press, 1976, pp. 71-72.

Young people like JA because she has a "sense of fun and fooling" and creates a world that "is the world of the young, of the young who, fighting their way out of the shell of self, emerge into the moral realm and frequently do not like what they see there."

908 Frye, Northrop. The Secular Scripture: A Study of the Structure of Romance. Cambridge, Mass.: Harvard Univ. Press, 1976, pp. 76-77 and passim.

"It is not that Jane Austen is a woman novelist expressing a woman's resistance to social conditions governing the place of women in her time. She accepts those conditions, on the whole: it is the romantic convention she is using that expresses the resistance. This principle that an element of social protest is inherent in romance is one" evident throughout her fiction.

909 Gaull, Marilyn. "Romantic Humor: The Horse of Knowledge and the Learned Pig." Mosaic, 9 (Summer 1976), 56-57.

Representing "some of the most central concerns and tenets of English Romanticism," NA's parody is threefold: it ridicules "the Gothic romance for its misrepresentation of human behavior," "the people who read it and believe in it," and "the world in which these romance-readers live."

910 "A Hard Sell: How Modern Packaging Can Shed a New Light on the Classics." STimes, 5 Dec. 1976, pp. 36 and 49.

(Cover drawing for P and P in the style of "to-day's light romancers.")

911 Haworth, H. E. "Romantic Female Writers and the Critics." TSLL, 17 (1976), 730 and 734-35.

In the early nineteenth century, English reviewers tended to see all women writers, including JA, as limited and, despite their possible merit, as "inferior to men."

912 Hinz, Evelyn J. "Hierogamy versus Wedlock: Types of

Marriage Plots and Their Relationship to Genres
of Prose Fiction." PMLA, 91 (1976), 900-903.

Just as P and P's opening "may be viewed as a
classic enunciation of the general connection between
wedlock and the novel," so E's conclusion "may be
regarded as a capsulized expression of the comic form
of the wedlock plot and its societal and ethical implications."

913 Kelly, Gary. The English Jacobin Novel, 1780-1805.
     Oxford: Clarendon Press, 1976, p. 65.

Lovers' Vows becomes a controversial subject in
MP "because of the impropriety of its social mores
rather than the Jacobinism of its political views."

914 Kennard, Jean. "Oates, Lessing, and Jong: The Burden
     of Tradition." Atlantis, 2 (Fall 1976), 14, 16,
     and 21. Kennard's comments on JA appear also,
     with the title "Jane Austen: The Establishment,"
     in her Victims of Convention (Hamden, Conn.:
     Archon, 1978), pp. 21-45; see no. 344.

The fictional convention involving the heroine
who must choose between two suitors works structurally in JA's novels but functions less well in later
writers "as the concept of female maturity becomes
more modern and, indeed, inseparable from the ideas
of independence and self-reliance."

915 LaJoy, Maureen. "No Laughing Matter: Women and Hu-
     mor." Women, 5, no. 1 (1976), 7.

JA's "literary humor lay in the innocent, proper
way that she broke with contemporary convention."

916 McFarland, Thomas. "Recent Studies in the Nineteenth
     Century." SEL, 16 (1976), 713-16.

The key to JA's greatness is that she "presents
human concern not as becoming, but as being." She
creates a world which, "like paradise, grants full-
ness of being to the most ordinarily unremarkable
actions of life."

917 Moers, Ellen. Literary Women. Garden City, N.Y.:
     Doubleday, 1976, pp. 215-29.

"Emma is a cautionary pedagogical tale in the

Genlis tradition, a tradition which Austen, as was
her way, satirized as she brought it to perfection."
The heroine "seems to have been ironically conceived
as stand-in for the novelist herself, the arrogant
romancer, the woman who arranges lives in order to
teach the world how to go 'on a more perfect plan.'"

918 Nielsen, Jørgen Erik. Den samtidige Engelske lit-
     teratur og Danmark, 1800-1840. (Publications of
     the Department of English, University of Copen-
     hagen, 3.) Copenhagen: Nova, 1976. I, 152 and
     433.

     Until 1855-56, when S and S was translated into
Danish, JA was almost unknown in Denmark.

919 Peacock, R. "The Ethics of Goethe's Die Wahlver-
     wandtschaften." MLR, 71 (1976), 341-42.

     MP explores "the middle area of human character;
it reaches neither to the evil of Les Liaisons Dangereuses, nor to the tragic intensity of Goethe's
Ottilie-image [in Die Wahlverwandtschaften]. And
also, at the side of the precise moral certitudes of
Jane Austen, Goethe's social picture appears toler-
antly neutral."

920 Priestley, J. B. English Humour. New York: Stein
     and Day, 1976, pp. 116-25.

     JA presents "a greater variety of feminine humour
than anybody else" yet resembles male rather than female novelists in that she indulges her comic characters, "stopping everything else to show them off."
Sometimes she even overexposes her creations, as she
does with Mr. Collins and Miss Bates, though on other
occasions, as with Mr. Woodhouse, she does not.

921 Ray, Gordon N. The Illustrator and the Book in Eng-
     land from 1790 to 1914. New York: Oxford Univ.
     Press for the Pierpont Morgan Library, 1976, pp.
     181-82.

     In his illustrations for an 1896 edition of E,
Hugh Thomson emphasizes not JA's rigorous examination
of human relations "but the Cranfordian elements in
her work. If Emma herself is simply one more pretty
young woman and Mr. Knightley is presented chiefly in
terms of his 'tall, firm, upright figure,' Thomson is
adroit in showing the surface peculiarities of the
novel's shallower personages."

922 Sacks, Sheldon. "Novelists as Storytellers." Mod-
      Phil, 73 (May 1976), pt. 2, S103-8.

      JA demonstrates in P "that an integral part of a
plot need not in fact add to the material progression
of the story she is telling just so long as it is
intuitively relevant to the power of that story."
Thus, while the book's central section creates an
appearance of movement, it is actually static,
ordered "to reveal as fully as possible the emotional force" of Anne's not changing her unhappy
condition.

923 Spacks, Patricia Meyer. Imagining a Self: Autobiog-
      raphy and Novel in Eighteenth-Century England.
      Cambridge, Mass.: Harvard Univ. Press, 1976, p.
      89.

      JA and Fanny Burney "confirm the implications of
works by less obviously gifted women. Their strength
derives from successful exploitation of the dichotomy
between public passivity and private energy that
weakened those women unable to use their sense of
division as material for strong images of female experience."

924 Steiner, George. "Eros and Idiom," in Reactions,
      vol. 3 of The Modern World. Ed. David Daiches
      and Anthony Thorlby. (Literature and Western
      Civilization.) London: Aldus, 1976, pp. 51-54
      and 77. Steiner's comments on JA appear also in
      his On Difficulty and Other Essays (New York:
      Oxford Univ. Press, 1978), pp. 95-99 and 131.

      In JA sexuality is "inside the narrative, not in
the sense of impulse hidden or unconscious, but as an
area of understood meaning so intelligently faced, so
publicly acquiesced in--the novelist and her reader
having, as it were, negotiated a treaty of mutual in-
tent--that there is no need of localizing articulation. Such a pact, in reference to sexuality, is the
underlying condition of Jane Austen's art."

1977

925 Armstrong, Nancy. "Character, Closure, and Impres-
      sionist Fiction." Criticism, 19 (1977), 329.

      In P and P's opening sentence JA "does not speak
as an individual but as a member of a reading public
of homogeneous class interests, and in such a situa-

tion the asseverations of an author naturally take on
the authority of a science that posits its source in
the world itself."

926 Carpenter, Andrew. "Double Vision in Anglo-Irish
     Literature," in his ed. of Place, Personality,
     and the Irish Writer. (Irish Literary Studies,
     1.) New York: Barnes & Noble, 1977, pp. 186-
     87.

     Unlike Maria Edgeworth, JA relies on "an irony of
     techniques and of surface rather than an irony which
     springs from the author's conception of the book it-
     self." As a result, though JA plays a game with her
     characters, she does not crucially involve us in it
     or allow us to participate "in any process of testing
     the impression we have received against our own sen-
     sibilities."

927 Carroll, David. "Introduction" to his ed. of Richard
     Simpson as Critic. Boston: Routledge & Kegan
     Paul, 1977, pp. 38-41.

     Simpson wrote so penetratingly of JA because she
     provided "a paradigm of his own theory of knowledge
     in which the mind works dynamically but in full con-
     trol of its powers, without imaginative or emotional
     excess. The creative process is controlled by a
     moral purpose which rescues the work of art from the
     merely emotional or aesthetic."

928 Cohen, Murray. Sensible Words: Linguistic Practice
     in England, 1640-1785. Baltimore: Johns Hopkins
     Univ. Press, 1977, p. 80.

     While JA excludes the grossness of her senti-
     mental and Gothic predecessors, "she retains their
     rhetorical representation of character," that is, the
     association of "intonation, evocative gestures and
     settings, and certain rhythms of speech and narration
     with particular effects."

929 Eagle, Dorothy, and Hilary Carnell, comps. and eds.
     The Oxford Literary Guide to the British Isles.
     Oxford: Clarendon Press, 1977, passim. An ex-
     cerpt from this book, describing JA's association
     with Dartford, Kent, appears in STimes Mag, 17
     Apr. 1977, p. 74; this book appears also in an
     edition revised by Dorothy Eagle, with the title
     The Oxford Illustrated Literary Guide to Great

Britain and Ireland (New York: Oxford Univ.
Press, 1981).

(Surveys JA's association with different English
localities.)

930   Fernando, Lloyd. "New Women" in the Late Victorian
      Novel. University Park, Pa.: Pennsylvania State
      Univ. Press, 1977, p. 35.

      JA shapes "trivialities of thought, speech, and
conduct into exquisitely designed plots highlight-
ing personal moral crises" but lacks George Eliot's
concern for "the 'hard non-moral outward conditions'
of the material world."

931   Joy, Edward T. English Furniture, 1800-1851.
      London: Sotheby Parke Bernet, 1977, p. 196.

      JA's novels reflect changing fashions in furni-
ture, P, for example, describing "how fashionable
taste in the arrangement of furniture was moving in
the direction of profusion and disorder, to the de-
light of the younger generation and the dismay of
the older."

932   Killham, John. "The Idea of Community in the Eng-
      lish Novel." NCF, 31 (1977), 384-87 and 390-
      91.

      Contrary to Raymond Williams's contention in
The English Novel from Dickens to Lawrence (1970),
JA's novels prove much more than "merely the product of high bourgeois society." Though concerned
with economics and class structure, and in more complex ways than Williams realizes, her works are
fundamentally "love stories" and "romantic, dream
fulfillments," which speak of "intelligence, character, and accomplishment."

933   Kincaid, James R. The Novels of Anthony Trol-
      lope. Oxford: Clarendon Press, 1977, pp. 52-
      53.

      "Despite the fact that in Trollope Jane Austen's
methods and assumptions are being tested under new
conditions, Trollope received from Austen what he
most needed: a confirmation of the wonderful potential in the comedy of manners tradition for exploring
human life with delicacy and profundity."

934   Lerner, Laurence. "The Triumph of Scylla: Lukács'
       Theory of Realism." Encounter (London), 49 (Aug.
       1977), 40. Lerner's comments on JA appear also,
       with the title "Lukacs' Theory of Realism," in
       his The Literary Imagination: Essays on Litera-
       ture and Society (Totowa, N.J.: Barnes & Noble,
       1982), pp. 144-45.

       Contrary to the view of some critics, JA is not
       "well aware of the forces of change in her society."
       Though she shows "the importance of economic con-
       straints on the individual," she does not study
       "their operation in society" or provide a sense that
       "institutional structures . . . could conceivably be
       different."

935   Levine, George. "High and Low: Ruskin and the Novel-
       ists," in Nature and the Victorian Imagination.
       Ed. U. C. Knoepflmacher and G. B. Tennyson.
       Berkeley and Los Angeles: Univ. of California
       Press, 1977, p. 137.

       Emma's irresponsibility and rudeness on Box Hill
       point to the idea that in novels "the heights are
       where society is not."

936   Low, Donald A. That Sunny Dome: A Portrait of Regen-
       cy Britain. Totowa, N.J.: Rowman and Little-
       field, 1977, pp. 158-65.

       Although JA excludes contemporary social crises
       from her fiction, she still does provide insights
       into the Regency period. Through her elegance and
       sense of proportion she projects an image of the time
       "as one of calm, leisured living, and equipoise."
       She shows also the dominance of material interests in
       the age.

937   Lucas, John. The Literature of Change: Studies in
       the Nineteenth-Century Provincial Novel. New
       York: Barnes & Noble, 1977, pp. x-xi.

       The kind of alliance JA's characters establish
       with houses, as Fanny does with Mansfield Park, be-
       comes problematic in later novels because it involves
       "the process of separation that really doesn't much
       enter Jane Austen's fiction. (The only painful sepa-
       rations in her novels are those of the outcasts, and
       such pain has to be assumed; it isn't dwelt on.)"

937a   Pratt, Mary Louise. Toward a Speech Act Theory of

Literary Discourse. Bloomington, Ind.: Indiana
Univ. Press, 1977, pp. 166-71.

We know P and P's first sentence is ironic not
because of the sentence's intrinsic features but because we know that "the circumstances under which
literary works are composed, edited, selected, published, and distributed" aim "to eliminate failures
which result from carelessness or lack of skill."

938 Ram, Atma. "An Interview with Anita Desai." WLWE,
       16 (1977), 102.

"When I first read Austen, I was left cold. . . .
Much later, I reread her and found her exhilarating.
I very much admire her particular and unique qualities, but something of my first reaction lingers--I
am still left cold. There is something about her
that is totally alien to my own writing."

939 Reed, Walter L. "A Defense of History: The Language
       of Transformation in Romantic Narrative." BuR,
       23 (Fall 1977), 52-53.

"In Fanny's sympathy for the ideals of the father
figure in ⌈MP⌉, Austen lays the basis for a Romantic
transfer of authority from one generation to the
next--a basis that lies not in nature but in Fanny's
peculiarly negative consciousness," which defines
propriety as defeat and absence.

940 Roberts, Warren E. "Social Customs and the Crafts: A
       Note." KFR, 23 (1977), 72-78.

The custom of touring the homes of the wealthy,
as Elizabeth and the Gardiners do in P and P, helps
account for the high quality of furniture, china,
paintings, and the like that date from about the
start of the nineteenth century: noble families like
Darcy's naturally wished "to appear to live in a manner worthy of their position and income and to have
proper tastes," as well as to display pride in their
histories.

941 Showalter, Elaine. A Literature of Their Own:
       British Women Novelists from Brontë to Lessing.
       Princeton, N.J.: Princeton Univ. Press, 1977, p.
       302.

The completion of Sanditon by Another Lady in
1975 provides an example of a modern writer, in the

continuing battle for private and artistic independence, reasserting her connection with a woman of the
past.

942   Woodring, Carl. "Nature and Art in the Nineteenth
        Century." PMLA, 92 (1977), 194-95.

        As evidenced by Mr. Knightley's reply to Mrs.
Elton concerning "the nature and the simplicity of
gentlemen and ladies" (E, vol. 3, chap. 6), JA agrees
with Schiller, Wordsworth, and Lamartine "that nature
is in us unless by artificiality we drive it out of
ourselves and into the mountains and seas."

943   Zeman, Anthea. Presumptuous Girls: Women and Their
        World in the Serious Woman's Novel. London:
        Weidenfeld and Nicolson, 1977, pp. 153-56, 170-
        72, and passim.

        JA treats Eros, among other ways, as humorous, a
subject for jokes, and as dangerous, notably when it
takes the form of seduction, whether of body or mind.
For her, "good sex is a moral good" because it constitutes "the basis of a woman's integrity."

                          1978

944   Cunningham, Gail. The New Woman and the Victorian
        Novel. New York: Barnes & Noble, 1978, pp. 20-
        21.

        In JA's fictional world, which proves more robust
than that of the Victorian novel, "sexuality is a
normal part of life." She does not allow "rational
perception of immorality to be overlaid with pious
amazement" that illicit passion should exist.

945   Gosling, Kenneth. "Scientists Preparing for New Wave
        of Art Forgeries." Times, 5 Apr. 1978, p. 4.

        Microscopic analyses of different hairs, "includ-
ing those of Egyptian mummies, Danish bog bodies, the
medieval English, Jane Austen and Napoleon Bona-
parte," have revealed that most of the hairs "are
contaminated by fungi and some have undergone subtle
surface degradation. Only in the case of Jane Austen's locks was it possible to glean information
about cosmetic habits."

946   Harvey, A. D. Britain in the Early Nineteenth Cen-

tury. New York: St. Martin's Press, 1978, p. 23.

Because it is historically accurate that the British Navy was, around 1800, less aristocratic in its upper ranks than the Army, Sir Walter Elliot has "some justification for the objection . . . that the Navy was 'the means of bringing persons of obscure birth into undue distinction, and raising men to honours [which] their fathers and grandfathers never dreamt of.'"

947   Heilman, Robert B. "Robespierre and Santa Claus: Men of Virtue in Drama." SoR, 14 (1978), 224.

Like The Way of the World JA's work demonstrates that "the most substantial charity is essentially the spirit of high comedy. It is the civility which survives, or triumphs over, mistakes and misjudgments (by ourselves and others), and which, by conceding, by tolerating, by accepting, introduces the graciousness that makes community possible."

948   Heinz, A. Elgin. "Murasaki Shikibu: The Tale of Genji." SocEd, 42 (1978), 342.

P and P and The Tale of Genji resemble each other in viewing human beings sympathetically but with no illusions, in treating a world more concerned with form than substance, and in concentrating not on political or economic issues but personal relationships.

949   Hunt, John Dixon. "Sense and Sensibility in the Landscape Designs of Humphry Repton." SBHT, 19 (1978), 23-26.

Many of JA's "descriptions and discussions of landscaping parallel Repton's ideas": in typically Reptonian fashion both Pemberley and Donwell Abbey carefully adjudicate "between natural and formal elements," and NA and S and S "submit landscape ideas," as he did, to common sense.

950   Kestner, Joseph A. The Spatiality of the Novel. Detroit: Wayne State Univ. Press, 1978, p. 121.

One detects the syllogism's form in the three-volume structuring of P and P and E. "The novels present a major premise, minor premise, and conclusion. In Pride and Prejudice, for instance, we have: (1) the rejection of Darcy; (2) the understanding of

Darcy; (3) the acceptance of Darcy by Elizabeth Bennet."

951   The Marxist-Feminist Literature Collective. "Women's
      Writing: Jane Eyre, Shirley, Villette, Aurora
      Leigh." I&C, no. 3 (Spring 1978), p. 31.

      "Austen's refusal to write about anything she
      didn't know is as undermining to the patriarchal
      hegemony as Wollstonecraft's demand for a widening
      of women's choices: the very 'narrowness' of her nov-
      els gave them a subversive dimension of which she
      herself was unaware, and which has been registered in
      critics' bewilderment at what status to accord them."

952   Raimond, Jean. "L'Évolution du roman anglais au XIXe
      siècle," in Le Roman anglais au XIXe siècle. Ed.
      Pierre Coustillas, Jean-Pierre Petit, and Jean
      Raimond. Paris: Presses Universitaires de
      France, 1978, pp. 80-83.

      "If it is possible to speak of the 'pure novel'
      by analogy with the idea of pure poetry, and if the
      'pure novel' is that which deals only with human
      beings and their interactions, then Jane Austen has
      written pure novels." In this sense her work is
      rather modern.

953   Shroff, Homai J. The Eighteenth-Century Novel: The
      Idea of the Gentleman. Atlantic Highlands, N.J.:
      Humanities Press, 1978, pp. 43-44.

      "The disdain for trade and other monetarily re-
      warding activities" evident in JA's novels, espe-
      cially E, often proves so extreme that one wonders if
      the author is satirizing her characters' snobbery "or
      revealing her own sentiments."

954   Swingle, L. J. "The Romantic Emergence: Multiplica-
      tion of Alternatives and the Problem of System-
      atic Entrapment." MLQ, 39 (1978), 273-74.

      Like Scott, Mary Shelley, and "other literary
      artists of her period, Austen is preoccupied with
      problems that evolve from consolidations of thought
      into systems of fundamental opposition. . . . The
      world gets divided into halves, and each becomes an
      order, The Order, unto itself."

955   Torrance, Robert M. The Comic Hero. Cambridge,

Mass.: Harvard Univ. Press, 1978, pp. 226-27.

Even in JA's civilized universe "the gulf sepa-
rating the thinking and feeling individual from a
polished and often cold-hearted society becomes--es-
pecially in her last novel, Persuasion--very nearly
too wide to bridge. In its quiet isolation the heroism of nonconformity seems painfully remote from the
comic."

956 Yanal, Robert J. "Denotation and the Aesthetic Ap-
     preciation of Literature." JAAC, 36 (1978), 471,
     474, and 476.

As passages in P and P and E show, denotative
features, those pointing "'outside of' or 'away from'
the aesthetic object," prove "relevant to the aesthetic appreciation of literature."

1979

957 Backscheider, Paula R. "Woman's Influence." SNNTS,
     11 (1979), 17.

"Self-discovery, self-respect, and harmony within
replace the overcoming of external obstacles to marriage as the subject of many novels by women. Austen's protagonists illustrate the emphasis on these
themes," as in E.

958 Bryant, John. "Emma, Lucy, and the American Situa-
     tion Comedy of Manners." JPC, 13 (1979), 248-49.

A "traditional forebear" of the situation comedies found on television, E resembles them in making
us feel both sympathy and embarrassment for a foolish
protagonist and differs in possessing a patrician
code and relying more on language for its humor.

959 Daiches, David, and John Flower. Literary Landscapes
     of the British Isles: A Narrative Atlas. New
     York: Paddington Press, 1979, passim.

(Surveys JA's association with different English
localities.)

960 Drabble, Margaret. A Writer's Britain: Landscape
     in Literature. New York: Knopf, 1979, pp. 130-
     34.

Very influenced by contemporary attitudes, JA "is
as aware as anybody of the emotional and literary at-
tractions of landscape." While her natural settings
do not rouse the imagination like Wordsworth's, they
are truly picturesque: "they are composed as for a
picture, with the appropriate ingredients, arranged
in an appropriate order."

961 Eagleton, Mary, and David Pierce. Attitudes to Class
     in the English Novel from Walter Scott to David
     Storey. London: Thames and Hudson, 1979, pp. 25-
     29.

     In contrast to much critical opinion, JA's con-
     cerns are not narrow; rather, though she sets her
     novels in the drawing room, she focuses on the public
     world, treating "historically significant themes."
     She analyzes profoundly the gentry and its reaction
     to social transformation, offering a conservative
     perspective, one "equally wary of fossilized tradi-
     tion and rapid change."

962 Edwards, Lee R. "Flights of Angels: Varieties of a
     Fictional Paradigm." FemSt, 5 (1979), 550-51.

     Like Charlotte Brontë, George Eliot, and others
     JA seems "caught in the grip of an irreconcilable
     paradox. Marriage, domesticity, and family life
     appear in these authors' works as absolutely neces-
     sary and absolutely confining to women of intelli-
     gence, energy, and vision."

963 Heilbrun, Carolyn G. Reinventing Womanhood. New
     York: Norton, 1979, pp. 135-36 and passim.

     Contrary to Lionel Trilling's assertion in Sin-
     cerity and Authenticity (1972), JA understood that,
     for a woman, the pedagogic relationship, in which the
     man serves as the educator, "not only cannot lead to
     an 'intelligent life,' but, in fact, altogether pre-
     cludes it."

964 Hilliard, Raymond F. "Desire and the Structure of
     Eighteenth-Century Fiction," in vol. 9 of Studies
     in Eighteenth-Century Culture. Ed. Roseann
     Runte. Madison, Wis.: Univ. of Wisconsin Press
     for the American Society for Eighteenth-Century
     Studies, 1979, pp. 361-64.

     The structure of E resembles that of many
     eighteenth-century fictions, such as Robinson Crusoe,

Rasselas, Clarissa, and Vathek: "desire prompts the
protagonist to break out of a situation that is felt
to be confining, but the indulgence of desire leads
eventually to a more restrictive form of confine-
ment."

965   Irwin, Michael. Picturing: Description and Illusion
       in the Nineteenth-Century Novel. Boston: Allen &
       Unwin, 1979, pp. 145-48 and passim.

On those rare occasions when JA provides random
or physical details, she does so not for the sake of
visualization but to make a point. Thus, in E "local
color" helps emphasize Highbury's "life as a social
community" and "reassure the reader of the range and
consistency of Jane Austen's imagination."

966   Jeffares, Bo. The Artist in Nineteenth-Century
       English Fiction. Atlantic Highlands, N.J.:
       Humanities Press, 1979, pp. 149-50.

Henry Tilney constitutes a good example of the
early nineteenth-century connoisseur, "a man whose
knowledge of art was but a single facet of his carefully cultivated and generally detached and erudite
mind." He can discuss artistic subjects like the
picturesque "without implying any close relationship
with professional artists as such."

967   Karlinsky, Simon. "Dear Volodya, Dear Bunny; or, Af-
       finities and Disagreements," the introduction to
       his ed. of The Nabokov-Wilson Letters: Corre-
       spondence between Vladimir Nabokov and Edmund
       Wilson, 1940-1971. New York: Harper & Row, 1979,
       pp. 17-18.

Wilson, who greatly admired JA, helped Nabokov to
appreciate her, thereby overcoming a "typically Russian prejudice against women novelists. . . . There
was also the fact of Jane Austen's total lack of
reputation in Russian culture." Nabokov later included MP in his course at Cornell University and
drew on the work for his Eugene Onegin commentary
and Ada.

968   Lerner, Laurence. Love and Marriage: Literature and
       Its Social Context. New York: St. Martin's
       Press, 1979, pp. 25-29.

"If marriage is made of prose, then Jane Austen
is just the writer for it," but, with the exception

of <u>P</u>, she did not seriously try "to express the experience of love."

969 Müller, Wolfgang G. "Charlotte Lennox' <u>The Female
     Quixote</u> und die Geschichte des englischen
     Romans." <u>Poetica</u>, 11 (1979), 389-93.

     <u>E</u> resembles <u>The Female Quixote</u> in portraying a
     heroine who has an active imagination, lacks experi-
     ence, and understands the world in terms of senti-
     mental novels. But through careful use of point of
     view and language JA presents her character's inner
     reality much more subtly and convincingly.

970 Olmsted, John Charles. <u>A Victorian Art of Fiction</u>:
     <u>Essays on the Novel in British Periodicals</u>, 1830-
     1850. (Garland Reference Library of the Human-
     ities, 100.) New York: Garland, 1979, pp.
     xix-xx.

     Reviewers in the 1830s tended to consider JA as
     merely another woman novelist, according her "praise
     mixed with condescension."

971 Stevenson, Anne. "Writing as a Woman," in <u>Women
     Writing and Writing about Women</u>. Ed. Mary
     Jacobus. (Oxford Women's Series, 3.) New York:
     Barnes & Noble, 1979, p. 163.

     "Spinster writers" like JA and Emily Brontë "may
     have suffered, but they suffered as women who at-
     tempted neither to fight male domination nor compro-
     mise themselves to suit it. Theirs was a narrow
     independence, even a selfish one, but it was real."

972 Stineman, Esther, with Catherine Loeb. <u>Women's
     Studies</u>: <u>A Recommended Core Bibliography</u>. Lit-
     tleton, Colo.: Libraries Unlimited, 1979,
     passim.

     (Bibliography.)

973 Stubbs, Patricia. <u>Women and Fiction</u>: <u>Feminism and
     the Novel</u>, 1880-1920. New York: Barnes & Noble,
     1979, p. 31.

     JA's treatment of Fanny Price's relationship with
     Edmund Bertram and of Emma Woodhouse's with Mr.
     Knightley possibly begins the tradition, so apparent
     in the Victorian novel, of merging different types of

love and using "age discrepancies between the part-
ners." This domestication of sexuality derives from
the demand of the middle class "for sexual restraint
and the consequent desexualization of relationships
generally."

974   Williams, Ioan. The Idea of the Novel in Europe,
        1600-1800. New York: New York Univ. Press, 1979,
        pp. 223-24.

        In contrast to the women novelists preceding her,
JA is "a practical moralist. . . . She found it possible to reconcile sense and sensibility by representing the forms of contemporary social life."

975   Wolff, Cynthia Griffin. "The Radcliffean Gothic
        Model: A Form for Feminine Sexuality." MLS, 9
        (Fall 1979), 105-6. Wolff's comments on JA ap-
        pear also in The Female Gothic, ed. Juliann E.
        Fleenor (Montreal: Eden Press, 1983), p. 216.

        Catherine Morland's fantasies concerning Gothic
novels "include not only the undefined, melodramatic
expectation of danger, but also a quite precise (al-
beit veiled) suggestion of sexual anticipation. . . .
If Austen had not had the language of Gothic fiction at her disposal, she probably could not have
conveyed this fact without violating the humorous and
ironic tone of her fiction."

                              1980

976   Bayley, John. "Family versus Group as Formal Tech-
        niques of the Novelist." ArQ, 36 (1980), 24-25.

        "Like Tolstoy, Jane Austen took her fictional
strategies from the eighteenth century and she shares
the same basically tough family view of life. Her
art also depends on some characters within the family
unit being understanders and some not."

977   Bernikow, Louise. Among Women. New York: Harmony,
        1980, pp. 220-23.

        The conflict in P between Anne and Lady Rus-
sell does not really concern Wentworth but "the
theme of separation, the development of one's own
influence over oneself, the ability to differ from
and stand one's ground against the persuasion of
another woman." And, because the conflict occurs

between two women, affection coexists with it.

978 Conger, Syndy McMillen. "A German Ancestor for Mary
     Shelley's Monster: Kahlert, Schiller, and the
     Buried Treasure of <u>Northanger</u> <u>Abbey</u>." <u>PQ</u>, 59
     (1980), 216-32 passim.

     JA's mention of <u>The</u> <u>Necromancer</u> in <u>NA</u> helps show
     the significant influence German literary figures had
     on English Gothic writers.

979 Doody, Margaret Anne. "George Eliot and the
     Eighteenth-Century Novel." <u>NCF</u>, 35 (1980),
     268.

     JA, Charlotte Brontë, and George Eliot owe much
     to the "women writers of the later eighteenth cen-
     tury [who] developed the ur-model of a new kind of
     novel." This "ur-model," among other things, tells
     the story of a gifted woman, often an orphan, who
     does not fit easily into her society, who has a fe-
     male character the same age as her foil, and who
     finds love with a man her equal difficult to achieve.

980 Duckworth, Alistair M. "Scott's Fiction and the Mi-
     gration of Settings." <u>ScLJ</u>, 7 (May 1980), 102-4.

     The description of Willingham in <u>The</u> <u>Heart</u> <u>of</u>
     <u>Midlothian</u> recalls that of Donwell Abbey in <u>E</u>. But
     where JA's portrait "suggests a cultural state to
     which it is impossible to conceive a better alterna-
     tive," Scott's "signifies a historically identifiable
     stage of culture which, in spite of all its charm, is
     not the only, or even the best, form of society."

981 Fisher, Lois H. <u>A</u> <u>Literary</u> <u>Gazetteer</u> <u>of</u> <u>England</u>.
     New York: McGraw-Hill, 1980, passim.

     (Surveys JA's association with different English
     localities.)

982 Kiely, Robert. <u>Beyond</u> <u>Egotism</u>: <u>The</u> <u>Fiction</u> <u>of</u> <u>James</u>
     <u>Joyce</u>, <u>Virginia</u> <u>Woolf</u>, <u>and</u> <u>D</u>. <u>H</u>. <u>Lawrence</u>.
     Cambridge, Mass.: Harvard Univ. Press, 1980, p.
     86.

     "The fiction of Jane Austen provides the clear-
     est, most polished example of the extent to which
     marriage--abstractly conceived as a harmonious
     union--governs the shape and symmetry of the nar-
     rative structure as well as its contents."

983   Lascelles, Mary. The Story-Teller Retrieves the
      Past: Historical Fiction and Fictitious History
      in the Art of Scott, Stevenson, Kipling, and
      Some Others. New York: Oxford Univ. Press,
      1980, p. 79.

      We cannot elucidate Sanditon "by conjectures
      framed on a reading of previous works," for it "ex-
      plores territory new to the writer."

984   Miller, Nancy K. The Heroine's Text: Readings in the
      French and English Novel, 1722-1782. New York:
      Columbia Univ. Press, 1980, pp. 151-52 and 155-
      56.

      "The feminocentric eighteenth-century novel . . .
      ends in France with Sade, and in England with Jane
      Austen. This unlikely pair in radically different
      ways establishes the outer limits and the culmination
      of the century's concern with the forms of a certain
      private life, with a self imagined in the bedroom and
      at home."

985   Mitgang, Herbert. "Publishing: Giving Books New
      Life by a TV Tie-in." NYT, 7 Nov. 1980, p.
      C24.

      Because P and P, like other books, may attract
      new readers when dramatized on television, a special
      paperback edition is planned to accompany the showing
      of the BBC adaptation in America.

986   Morley, Frank. Literary Britain: A Reader's Guide to
      Its Writers and Landmarks. New York: Harper &
      Row, 1980, passim.

      (Surveys JA's association with different English
      localities.)

987   Ní Chuilleanáin, Eiléan. "Woman as Writer: The
      Social Matrix." CB, 4, no. 1 (1980), 101-
      3.

      Though writers like JA and Maria Edgeworth
      "analyse society acutely, they do so from above,
      and they identify with their own class, or at least
      with the enlightened, educated part of it. Their
      intellectual emancipation appears to be a function of
      aristrocratic [sic] culture, still cultivating the
      Renaissance values of amateurism and accomplishment,
      in the largely unchanged Renaissance setting of the
      household."

988 Nicolson, Nigel. "A Definition of a Snob." EDH, 41
     (1980), 62.

     Although JA did not invent him, "she was the
     first to describe the snob in all his delightful
     vagaries."

989 Tiger, Virginia. "The Female Novel of Education and
     the Confessional Heroine." DR, 60 (1980), 475.

     Like Charlotte Lennox's The Female Quixote and
     Maria Edgeworth's Angelina, E takes as its "moral
     core the necessity of emancipating [its heroine] from
     the sexual and social fantasies stimulated by reading
     romantic literature."

                          1981

990 Barish, Jonas. The Antitheatrical Prejudice.
     Berkeley and Los Angeles: Univ. of California
     Press, 1981, pp. 299-307.

     MP does not clearly explain its intense objec-
     tion to the acting of plays. The novel's anti-
     theatricalism derives, though, from JA's
     "uncomfortable personal memories" concerning her
     brother Henry, an antagonism to impersonation, a
     retreat to severer ethical standards than once
     espoused, and "an abdication of the freedom the
     author had implicitly claimed for herself" in P and
     P.

991 Baruch, Elaine Hoffman. "The Feminine Bildungsroman:
     Education through Marriage." MR, 22 (1981), 338-
     39.

     Unlike the male protagonist of the Bildungsroman,
     who, no matter what he suffers, corrects himself
     without a mentor, "Emma accepts a guide to lead her,
     after not suffering very much. It would seem that
     womankind cannot bear much reality."

992 Berland, Alwyn. Culture and Conduct in the Novels of
     Henry James. New York: Cambridge Univ. Press,
     1981, p. 78.

     "The characteristic and remarkable lightness of
     Jane Austen which sees her through even the quasi-
     tragic episodes of her novels, where the lightness of
     touch is as of a wise but polite aloofness, is dis-

carded for better or for worse by both George Eliot
and James for a fuller register."

993 Blake, N. F. Non-standard Language in English Liter-
      ature. (Language Library.) London: Deutsch,
      1981, pp. 144-46.

      In JA "an appropriate use of words is a desirable
accomplishment and meaningless vogue words meet with
disapproval. This situation arises through the
eighteenth-century insistence on correctness in language use, which continued to exercise a strong influence over the nineteenth century."

994 Bratton, J. S. The Impact of Victorian Children's
      Fiction. Totowa, N.J.: Barnes & Noble, 1981, pp.
      175-76.

      S and S inspired "the use of characters as the
organising principle" in Charlotte Yonge's Scenes and
Characters.

995 "Britain's Students Favor Classics, Not Best-
      Sellers." NYT, 3 Jan. 1981, p. 19.

      JA ranked second in a survey of favorite authors.

996 Curtis, Laura A. "A Case Study of Defoe's Domestic
      Conduct Manuals Suggested by The Family, Sex, and
      Marriage in England, 1500-1800," in vol. 10 of
      Studies in Eighteenth-Century Culture. Ed. Harry
      C. Payne. Madison, Wis.: Univ. of Wisconsin
      Press for the American Society for Eighteenth-
      Century Studies, 1981, pp. 424-25.

      The clash in MP "between the system of family
governance adhered to by the country gentry and the
affective individualism espoused by the modish upper
middle class" provides evidence of the "persistence
in the early nineteenth century of the discord . . .
in the early eighteenth century between Addisonians
and Lockeans" regarding education, morality, and
parent-child relations.

997 Duckworth, Alistair M. "Fiction and Some Uses of the
      Country House Setting from Richardson to Scott,"
      in Landscape in the Gardens and the Literature of
      Eighteenth-Century England. Papers Read at a
      Clark Library Seminar, 18 March 1978, by David C.
      Streatfield and Alistair M. Duckworth. Los

Angeles: William Andrews Clark Memorial Library, Univ. of California, Los Angeles, 1981, pp. 108-9.

In P and P, JA follows Richardson in using the estate "as a metonym of an ideal culture," but her treatment differs from his because the description of Pemberley proves "far more dramatic and pivotal" than that of Grandison Hall and mediates a social vision emphasizing nature rather than fashion.

998   Gilmour, Robin. The Idea of the Gentleman in the Victorian Novel. Boston: Allen & Unwin, 1981, pp. 31-32.

JA transforms Richardson's "heightened vision of ideal heroines and satanic seducers" into portraits of ordinary human beings. "If Sir Charles Grandison is the grandfather of Mr Knightley, then Clarissa is the grandmother of Elizabeth Bennet and Fanny Price," and the rake becomes "a dissembler who gives himself away by leaving doors open, like Frank Churchill in Emma."

999   Hanzo, Thomas A. "Paternity and the Subject in Bleak House," in The Fictional Father: Lacanian Readings of the Text. Ed. Robert Con Davis. Amherst, Mass.: Univ. of Massachusetts Press, 1981, p. 29.

"Weak--powerless, defeated, supplicating, appealing--fathers abound in fiction as structural complements to vigorous daughters full of promise (Emma is Jane Austen's definitive portrait of the relation)."

1000   Hart, Francis Russell. "The Regency Novel of Fashion," in From Smollett to James: Studies in the Novel and Other Essays Presented to Edgar Johnson. Ed. Samuel I. Mintz, Alice Chandler, and Christopher Mulvey. Charlottesville, Va.: Univ. Press of Virginia, 1981, pp. 100-101.

"The structure of Cecilia is a large-scale anticipation of Austen's Northanger Abbey: the world of painful public frivolity is succeeded by a narrower world of rigid vanity; the discomforts of both are aggravated by vulgarity--bourgeois avarice and pretension."

1001   Kestner, Joseph. "Secondary Illusion: The Novel and the Spatial Arts," in Spatial Form in Narrative.

Ed. Jeffrey R. Smitten and Ann Daghistany.
Ithaca, N.Y.: Cornell Univ. Press, 1981, p. 126.

"In her first paragraphs, Jane Austen gives an
indication of the speed of the narration to follow.
The short aphoristic single-sentence paragraphs of
Pride and Prejudice and Emma contrast with the extended analysis of the first paragraph of Mansfield
Park. From his first entrance the reader experiences the rhythm of narration."

1002   Lanser, Susan Sniader. The Narrative Act: Point of
        View in Prose Fiction. Princeton, N.J.:
        Princeton Univ. Press, 1981, p. 175.

On the rare occasions when the narrator of one
of JA's novels says "I," "there is no real departure
from the text's decorum because the authorial voice
is overtly present in the narrative act. The 'I'
might be momentarily surprising, but it is not likely to receive much further note."

1003   Leavis, Q. D. "The Englishness of the English Nov-
        el." ES, 62 (1981), 129. Leavis's comments on
        JA appear also in NUQ, 35 (1981), 150, and in
        her The Englishness of the English Novel, vol. 1
        of Collected Essays, ed. G. Singh (New York:
        Cambridge Univ. Press, 1983), p. 304.

An innovator, a "true major novelist on whom the
maintenance of the tradition depends," JA grows
throughout her career: "starting, in Sense and Sensibility, with an attempt to endorse the moral conventions of her youth regarding the duties of the
individual to society but concerned also to find
what rights the individual is entitled to," she
moves gradually in each novel until "she reaches
in Persuasion an almost opposite position from her
starting-point."

1004   Leech, Geoffrey N., and Michael H. Short. Style in
        Fiction: A Linguistic Introduction to English
        Fictional Prose. (English Language Series, 13.)
        New York: Longman, 1981, pp. 272-75, 291-94,
        325-27, and passim.

As examples from JA's novels make clear, a good
deal of what we discover about fictional characters
comes "not only from direct statement and attribu-
tion but from other clues," notably inferences from
language expressing value, from sentence structures,
and from speech patterns.

1005 Lewis, Paul. "Mysterious Laughter: Humor and Fear
      in Gothic Fiction." Genre, 14 (1981), 315-18.

      As a mock Gothic novel, NA "uses humorous irony
      and exaggeration to repudiate the encounter with the
      unknown and feared." Yet it ends by substituting
      "one limited view of the nature of evil for anoth-
      er," excluding "not only extreme mental states" but
      much obvious contemporary misery.

1006 McEwan, Neil. The Survival of the Novel: British
      Fiction in the Later Twentieth Century. London:
      Macmillan Press, 1981, pp. 91-92.

      Though Kingsley Amis attacked JA in "What Became
      of Jane Austen?" (1957), in his fiction "he judges
      by the standard which she created for the English
      novel," satirizing "the same refusal to be aware of
      other people's feelings" she did.

1007 McVeagh, John. Tradefull Merchants: The Portrayal
      of the Capitalist in Literature. Boston:
      Routledge & Kegan Paul, 1981, pp. 119-20.

      As suggested by the contrast between Sir Thomas
      Bertram the decorous head of Mansfield Park and Sir
      Thomas Bertram the West Indies plantation owner and
      thus presumably owner of slaves, JA, though aware of
      the conflict between money and spirit, does not ex-
      plore "how her condition of society came into exist-
      ence."

1008 Martin, Graham Dunstan. The Architecture of Experi-
      ence: A Discussion of the Role of Language and
      Literature in the Construction of the World.
      Edinburgh: Univ. Press, 1981, pp. 79-80.

      Although the style of E does not present the
      mind's inner processes as concretely as Joyce or
      Woolf, it does perform some of the same functions
      as the modern novel's technique of stream of con-
      sciousness, manipulating diction, syntax, and sen-
      tence rhythm so as to dramatize "a controlled turmoil
      of emotion."

1009 May, Keith M. Characters of Women in Narrative
      Literature. New York: St. Martin's Press, 1981,
      pp. 58-62.

      Because she believes "that the sexes should en-
      joy frank comradeship based upon much similarity of

interests and an absolute sameness of values," JA
attacks "cultivated sex-distinctions." She endows
her heroines with "some of those qualities which it
has often been thought no woman should possess,
while investing her lesser women with traits it is
supposed no woman should altogether lack."

1010 Morse, David. Perspectives on Romanticism: A Trans-
      formational Analysis. Totowa, N.J.: Barnes &
      Noble, 1981, p. 179.

P and P resembles other Romantic novels like
Caleb Williams, Frankenstein, and Waverley in its
psychological dynamism, portrayal of contradictions
between one's social and private reality, and use of
key emotional scenes precipitating a character's
change of heart.

1011 Mussell, Kay. Women's Gothic and Romantic Fiction:
      A Reference Guide. (American Popular Culture.)
      Westport, Conn.: Greenwood Press, 1981, pp. 51-
      52.

JA influenced the development of women's Gothic
and romantic fiction in the nineteenth century, "especially in her portrayal of the primacy of the
courtship ritual for young women" and her use of
such character types as unhelpful parents and un-
welcome suitors.

1012 Neale, R. S. Class in English History, 1680-1850.
      Totowa, N.J.: Barnes & Noble, 1981, p. 200.

An existential figure, Fanny Price defends
"property and existing political conditions" in her
condemnation of the theatricals and also refuses
"to sell herself to property." JA thus suggests
"the impropriety of conventional propriety" while
revealing Fanny's alienation.

1013 Paulson, Ronald. "Gothic Fiction and the French
      Revolution." ELH, 48 (1981), 532-34. Paulson's
      comments on JA appear also in his Representa-
      tions of Revolution (1789-1820) (New Haven:
      Yale Univ. Press, 1983), pp. 215-18.

In NA the Gothic serves as a metaphor for a grim
reality, and ironically Catherine's fantasies signi-
fy "not a Gothic but rather a worse, because more
banal, more historical evil--one perhaps like the
French Revolution itself: General Tilney's abrupt

dismissal of Catherine because he thinks she will
interfere with his dynastic plans for Henry."

1014   Pearson, Carol, and Katherine Pope. The Female Hero
in American and British Literature. New York:
Bowker, 1981, pp. 117-20.

"Emma rejects the egotistical maternal captor
role, but she clearly identifies her fiancé as her
mentor and superior in wisdom. Thus, it is not
clear at the end of the novel whether she has found
that ideal of personal responsibility which pre-
cludes the inclination to run others' lives or to
turn over one's life to another."

— 1015   Pratt, Annis, with Barbara White, Andrea Loewen-
stein, and Mary Wyer. Archetypal Patterns in
Women's Fiction. Bloomington, Ind.: Indiana
Univ. Press, 1981, pp. 15 and 44.

Like Fanny Burney and Maria Edgeworth, JA uses
"the ambivalences of dual plotting to satirize excesses in courtship norms by, for example, comparing
the hero's pragmatic choice of mate to a less sensible couple in a subplot." She thus balances criticism of existing concepts of marriage and womanhood
with acceptance, rebellion with conformity.

1016   Prickett, Stephen. "Romantic Literature," in his
ed. of The Romantics. (Context of English Literature.) New York: Holmes & Meier, 1981, pp.
206-7.

JA proves only superficially "an anti-Romantic.
. . . In her feeling for the differentness of the
past and the present, and of the tensions and contradictions within her society, she shared a common
consciousness with her great Romantic contemporaries."

1017   Pritchard, William H. "Fabulous Monster: Ford as
Literary Critic," in The Presence of Ford Madox
Ford: A Memorial Volume of Essays, Poems, and
Memoirs. Ed. Sondra J. Stang. Philadelphia:
Univ. of Pennsylvania Press, 1981, pp. 126-27.

Ford admired JA for what she avoided, namely,
moral preoccupations, ideas, idealizations, and
for what her "pure imagination" included, particularly the "activity of listening to the 'gossip,'
or watching Mrs. Norris prepare conserves, or

hearing about the troubles of a neighbor."

1018 Robertson, P. J. M. The Leavises on Fiction: An
      Historic Partnership. New York: St. Martin's
      Press, 1981, pp. 56-57 and passim.

      Q. D. Leavis's "A Critical Theory of Jane
      Austen's Writings" (1941-42 and 1944) sought "to
      demolish the notion that the art was miraculous,
      limited and lightweight" by demonstrating the pains
      JA took to achieve perfection. "If in her enthu-
      siasm speculation exceeded probability, Mrs Leavis
      certainly gave a backbone to modern Jane Austen
      studies that was not there before she wrote."

1019 Ruthrof, Horst. The Reader's Construction of Narra-
      tive. Boston: Routledge & Kegan Paul, 1981, pp.
      149-50.

      As a parody of the Gothic novel, NA primarily
      perverts story "rather than language. This is not
      to say that the surface structure of language is not
      parodied," only that the linguistic patterns do not
      prove essential.

1020 Spacks, Patricia Meyer. "The Difference It Makes."
      Soundings, 64 (1981), 343-44 and 353-57. Part
      of Spacks's comments on JA appears also in her
      "Afterword" to S and S (New York: Bantam, 1983),
      pp. 332-43; see no. 677.

      Feminist criticism, asking new questions and
      offering new viewpoints about female experience, has
      made a difference in the way one reads JA. It has
      enabled one to see, for example, that S and S, like
      the story of the two Elizas in it, portrays woman's
      condition as one that involves making do with lit-
      tle. "Properly schooled in repression and denial,
      a woman will get something out of life: something,
      but probably not much."

1021 Torgovnick, Marianna. Closure in the Novel.
      Princeton, N.J.: Princeton Univ. Press, 1981,
      p. 17.

      The relationship JA and George Eliot establish
      with the reader during closure is "complementary," a
      term meaning that "the reader accepts--more or less
      uncritically--both the ending itself and whatever
      meaning (or lack of meaning) the author wishes it to
      convey."

1982

1022   Armstrong, Nancy. "The Rise of Feminine Authority
       in the Novel." Novel, 15 (1982), 138-41.

       JA could not, in a novel like P and P, "choose
       to depoliticize sexual relationships, but she could
       modify the existing strategies for resolving the
       conflict among competing social groups." She thus
       subtly redistributes "sexual features between
       Elizabeth and Darcy," thereby making "it possible
       for the novel to imply that such a marriage actually
       democratizes social relationships while it also
       reestablishes the traditional patriarchy."

1023   Banfield, Ann. Unspeakable Sentences: Narration and
       Representation in the Language of Fiction.
       Boston: Routledge & Kegan Paul, 1982, p. 218.

       As an example from E illustrates, "sentences
       representing a third person consciousness and sen-
       tences of narration have different empirical conse-
       quences" and "cannot be correctly read in both ways
       simultaneously."

1024   Elsbree, Langdon. The Rituals of Life: Patterns in
       Narratives. (National University Publications,
       Series in Modern Literary Criticism.) Port
       Washington, N.Y.: Kennikat Press, 1982, p. 31.

       Because she writes about people of leisure, JA
       pictures community as largely a matter of play,
       focusing on card tables, riddles, picnics, and
       amateur theatricals. "The relationship of the
       individual to her society in Austen's novels is
       her relationship to a play community, and her
       success depends upon how faithfully she follows
       the rules and how skillfully she performs, whether
       in dancing or marriage."

1025   Garver, Joseph. "The Context of the 'Interesting'
       Heroine." ES, 63 (1982), 321 and 327-29.

       JA uses the word interesting in its original
       sense of "vitally concerning"; in its Romantic "con-
       notations of pity and admiration, but in a way which
       made light of her own fascination with the theme of
       persecution"; and in its Victorian euphemistic mean-
       ing of "sexually attractive."

1026   Hartog, Dirk den. "Morality and Psychology in Some

Nineteenth-Century Novels." CR, no. 24 (1982), p. 5.

"Jane Austen is perhaps the last figure for whom the discrimination between morally sanctioned and thus good feeling, and immoral and thus bad feeling, can be regarded as unproblematic; and even in her the curtness with which she dismisses 'the high spirit and strong passions' of Maria Bertram sounds reactionary."

1027 Jacobson, Dan. "Ethics and Fantasy." CR, no. 24 (1982), pp. 35-36.

In E, JA chastises her heroine for making fun of Miss Bates and trying to manage other people's lives, actions the author herself commits. "In her portrait of bossy, fantasizing Emma is Jane Austen punishing or rewarding herself for being a novelist? (She is certainly laughing at herself, I think, though not without a certain degree of bitterness.)"

1028 Kuhns, Richard. "The Beautiful and the Sublime." NLH, 13 (1982), 295-99.

In S and S's social world "beauty suffers disruption through a force that is generated in the women by the destruction money wreaks upon trust, love, and position. Accommodation to the economic or bourgeois sublime . . . comes not through the affirmation of one's moral self, nor through the reconstitution of the world through beauty, but in submission and the subordination of women to men."

1029 McMaster, Juliet. "Trollope's Country Estates," in Trollope Centenary Essays. Ed. John Halperin. New York: St. Martin's Press, 1982, pp. 71-72.

Both JA and Trollope describe characters by telling us about their estates and judge estate-owners according to the manner in which they fulfill their moral responsibilities as landlords.

1030 Modleski, Tania. Loving with a Vengeance: Mass-produced Fantasies for Women. Hamden, Conn.: Archon, 1982, pp. 36 and 49-51.

P and P, which presents "feminine fantasy under the guise of 'realism,'" resembles modern romances for women. Both Elizabeth Bennet and the typical protagonist of a Harlequin Romance, for example, at

first dislike the hero for his arrogance, a dislike
that simultaneously absolves them of mercenary motives and becomes the means by which they obtain the
hero's love and fortune.

1031   Morse, David. Romanticism: A Structural Analysis.
Totowa, N.J.: Barnes & Noble, 1982, p. 29.

"The blurring, the inmixing of moral and social
criteria that we find in Jane Austen's Mansfield
Park, so that sound judgement and moral courage are
seen as the indispensable precondition for an entree
into the aristocratic world--such a confusion is un-
thinkable in the radical vision of Holcroft and
Bage."

1032   Munday, Michael. "The Novel and Its Critics in the
Early Nineteenth Century." SP, 79 (1982), 205-
26 passim.

Scott's review of E (1816), together with other
evidence, suggests "that the most impressive
achievement of the periodical critics of the novel
lies in their discussion of the way in which the
realist novel was beginning to emerge at this time."

1033   O'Neill, John H. "The Experience of Error: Ironic
Entrapment in Augustan Narrative Satire." PLL,
18 (1982), 278 and 283-84.

JA "inherited and modified a narrative strategy
of entrapment which was traditional in the satirical
literature of the Restoration and the eighteenth
century--the use of the reader's identification with
a central character as a means of teaching a moral
lesson." And she is the first English novelist "to
use the third-person limited narrative voice" to
create this "experience of error."

1034   Rogers, Katharine M. Feminism in Eighteenth-Century
England. Urbana, Ill.: Univ. of Illinois Press,
1982, pp. 225-31.

Though aware of women's disadvantages and intelligence, JA yet rejects "systematic feminism," creating heroines, convincing models for their sex, who
prove noteworthy both for their unconventional as-
sertiveness and passion and their more traditional
"self-discipline, humility, duty to others, and
sober acceptance of reality."

1035   Spacks, Patricia Meyer. "In Praise of Gossip."
       HudR, 35 (1982), 24-25, 27, and 32.

       As the relationship between Mrs. Smith and
       Nurse Rooke in P suggests, gossip offers both
       pleasure and profit, enlarging the world and
       penetrating to the reality of human littleness,
       but it also generates guilt. And, as P and P and
       E indicate, "as a social phenomenon, gossip often
       appears to blunt moral discrimination."

1036   Tytler, Graeme. Physiognomy in the European Nov-
       el: Faces and Fortunes. Princeton, N.J.:
       Princeton Univ. Press, 1982, pp. 311-15 and
       passim.

       Writing in "the moralistic tradition of Field-
       ing," JA uses physiognomical details and judgments
       in E for the sake of characterization and struc-
       ture. She manages as well "to bring the physi-
       ognomical atmosphere of her day into the novel
       without making it seem banal or obtrusive."

                              1983

1037   Bell, Michael. The Sentiment of Reality: Truth of
       Feeling in the European Novel. Boston: Allen &
       Unwin, 1983, pp. 188-89.

       JA's achievement lies in the fact that her
       "comic structures manage to accommodate a minutely
       observed verisimilitude with respect to locale, in-
       come and the gradations of contemporary society," at
       the same time that "they never lose their clear val-
       ue as universal, partly idyllic, forms" that express
       "an ideal order of principle and feeling."

1038   Conrad, Peter. "The Englishness of English Litera-
       ture." Daedalus, 112 (Winter 1983), 169-70.

       Not an idyll, as Trilling believes, but "a
       spoiled idyll," like all Edens in English litera-
       ture, E in its course proves menaced from without
       and within and ends "as the 'small band' of like-
       minded castaways unite to defend their communal
       island against its enemies."

1039   Crowl, Philip A. The Intelligent Traveller's Guide
       to Historic Britain: England, Wales, the Crown

Dependencies. New York: Congdon & Weed, 1983, passim.

(Discusses Chawton Cottage.)

1040   Davies, Simon. "Laclos dans la littérature anglaise du XIXe siècle," in Laclos et le libertinage, 1782-1982. Actes du colloque du bicentenaire des Liaisons dangereuses. (Publications du Centre d'Études du Roman et du Romanesque, Université de Picardie.) Paris: Presses Universitaires de France, 1983, pp. 256-58.

Lady Susan shows that JA probably knew Les Liaisons dangereuses, for the two works significantly resemble each other in characterization, plot, and style. "And what could be more natural than that the young Jane Austen, daughter of an Anglican clergyman, living in the countryside, should become interested in the perplexing world of Les Liaisons dangereuses?"

1041   Hobsbaum, Philip. Essentials of Literary Criticism. London: Thames and Hudson, 1983, pp. 116-23.

As a comparison of passages from Sir Charles Grandison, Evelina, and E makes clear, JA "refined the frequently crude usages of her predecessors into literature." She avoided Richardson's echoes of stage melodrama and Burney's unstable tone to create her characteristically precise comedy and a style noteworthy for its "dexterity and variegation of nuance."

1042   McGann, Jerome J. The Romantic Ideology: A Critical Investigation. Chicago: Univ. of Chicago Press, 1983, pp. 18-19 and 29-31.

Many recent attempts by critics to demonstrate JA's romanticism prove "thoroughly misguided," obscuring her "special historical significance" and confusing "the entire subject of Romanticism both in its structural and its historical formations."

1043   Sales, Roger. English Literature in History, 1780-1830: Pastoral and Politics. New York: St. Martin's Press, 1983, pp. 30-35.

JA's "universally acknowledged truths turn out to be political prejudices": she actually treats only a very limited segment of country society, the "dictators," and endorses "agrarian capitalism," succeeding in uniting the rural gentry's conservatism with capitalist production's ethics.

1044   Stonyk, Margaret. <u>Nineteenth-Century English Literature</u>. (Macmillan History of Literature.) London: Macmillan Press, 1983, pp. 48-52.

A "subdued" but "surprisingly pure" Romantic, JA "values integrity, a fresh and candid response to nature, pure emotions, and a treasuring up of past associations." More particularly, <u>NA</u> shows imagination deepening one's grasp of life; <u>S</u> <u>and</u> <u>S</u> comprehends violent feeling; and <u>E</u> "develops a Romantic subject--the human need to create."

1984

1045   Jarrett-Kerr, Martin. "The Mission of Eng Lit." Letter in <u>TLS</u>, 3 Feb. 1984, p. 111.

During World War I the Oxford tutor H. F. Brett-Smith, advising hospitals "on reading matter for the war-wounded," used to select JA "for the severely shell-shocked."

Indexes

Index of Authors

Reference is to item numbers.
"R" prefix indicates a book review.

Index of Jane Austen Titles

Index of Subjects

Acting, 10, 78, 146, 248, 322, 990

Adaptations, 55, 114, 132, 140, 181, 187, 246, 472, 474, 487, 505, 520, 537, 539, 556, 584, 638, 650, 985

Addison, Joseph, 10, 886, 996

Aesthetics, 61, 63, 78, 212, 310, 359, 360, 421a, 424, 547, 680, 682, 739, 752, 806, 844, 956

Amis, Kingsley, 1006

Architecture, 73, 78, 577, 889

Aristocracy. See Social classes

Augustan Age, 58, 690, 887

Bage, Robert, 110, 1031

Balance, 19, 30, 44, 49, 65, 77, 229, 344, 360, 405, 408, 479, 515, 559, 598, 608, 671, 682, 688, 690, 711, 719, 873, 1015

Barrett, Eaton Stannard, The Heroine, 651

Barth, John, The Sot-Weed Factor, 817

Bath, 9, 94, 142, 193, 204, 577, 629, 651, 679

Beckford, William, Vathek, 964

Bentley, Richard, 584

Beowulf, 680

Bibliography, 16, 37, 39, 42, 65, 71, 77, 78, 90, 91, 101a, 108, 126, 132, 153, 156, 177, 188, 191, 201, 220, 223, 228, 229, 264, 302, 310, 341, 380, 391, 402, 412, 469, 515, 517, 521, 523, 528, 536, 548, 559, 561, 567, 584, 595, 610, 613, 643, 676, 677, 688, 972

Bicentennial, 56, 60, 74, 86, 100, 101a, 103, 104, 109, 112, 115, 117, 119, 121, 122, 123, 128, 132, 134, 135, 136, 137, 138, 141, 144, 147, 151, 154, 162, 166, 168, 170a, 182, 183, 187, 194a, 213, 218, 221, 230, 232, 265

Biography, 3, 7, 23, 27, 39, 41, 62, 65, 66, 69, 86, 100, 101a, 108, 112, 114, 127, 128, 132, 133, 135, 140, 141, 148, 150, 154, 157, 158, 162, 164, 165, 167, 175, 178, 189, 192, 195, 198, 208, 209, 214, 228, 263, 266, 281,

History, 18, 63, 95, 177,
231, 235, 345, 349, 386,
409, 414, 431, 489, 493,
518, 547, 565, 680, 772,
946, 980, 1013

Hogg, James, 888

Holcroft, Thomas, 1031

Hoole, Barbara, Ellen, the
Teacher, 822

Horney, Karen, 360, 461a,
782

Hungary, 334

Hutcheson, Francis, 656

Illustrations, 39, 65, 73,
80, 150, 157, 320, 336,
340, 382, 428, 569, 921

Imagination, 10, 30, 49,
78, 108, 110, 126, 133,
231, 310, 331, 337, 405,
454, 479, 481, 507, 509,
511, 516, 547, 560, 680,
685, 744, 762, 770, 816,
831, 832, 856, 883, 894,
927, 960, 965, 969, 1017,
1044

Improvements, 78, 151, 218,
283, 531, 807, 866, 904

Incest, 45, 69, 132

India, 610

Intimacy, 78, 187, 292,
491, 632, 676, 820

Irony, 3, 4, 10, 13, 30,
34, 39, 46, 48, 50, 52,
57, 58, 71, 94, 120, 151,
166a, 177, 179, 184, 185,
187, 190, 213, 218, 231,
235, 244, 255, 264, 279,
287, 307, 310, 313, 323,
331, 334, 346, 347, 365,
371, 386, 398, 399, 401,
413, 414a, 425, 439, 461,

469, 515, 524, 543, 548,
549, 574, 588, 610, 620,
624a, 626, 632, 639, 641,
651, 657, 683, 760, 771,
813, 817, 820, 828, 843,
846a, 860, 870, 893, 917,
926, 937a, 975, 1005,
1013

Isolation, 15, 108, 187,
386, 404, 480, 488, 509,
517, 676, 767, 804, 955,
1012

Italy, 585

James, Henry, 184, 199,
218, 799, 820, 830, 992;
"The Lesson of Balzac,"
132; The Portrait of a
Lady, 43

The Jane Austen Society,
27, 73, 144, 146, 211,
254, 273, 341, 412, 434,
469, 531, 595, 643

The Jane Austen Society of
North America, 390, 410,
424, 446, 489, 551, 608,
609, 652, 658, 667, 673,
684

Janeite, 285, 652

Japan, 543, 593

Johnson, Samuel, 39, 118,
143, 174, 275, 454, 547,
643a, 644, 741, 748, 818;
The Rambler, 486; Ras-
selas, 648, 964

Joyce, James, 717, 726,
824, 833, 1008

Judgment, 10, 21, 34, 39,
44, 64, 65, 92, 94, 96,
102, 108, 132, 143, 151,
187, 218, 239, 245, 253,
306, 312, 334, 365, 374,
376, 394, 454, 456, 470,
480, 481, 512, 515, 548,
632, 639, 648, 655, 660,

674, 680, 683, 689, 692,
700, 715, 720, 723, 725,
726, 738, 739, 740, 749,
752, 759, 768, 777, 778,
783, 786, 789, 790, 791,
805, 806, 812, 818, 819,
821, 825, 832, 834, 845,
855, 856, 866, 867, 868,
870, 877, 886, 890, 892,
896, 900, 903, 905, 907,
912, 919, 927, 930, 943,
944, 974, 989, 990, 996,
1003, 1017, 1026, 1028,
1029, 1031, 1033, 1035,
1036, 1043

Mozart, Wolfgang Amadeus,
682

Murasaki, Baroness, The
Tale of Genji, 948

Music, 15, 79, 428, 584a,
667, 682

Myth, 95, 132, 184, 680,
695, 777, 817, 884

Nabokov, Vladimir, 967;
Ada, 967

Napoleon I, 945

Narrative point of view,
10, 25, 34, 38, 68, 78,
84, 94, 133, 151, 156,
166a, 206, 213, 231, 243,
255, 259, 287, 295, 322,
345, 348, 377, 398, 409,
423, 435, 447, 461, 470,
490, 515, 517, 529, 547,
548, 550, 575, 586, 600,
631, 633, 648, 680, 685,
698, 699, 710, 727, 746,
752, 770, 778, 790, 799,
800, 805, 814, 817, 828,
845, 849, 868, 969, 1002,
1023, 1033

Narrator. See Narrative
point of view

Nature, 10, 15, 30, 105,
110, 132, 200, 212, 255,

277, 296, 313, 365, 420,
424, 426, 443, 452, 514,
562, 572, 585, 598, 637,
651, 715, 744, 763, 771,
939, 942, 949, 960, 997,
1044

Navy, 193, 208, 234, 443,
608, 946

Netherlands, 282a

Newton, Sir Isaac, 815

Novel as genre, 133, 166,
199, 213, 218, 322, 337,
392, 429, 440, 466, 524,
537, 612, 695, 727, 748,
843, 873, 880, 883, 912

Novel conventions, 34, 39,
88, 110, 130, 270, 310,
385, 386, 405, 547, 576,
632, 664, 698, 777, 831,
846a, 906, 914

Novel, domestic, 440, 680

Novel, epistolary, 10, 62,
213, 395, 419, 440, 453,
476, 774, 848

Novel of manners, 53, 184,
343, 407, 420, 860, 904

Novel readers, 10, 24, 49,
85, 88, 102, 156, 184,
207, 217, 231, 252, 319,
366, 377, 381, 386, 508,
515, 548, 550, 555, 596,
597, 600, 605, 610, 632,
639, 648, 672, 700, 718,
721, 765, 766, 770, 795a,
805, 810, 814, 845, 846a,
870, 909, 924, 925, 926,
985, 1001, 1021, 1033

Novel, sentimental, 13,
110, 126, 213, 373, 586,
632, 651, 758, 928, 969

Novel structure, 3, 8, 10,
31, 38, 58, 65, 89, 94,
97, 110, 126, 132, 156,
166, 184, 187, 197, 213,